HELP!

I'm a Parent

Christian Parenting in the Real World

Family Ministries Department of the North American Division
CLAUDIO CONSUEGRA, D.MIN., DIRECTOR
PAMELA CONSUEGRA, PH.D., ASSOCIATE DIRECTOR
KAREN PEARSON, EDITOR

Karen Pearson, editor

Karen Pearson lives in Nampa, Idaho, where she serves as the director of publicity and public relations at Pacific Press® Publishing Association. She is an author, a speaker, and an avid storyteller. One of her greatest joys is to work with authors to help them develop their skills and craft their stories.

Karen has been married to Michael, a pastor in the Idaho Conference, for 35 years, and they have two adult children. Carey and Bruce are both professional musicians who live and work in Seattle.

This is the second devotional Karen has edited. She previously edited a women's ministries devotional for the Southern Africa Union Conference.

Her favorite topic on which to write and speak is the wild and wonderful love of Jesus—for it is only through His love that we have the ability to rewrite our stories. Jesus still mends broken things and makes all things beautiful in His time.

You can reach her at karen.pearson3@gmail.com.

Copyright © 2014 Review and Herald® Publishing Association

Published by Review and Herald® Publishing Association, Hagerstown, MD 21741-1119

This book was
Edited by Karen Pearson
Copyedited by Delma Miller
Designed by Derek Knecht/Review and Herald® Design Center
Cover Photos © Think Stock
Typset Minion Pro 11/13

Library of Congress Control Number: 2014942471

ISBN 9780828028073

Parents,

What if someone gave you a block of the finest marble with the task of creating a masterpiece that would be displayed in the most prominent place for the entire world to see? Unless you are a gifted sculptor, and hiring one is not an option, what would you do? And what if you were given only a few years to create this monument that will last a lifetime?

Parenting is like that, except that instead of a block of hard, cold marble we are given the delicate life of a child for us to begin to shape and mold so they can become lifetime disciples of Jesus Christ. What an awesome task and responsibility! Where do we begin? When you face the daily parenting grind of never-ending challenges, do you feel like giving up?

In a national survey of the state of families in America,[1] parents reportedly believe that raising children today is more complicated than it used to be. Along with that, most perceived that the quality of American family life was declining. In addition, 55 percent of the parents surveyed expressed a concern that they were not doing a very good job of parenting. In essence, the study concluded that "for today's mothers and fathers, there is no clear map that charts the path for nurturing the next generation of adults."[2]

We bring you good news! There is a how-to manual in God's Word. The principles of parenting in Scripture are timeless and still relevant to parents today. The purpose of this devotional is to inspire, encourage, and equip you on your journey to be the disciple makers of your children. You will be motivated to take up the exciting challenges and blessings of parenthood. We invite you to journey with us over the next year as we explore your God-given role of parenting.

Claudio and Pamela Consuegra
*Director and Associate Director of the Family Ministries
Department of the North American Division
of the Seventh-day Adventist Church*

---

[1] Carl D. Bowman, *Culture of American Families: A National Survey* (Charlottesville, Va.: Institute for Advanced Studies in Culture, University of Virginia).

[2] *Ibid.,* p. 10.

January

Each Child Is Unique and Precious

New Beginnings

Because of the Lord's great love we are not consumed,
for his compassions never fail. They are new every morning;
great is your faithfulness. Lam. 3:22, 23.

Dear Father,

It's the beginning of a new year for us, and though I know You don't mark time as we do, I thank You for new beginnings. Your mercies are truly new each morning, and as a parent I know that is a good thing!

I look into these little faces that You have blessed us with and see so much I recognize: their father's chin, my bright eyes, and the sweet dimples that form with each smile. I see love and hope growing as life expands so quickly I can hardly keep up.

But there is so much in each little one that I have no idea where it originated: the stubbornness of our youngest, and the decisiveness of our oldest. Where do these traits come from so early in life? Was I ever that stubborn or sure of myself?

I know the new year will bring many joy-filled days. I pray we will lead them, by example, to the feet of their Abba Father as gently as a shepherd leads their sheep. As they walk further into the life You have created for them, I pray they will see You standing by their side. May they use those God-given talents to decisively and stubbornly commit themselves to You.

There will be hard days too. There always are. I see the world pulling at my children, pushing them to make choices that are sometimes discouraging and heartbreaking. May we show by our example that You are a God who forgives. May our lives demonstrate how Your mercy has the power to transform and renew.

I pray for patience not to provoke them and for a love that will never quit, never give up, never grow old. No matter what this new year brings, we commit ourselves to You, Lord. Make us the parents You designed for these little ones.

Father, please help us raise these children, these precious gifts You have lent to us, in such a way that their lives will honor You.

Kimberley Tagert-Paul

Each Child Is Unique

God has given each of us the ability to do certain things well. Rom. 12:6, TLB.

If you have more than one child, then you already know that they are different. It is amazing how children can grow up in the same home, go to the same school, and be exposed to the same environment, and yet be so very different.

We are often tempted to compare our children. "Why can't you get good grades like your brother?" "Your sister plays the piano, and so will you." The scripture for today reminds us that God made each of us with different abilities and gifts. If we all had exactly the same gifts, we would miss out on so much beauty in this life.

As parents we need to recognize the uniqueness in each of our children. What distinctive gifts and talents do we see in them? How can we encourage and equip them to maximize those gifts and talents? Don't compare your children but instead, celebrate their differences! For example, if you see your child with an aptitude toward and interest in astronomy, take them to the library and check out books on the planets, stars, and space program. You can also purchase or rent DVDs on these things. Just be certain that all materials agree with the Bible. We have an awesome God-given responsibility as parents to nurture the gifts in each child. We can partner with the Divine and then watch how God opens the doors for each of our children by giving them opportunities to use those gifts to serve Him.

Consider a beautifully woven tapestry. It is the various colors and threads woven together that make it a masterpiece. The same applies to our families. Every member brings a different character trait and gift. Let that uniqueness shine through. Celebrate the differences of each individual as well as the beauty of the whole that is created as we come together as a family.

Reflect on the gifts and talents God has given each of your children. Affirm them and determine how you can encourage them to grow in that area.

Dear Lord, open my eyes and help me to recognize each of my children for their uniqueness. Help me to encourage them to use their individual gifts and talents for Your service.

Claudio and Pamela Consuegra

Unique and Precious

Indeed, the very hairs of your head are all numbered.
Don't be afraid; you are worth more than many sparrows. Luke 12:7.

Our first child was a fabulous textbook baby. He was up by 7:00 a.m. and down by 7:00 p.m., with regular feeding and sleeping times throughout the day. The next two babies, however, not so much. It didn't take long to realize that even though they were all boys, they were each unique and precious in their own ways.

As they grew and formed their own talents and personalities it was fun to see how they changed. They have some characteristics that are the same and some that are very different, but each one is special and unique, just as God made them.

It would have been incredible to be Mary, the mother of Jesus, watching her child grow and change in different ways than other children. Most parents are proud to see their child excel at things beyond their imagination, but how would you feel to be Mary? Her child went through some incredible situations and ultimately died on a cross.

Mary must have had incredible faith. First, to truly believe the child growing inside her was Jesus, the Messiah. Second, to allow Him to go and be the person He was supposed to be.

We need to have that faith believing that God loves our children even more than we do. I know for some that may not seem possible, but He does. Reread the Bible verse above. He knows the number of hairs on your head. Yes, that may be more for some than others, but make sure to read the whole verse. He says we are worth more than many sparrows. He is talking about you and your children.

We need to develop true acceptance, as Jesus has. Being able to accept each child as God created him or her to be. Not conformed to our will, but God's will. That's not always easy to do, especially when the child's temperament or talents are different than our own.

Martin Luther King, Jr., is quoted as saying, "I have a dream that my four little children will one day live in a nation where they will not be judged by the color of their skin, but by the content of their character." Wouldn't it be nice if all people's character were like that of Jesus?

Lord, thank You for making each one of us unique and precious. Help us to appreciate other qualities that are different than our own.

Tamara Michalenko Terry

Nurturing Your Child's Spiritual Growth

The fruit of the righteous is a tree of life,
and he who wins souls is wise. Prov. 11:30, NKJV.

A few years ago I received a gift of a planter with three cacti from Arizona. I placed the pot on my kitchen windowsill along with several other plants. Every time I watered the other plants, I felt the urge to water the cacti. And even though the instructions said to water them with one tablespoon a month, sometimes I would give them an extra little sip, thinking they would be happy for some moisture. But after several months, one of the cacti started leaning a bit and changing color. I had watered it too much. I was killing it with kindness.

In order to thrive a child needs food, water, and shelter, as do plants. But each type of plant needs the best kind of soil, fertilizer, and water to meet its particular needs and to flourish and grow.

All children need three things. First, a child needs to live in a family with a strong sense of ethics and values. That is, the way we treat ourselves and others, and the core beliefs of the family. These provide a child with a sense of security that helps take them through the pain and disappointments of life. We build the foundation of a child's prayer life by praying with them and for them in times of celebration and concern.

Second, a child needs a sense of tradition and community. Familiar rituals of worship, church services, and attending special events all strengthen a sense of belonging for a child.

And third, a child needs to know they are loved for who they are, not for what they do or do not do. We need to ask "How do I unconditionally show love toward my child and yet instill in them the religious beliefs I value so dearly?" Parents provide the most important source of spiritual direction in the lives of their children.

Maybe you like violets, but the Lord placed a cactus in your care. Or maybe you like pine trees, but the Lord placed a rhododendron for you to raise. Ask Him for wisdom to know how best to nurture the little plants in your care.

Lord, bless my child in the ways they need today.

Susan Murray

Individuality

Now there are varieties of gifts, but the same Spirit; and there are varieties of service, but the same Lord; and there are varieties of activities, but it is the same God who empowers them all in everyone. 1 Cor. 12:4-6, ESV.

Every few years I try to update the family photos on display in our home. I always make sure to have the same number of photos for each of us, as I will never forget the day I overheard my son and daughter counting how many pictures of each other there were in a family collage, each declaring the other to be the favorite. It was at that moment I realized my brilliant idea of telling them they were each my "favorite daughter" or "favorite son" was less than effective.

This sibling rivalry shouldn't have come as any surprise to me because my sister and I fought very similar battles as children. Our parents would tell us they loved us the same, but even the faintest hint of any extra privilege was always an indicator to us that the scales were balanced in favor of the other. We each wanted to be loved just a little more, and even today, when we call home we say, "It's me, the favorite." The truth is, we can joke about it now only because we are confident of our parent's love.

In trying to figure out how to be the best parent I can be for my children, I have to consider that my children are very different from each other, so I can't treat them the same. I have to raise them as individuals. They have different abilities, personalities, sensitivities, struggles, and expectations. I also have to help them recognize the unique place they each have in our family. I need to teach them how to value their own and each other's individual gifts and differences, rather than compete with each other. Sometimes it's exhausting. It would be so much easier if I could figure out a way to streamline parenting a little more.

I am thankful though that God doesn't streamline the grace He extends to us. He treats us as individuals, He knows our needs, our strengths, and our shortcomings, and provides for us accordingly while loving us consistently.

Lord, thank You for Your consistent and individualized love. Help me teach my children how to value their unique qualities while being a consistent representation of Your love.

Colleen Duncan

Crazy Love

My little children, let us not love in word, neither in tongue;
but in deed and in truth. 1 John 3:18, KJV.

After one less-than-successful discipline session, our son Jamel made a penetrating remark that pierced my soul. I wrote it down and said if he lived what he preached as a 6-year-old, he would make a wonderful husband. "When I am a daddy," he said, "I'm not going to shout at my children or hit them. I'm going to talk to them and say, 'Now you shouldn't do that.' I'm going to love my wife. I'm not going to divorce her. I'm going to kiss her every morning and every night and tell her, 'I love you,' and sleep with her in the bed."

I still marvel every time I read these words. I see three important things here: discipline, modeling, and love. First, discipline, which comes from the root word *to disciple* and conveys the idea of planned prevention rather than panicked punishment. Hold your child's hand to stop them from running all over the store.

Second, modeling. Nothing impacts children more than watching how their parents treat each other. We are their superheroes, at least for a while, and we can't let them down. Let's show what I call *limited public affection* to each other in front of our children. Let's not raise our voices at each other. Don't you know, fathers, that you are shaping in your daughter's mind her choice of a future husband?

Third, love. Love your spouse, yes, but love your child as well. In his book *Little Lamb, Who Made Thee?* Walter Wangerin, Jr., said: "So give your children . . . golden days, their own pure days, in which they are so clearly and dearly beloved that they believe in love and in their own particular worth when love shall seem in such short supply hereafter."

Cornell University professor Urie Bronfenbrenner said every child should spend a substantial amount of time with someone who is crazy about him or her, someone willing to make an "irrational commitment" to their child. Maybe we could kiss someone every morning and every night and tell them, "I love you."

Dear Lord, thank You for the privilege of giving me a child that loves me. Please help me with the awesome honor of pouring into my child the love of God by what I say and do.

Jeffrey O. Brown

Family Days Are Fun!

Jesus said, "Let the little children come to me." Matt. 19:14.

When Jesus was on earth, He took time for children. Other adults tried to keep them away, thinking they weren't important or that they might be bothering the Master. But Jesus had a special spot in His heart for children. He loved spending time with them. As parents, I believe Jesus would have us do the same thing. Children are only young once. No matter how many projects demand our attention, it's important to spend time with our kids.

When our children were small, we talked it over and decided to set aside one day a week to spend time together as a family. On that day we didn't answer the phone or plan things with other people. Instead we did things with just the four of us. Our kids loved it. They counted the days until "family day," and it brought a closeness to our family we wouldn't have otherwise enjoyed. If you'd like to start a family day too, here are a few ideas to get you started.

- Draw an imaginary two-hour radius around your home and find out what there is to do within that area.
- Don't make your outings expensive, or you'll soon quit because of finances. Keep in mind that some museums have a free day once a month.
- Keep it simple, so it doesn't take a lot of time to prepare.
- Let everyone have input into what you choose to do.

We've gone to the beach, the lake, and the zoo—yearly passes can significantly cut costs. We've had picnics in the park, and we've even taken our picnic basket to the food court at the mall during the winter months! We've gone for walks, out to baseball games or bowling, or to get ice cream. But we also love the simple things, such as playing board games, reading aloud in the hammock, or watching a video together while munching on popcorn. It's not so much what you do as it is that you are doing something together as a family. Start your family day this week. You'll be glad you did!

Father, help us to take time with our children and enjoy the wonderful gift You have given to us through them.

Jeanne Hartwell

Children and Apple Trees

*And let us not grow weary of doing good,
for in due season we will reap, if we do not give up. Gal. 6:9, ESV.*

Last night my husband and I took a walk and looked at our apple trees. For five years he has nurtured, fed, and protected them with the anticipation of one day being able to enjoy great-tasting apples. This is the first year blossoms have appeared, and I can't wait to taste the fruit of his labor. It's important to feed our family healthy food, and what's better than homegrown?

Children are similar to apple trees. It took my husband five years of *hard work* before he started to see the fruits of his labor. Isn't that how it is with children? When they're first born, they are completely dependent on their parents for food, shelter, protection, and love. They need to mature in order to survive on their own. And we as parents take on the challenge to provide for their needs. We know one day they'll fulfill their purpose in life in part because of our hard work and dedication to helping them develop the traits necessary for a successful life.

Our relationship with God is very similar. We begin our spiritual journey dependent on Him. Our maturation progresses over time as we discover how to become more like Christ. As we learn how to demonstrate His love toward others, our dependence on God stays constant with our lives as living proof of the fruit of our spiritual growth.

When our children are little, we're in the season of hard work and sleepless nights, with enormous demands on our time and energy, and lots of hands-on instruction. But if we continue to provide structure, boundaries, protection, and love, there will come a day we'll be able to sit back and enjoy the fruits of our labor. Until then let's encourage each other through the sleepless nights, puberty, endless homework, and high grocery bills. Let's not get so busy we forget to enjoy each and every stage. They are fleeting and will disappear sooner than any of us want them to.

Lord, thank You for the privilege to nurture, protect, and guide the children You have lent to us. Let us never grow weary in training them to love and serve You so their harvest may be bountiful and please You.

Cheri Swalwell

Beautiful in His Eyes

For you created my inmost being; you knit me together in my mother's womb. I praise you because I am fearfully and wonderfully made; your works are wonderful, I know that full well. Ps. 139:13, 14.

Each morning about 11:30 a.m. I have the privilege of sitting down with three or four toddlers and we enjoy eating lunch together. One particular morning I was asked, "Teacher Darla, are you gorgeous?" I was taken aback somewhat and not sure how to answer, so I did what I always do and asked a question myself. "Amy, are *you* gorgeous?" She very sweetly and assuredly answered, "Yes!" So I ventured a little further. "Who told you that you are gorgeous?" Again she answered with confidence, "My daddy did."

Oh, for the self-assurance and faith of a little child to know that we are "gorgeous" in our Father's eyes. To know that God made us the way we are to uniquely fulfill the purpose that He has for us. At times that purpose may seem unclear or out of reach. We have a hard time deciphering what it might be and become discouraged and disheartened. Life can sometimes batter us so hard that we feel ugly and void of anything good, or gorgeous.

God has promised that He can make us clean and new no matter what has happened in the past. Paul reminds us that "if anyone is in Christ, the new creation has come: The old has gone, the new is here" (2 Cor. 5:17).

We all make mistakes and become discouraged, but when we really want to find out who we are, or if we just need reminding, all we need to do is look to our heavenly Father.

Moms and dads, remember, just as your children are beautiful in your eyes, in God's eyes you are the most beautiful of all His creation. You are unique and are precious in His sight. And in case you need to hear it—you are gorgeous!

Dear Father, as I wind my way through each day, please give me the confidence that comes from knowing I am beautiful in Your eyes and that my life has purpose whether I can see it now or not. Thanks for Your promise and for the joy found in knowing I am Yours.

Darla L. McCarty

Fat Love

Hearken diligently unto me, and eat ye that which is good, and let your soul delight itself in fatness. Isa. 55:2, KJV.

People used to tease me about my chubby babies. I didn't mind. Babyhood is the only time in life when chubby equals cute. Infants' small bodies need more fat to survive, so God layers them with soft padding against fevers and other bumps and bruises that can come with some of life's hardships.

Since raising my babies I have come to understand that God packs on the pounds in more ways than one. During those early years He provides emotional calories—emotional and cognitive energy—to the tiny members of the human family through the mysterious phenomenon of bonded relationships. Incredibly, mom's and dad's tickles, kisses, hugs, and knee bounces help build the brain, and the future, of the infant. What an awesome responsibility we have as parents to impact the lives of our children at such a fundamental level.

In the first three years of life the attachment between infant and parent provides the basis for all subsequent relationships the child will develop. The loving interaction of the child with its mother or father literally grows the relational genius of the brain, the prefrontal cortex, from almost nothing in infancy to a vibrant mass of sizzling connections in adulthood. It is interesting to note that the healthy growth of this part of the brain is not automatic—it requires a rich and stimulating environment. Affection shown to a baby releases growth hormones that help the brain to grow to its true capacity. Without that affection the brain will never develop to reach its potential.

As we grow our children's brains through countless affectionate interactions, let's remember God, the ultimate parent, who loves us with an unending, unchanging, unfailing, and unfathomable love.

Dear heavenly Caregiver, teach us to love and to receive love, that we may grow and reach the potential You envision for us, and may we fully reflect You to one another and the world.

Jennifer Jill Schwirzer

Loving the Differences

*Each of you should be concerned not only about your own interests,
but about the interests of others as well. You should have the same attitude
toward one another that Christ Jesus had. Phil. 2:4, 5, NET.*

A friend once admitted his two children were so different from each other that it was difficult for him to like them equally. He tended to favor the child who was more like him, until he realized the Lord had given him exactly the children he needed to help him grow into the image of Christ. He came to understand and appreciate his children for the unique individuals they were.

A meticulous mother had a sloppy son. After years of trying to change him, she finally admitted there was nothing morally wrong with his behavior. Once she realized that a neat person is not morally superior to a messy one, she began to enjoy him, and helped him with his weaknesses and developed his strengths.

Four questions will help us understand and celebrate our children's differences.

First, "What energizes my child?" Do they love being with other people or do they prefer to be alone? While both my children enjoyed their friends growing up, our son brought all of his buddies home where there was always lots of action and food to eat. Our daughter, on the other hand, enjoyed home as a place to come aside and reenergize herself.

The second question, "How does my child process information?" Some rely heavily on their five senses, while others rely more on intuition. Caring about details doesn't come naturally for them. They need more patience and encouragement and are typically creative.

Third, "How does my child make decisions?" The thinking child will drive you crazy asking questions. And finally, ask yourself, "How does my child relate to the outside world?" Some have strong opinions, like to make choices, are more orderly, and thrive on schedules and plans. They need to know what's happening and need help in making good decisions.

When we recognize these needs and refrain from making value judgments, we give our children the freedom to thrive and become who they were born to be.

Lord, may I see my child through the eyes of Christ: unique, irreplaceable, and likable!

Susan Murray

A Mother's Love

But we proved to be gentle among you, as a nursing mother tenderly cares for her own children. Having so fond an affection for you, we were well-pleased to impart to you not only the gospel of God but also our own lives, because you had become very dear to us. 1 Thess. 2:7, 8, NASB.

The apostle Paul developed such a close relationship with the people he brought to Jesus that he considered them more like his children than his pupils. He compared his affection for them to the love that a mother has for her children.

About 35 years ago social scientists began to teach the importance of early bonding with babies. Studies of newborn monkeys who were given mannequin mothers at birth showed that even when the mannequins were made of soft material and provided formula, the babies were better socialized when they had live mothers with whom they could interact. The baby monkeys with mannequin mothers were more likely to suffer from despair. Scientists suspect that lack of bonding in human babies can cause similar problems.

Most babies are ready to bond immediately upon their birth. Parents, on the other hand, may have mixed feelings about it. Some parents feel an intense attachment within the first few minutes or days after their baby's birth, while for others, especially if the baby is adopted or has been placed in intensive care, it may take longer.

At any rate, bonding is a process, and not something that has to happen within a certain time period after birth. For many parents, bonding is a by-product of caring for their baby on a daily basis. You may not even know it's taking place, but then you see your baby's first smile and suddenly you realize that you're filled with love and joy for that little child of yours.

This is not a skill you learn, it is a natural feeling that God places inside your heart. Those of us who are parents love that feeling and flourish in the glow of our bond with our children. Enjoy every minute of the experience.

Thank You, Father, for letting Your love shine through our hearts to our children. Help us to enjoy the experience as long as possible so they too may experience Your love through us.

Claudio and Pamela Consuegra

Dirt Trails and Little Boy Tales

I praise you because I am fearfully and wonderfully made. Ps. 139:14.

The first time my boys played in the dirt it was love at first sight, and the love affair has only grown over time. There's something about dirt and gravel that is good for the heart of a boy. With their trucks and tractors, my boys excavate roads, parking lots, and lakes in our driveway. Then they use the hose to fill these creations with water, which of course creates mud. By the end of the day they are thoroughly covered in dirt and grinning from ear to ear. Life could not be better.

I love to have a sparkling clean home but I understand the importance of letting my boys be boys. So often our society tries to fit little boys into molds that are decidedly *not* little-boy shaped. They must sit still at their desks; they must not get too dirty or climb too high; they must not roughhouse and tumble about with their friends. This mentality causes all kinds of pinching and chafing and general grumpiness, because boys were meant to be—well, boys! They were meant to conquer, overcome, and use their strength wisely. When our culture tries to adapt what it means to be a boy, we are in danger of developing a generation of boys who are trying to figure out who they are and what it means to be a man. Boys should be allowed to be boys.

Here are a few of the rules that we have for our kids:

- Work hard at chores. Play harder.
- Shout, holler, yell, and climb things.
- Conquer your fears by trying new and difficult things.
- Create your dreams and fantasies in bright colors, using a variety of media.
- Always try to do better than you did last time.
- Know the One in whom your strength truly lies.

My husband and I want to raise happy, self-confident children who are ready for the challenges and joys of adulthood. Their success lies in the freedom to discover their talents and strengths within the supportive environment we provide them as parents.

Thank You, Lord, for the opportunity to learn more about who You are as I nurture my children—even when their interests are different from mine.

Kirsten Holloway

Finding the Balance

Can a woman forget her nursing child and have no compassion on the son of her womb? Even these may forget, but I will not forget you. Isa. 49:15, NASB.

The most heartbreaking lesson I have learned came through finding the balance when you have both a strong-willed child and a mellow, tenderhearted child. The attention needs of the high-maintenance child can often eclipse those of the undemanding child. Unfortunately, it's not always easy to see the damage being done until it is too late.

Toward the end of summer, when the children were 6 and 4, I finally realized just how bad things had become. We were all enjoying swimming at Grandma's house when I noticed someone was missing. The littlest boy had retreated, unnoticed, to a far corner of the backyard and was sitting silently by himself. I left his boisterous sister to play noisily in the pool and, following the pathway, I made my way toward him and joined him in a shady place under the oak tree.

"What's wrong, darling?" I asked.

No response. He sat still a moment longer, then he picked up his rubber toy snake, which he had creatively named "Snake," and began talking to him. He gave no indication that he had even heard me. Since he wouldn't talk to me, I pretended to be the snake. His little face lit up, and he happily chatted away with Snake. That conversation broke my heart in pieces. I realized that somehow, in his noisy household, he'd given up on being heard and had turned instead to inanimate objects to get the attention he craved.

I felt like the worst human being on the planet for allowing this to happen. It took time and a great deal of effort before he slowly began to respond to me again. The lesson I learned in all this is to always be aware. While one child devours your attention, another may be starving for it.

Dearest Father, we thank You for Your unfailing love. Thank You for being the perfect parent. Forgive us where we have failed. Open our eyes to those who have neither the courage nor the ability to alert us to their needs.

Carey Pearson

Sing to Your Children

The Lord your God in your midst, The Mighty One, will save;
He will rejoice over you with gladness, He will quiet you with His love,
He will rejoice over you with singing. Zeph. 3:17, NKJV.

She was 9 years old and had been in the orphanage since the age of 4. We will call her Carla. Of all the girls in this home at Los Pinos, she was the one that I, as housemother, had the most difficulty with. Each child had daily home duties, and usually they were carried out without excessive dallying or excuses. But not with Carla! Her excuses were many, her grumbling and rebellion were loud and long.

One morning I called her into my room, amid wide-eyed anxiety from the other children. They knew this was serious! I sat down on the bed and patted the place beside me. My Spanish was at best "Spanglish"—and very limited. Carla complied rather sullenly. Putting my arms around her and rocking her gently, I sang in English, "I was sinking deep in sin. . . . Love lifted me!" Slowly her body relaxed, and as I smoothed her dark hair, she began to sob. In my halting Spanish, I told her, "*Yo te amo, y también Jesús* [I love you, and Jesus loves you too]."

When we returned to the living room, she quietly swept the floor. No more angry words, no more excuses. From that time forward, she would often come to me, snuggle into my arms, and ask me to sing to her. Of course, she wasn't a perfect child, but she knew love was there for her.

Singing has never been my forte, but love is the same in every language and culture. Children need to be sung to. Our heavenly Parent promises to rejoice over us with singing. Oh, how I long to slip into God's arms, lay my head on His shoulder, and know I am safe, and I am loved. I know that He loves me, even when I am angry and rebellious. He loves me, He saves me, He rejoices over me! Our children will learn to love and trust God when we are loving and trustworthy to them.

Thank You, God, for singing over me and loving me with everlasting love.

Dorothy Duncan

Motherhood Came Gently

See, I am doing a new thing! Isa. 43:19.

As a young bride I was told that I would probably have trouble becoming pregnant. I didn't think much about it. Having a baby was the last thing on my mind. Six months later I was dumbfounded at the weight I was gaining. A wise friend suggested I see a doctor, who promptly told me I was pregnant. I didn't know how to relate to this news and simply went about learning to cook, clean, and work in our new business. The only conscious awareness I had during pregnancy was how tired I felt.

The humid summer was full-blown, the baby's room as ready as could be on a tight budget, when finally the night arrived to rush to the hospital. The long hours that followed were foggy as the nurse pumped me full of painkillers and I groaned through fear and pain. I was so ill-prepared for birth, let alone motherhood. This was before the days of parenting lessons, learning the Lamaze technique, or even the most basic birth instruction.

When it was over, I remember being alone with a tiny little girl in a room at the end of the hallway. I looked at the swaddled baby lying in her bassinet next to me and remember feeling so disconnected and filled with disbelief that I was a mother. I knew she was mine—she had my nose, mouth, and eyes. "O Jesus," I prayed, "please let her have her father's legs."

At that moment all the mommy instincts kicked in. I wanted to protect her and longed for the best of everything for her. Every day I'd stare at her, hold her little fingers in mine, press her little head to my chest, and hum softly. The nurses taught me how to feed her, wash her, and swaddle her. I was in the hospital for 10 days and gained some strength back before we went home.

Lianro was very much mine as her father worked, studied, and built a career. She went everywhere with me, sharing the lonely times as well as the joy found in exploring new things. Slowly, tenderly Jesus did this new thing in my life. The gift of motherhood came gently, and it has been one of life's most beautiful gifts.

Thank You, Jesus, for giving me the gift of motherhood, in spite of me. Give young mothers hope, strength, and courage, for it is You who equips us for motherhood.

Emra Wagener Smith

A Blue-eyed Bundle of Hope

Blessed are those whose help is the God of Jacob, whose hope is in the Lord their God. Ps. 146:5.

There had been many tears. Too many to count. They poured from my eyes at random moments. I watched frequently as our only son looked with longing at other families with siblings galore. My heart broke as my husband spotted a little redhead, that by looks alone could have been our daughter, and he turned his face away. Infertility was taking its toll.

Wanting at least one more child filled our hearts. But each pregnancy ended with the same result, and we were about out of hope. Then came the surgery that ended our dreams. Adoption was not in our budget. We were out of hope . . . or so we thought.

He was born on a Sabbath day—one cold January morning. We had known he was coming into the world, and would most likely be given a home other than with his birth parents, so we prayed. We prayed and prayed and prayed. He was a blue-eyed bundle of hope.

And three weeks after his birth, he joined our family. It would take three years for the courts to make it official, but this precious boy had already become our son. Our nephew by birth, but our son by choice and the answer to many prayers.

The road wasn't always easy. Ending parental rights became a scary time, and the process seemed to take forever. But watching this little one grow into a sweet toddler, then a growing boy, put hope back into our hearts. A miracle in every sense of the word. God's gift to remind us never to give up hope.

When our hope was almost gone, God found a way to renew in us His Spirit. He fulfilled our dreams against all human odds. His ways were so far above ours, we didn't even understand until He placed in our arms the dream we had prayed for. Never give up hope! It is the stuff of dreams . . . ours, and God's for us. He tells us that in Jeremiah 29:11.

Father, forgive us when we let our human sight make us believe that all hope is gone. Help us see what You see: that hope should never die. That love is Your choice for us.

Kimberley Tagert-Paul

My Atonement Child

For you created my inmost being;
you knit me together in my mother's womb. I praise you
because I am fearfully and wonderfully made. Ps. 139:13, 14.

I circle my rounded abdomen with my hand and utter a prayer for the baby I can feel moving about inside. This is my second chance.

But my first chance as a believer.

It seems like that long-ago time at age 16 is so far away. I was so young. So alone. And so scared. I had never read Psalm 139. I never knew the One who had formed me and called me "wonderful!" The only thing I knew for sure was that I could not raise a baby by myself. Oh, how I longed for my baby to go to a loving home.

God was far away at that point in my life, but now, as I circle my baby's form once more and settle into a sweet spot, I offer praise to a God who is faithful even to those of little faith. He never gave up on me. He never abandoned me. He blessed me with a loving husband beyond my wildest expectations. A husband who loves and serves God and wants only the highest and best for me.

All of God's words about the sanctity of life and my body being His temple, I now hold as personal articles of faith that help keep me anchored as a Christian. I now know I am precious and honored in God's sight, and so is my baby. I know I have been bought with a price and my body is not my own. It is the temple of the Holy Spirit.

I know He places us in families. It is not something accidental. Rather, it is ordained by God. I hold tightly on to that thought, hugging it to myself as I pray for my first baby's adoptive family.

And this baby who kicks against me now is my atonement child.

I am the recipient of redeeming love.

Lord, grant me selfless love for my child and an understanding of the great love with which You have loved me.

Jude Urbanski

The Yellow Chair

*Therefore, if anyone is in Christ, he is a new creation; old things
have passed away; behold, all things have become new. 2 Cor. 5:17, NKJV.*

My grandpa was in his late 80s when I was born. My dearest memories of him included his favorite—an old yellow one. He loved to sit and rock in it. I thought it was the most wonderful thing in the world—because it could also spin around. I felt so loved and special when I sat with Grandpa in his old yellow chair. My favorite game was to run around the chair while he spun and tried to catch me. It would get us both giggling and laughing.

When I was 3 years old, Grandpa passed away. It was a sad and confusing time, and I remember it clearly. After he was gone, I would often sit alone in his chair and spin around and around. I made sure my mom kept Grandpa's yellow chair. Every time we moved she would ask me if she could just get rid of that old thing, but I wouldn't let her. The memories of my grandpa were just too precious to let go. The chair wasn't worth much—but the sentimental value of it was priceless. In a life of constant chaos and change, Grandpa's chair anchored me to something solid and good.

I finally let Mom get rid of it after I graduated from college and we decided to move back home to the West. For an old yellow chair it was no longer very pretty, and it had started to become uncomfortable after so many years of use.

How often do we hang on too tightly to certain *stuff* because of the memories, or because it is easier to keep it than getting rid of something that is comfortable. Does this have a spiritual parallel? Do we do it with God? Keep hanging on to the comfortable sins, the old and familiar sins, instead of letting God change our hearts and dump our sins in the deepest ocean. Where do we anchor our hearts? Do you have an old yellow chair in your life that you need to let go of?

Dearest Father, please come into our hearts and obliterate our sinful nature and fill us with memories of Your love and care.

Wanda L. Davis

Interlude in the Foyer

Be still, and know that I am God. Ps. 46:10, NKJV.

It's 6:30 a.m. The alarm goes off. 6:35. My mind wakes up slowly, then sluggishly picks up speed like a cold engine insufficiently warmed. And the race begins. Get self dressed, kids dressed. "Did you pack your gym clothes? Where is that lunch order? Did you find your mittens? Where are the car keys? Let's go; it's almost 8:00. Who didn't finish their breakfast? Eat it now. Let's go! Put on your coat. Take off those shorts—it's winter outside!"

I run this way and that, grabbing bags, lunches, briefcase, coats, all the while thinking about work, after-school activities, what to make for dinner. I need to visit my mother in the nursing home today and get cracking on that script for Easter. My husband hints that it's my turn to plan our next date night, but I am so tired. One kid had a nightmare last night and chose me to be the demon-chaser. Why didn't she pick her dad? I'm tired.

I'm running late again, and my nerves are shot from insufficient sleep. We need to leave by 8:00, and these kids are not cooperating. "Let's go," I yell. "Come on; all you have to do in the morning is eat and get out the door. Let's go!"

There in our small front foyer, hands laden with bags, lunches, and keys, I yell them into speed. One child starts to cry while the other spins out of control. I stop. Look at them. My heart breaks at the sight of the devastation I've created. This is not the way to start their day!

I drop the stuff in my hands and fall to my knees. Pulling them to myself for a long hug, I repent. "It's OK. Hush. Mommy is sorry for yelling. Today is not starting out well, but let's ask God to help me be patient and help you guys to have a good day."

They nestle against me as the mom they know and love comes back home to her mind. All three of us pray, and God does His thing once again. He brings calm to our chaos. Within five minutes my foyer is transformed. Happy children walk with me to the car. I am going to be late for work, one child will be late for school, but today this mother was reminded of the power of God to calm storms in the foyer.

Lord, I know my life is crazy at times, but please, please help me to take time to be holy.

Yvonne Rodney

Savor the Moments

Come to Me, all who are weary and heavy-laden,
and I will give you rest. Matt. 11:28, NASB.

The children have been tired today. I think my eldest is coming down with a fever, and it doesn't help that our schedule has been thrown off-kilter. It started this morning when we woke up to an inch of new snow on the ground. I opt for a snow day. The children put on their coats, snowsuits, gloves, and boots and head for the door. What's that smell? One of the boys apparently had exercised his ability to write in the snow yesterday instead of coming in to use the bathroom, and consequently his coat needs washing.

I quickly help him remove the offending garment and toss it in the laundry hamper. We've recently moved, and I don't have any extra coats unpacked. But I want him to enjoy the snow, so I dig through the closet and thankfully find several sweatshirts that fit. I layer him up and send him out.

They all have a great time playing outside, but the snow melts by lunch-time. I call them indoors hoping to avoid more laundry tomorrow. Soon they are bored and hover around me, throwing me little "lost" looks, then lying on the couch they start to pick at each other. Finally my oldest begs to do schoolwork, even though it is after 3:00. I halfheartedly copy some math assignments and some Bible coloring sheets, and we dig in.

My 7-year-old and the youngest child finish their assignments quickly, but my 6-year-old dawdles. After nearly an hour I inform him that he is done for the day. We will finish the assignment tomorrow. He collapses into a puddle of tears because he did not get a chance to write his name on his paper. My eldest suggests we listen to some soft music. It's a good idea and we relax on the couch, all four of us snuggled together, enjoying the first peaceful moment we've had all day. And this is how my husband finds us when he arrives home—dishes still in the sink, beds only half made, and me with three cuddle-bugs in my arms.

Thank You, Lord, for this time to slow down and pursue peaceful moments with my children—even when there is still work to be done; even with disorder all around.

Kirsten Holloway

Understanding God's Love

Behold, what manner of love the Father has bestowed upon us,
that we should be called the [children] of God. 1 John 3:1, KJV.

From that first moment when his dark eyes locked with my own, when his tiny fingers grasped one of mine, my heart was instantly captured by this precious little babe that Bob and I had created together! I thought of how God must have felt as He looked at His new creations, Adam and Eve.

As I cared for my baby's needs—changing his diapers, feeding him, cuddling and rocking him to sleep—I felt a warm sense of fulfillment because I was able to keep him happy and contented. But when he developed an earache in the middle of the night, ran a high fever, or had an upset stomach, I was frightened by my inability to relieve his pain.

At each amazing stage of his development—his first smile, his first little teeth, the first time he rolled over, sat up, started crawling, then walking, his first real words, first sentence—I marveled anew that this adorable little boy came from our own bodies! I began to think about how my parents felt about me, their first baby, and how God smiles down on His earthly children, enjoying this ability to create.

As he grew, there were always new challenges: Keeping him safe from falls and away from things that might hurt him sometimes seemed like a full-time task. Helping him learn to play nicely with others was an even more difficult job. It began to dawn on me what it had been like for my parents to take care of me, a little preemie born at home.

It was interesting to see little traits of Bob's or mine show up in his personality. He inherited a double dose of stubbornness and determination from both of us, and we gently tried to curb some of these tendencies. Our child not only helped us learn the important lessons of unselfishness, patience, and dependence on God's wisdom, but he also reminded us of God's loving care for, and yearning over, each of us, His imperfect children.

Thank You, God, for showing me Your great love through my children. Help me to demonstrate Your love to them.

Carrol Grady

Crazy Prayer

*For this child I prayed; and the Lord hath given me my petition
which I asked of him: Therefore also I have lent him to the Lord;
as long as he liveth he shall be lent to the Lord. 1 Sam. 1:27, 28, KJV.*

Erma Bombeck once wrote, "Somebody asked me if I had my life to live over, would I change anything? At first I thought, *No*, but then I began to think. I realized that instead of wishing away nine months of pregnancy, I'd have cherished every moment and recognized that the wonderment growing inside me was my only chance in life to assist God in a miracle." I was blessed to have had that chance. But it didn't last nine months. Far from it.

"We're keeping you in the hospital, Mrs. Brown." I was only six months pregnant when I heard those words and learned more than I wanted about toxemia, preeclampsia, and protein in the urine. As the nurses took me down the hallway, my mother in Bermuda called my husband in England, where he sat anxiously awaiting news.

"Has Pattiejean had the baby?" Jeffrey asked the nurse. The nurse repeated the question into the phone. "Yes," she answered. Slightly mystified that he hadn't been told, he asked, "What is it?" He looked at the nurse again. "What is it?" she asked. "It's a girl, and she weighs one pound and one-half ounce!"

For the next two months we went to the hospital twice a day. Sometimes our baby would stop breathing and would have to be returned to intensive care. We were told to bathe and dress her as quickly as possible because she didn't have much fat to keep her warm. In spite of the challenges, praise God, she survived and grew.

We named her Kristle, from the German *Kristel,* which is the English form of Christine, the feminine of Christian, which means follower of Christ. As she continues to grow, I am learning to cry out to God on her behalf. My husband fasts each Thursday morning. Why do we do this? Because I believe this is our second chance in life to assist God in a miracle.

Dear Lord, thank You for selecting us to look after Your child. We know she is ours on loan. We pledge to surround her with loving care and unceasing prayer.

Pattiejean Brown

God's Great Plans for Your Child

For I know the plans I have for you . . .
plans to give you hope and a future. Jer. 29:11.

Children believe what their parents say about them. Have you ever heard a parent say to their child, "Don't try jumping rope; that's just for kids with good balance"? Or "Don't try out for the play at school; that's just for kids that do well up front. You'll get nervous and just mess up"? What message does that give to your child? It tells them bluntly you don't believe in them and you don't expect much from them in the future. It also tells them they aren't worth much.

What if, instead, you let your children know you picture a bright future for them? Be intentional in the way you show your child that you have faith in them and in their future. Let them know that you admire their abilities and that you are willing to invest in them. As you encourage them to use and develop the abilities God has given them, they will thrive, and will bless others as they learn and grow.

That's something my parents did well. They often told me the story of when I was a baby and failing to thrive. At the age of 1 month I weighed less than when I was born. My parents were worried because I just couldn't seem to keep food down. They prayed and told God that they would dedicate me to Him if He would save my life. After that I started doing well, and actually became a chubby-cheeked little baby. They always let me know that God had something special in my future because He had saved my life. That gave me confidence that I had potential and helped me work harder when things were tough.

Letting your child know that God has a special future for them can help determine the course of their whole life. So starting today, encourage your children when they do well, help them master new things, and let them know you believe in them. God has planned a future full of hope for your child.

Lord, help me to look for the good in my children and to cheer them on as they grow and become who You have called them to be.

Jeanne Hartwell

To My Firstborn

You are precious to me, you are honored and I love you. Isa. 43:4, GW.

When I saw you for the first time, many hours after you were born, I held you and spoke such special words to you. The secret language known and spoken only between mothers and their just-born babes. You were my firstborn and you lay, calm and content, in my arms. I loved you beyond description.

When we took you home, it was just the three of us. You settled into your little nest, and we thought you were beautiful, awake or asleep. I would watch you for hours while you slept so contentedly. You placed your trust, so fully and completely in me . . . your naive mother. We said a prayer over you as you faced the big wide world.

As a toddler you brought such joy to the neighborhood. You loved your friends' company and played to your heart's content. You loved every insect or bug you could find. You were the adventurer among your little friends. You needed, and found, a daily challenge!

Watching you ride your blue plastic bike was the highlight of our day. The faster you could move, the happier you were. You still did this even when you had "grown up" and left your training wheels behind.

When you decided to swim the individual medley in the school gala, you threw yourself into the adventure. I don't think you realized how far you'd have to swim, or how hard it would be, but you never gave up. You determined to finish that race no matter what. Your dad and I, along with all the other parents, gave you a standing ovation when you finished. And I wept with pride and respect for you. Your determination to challenge whatever crosses your path is a constant inspiration. I love the way you never look at anything as being impossible.

Your gentle heart and compassion for others still shines through you. Your sense of adventure has not waned. You have taught me to trust you, as you trusted me from the start, and I thank God for His guidance and protection over you daily.

Father God, I praise You! Thank You for the gift You have given us in our children. Every day they teach us something new, inspiring us and drawing us closer to You.

Debby Botes

In His Time

He has made everything beautiful in its time. Eccl. 3:11, NKJV.

I had a late potty-trainer. It wasn't for lack of trying on my part. His skin got irritated from diapers, so at 18 months I decided that potty training would be the perfect solution. Unfortunately my son wasn't as ready as I was. It wasn't until he was almost 4 that he was completely potty-trained.

At times I wondered if I'd be changing wet pants for the next 20 years. He just wasn't catching on and didn't seem to care. I thought it would last forever, and then one day it stopped. He decided he was big enough to use the toilet, and that was that.

Looking back on those years, I wish I'd relaxed more and worried less. That's easy to say when your carpet isn't getting sodden with urine daily, but potty training isn't the only time we face this helpless feeling.

How about when your child hasn't started walking yet, and people are starting to ask pointed questions? Or when they cry every single morning as you drop them off at playschool, and you worry that they'll still be sobbing for you to come back when they're 10?

How about when no one but you can understand what they say, and it doesn't seem to be getting any better? How about when your child just isn't catching on at school, and all the other kids seem to be forging on ahead, leaving your child behind?

The truth of the matter is, kids mature at different rates, and they will all have different strengths and weaknesses. It isn't fair to judge your child against your friends' children. Your child is a unique compilation of you and your spouse, and God created them to be exactly the way they are for a specific purpose.

In His time they will learn to use the toilet, they will learn to be brave, they will learn to read, and they will grow tall enough to reach their own cups of water. In His time we parents will learn patience and will gain wisdom. When He is finished with both us and our children, He will have created a family filled with love and faith, a legacy to be passed down to the generations that come after us.

Father, give me patience as I raise this child, and help me to trust in Your perfect timing.

Patty Froese Ntihemuka

Tender Hearts Need Gentle Words

*Jesus said, "Let the little children come to me,
and don't prevent them." Matt. 19:14, TLB.*

Last fall our congregation held an evangelistic series. A well-known evangelist came to town, and I looked forward to hearing him. However, before the meetings began, our pastor asked for volunteers to help with the children's program, and I decided to help them out.

As I walked into the room that first evening and looked around I noticed a mannequin dressed to look like Jesus. We were told not to let the children play near it during the meeting.

Finally, they began to arrive, and by the time we started, about 50 energetic 5-year-olds filled the room. We sang together, told stories, and enjoyed making crafts and eating snacks. As the meeting wound down and parents came to collect their children, I stayed behind to clean up. The few children that remained played quietly.

Then a little boy walked up to the mannequin. "Is that Jesus?" he asked. We assured him that it was. Inquisitively he reached out to touch "Him," and as he did, it fell to the floor in pieces. We scrambled to put it back together when a voice cried out from the back of the room, "Oh no, Ben! You killed Jesus!" The little boy burst into tears.

Once she realized what she had said, the teacher hurried to comfort the child, but he was not easily convinced. In our hasty, get-it-done world, it's so easy to forget that children are tenderhearted and take things literally.

When the disciples wanted to chase away the children, Jesus told them, "Leave them alone. Let them come to Me." There was something irresistible about Jesus that drew the little ones to Him. He noticed each one. Made every one of them feel unique and precious. No wonder they loved Him!

Do our words draw children to Jesus? Do we show them, through gentle acts of kindness, that they are precious? Do they know that Jesus loves them?

Dear Lord, please speak Your love through me so that the little ones will know how much You love them.

Carey Pearson

The First Day of School

I wish that all of you were as I am. But each of you has your own gift from God; one has this gift, another has that. 1 Cor. 7:7.

Wiggly children. Nervous children. Tearful parents. Crisp bulletin boards. Sparkling desks. Colorful name tags. Fresh textbooks. Smiling teachers. Clicking cameras. New friends. Old friends. It's the first day of school and the children have arrived! In the coming weeks each class will take on its own character and personality as the new students create their school family. As a first- and second-grade teacher I've experienced the first day of school almost 30 times.

One of my fondest memories is of a young girl bouncing on her feet, while her ringlets bobbed up and down. Her smile lasted almost the full day. One young fellow expressed his enthusiasm almost daily for two months. Unfortunately not all children make such an easy transition, yet I believe God has lovingly placed each unique and precious child in my class.

You, as a parent, are the most important earthly teacher in your child's life. You have eagerly anticipated each milestone of your child's life so far. On this day, your child's first day of school, there will be conflicting emotions. It's time to begin to let go as they start a new journey of learning. Others will now be part of this process of educating and pointing them to the Savior.

Look to Christ to lead you to a school with Christ-centered teachers. Pray for your child's teacher and all those in the school who will touch your child's heart. Pray for your child and the interactions they will have with their peers. Pray for yourself, that you will continually recognize your needs for God's strength and wisdom.

As you work with and support your child, your child's school, and teacher, you will find God's blessings each day of your child's learning journey. You will still have a major part in teaching your child and leading them to Christ. Trust in God's faithfulness to help your child grow into the person God designed them to be.

Dear Lord, my heart is overflowing with gratitude for the blessing of my child and for the unique gifts and talents You have given. Please fill their heart with the joy of learning and an ever-deepening love for You.

Verna Reinbold

HP-2

The Grace of Flowers

O Lord, how manifold are Your works!
In wisdom You have made them all. Ps. 104:24, NKJV.

I feel fortunate that we were able to raise our children in the country with a simple lifestyle. This is not an option for all parents, but regardless of where you live, it is possible for families to spend time in nature. God's creation is filled with spiritual lessons waiting to be discovered and shared with our children.

When our family first moved into our neighborhood, the roads were lined with wildflowers. Our toddler gathered the different varieties to make a lovely bouquet. When our daughter was older, we bought her a microscope under which she could closely examine flowers. Each flower is individually patterned with intricate designs and minute details. The lacy center of a purple passionflower, the violet's little face, the perfect petals of a white daisy, all reveal something about the character of our Creator.

God likes variety, in flowers and in children. The flowers don't worry about where they are planted, when they will bloom, or who might notice them. Some, such as the daylily, bloom only for one day, while asters lend roadsides splashes of yellow, lavender, and white flowers for weeks. I've never heard a flower complain. They just lift colorful faces toward the sunshine or rain and keep growing. From the flowers we can teach our children lessons of contentment, and trust in God to take care of us. Children may bloom with grace as lovely as the flowers.

Ellen White penned these words of counsel. "Teach the children that because of God's great love their natures may be changed and brought into harmony with His. Teach them that He would have their lives beautiful with the graces of the flowers. Teach them, as they gather the sweet blossoms, that He who made the flowers is more beautiful than they. Thus the tendrils of their hearts will be entwined about Him" (*Thoughts From the Mount of Blessing*, p. 98).

Father God, let me see the uniqueness of each child as a beautiful flower. Grace my children with the loveliness of Your character.

Barbara Ann Kay

He Knows Each One by Name

Are not two sparrows sold for a penny?
Yet not one of them will fall to the ground outside your Father's care.
And even the very hairs of your head are all numbered. Matt. 10:29, 30.

Ours was a high school romance. I met my husband when I was sweet 16, and our friendship blossomed into a steady and loving relationship. We married five years later and soon added a precious baby boy to our little family. He was the absolute love of our live. We felt complete. God had given us all we needed. Or so we thought.

However, one evening while watching the news on television we heard a report of a horrific air disaster in which Korean Air Lines Flight 007 had been shot down by a Soviet interceptor in the Sea of Japan. All 269 passengers and crew lost their lives. The news report included an interview of a young woman who had lost both parents in the crash. She was an only child, and my heart broke just watching her standing bewildered in front of the camera. When asked how she felt, she said, "I am all alone now. I have no one left."

The next day those words kept going round and round in my mind, "I am all alone." I began to imagine how our son would feel if he ever faced that situation. By now he was 9 years old and content as an only child. He had cousins who kept him company and friends who came over to play. Still, those words, "All alone—no one left," kept haunting me. I knew we had to do something soon.

Finally, one afternoon I called my husband at work and told him we needed to talk about having another child. Was he ever surprised! After much discussion and prayer we decided it was the right thing to do. By God's grace two years later Julian was born into our family. He has brought untold happiness and joy to all our lives. We thank God for His blessing of two sons. In spite of the 10-year age gap, they are brothers. Now we are a complete family.

Our Father, I thank You for the way You have blessed our family. I thank You for waking me from my complacency. Thank You for my two precious sons. Please continue to bless them that they may be faithful to Your voice at all times.

June Jepthas

The Birth of a Mother

Being confident of this, that he who began a good work in you will carry it on to completion until the day of Christ Jesus. Phil. 1:6.

Maybe because I was the last born of six children I was never overly fond of babies or little children. Time and exposure to my nieces and nephews never gave me any good reason to change my opinion that while children might be fine for everyone else, they were definitely not for me. However, back in my 20s, and the four years after marriage, when I did spare the time to think about the future, I kept seeing a family there. But there was one problem: The kids in my future vision were fully grown and independent. I didn't need an appointment with Sigmund Freud to tell me that if kids were to be in my future, sooner or later they'd have to be in my present.

So what prompted me into motherhood? It was not a maternal urge. I was not swept up in some nesting instinct. Nor was it an appointment with my biological clock. It was a research decision and a leap of faith.

And then it happened. I was pregnant. And . . . and . . . I hated it! For nine months I called myself all kinds of foolish. Forced bed rest for six months of the pregnancy, heartburn like I've never known, stretch marks, acne, and no pregnant "glow." Hello! Then the dreaded labor pains took control of my body, and as I prayed for God to see me through this travesty I'd inflicted on myself I vowed, "never again!"

Now I have two children and am living the future I envisioned: A creative son who can light up a room with his smile; a beautiful daughter who is focused, deep, and restful. And me, I survived those crazy early years by the grace of God—managing, living, striving and growing, loving and leaning. The journey continues. I pray for their walk with God to be more important than their love for anything or anyone else—even me. I became a mother by giving birth and in the process experienced my own rebirth.

Holy Spirit, inject Your reviving breath of peace into the lives of busy mothers.

Yvonne Rodney

February

A Parent's First Work Is to Seek Christ

Talking With God

*My son, never forget the things I've taught you. If you want
a long and satisfying life, closely follow my instructions. Never tire of loyalty
and kindness.... Write them deep within your heart. If you want favor with
both God and man, and a reputation for good judgment and common sense,
then trust the Lord completely; don't ever trust yourself. Prov. 3:1-5, TLB.*

From the day Jesus' parents found Him in the Temple, His behavior was a mystery to them. He seemed very different. He was happiest spending time alone in the fields or forests talking with God. In the early morning often He was in a quiet place meditating, reading the Scriptures, or praying.

Jesus always treated His mother with love and respect. Mary believed in her heart that her child was the promised Messiah. But she didn't dare say this to others. All through His life, she suffered when He did. She saw how He was treated and was often caught in the middle trying to defend Him. She believed that the home life and the care of the mother were very important in forming a child's character. She worried about how Jesus' character was being formed in her home.

Mary often urged Jesus to follow the rabbis' rules. But even she couldn't persuade Him to give up His time with God in nature or to stop helping people and animals whenever He saw them in need. Mary became very upset when the rabbis expected her aid in controlling Jesus. When He explained His actions by showing her scriptures, peace filled her heart.

He walked every day with people who were rude and thoughtless. He dealt with soldiers, Samaritans, and peasants. He helped carry their heavy burdens, spoke words of encouragement, and told them what He had learned about God's love and kindness.

O Father, if Jesus came aside to talk with You, how much more do we need it today? In the middle of the conflicting expectations of others, please help us keep our eyes on You and Your Word. May we seek You first. Always.

Jerry D. Thomas

Reach Forward

Forgetting those things which are behind,
and reaching forth unto those things which are before. Phil. 3:13, KJV.

The year I turned 38 I hit a wobble. Time was running out! My life was half over, and what had I done with it? Compared with others my age, I was decidedly behind when it came to career and the development of my talents and abilities. A painful reflection.

The morning after my birthday the Lord brought my attention to Philippians 3:13, 14 and reminded me to forget about the things I'd thought I'd missed. It was time to reach forward, create opportunities, and make the very best effort with the time I had left. Instead of moping around, I realized it was never too late to make life better for myself—and for my family.

Choosing to follow the conviction that my place is in my home has not come without some sacrifices. Putting my children and their education first has meant that I have missed some of the opportunities out there for women. In the eyes of the world I have missed out on personal growth and development. Yet this so-called loss cannot compare with the character work that God has been doing in me while at home raising my children. I may lack a career, but God has given me a new character, which is the ultimate in personal growth. I've developed such traits as endurance, perseverance, diligence, neatness, patience, and a string of others, and the growing is not over. Watching the Lord at work in my life has been awesome.

In making my husband, my home, and the education of my children my career I have in fact grown personally. Surprise! In taking up the work that lies nearest at hand, I have been forced to face challenges that I might have avoided otherwise, and in facing these I have grown. I may not have time to pursue a career, but as I wisely improve daily opportunities, and diligently cultivate my entrusted talents—as I have time—I *am* improving myself.

Lord, help me to realize that what's behind me does not have to keep me from becoming the person you want me to be. Thank You that as I seek to know You more, You will grow me and change me in untold ways.

Jenny Lovemore

Life in the Fast Lane

Come to me, all who labor and are heavy laden,
and I will give you rest. Matt. 11:28, ESV.

Trying to balance work, running the household, taking the kids to and from school, to doctors' appointments, after-school games or rehearsals, birthday parties, music or other classes, and on and on and on, life can seem like we are living it in the fast lane sometimes. Especially with kids and the endless appointments and things going on, every day is a rush, and we are happy to see the Sabbath at the end of the week, just to take a breath and recover. Sound familiar?

Among the hustle and bustle of life going on, try to take time to enjoy and appreciate moments, especially with your kids. They grow up way too fast, and someday you will look back and want more time with them. Life can be really crazy and stressful sometimes—OK, a lot or most of the time—but I have learned to take time to appreciate the experiences.

I have three boys all close together in age, and when they were younger, there were times life was just a whirlwind of activity and it was all I could do to make it through a day or a week. Enjoy the time you spend with them and cherish those moments, just don't forget to make Christ a daily part of your life, even if you whisper your prayers to Him throughout the day while you are frantically running through the schedule of activities.

Develop a relationship with God, and He will help you to find joy and contentment in the busyness of everyday life. He will grant you both mental and physical rest, both of which are important. You cannot take care of everyone else if you do not first take care of yourself. As the saying goes: "Take time to smell the roses." When you do, you will find you benefit from the experience of raising your children every bit as much as they do.

Lord, please help us to take time to pause and acknowledge You, and not to get so caught up in the fast lane of life that we forget to enjoy the precious, simple moments and our relationship with You.

Shirley Jones

Exhausted?

They who wait for the Lord shall renew their strength;
they shall mount up with wings like eagles;
they shall run and not be weary; they shall walk and not faint. Isa. 40:31, ESV.

Excuse me, Lord. I can't count to five. Could we talk about this? When I discovered I carried my fifth child, I freaked. I already had four children and homeschooled. My house buzzed with activity, chatter, and teasing. While juggling schoolwork, meals, housekeeping, and piano lessons, I didn't welcome pregnancy. What was God thinking? Parenting involves serious work, and I thought He should have consulted me.

Fatigue and nausea plagued me. Every morning I gave out assignments and then crumpled in the nearest soft chair, trying not to think about my stomach. At night I collapsed into bed around ten in the evening, and slept until eight or nine. Even after that much sleep, I longed for rest after an hour on my feet. My heart reached out to God in desperation and sometimes in anger. What are You doing, Father?

I got my answer. One week at church the teacher, who happened to be my husband, taught on Isaiah 40. Tears burned my eyes as I listened to him explain our human weakness. We can't face life alone, ever. The Lord can and will renew our fragile strength when we rely on Him. In each moment, the Father can provide what we need for the next step, and then the next. He doesn't grant power for future struggles until the time comes. A few days later the same verse came up in one of my kids' lessons. God made His message obvious.

Before I heard those words, I knew the verse. I could quote it, but it rolled off my tongue without grabbing me. My pregnancy created a desperate need that made me thirsty for something more than I had. I learned to seek God in weakness, and I saw Him provide stamina each day.

When I finally gave birth to a precious baby boy, I knew God could and would empower me to add one more child to my home. Though I hadn't the power to do this on my own, He would give me all the strength I needed.

Lord, thank You for teaching me how much I need You.

Cynthia L. Simmons

Approach

*And they heard the sound of the Lord God walking in the garden
in the cool of the day, and Adam and his wife hid themselves
from the presence of the Lord. . . . Then the Lord God called to
Adam and said to him, "Where are you?" Gen. 3:8, 9, NKJV.*

The perfect pair was in hot water. They had disobeyed and ignored
the warning of dire consequences that would follow if they ate the
glistening fruit from the tree of the knowledge of good and evil. Now, to
top it all, they did not want to 'fess up, so hid as far away as they could.
What would the divine Parent do?

What was the Divine's approach? First, He asked a question: "Where
are you?" Of course, it was not because He needed the information to find
them, as God knows everything. And then, another question: "Have you
eaten from the tree of which I commanded you that you should not eat?"
(verse 11, NKJV). Of course, He knew the answer to that, too. In His desire
for dialogue with His disobedient children, He showed just how interested
He was in preserving His relationship with them. Now that the facts were
brought to light, how did God respond? Did He scold them for their sin?
Amazingly, the answer is no. No anger, no scolding, no frowning, no harsh,
impatient tone.

But, you ask, was the sin really dealt with? Yes, indeed, and ever so
kindly and firmly.

They did have to leave their home and face death one day. They must
have cried at the thought of these bitter consequences, but our loving Father God did not leave them without hope. A Savior would come. There
was the promise of reclaiming eternal life.

Think with me for a minute: Does approach matter? I should say it
does. It makes an enormous difference. Even we as adults appreciate it
when someone approaches us gently and pleasantly and gives us hope,
even if we don't relish what they have to say. How much more with children! As I look at God's way of dealing with me, a sinner, I thank Him for
His approach.

*Dearest Father, today let me take time to ask questions, and not to frown and
scold. May I allow my children to experience the right degree of consequences
for their actions, while offering them hope instead of anger.*

Heather Krick

Sanctuary

*But when you pray, go into your room, close the door
and pray to your Father, who is unseen. Then your Father,
who sees what is done in secret, will reward you. Matt. 6:6.*

How do I grow closer to God while the children absorb so much time?"
The short answer is "Sanctuary." A sanctuary is a quiet spot where
nothing else can distract you from your spiritual focus. In Jesus' day people
wore prayer shawls that could be pulled over the head to form a little linen
tent. The sights of family and friends, dust and din would be instantly zip-
locked out of the visual field, and prayer could progress in that environment without distraction. You need to find two kinds of sanctuaries.

The first is your daily time sanctuary, when children are sleeping or out
of your care. My wife and I take turns watching Melody while the other has
their hour of prayer. One father I know was burdened by his son's tendency
to wake up at 6:00 a.m. and ended up waking up at 5:00 a.m. How did he
keep from falling asleep? He went to bed an hour earlier too. He skipped
television, neglected his social networks, and remembered the exceeding
importance of conversation with his divine Father.

The second kind of sanctuary is what I call a "break." One mother I
heard of created a rule for her children: if she pulled her apron up over her
face, they couldn't disturb her. What did she do during these times? She
prayed fervently. Sometimes parents need time-outs too! We have all been
frustrated, and to create a spontaneous sanctuary for some teeth-gnashing
prayers of deliverance is far superior to losing your temper.

We all need reminding of Jesus' words from today's Scripture reading
from time to time. Jesus was stressing the importance of having a quiet
spot where nothing else could distract us from the Father. Sanctuary is a
key to success. It is important to be fed by your heavenly Parent, because if
you aren't, your own parenting will suffer.

*Heavenly Father, we praise You that in the busyness of life, we can find sanc-
tuary in You. Teach us the importance of coming aside to a quiet place and
seeking Your presence as a daily practice.*

Jesse Ferguson

Delight Yourself in the Lord

Delight yourself in the Lord. Ps. 37:4, ESV.

I stood at the kitchen window washing the dishes. Our Labrador retriever, Husky, seemed to have spotted me through the light kitchen curtains. I could see him just staring at me through the curtains, probably trying to get a better view. I moved the curtain so we could both get a better view of each other. As soon as he saw me clearly, he wagged his tail furiously. I closed the curtain and his tail stopped wagging immediately, but he kept on "looking intently," as my then-5-year-old daughter liked to put it. I opened the curtain again, which evoked the same response from Husky. I did this a few times, and had fun watching how I received the same response every time—consistent and predictable! It got me thinking . . .

How do I respond to my children? Do I show them that I am happy to be with them, irrespective of the circumstances? Do I take delight in them, love them consistently, irrespective of their behavior? Do I, at times, stop what I am doing, look directly at my children and listen to them, showing genuine interest in them? H'mmm . . . How do I respond to Jesus? Am I happy to be in His presence? Do I let Him know that I am so glad to have Him with me—all the time? Do I "see" Him? Or is there a "curtain," or something else in my life, that, at times, obscures my vision of Him? Could it be my busyness? My self-interests? My preoccupied thoughts? H'mmm . . . What is Jesus' response to me? How does He feel when I am in His presence?

"The Lord your God is in your midst, . . .
He will rejoice over you with gladness,
He will quiet you with His love,
He will rejoice over you with singing" (Zeph. 3:17, NKJV).

Dear Jesus, there are so many lessons that You would like to teach me. What an awesome reality that the God of the universe takes delight in me, actually rejoices over me with singing! Lord, may I focus on You intently today, and may the love, joy, and peace that will come from that experience serve to draw my children to You.

Belinda Solomon

Recharge Your Batteries

However, the report went around concerning Him all the more; and great multitudes came together to hear, and to be healed by Him of their infirmities. So He Himself often withdrew into the wilderness and prayed. Luke 5:15, 16, NKJV.

Have you ever felt that you needed to escape? Are you besieged with endless to-do lists and a calendar that is relentless? The verse above reminds me that Jesus Himself needed time alone. Wow! That gives me permission to withdraw and recharge my own batteries without feeling guilty.

Parenting is a lot of work. It makes great demands on our time and energy. These demands start before our children even get out of bed and continue long after they've fallen asleep. Jesus understands these demands. Many people besieged Him when they discovered He could heal the sick and perform miracles. There was no end to the ingenious ways they devised just to touch Him or get His attention (see Luke 5:18, 19).

Jesus recognized the huge demand for His time and knew that the only way He could deal with this well would be in spending time alone with His heavenly Father to rest, pray, and recharge His batteries. It wasn't selfish; it was the most loving thing He could do for His children. It gave Him the energy and strength He needed to deal with their many issues. Your own need for time alone with God isn't selfish either.

Sometimes you need to say no to your children so you can spend quality time with your heavenly Father. It is one of the most loving things you can do as a parent. It also models the importance of a daily devotional life to your children.

Do your children witness you spending time in prayer and with the Word? Do they see that this is a priority in your schedule? Teaching your children this is one of the most important lessons that they will ever learn, and it will help keep you refreshed and recharged to meet the challenges of each day.

Dear Lord, please help me to slow down. I need to drink deeply from the springs of living water that flow freely from Your Word. May this be my first priority each day.

Claudio and Pamela Consuegra

God's GPS

Trust in the Lord with all your heart and do not lean on your own understanding. In all your ways acknowledge Him, and He will make your paths straight. Prov. 3:5, 6, NASB.

I have heard since I was a little girl that God has a plan. He has mapped the course of my life and if I just follow His directions, He'll get me where He wants me. I have never doubted that God has a plan, but what happens if I make a wrong turn? What if I refuse to listen at a crucial crossroads? Does that mean I've forever ruined God's plan for my life?

A few years ago I was driving with a friend who had a GPS system in her car. The GPS told us where to turn, but we thought we knew a better way, and ignored its automated voice time and again. Each time the voice would say, "recalculating route," and a moment later we would have revised directions to follow. It wasn't long before we were hopelessly lost. Finally deciding to listen to the GPS, we got where we needed to be, but it took us nearly twice as long as it would have if we'd just followed the instructions in the first place.

My wrong turns in life left me feeling as though I'd rendered myself unusable by God. Each wrong turn had taken me further from Him and all He had in store for me. When I cried out to God, He did something amazing. He began recalculating my route. Looking back to that moment, I realize God was recalculating all along. I was just not willing to listen to His directions. God infused renewed purpose, direction, and hope into my life.

I still make wrong turns, but God has never failed to recalculate my route to lead me back to Him. I want to be in the center of His will for my life, for it is the only place where I truly experience joy, hope, peace, and pure, unconditional love. He is ever faithful. He will never stop recalculating your route. Just turn on your spiritual GPS and follow His directions.

Lord, thank You for Your endless mercy. I want to make Your will my destination. Please recalculate my path until it leads straight to You.

Andrea Michelle Wood

The Redwall Descent

*Have I not commanded you? Be strong and of good courage;
do not be afraid, nor be dismayed, for the Lord your God
is with you wherever you go. Joshua 1:9, NKJV.*

Last week, while my wife (who is five months pregnant with our first child) was visiting family, I had the opportunity to take a few days off work to go backpacking in the Grand Canyon. I was glad to follow my friends' lead down the Grandview Trail, though I soon realized I was carrying too much and was not in good shape. I'd also forgotten my map, and I missed the "dangerous and difficult" designation of the descent we were taking.

Fear began taking over when I found my pack touching the cliff wall to my right and the path fell away into a several-hundred-foot drop four inches from my left shoe. This triggered my fight-or-flight response, but with no one to fight and no safe way to flee, I set about fighting the urge to hyperventilate while I begged my knocking knees to hold me up and keep moving until I reached a safe resting place. I also fought the urge to make unreasonable promises to God concerning what I would do in exchange for my life.

Days later, the thought came to me: *I risked my life for almost nothing.* A few pictures, a few memories, maybe, but nothing of real significance was gained from that risk. The next thought I believe was God-inspired: *I haven't been very willing to risk my life for something that matters.* Many of my decisions are based on reducing risks rather than achieving worthy goals. Like Joshua before the march around the walls of Jericho, I am in need of my Captain's call and promise: "Be strong and of good courage; do not be afraid, nor be dismayed, for the Lord your God is with you wherever you go." And with that call He has given me a "Map" for the journey to follow His lead, and the courage in turn to lead my growing family in His path.

Dear God, thank You for being our captain and friend through life, both in the valley of the shadow and beside the still waters, and for the courage to follow You to the end. Amen.

Joseph Earl

Yesterday's Regrets

Brothers and sisters, I do not consider myself yet to have taken hold of it.
But one thing I do: Forgetting what is behind and straining
toward what is ahead, I press on toward the goal to win the prize for which
God has called me heavenward in Christ Jesus. Phil. 3:13, 14.

Yesterday I didn't give out enough hugs. Yesterday I ignored my children when I really should have taken time to give them my full attention. Yesterday I wasn't consistent with my discipline. Have your yesterdays ever looked like mine? I've had more than a few parenting regrets over the years, and chances are, so have you. I am so very glad that God has given us His Word to instruct and uplift. Today's scripture encourages and reminds me that yesterday is gone and I must press forward regardless of what is past.

I've heard it said more than once that parenting is a journey. While each day presents us with a new challenge, it also presents us with a new opportunity to try again. Being honest with yourself about your mistakes, taking responsibility for the things you can change, and moving forward in God's grace is the best way to redeem what was lost yesterday.

"I do not consider myself yet to have taken hold of it." This scripture reminds me that it is OK that I am not a perfect parent, and that I have the opportunity to improve each and every day. So I press forward. I press forward in my efforts to be peaceful and use a variety of parenting tools to teach my children. I press forward as I show love to my children every opportunity I get. I press forward as I endeavor to give my children attention in appropriate ways. I press forward as I learn from my mistakes and become a consistent and loving disciplinarian. I press forward toward parenting in a way that will bring glory to God.

Dear Father, You see my mistakes. Forgive me for what is past. Strengthen me as I move forward and, by Your grace, become a better parent each and every day. Give me the tools I need to raise my children for You. Give me the courage to press forward.

Kelly D. Holder

Mocha Mischief

How sweet are Your words to my taste!
Yes, sweeter than honey to my mouth! Ps. 119:103, NASB.

My sons looked like adorable miniature college students in their matching red-and-blue oxford sweaters and patent-leather shoes, and we still had 15 minutes to spare. It had been more than a year since I'd visited my former workplace, and today my boys and I were invited back for a visit. I was eager to show them off to my former coworkers, happy to have a day out of the house.

Suddenly an awful truth hit me: it had been silent for more than five minutes. Running through the kitchen, I turned into the hall and looked into the boys' corner bedroom.

Four "raccoon" eyes stared back. In front of me sat two of the stickiest, dirtiest toddlers ever. Their once-washed, gelled-back hair now resembled dirty mop heads. Their matching red-and-blue oxford sweaters were entirely caked in brown. Their collars, once starched and white, were now barely visible, bobbing and drowning amid a sea of milk chocolate.

Todd, my oldest, muttered, "Hide!" and my two Mocha Monsters dropped their chocolate container to the floor and looked up angelically, a vapor of cocoa dust spiraling up into the air. The boys smiled, their little mocha mustaches serving only as iconic mockeries to the clean boys they had been just minutes before. "Y-e-s, Ma-ma, we red-ee ta-g-go," they stuttered, Hershey syrup dribbling down their chins.

In the words of the famous Uncle Arthur, "I'll draw a curtain around what happened next." Let's just say it wasn't two well-dressed little boys that went to the office that day. Instead, two boys in sweat suits and baseball caps made a hurried visit, all the luster gone from the morning excursion.

I have long thought about that chocolate-dumping day, and like sweets gone sour too fast, sin goes down sweetly but leaves huge stains. Much like toddlers, we lack the perspective to see our true condition, and, after time, leave dirty habits and footprints everywhere we go. The only moral hygiene is to "shower" every day in God's presence and feast often in the rich milk chocolate of His Word.

Father, may we feast ourselves daily on the richness of Your Word as we strive to become more like You.

Cindy R. Chamberlin

Puzzle of My Life

For I am confident of this very thing, that He who began a good work in you will perfect it until the day of Christ Jesus. Phil. 1:6, NASB.

Another puzzle. I so enjoy the peace that puzzles bring, but suddenly that is interrupted. "I've looked everywhere, Mommy, and it isn't here! It's green, and there are no green ones." And he jumps down from the chair and heads into the other room where the puzzles are stored. He is so sure that the missing piece is stopping all progress. Oh, my little child. You have so much to learn.

"Honey, just come back and put together the pieces you do have, OK? After you figure out these, then we will look for the one that is missing."

Reluctantly he turns around to continue working on the puzzle. But here's the thing. Ten to 20 minutes later, when the puzzle is finished, there are no missing pieces! He had been so very sure one was missing, but in the end it was here all along.

I think of my life, which feels all too much like a puzzle sometimes. Jumbled. In pieces. I want so very badly to get those pieces together and see the finished product. Then suddenly I get stuck. A missing piece? It must be. It has to be! But where is it? "God, I'm missing a piece of my life, and I can't continue on without it. I have to find it right now! Now! Have You seen it?"

His reply sounds strangely familiar. "My child, sit back down and relax for a while. Look at the pieces in front of you. Everything you need to complete this puzzle, to live your life, to be complete, is already there."

And here's the thing. Ten to 20 (or more) years later my puzzle is looking more and more complete. I keep finding the pieces I need right in front of me. At times I think I'm stuck, but then I see it, right in front of me. Piece by piece. One by one. Slowly I learn that God has already given me everything I need to become the beautiful picture He intended me to be.

God, help me trust You, believing that all these jumbled pieces will someday be a masterpiece.

Elizabeth Fresse

Becoming Full-term

But grow in the grace and knowledge of our Lord and Savior Jesus Christ. To him be the glory both now and to the day of eternity. Amen. 2 Peter 3:18, ESV.

When I was about eight months pregnant with my third child, I attended a midweek Bible study focusing on spiritual maturation and how to be a mature disciple for Christ. While we were studying, my son began to kick in a most feisty manner, and I couldn't help thinking how glad I was going to be when my pregnancy was finally over.

At that point it dawned on me that spiritual maturity is a lot like having a baby. When we first give our hearts and our lives to God, we become a new creation. We start off small and completely unable to survive on our own, completely dependent on our heavenly Father. Yet as long as we are connected to God we continue to grow and thrive, and eventually we are able to function in the world as a living, breathing, fully mature Christian. If during this time something ever goes wrong, then our gestation is at risk, and sadly, we may never reach full maturation.

I picture God being something like an anxious mother, counting the days until her pregnancy is over and her baby is delivered. He waits for the day when sin is no more, when Jesus comes to claim His children. He waits for that day with longing, wanting to be with us so badly, but knowing if that day comes too soon, not everyone will be ready. So He continues to wait, knowing His people need a little longer to reach their full development.

In the meantime, we need to continue to cling to God, realizing just how dependent we are upon Him for our spiritual growth and development. Let us gather as much nourishment from Him as we can so that we can be fully mature Christians when the day of our delivery finally arrives and we are united with our Father in heaven.

Father, thank You for giving us time to grow and mature in You. Please help us develop into the Christians You want us to be, ready for the world and ready for our deliverance.

Asheley Woodruff

A Matter of Priorities

But seek first his kingdom and his righteousness,
and all these things will be given to you as well. Matt. 6:33.

When children enter the picture, life becomes busy. It doesn't matter how organized you are—life changes drastically when the first child comes home. Life now tends to revolve around the children, and spare time, if you had it before, comes at a premium, if it comes at all.

It is so easy for devotional time to evaporate as we spend time with our children and everything else parenthood entails. There are always toys to pick up, clothes to wash, dishes to take care of, not to mention the mundane duties of shopping and errands. It is easy to get busy with life and forget our spiritual priorities.

One of our first priorities as parents should be seeking to maintain our relationship with our God and Savior. As our children grow, we begin worshipping with them before bed, and while this is good, it should not substitute for our own personal time with God.

Let your children see you having your devotions, rather than putting it off until they are in bed. How much better it is to take the time to worship while they are still awake and can observe from their earliest years that this is a priority for us. Dishes can wait, folding clothes can wait, picking up toys can wait, because worship is more important.

Our children will be observing us as they grow. What will they perceive our priorities to be? It is OK that they see us vacuuming, mowing the lawn, cleaning the garage, reading and relaxing. These are good things. But remember, they also need to see us spending time building our spiritual relationship with God and with our spouse. If God thought it was a priority to provide a way of salvation for us, it is only right that we take advantage of this and spend the time we need to maintain this relationship. The example for our children has eternal benefits.

Lord, thank You for the gift of time. Help us to use our time and set our highest priorities on our spiritual life to give our children an example worthy of the gift of Your Son.

Gary Reinbold

Closer, Daddy

But it is good for me to draw near to God. Ps. 73:28, NKJV.

We all know we should be nurturing and strengthening our relationship with our heavenly Father on a daily basis, but in this crazy life it's easy to let our quiet time with Him get shortened or even forgotten. How kind of God to remind us, through our children, of what He desires for us.

At dinnertime one evening when my son was about 2, he leaned over in his high chair and said, "Closer, Daddy." How that melted my heart. It became a common refrain at mealtimes.

A few Fridays later I was feeling run-down. Long hours at work had shortened my time with my son, and several times I had gotten home after he'd already gone to sleep. On top of that, I had a sermon to prepare for the coming Sabbath and still didn't know what I'd be preaching. When a box of doughnuts showed up, I ate one, thinking I needed a pickup. Shortly after, I felt a fever and headache coming on, then became sick to my stomach. I told my boss I was headed home. My wife and son were astonished to see me so early on a Friday looking green as can be. Andrew ran up to me and said, "I want up with Daddy." This tugged at my heart because we hadn't been close all week, but I was very hesitant to hold him. Who wants to pass the flu or cold virus to a 2-year-old?

As I considered my looming sermon, I had a hard time finding anything redemptive about this ordeal. That's when it struck me. God desires a closer relationship with me. Yet many times, because of my selfish choices and lack of self-control, I find myself run-down, feeling sick and unable to be close to my heavenly Father. But my heavenly Father is actively pursuing that closer relationship with us.

How thankful I am that He will take me, broken and worn-down as I am. Oh that we may "lay aside every weight" and run to our Daddy, who loves it when we move closer.

Dear Father, thank You for being a Father who yearns for His children. Help me remember to draw close to You and snuggle close in Your arms.

Aaron and Jennifer Martin

Letting Go of the Pain

Peace I leave with you; my peace I give you. I do not give to you as the world gives. Do not let your hearts be troubled and do not be afraid. John 14:27.

Pain is a part of life! Unfortunately, unresolved pain can keep us from being complete and content people. We may not even be aware of this pain on a daily basis, but when someone touches that hurtful place, we react!

When my children were quite young, I became aware that the pain of a certain relationship was still very much affecting me. I carried around some unanswered questions, frustration, hurt, and even anger; and these burdens were becoming so heavy!

As I examined my hurt and pain, I realized I had internalized this message: If you love God and study and pray enough, you shouldn't have problems. I had believed that if I was really filled with the Holy Spirit, my emotions should always be in good order and my relationships would always be good. It was all up to me.

This situation, however, I couldn't seem to fix. In my quiet moments I realized that too much of my energy was wasted in trying to do the impossible, and I had less and less energy for my family. So I wrote the most difficult letter of my life. In that letter I shared my perception of the situation, my desire to continue the relationship, and my need to give my best energies to my husband and children.

The potential for loss was there, but I had to take the risk. It was incredibly scary to fold that letter, address the envelope, and drop it in the mailbox. I wasn't used to being so direct in addressing difficult issues, for I had been taught as a child, "Don't rock the boat," and "Don't talk about difficult things." Yet, somehow, sending that letter gave me a gentle sense of peace. In letting go of the past, I began to heal.

I remember calling to Marci and Ryan. When they came to me, I hugged and kissed them, told them how much I loved them and how much I enjoyed being their mother. They didn't really understand what was going on, but they liked it!

Lord, thank You for granting me peace in painful times.

Susan Murray

Ripples in a Slippery River

For we do not have a High Priest who cannot sympathize with our weaknesses, but was in all points tempted as we are, yet without sin. Let us therefore come boldly to the throne of grace, that we may obtain mercy and find grace to help in time of need. Heb. 4:15, 16, NKJV.

About a month ago I went camping with one of my best friends and her sons. The water sparkled and babbled as it flowed onward toward the next bend in the river. At one point while creek walking, I found a walking stick just the right size for one of the younger boys to use to maneuver better among the slippery rocks of the river. We all enjoyed playing in the ripples where there were miniature rock dams.

One afternoon I sat down on the edge of a dam and let the water flow around me. The boys pretended they were boats in the water and were having a grand time. Then the boy with the walking stick decided to use it as a boat, wanting to watch it flow down the current to me. It worked fine until he decided to put the stick on the other side of the rock barrier. The current was much faster over there, and it very quickly took that little stick just out of my reach. No matter how far I reached for it, the stick floated farther and farther away until it was lost.

To us it was just a simple stick, but it made me think about how careless we are, how we like to push the limits with God. He gives us the tools we need to navigate the rapids and slick rocks of life, yet we often think we know better, that crossing the barrier just a little surely can't hurt us. We quickly lose our footing and are carried farther and farther away from Him. God's reach, however, can find us no matter how far from Him we drift. Oh the joy He has when we finally reach up to take His hand, which pulls us into the safety of His loving arms.

Thank You, Father, for rescuing Your children from the rapids of life and for staying right beside us no matter how many times we break through Your safe barriers.

Wanda L. Davis

Remember Elim

I pour out my complaint before him; before him I tell my trouble. Ps. 142:2.

A most effective conversation starter is to complain about something. Complaining is contagious, and soon you are surrounded by a storm of negativity. Consider the Israelites.

The story in Exodus 17:1-7 deals with one of Israel's many complaints. We are told the Israelites were led by God through the desert to Rephidim, but when they got there they were dissatisfied because there was no water. They were aggressively rude to Moses, but essentially they were complaining about God, until they began to question whether God was with them at all.

We tend to forget God's past providence when we are frustrated and concerned. Amnesia sets in. Just a short period before, God had miraculously sweetened the bitter waters of Marah and led them to picturesque Elim, where there were 12 springs and shady palm trees, yet the Israelites forgot. Now they doubted whether He was with them, as they anticipated dying of thirst in the empty wilderness.

In Isaiah 43:19-22 God says that He would have given His chosen people water in the desert, but they did not ask Him. Was the remedy that simple? Yes! All that was needed was to ask. God's heart of love longed for His people to remember how He had provided for them before, and realize He held the key to heaven's storehouse of blessings.

Despite their grumblings, God graciously provided water from a rock in the desert. What a loving and merciful God we have. Water gushed out and streams flowed abundantly (Ps. 78:20), more water than you could ever hope to find in a desert.

How do you handle your "Rephidim" experiences? Do you remember Elim or do you complain incessantly to God? Whenever you struggle to see God's hand, trust in His loving heart. Wherever He guides you, He will abundantly provide. His resources are limitless. Joyfully declare God's omnipotence, gratefully remember His past goodness, and humbly make your needs known to Him. Experience how prayer quiets the soul and calms the spirit.

Heavenly Father, we praise You for Your steadfast love toward us. Thank You for standing beside us even when we forget You are there. Help us to place our trust in You when we are tempted to complain.

Cheryl Williams

Let Your Heart Shine

For God, who said, "Let light shine out of darkness,"
made his light shine in our hearts to give us the light of the knowledge
of God's glory displayed in the face of Christ. 2 Cor. 4:6.

My boys love to make me paintings, cut-out hearts, colored pictures. Most of their art depicts their favorite outdoor activities and how much they love Mommy.

As I am writing this, I'm looking out my window. The sun is shining in, and I can see all kinds of smears and smudges on the window, tiny fingerprints all over the once-clean glass. I start to smile, because I remember my sweet Samuel taping his artwork to the window recently, his precious little hands working so diligently to display the heart he had cut out for me where I would see it. My first thought as I look out the window is how dirty it has become, but I look closer, and I see most of the smudges are around this perfect, clean shape of a heart. The sunlight streaming through the window illuminates it, reminding me of my precious son's love for his mommy.

Isn't this what God has done with each of us? Diligently He works on us with His precious, loving hands, cutting us out, perfecting us. Yes, we've been marked on, taped up, gotten smudges all over us, but take a breath. Step back and look at the picture of your life. When all is said and done, what do you see? Can you see it? Shining through the apparent mess of our lives, God's love is shining through us, displaying His love for all to see.

I see it. And I KNOW others do too.

If my window had never been covered in these little handprints, I would never have seen that special heart. It would have blended in and not been visible to shine. God is so awesome!

Father God, thank You for Your love. Thank You that even though our lives may seem messy and smudged and stained with the cares of life, there is more to it than that. We are Your artwork, Your message of love to the world around us. May we never get so caught up in the smudges that we forget to see the beauty of Your love. Amen.

Tami Faudi

God Carries Me

Listen to me, O house of Jacob, all the remnant of the house of Israel,
who have been borne by me from your birth, carried from the womb;
even to your old age I am he, even when you turn gray I will carry you.
I have made, and I will bear; I will carry and will save. Isa. 46:3, 4, NRSV.

From the time of the miracle of conception until birth, this child
inside me will have had everything provided for by my body. What an
amazing concept! Every cellular component and need of my baby has been
generated, gleaned, and maintained exclusively from my body's resources.
As I feel the growing baby inside me move and kick, joy grows in my heart
and I desire to make sure I provide all he or she needs to develop into a
healthy little one.

As incredible as that desire becomes, it is a mere echo of God's heart
toward me. As Acts 17:28 says: "For in Him we live and move and have our
being, . . . for we are also His offspring" (NKJV). How beautiful to stop and
ponder! What an intimate picture: God has carried us like a mother carries her child in the womb. Everything I need, everything I call my own,
everything I am comes from God's own resources.

So many times I fall the way of the Pharisees to fret over my own works
in this regenerative process, when I have no more claim to origination than
my growing fetus does.

How can I doubt God's lavish provision when He has given all of heav-
en to me in Jesus? What I needed God gave, even at the cost of His own
body. God suffered to offer me life, yet He does not resent His suffering.
All He desires is to take me closer to His heart for all eternity. As my needs
grow, His provision grows more abundantly. I cry tears of joy and thankfulness to be carried by this Savior.

*Dear Jesus, thank You for giving all of Yourself to me so that I can be re-
created in Your image. I accept the work You have done on my behalf, and
surrender all my heart to be reborn by Your Spirit. Thank You for making me
a forever child of the King.*

Jessica Earl

First Things First

But the Lord said to her, "My dear Martha, you are worried and upset over all these details! There is only one thing worth being concerned about. Mary has discovered it, and it will not be taken away from her." Luke 10:41, 42, NLT.

It seems as if the laundry basket is always full of dirty laundry. Dust settles on the furniture, toilets need to be cleaned, and floors need to be scrubbed, and that doesn't even take into account the car shuttles to soccer practice, piano lessons, doctor appointments, and grocery store runs. The calendar is full, and it seems overwhelming to attempt to fit one more thing in. Where does time with Jesus belong in the long to-do list?

In the Scripture verse for today, Jesus reminds us that we spend so much time and energy focusing on things that are of little significance. Instead, perhaps we need to take a look at how we are spending our time with a set of fresh eyes—eyes that see things from an eternal perspective. Journal for a week how you are spending your day. You may be surprised. Jesus' words "there is only one thing to be concerned about" cause us to pause and reflect. What is it that we are concerned about? What occupies our thoughts and our time? What can we change?

Is it time to set our homes in order so that there is time for family devotions? Our children will grow to become the father or mother that they see modeled in the home. Time management and the setting of priorities are skills that must be modeled and taught to our children. A good start is to schedule time daily for family worship. Keep this time as a sacred commitment. Do not allow anything else to push this time aside as unimportant. Put your house in order.

Daily sit as a family as the feet of Jesus. And, in the process of setting our priorities straight, we may end up discovering that our productivity as well as our energy level will actually increase.

Dear Lord, please help me set my priorities according to Your will. I pray that the busyness of life will not distract me from spending quality time with You.

Claudio and Pamela Consuegra

The Most Important Thing

Seek the Kingdom of God above all else. Matt. 6:33, NLT.

Raising a child seems as though it should be so easy, yet sin has marred this some. As difficult as the reality proves to be, however, let us not lose sight of the fact that God created us to fulfill a purpose. When we become parents, our purpose becomes, in part, demonstrating to our children God's outrageous love for them!

Our calling to represent God to our children cannot be something we take lightly! Before you allow the pressure of child rearing to overwhelm you, stop. None of us are perfect.

I was young when I had my firstborn, and I made so many mistakes! Just when you think you've learned something, another child comes along and you realize each child is different and what worked with one doesn't necessarily work with the other.

What, then, do we do? Put your child in God's hands from the first, even before your pregnancy begins, even before your child is born. Begin praying for them before they are born. Realize that if you want God to help you raise your child for the kingdom, you must first know your own way there. If you want to represent God to your child, be sure you have a relationship with Him yourself!

This is how my journey began! I became intentional about spending time with Jesus and developing my Christian life. When our daughter was born, she was such a joy! I don't know about you, but to me firstborn children are always a little scary. Did I make mistakes? Of course. But God was always there! I learned to bring everything to Him in prayer, and when things didn't go well, He was there to sustain, encourage, and guide the not-so-good into something better!

Whatever situation you find yourself in while raising your child, remember, your first job as a parent is to seek Him! By so doing we become like Him and are enabled to pass His character on to the next generation! It's never too late to turn to Him, and build that relationship that will carry us and our children to eternity!

Father, help us today to be more like You, to live and represent You to the children You've given us, so they are prepared for the kingdom!

Z. Kathy Cameron

God's Adopted Family

*God decided in advance to adopt us into his own family
by bringing us to himself through Jesus Christ. This is what he wanted to do,
and it gave him great pleasure. Eph. 1:5, NLT.*

As someone who has been adopted and is herself considering adoption, I am always amazed by the idea that God is in the same business Himself. Time and again in Scripture the great Creator of the universe is depicted as a parent engaged in the process of adoption. He loves His wayward people so much that He wants to incorporate us into His family! It is astonishing if you think about it. This is why God was willing to pay the ultimate sacrifice through His Son, Jesus. The Lord of everything could not bear to see His creation Fatherless and without a home, and so He decided to do something about it.

All children are God-given miracles, but there is something unique about adopted children. Adoption is not an event that happens on a whim or by accident. Neither does it happen quickly. Adoption requires months of careful planning and preparation, and all the time there is the anxiety of knowing that everything might fall apart at the last minute, just before the process is complete, before you can become family. On both sides, too, there is the worry "what if they don't like me?"

Surprisingly, these are the same worries God has over us. We are the children He is waiting to adopt. God has worked everything out so that we can join His family. He did it because He wanted to and it made Him happy, because He loves us immeasurably, and like all adoptive parents, God wants to know, "Do you want to be My child? Will you love Me?"

What a wonderful gift we have before us: to go from being lost and without a future, to becoming the adopted sons and daughters of God; heirs to the very kingdom of heaven.

Father, we want to thank You for making a way, through Jesus, to reclaim us as Your children. Thank You for loving us enough to adopt us into Your own heavenly family. Thank You for the future we have to look forward to in You.

Asheley Woodruff

Hummingbirds and Penguins

In the morning, Lord, you hear my voice;
in the morning I lay my requests before you and wait expectantly. Ps. 5:3.

We all know the differences between penguins and hummingbirds. Both are birds, but this is where the similarities end, for while penguins can't fly, hummingbirds can. They are among the smallest of birds, yet they beat their wings so rapidly—up to 80 times per second—that they appear to be hovering midair rather than flying.

Hovering is expensive—more metabolically expensive than any other type of flight, but as the hummingbird has found, nectar from a flower is an even bigger payoff than the energy it has to expend to get that nectar!

Penguins are really cute! They are great swimmers. They have been featured in a number of movies, and they grace the covers of numerous books and calendars, but that still doesn't change the fact that they never leave the ground.

Do you sometimes feel like a penguin when it comes to meeting the needs of your children? You flap your wings as hard and as fast as you can, yet so often it feels as though you never make it off the ground?

As parents we can learn from the hummingbird. The time we spend with our children should be proportionate to their needs. There are times we may need to "hover," or sustain our efforts for longer periods of time to meet those needs. It's costly. It takes extra energy and, most important, more time in prayer. This means either getting up earlier or staying up later, and can feel overwhelming when we look at our already crowded schedule.

Instead, we need to start looking at our time in prayer as our fueling station. This is where God can give us that extra burst of energy so we not only make it off the ground but can "hover" for sustained periods of time when needed. When we make Him our priority, we will discover that this is where the good stuff is to be found!

Father God, thank You for Your faithfulness to us. Help us never to forget that it is in the quiet moments we spend with You that we receive the strength with which to make it off the ground.

Tawny Sportsman

Come to Me

Come to Me, all you who labor and are heavy laden,
and I will give you rest. Take My yoke upon you and learn from Me,
for I am gentle and lowly in heart, and you will find rest for your souls.
For My yoke is easy and My burden is light. Matt. 11:28-30, NKJV.

I found myself feeling flustered. I had so much to do in such a little time—the story of my life! But it occurred to me yet again that there was no need to rush—as long as I was truly being led by the Lord, that is! I thought about Jesus. It is said that He never rushed. He was always calm and serene. At times He "sat on a mountain" (Matt. 15:29-31). When the crowds arrived, He taught them, healed them, and met their needs, and they in return glorified God. Does that kind of attitude seem possible for busy parents to emulate?

The thought that I did not have to rush was strangely comforting, because not having to feel rushed, not having to feel anxious while pushing so hard to tick off all my items on my to-do list, really went against the very grain of my being. Have you noticed, parents, that when you are taking care of young children all day, your to-do list somehow just doesn't get done?

I love the Bible account of Jacob and Esau's reunion. Esau was keen that they travel together, but Jacob told his brother to go ahead because he had to progress slowly for the sake of the children. He wanted to move at a pace that they could "endure." If we try to move at our own rapid pace, dragging our children along with us to keep up with our agenda, we will end up feeling frustrated, or even resentful—and this of course is not good for our children either! We have a Friend who beckons us to "come . . . and rest a while" (Mark 6:31, NKJV) and find refreshment and a new perspective.

Lord, forgive me for selfishly following my own agenda at times. Teach me how to slow down and meet my children's needs, as You did for the people who were with You every day.

Belinda Solomon

Preparation

*I am the vine; you are the branches. If you remain in me and I in you,
you will bear much fruit; apart from me you can do nothing. . . .
If you remain in me and my words remain in you, ask whatever you wish,
and it will be done for you. John 15:5-7.*

We're having a baby! These are some of the most exciting words a couple can say. Now the preparations begin.

My husband came home with books on exercise for the pregnant woman, books on nutrition for the pregnant woman, books on the growth and development of the fetus, and books on how to care for a newborn. I was exhausted just looking at them, but so pleased that he was so excited and involved in the process.

We signed up for prenatal classes, started reading all the books, and felt we were really getting our act together in this great adventure that we were on.

I will always be grateful for the wonderful Christian nurse practitioner who led our prenatal class. She took us through pregnancy, labor, and the delivery process, but then the questions came: "What is your relationship with Christ like?" "Have you committed yourselves and this child you carry to Him?" "Have you asked Him to develop your parenting skills in a way that is pleasing to Him?"

When I left class that evening, my head was spinning. Yes, I told myself, I am a Christian, I believe in prayer and faithfully pray every day. But have I specifically asked for God's wisdom concerning my unborn child? Have I even thought about what kind of parenting skills I have, and is God involved in my thoughts and actions as I prepare for this miracle?

That night my husband and I realized that this journey we were embarking on would take more than just our strength and feeble efforts, but would need a huge infusion of Christ's wisdom, love, and mercy.

Through the years we have come to depend on the time spent with God in prayer for our children. Check in with Christ each morning before you face your children, and He will not disappoint you!

Dear Father, I will face today with Your grace and love because You have told me I can, and I will lean on You as You direct my path.

Darla L. McCarty

Waiting Quietly

The Lord is good to those whose hope is in him, to the one who seeks him; it is good to wait quietly for the salvation of the Lord. Lam. 3:25, 26.

When there are small children in the house, it is not too often that the house becomes quiet. And if it becomes quiet, the question becomes, "What are they doing?" Are they in the bathroom filling the toilet with paper? Could it be that they are covering themselves with lotion—while fully dressed? Has someone discovered the hiding place for the scissors and begun giving out free haircuts? As much as parents desire peace and quiet, the sound of quiet is sometimes more alarming than the shrillest squeals. However, in my house, the direct opposite of this is the constant request of help. I hear "Mommy, Mommy, Mommy!" all day long. And often it's over the same request. I have answered my children, but they are unable to wait patiently for me to fulfill the request.

My relationship with God sometimes echoes what is happening in my relationship with my children. I find myself making a lot of noise, repeatedly asking for help, and trying to get God's attention. I sometimes forget that God sees me. He knows what I am doing. He hears my requests, and an answer is on its way. All I need to do is patiently wait on Him. Patiently waiting, however, can be one of the hardest things to do, and our ability, or lack of ability, to patiently wait is, I think, a good indication of our level of trust in God. It is obtained by putting our trust in the one we are waiting for.

I want my children to trust me, to wait for me to do what I said I would do. How much more does God want us to patiently wait on Him? I believe when we as parents learn to wait, we are much better equipped to teach our children how to wait. I challenge you to increase your trust by quietly waiting on the Lord.

Dear God, teach us how to wait quietly for You. Show us how to teach our children how to wait quietly. We thank You for answering.

Kelly D. Holder

March

Teaching Children That God Is Love

God Is Love

*The one who does not love does not know God,
for God is love. 1 John 4:8, NASB.*

J esus gave His listeners a new name for the ruler of the universe: "Our Father." He wanted them to understand what tender love God had for them and how He longed for them. He taught that God cares for every person, that "the Lord has mercy on those who respect him, as a father has mercy on his children" (Ps. 103:13, NCV).

This concept of God as a loving Father is unique among the religions of the world. Other religions teach that the Supreme Being should be feared rather than loved. They worship a cruel deity that needs to be appeased by sacrifices rather than a Father who showers His children with love. Since the Jews of Jesus' day had become so blind to this precious teaching of their prophets, Jesus' revelation of God's fatherly love was a fresh new gift to the world.

The Jews taught that God loved those who served Him—that is, those who lived by the strict rules of the rabbis—but that He had only anger and curses for the rest of the world's inhabitants. "That's not true," Jesus said. "The whole world, both the evil and the good, basks in the sunshine of God's love." They should have learned this truth from nature itself, for God "causes the sun to rise on good people and on evil people, and he sends rain to those who do right and to those who do wrong" (Matt. 5:45, NCV).

God loves us with an astounding love. As our love for Him grows, we will begin to appreciate the length and width and height and depth of this love that can never be measured. God never forces anyone—love is His tool to push sin from the human heart. With love, He changes pride into humility and turns hatred and skepticism into love and faith.

God is love. Like rays of light from the sun, love and light and joy flow out from Him to all His creatures. It is His nature to give. His whole life is about unselfish love. He tells us to be perfect as He is—in the same way. We are to be centers of light and blessing to our little circle, just as God is to the universe. We have no light of our own, but the light of His love shines on us, and we can reflect it.

Father, may we know how much You love us, and share it with the world.

Jerry D. Thomas

A God to Love

May the God of hope fill you with all joy and peace in believing, so that by the power of the Holy Spirit you may abound in hope. Rom. 15:13, ESV.

My sister recently told me that when we were growing up she was always afraid whenever my father was away from home because she believed that if she wasn't "good," God would punish her and something terrible would happen to him. He traveled an incredible amount, so this was a very heavy burden for a little girl to carry.

We grew up in Africa, in the country of Zimbabwe, and during our childhood it was a country at war. Each evening the news was full of reports of terrible atrocities, stories of people who had been ambushed or attacked while going about their daily lives. When our father was away from home, we would sleep with our mother, who would arm herself with prayer and, for some reason, the detachable leg of the dressing-table chair.

We believed in God. We prayed for safety for all of us, adding "Thy will be done." We were very aware that we didn't know what God's will was, and how we hoped that it included returning our father to us safely—which He did time after time.

When my sister told me about her childhood fear, it got me thinking about how we teach our children of God. It can be so easy for children to develop the idea that if they mess up, God will punish them or will no longer love them. In our desire to teach them obedience, we must be careful they don't develop the impression there are too many rules and expectations that they will never be able to live up to. In this way, they learn to anticipate failure.

How do we respond when our children mess up? What do we teach them about the love of God in those moments? How do we teach our children from the Bible? It is so important to remember that the stories of the Bible are there to show them just how much God loves them and just how far He will go to save them, and that He will never, ever give up on them.

Lord, help me represent You accurately to my children as the God who loves them so much He died for them and wants what is best for them. Help me show them You are love.

Colleen Duncan

Teaching Children That God Is Love

Apart from me you can do nothing. John 15:5.

Snuggle with me, Mama," the little voice pleaded, as I shut the storybook and tucked her in for her nap. I groaned inwardly. This was also my personal quiet time and my to-do list was long. Stifling frustration and breathing a silent prayer, I smiled at her wistful 3-year-old face.

"Just for a few minutes," I melted, laying down my agenda. I scrunched up on her bed and nestled my chin in her curly hair. She closed her eyes, both of us supremely content. Our arms wrapped around each other, I thanked God for the chance to hold my daughter, to give her a picture of what God's love means on her terms.

There are as many ways to teach our children God's love as there are moments in our day: Reading, playing and working alongside them, drawing them close to help instead of shooing them away, and showing our children how to love through service. God's love is baking cookies together. It is also picking up the doggy doo together. It is folding dish towels together, as well as drawing pictures to give away at the retirement home.

As parents we scribble pictures of God for our children to see. We show God's consistent, persistent love when we, too, persevere, never giving up on our goal to show them Jesus. Holding our children accountable, with loving communication and consequences, will open their hearts and win their respect. We teach God's love through a God-centered home.

Love takes the time to patiently teach children the way they should go. We show God's love by how we react to conflict. Do we ask our child for forgiveness when we've messed up, scolded them, or acted unloving? Do we practice with our children specifically how to "be nice," or do we snap at them, fed up with their childish ways?

"Apart from me you can do nothing," Jesus says. I can't show God's love unless I trust in His forgiving, loving heart for myself and my many failings. He graciously gives me what I do not naturally have: His cheerful, self-sacrificing love.

Dear Father, I pray that my children will see a picture of Your heart and know Your giving, forgiving, consistent, generous, playful, and snuggly love—on their terms.

Sophie Berecz

Living God's Love

And, ye fathers, provoke not your children to wrath: but bring them up in the nurture and admonition of the Lord. Eph. 6:4, KJV.

Recently a mother came to us for counseling, with her 7-year-old son. She had requested counseling to assist her and her son regarding communication and anger. As the session progressed a few things continued to come to the forefront. The mother kept asking, "Why is my child so angry? What can I do to get him to open up to me?" And from the little boy: "No matter what I do, my mom doesn't see the good in me." Our hearts broke when we heard him make this statement.

Imagine growing up without hearing nurturing words of encouragement and love. How unbearable for a child, or anyone, for that matter. We all require sensitivity and tenderness that keeps love growing between each other. In Romans 5:8 God showed His love for us in that while we were still sinners, Christ died for us.

Recognizing our own shortcomings can allow us to overcome the barriers that prevent us from reaching out to our loved ones. In order to correct a difficult situation it is not unusual for risk to be involved as we prepare to leave our comfort zones. Making changes in our behavior is never an easy undertaking, but our relationship with our children and family should be important enough to us that we will be willing to take the risk, improve our attitude and behavior, and exhibit compassion.

In many cases, taking the first step becomes a difficult process because of our inability to recognize our personal inadequacies. If we understand our character defects, we can begin the process of taking the risk to communicate our differences.

If we are not demonstrating patience, understanding, and love, it becomes paramount to discover why not and to take whatever steps are necessary to improve the situation. As parents, we are responsible for the tone and atmosphere found within our homes.

Lord, please help me to take the first step to release my burdens to You. Help me support, nurture, and love my children as You love them.

Arthur E. Nowlin and Kim Logan-Nowlin

There's Nothing My God Cannot Do!

The name of the Lord is a strong tower;
the righteous run to it and are safe. Prov. 18:10, NKJV.

Have you ever taken a moment to enjoy hearing children sing? Have you watched the changing expressions on their little faces as they sing each phrase? I enjoy it each morning at nine o'clock when we gather together in the toddler room at our day-care center to sing worship songs and to ask God to bless and keep us safe.

One morning when I asked the children which song they would like to sing, one 3-year-old boy shouted out, "My God Is So Big!" I answered, "That is a great song!" And then I asked him, "Cole, why do you want to sing that song?" Without hesitation he replied, "Because God is so strong and He keeps me safe like my dad."

As parents one of the things we so desperately want to do is to keep our children safe. Safe in the womb, safe on the playground, safe at their day care, safe at their school, and safe while traveling. And when they protest, as they inevitably do, we tell them, "Listen to Mommy and Daddy. We just want to keep you safe."

But what about us? Do we believe Him when says, "I am your tower; I will keep you safe"? The Bible is filled with stories that show God's everlasting love. He has promised to be our tower and defense: "I will be a place of safety to all who put their trust in Me."

Parenting is a rewarding but difficult journey. Have you committed it to God? I believe it is our duty as Christian parents to take God at His word in all our trials, big or small, and rest in the confidence of His Word. Then we can sing with the faith and confidence of the children, our faces aglow with the assurance that comes with knowing that "my God is so big, so strong, and so mighty there is nothing my God cannot do!"

Father, thank You for Your love and patience. Guide us as we teach our little ones to trust in You in all they do. May they see You as the strong tower, the mighty fortress, and God of all.

Darla L. McCarty

Keep Your Eyes on the Prize

*What good is it for someone to gain the whole world,
yet forfeit their soul? Mark 8:36.*

At the age of 9 I discovered what I thought was the eighth wonder of the world: a restaurant that served pizza and had video games. It was all a boy could wish for: piles of pizza, and a room full of video games. Some things are just meant to go together, and in my opinion, whoever had thought up the idea was a genius.

When my son was 6, we accepted an invitation to a friend's birthday party that was to take place at the same pizza-and-video-game restaurant. When we walked through the front door, I don't know who was more excited, me or my son! The atmosphere had improved a lot since I was a kid. No more dark rooms and stingy token distribution. The kids each received handfuls of coins and had the chance to win prizes for playing the games. Naturally, I volunteered to chaperon the kids on the game floor.

We played for hours and were really rolling in the prize tickets. After a couple of hours we had a wad of tickets and headed to the counter to redeem our prize. We were elated, until we noticed the Grand Prize Wall, where the prizes began with 1,000 tickets. We came away with plastic vampire teeth, a microscopic box of nerds, and some other "prizes" that didn't survive the night in the hands of a 7-year-old boy. We felt, in a word, cheated!

Though it had been fun, the payoff proved to be less than great. The investment wasn't really worth the money. Many things in life are the same way, with the promises rarely living up to the hype, leaving people to wonder, "Really? Is this all there is?"

That day served as a great teaching moment: Don't try to gain the whole world, only to lose your soul in the process. Invest in things that last, keep your eyes on the true Prize—Jesus, and hold fast to His teachings. The pursuit of entertainment only leaves us feeling empty.

Father, help us to see what is really important in this life. Help us to keep our eyes on the true Prize, and may we find our deepest joy spending time in Your Word.

Jason Hanselman

Show, Don't Tell

*But God was merciful! We were dead because of our sins,
but God loved us so much that he made us alive with Christ,
and God's wonderful kindness is what saves you. Eph 2:4, 5, CEV.*

My friend and I pushed our carts down the aisles of the grocery store planning our meals and judiciously choosing the best buys to meet our budgets. Both our husbands worked the evening shift at McKee Baking Company, and Cilla and I passed our evenings together; we had it down to a science. She would bathe the kids and read their Sabbath school lesson while I prepared supper. Lately the favorite story was Elijah and Mount Carmel, from *My Bible Friends*.

While we were filling our grocery carts one day, Timothy suddenly threw his hands up in the air and yelled at the top of his voice, "Pray to Baal! Baal, send the rain!" Michelle and Elisa joined in, while Cilla and I wanted to die of embarrassment right there on the spot.

I've asked myself many times why that was the message the kids remembered. Was that all the "take away" they got? And less important, but much more relevant to us that day, what did all the people in the grocery store think about us? Teaching that God is love isn't always easy. We can read them the stories, but we don't always know what they're going to remember. It takes more than *telling* to teach about God's character of love. We must *show* His love

The morning after our foray into the Red Food grocery store I was awake at 5:00, sitting in my favorite chair reading my Bible. Michelle crawled out of bed and came padding into the room. She crawled up on my lap and lay still, sucking her thumb while I prayed. I stroked her head and held her close, so thankful to have a precious daughter to love. She knew Mommy was talking to God, and she knew it was a love-filled experience.

We never heard about Baal again. Perhaps it was the shushing we did and the "Don't say that!" that did the trick. But I prefer to believe that it was the time we spent at home, showing by our example, that it is a loving God who honors the faithfulness of His children and sends the Living Water to those who seek after Him.

Remind us, Lord, that children best learn of Your love when they see it demonstrated in the lives of those they love and trust.

Candy Graves DeVore

A True Parent

For my father and my mother have forsaken me,
but the Lord will take me in. Ps. 27:10, ESV.

I grew up in a very loving home. We didn't have much, but we had one another. We were tucked in at bedtime and had family game nights. Basically, my siblings and I were given the freedom, love, and support needed to find out who we were. We knew our parents made sacrifices so we could be blessed. They were true parents. I dedicated the last book I wrote to them.

As I grew up I was surprised to find out how many false parents are out there. Parents, such as my husband's father, who would punish his children with a punch to the face. And many of my friends had parents who would provide for their monetary needs but deprive them emotionally: The kind of parents who never hugged them, or would crush their childish dreams. I'm sure many of these parents didn't even realize the damage they were inflicting. They simply parented the way they were parented. But this cycle doesn't have to continue.

God is a loving father. We can all learn from Him what it means to be a true parent—how to live with a spirit of adoption rather than an orphaned spirit.

But no matter what kind of parents you had, Father God will give you the freedom, love, and support you need to find out who you are. He has made sacrifices so you can be blessed. He's dedicated His Book to you.

The Bible is a great place to look for parenting advice. While reading to myself during breakfast the other day, my kids were using horrible table manners. I read out loud the verse I was on in *The Message* translation of Proverbs: "Don't gobble your food, don't talk with your mouth full" (Prov. 23:2). My kids thought I had made it up, so I had to show them the scripture.

I was actually surprised, too. But God's Word is like receiving counsel from a loving father. He gives us good advice because He wants what is best for us. He is the only example we need for how to parent.

Lord, help me forgive my own parents for any pain they caused me and teach me how to love my kids the same way You love me.

Angela Ruth Strong

God's Good Plans

"For I know the plans I have for you," says the Lord. "They are plans for good and not for disaster, to give you a future and a hope." Jer. 29:11, NLT.

When my husband accepted a new job position across the country, we were nervous about how the move would affect our children. How would they feel about being taken from their friends, their school, and the only home they had ever known? Would they be able to adjust to vastly different surroundings? How could we explain that God wanted us to make this move?

We had many concerns and endlessly second-guessed ourselves. Both my husband and I had moved across country with our families as young children. We had not adjusted well, and the memories of that trauma were now surging to the surface. Had we just made a huge mistake?

However, God was right there with us, reminding us both that He had set this plan in motion. We were not acting on our own wisdom, but at God's bidding. If God had orchestrated the move for our benefit, then why were we worrying over our children? Didn't God love them infinitely more than we could imagine? Why would our loving Father prosper my husband and me at the expense of our children? We decided to close our ears to Satan's attempts to make us distrust God, and we both took a few deep breaths.

I will not say that the move was easy; we were moving across country after all. Yet it was far better than we could have imagined. Our children became increasingly excited to see their new home and school. And every time they expressed worries about leaving their friends, we reminded them how much God loved them, and that He had good things planned for them.

It is one of the greatest truths. God loves our children infinitely more than we have the capacity to understand. And if He loves us that much, then it makes sense we can trust that when God asks us to step out on faith, He's looking after our children's best interests too.

Thank You, Lord, that You are a God whose plans are perfect. Thank You, Lord, that Your plans for us are good and that You will see to our children's needs, just as You see to ours.

Asheley Woodruff

Safe in Daddy's Arms

Whenever I am afraid, I will trust in You. Ps. 56:3, NKJV.

Thunder boomed and lightning flashed. I was just a little girl and I was afraid. Crawling out of bed, I went running into the living room where my parents were. Shaking and sobbing, I wrapped my tiny arms around my daddy's legs. Reaching down, he pulled me up into his strong arms and held me close. For a long moment I snuggled against my strong daddy and eventually I quit shaking. But at the sound of another lightning strike, I buried my face tight against his shoulder as the thunder rumbled across the sky.

For a while he just held me. Then, carrying me toward the window, Daddy began talking softly. "Look, honey. Let's watch the lightning show in the sky."

Cautiously I raised my head and peered outside. FLASH! Jagged streaks of light split the dark sky. Thunder followed. Daddy squeezed me tighter and whispered in my ear, "It is God's night show. Isn't it beautiful? It is outside, honey. It won't hurt you, because you are safe inside with me."

Held securely in my daddy's arms, I continued watching God's night show until the clouds rolled away and the thunder subsided. Daddy headed toward my bedroom, where he gently tucked me into bed. Then he bent over and kissed me good night. I fell asleep immediately.

I was probably only 3 years old when Daddy helped me overcome my fear of storms. It is the first memory I have of Daddy; the first lesson he taught me about my Father God. Just as my earthly parent soothed me in the darkness of night when I was afraid, so I find security in my Father's arms as I face the storms of life. I can trust my Father to take care of me, to comfort me, and to calm my fears. In His arms I am safe.

Father, hold me close when I feel afraid. May I show my children that Your arms are a safe place to be.

Barbara Ann Kay

Forgiveness

Be gentle and ready to forgive; never hold grudges.
Remember, the Lord forgave you, so you must forgive others. Col. 3:13, TLB.

Strong-willed children present challenges you just don't find anywhere else. How do you discipline a 4-year-old child who constantly punishes her little brother for undermining her position as sole attention-winner in the family? Never-ending sibling rivalry can so easily get out of hand, and it's not always easy to know how to handle these emotion-laden situations. I struggle to know what to do, yet not knowing all the answers has taught me the value of taking every situation to God in prayer.

One day I'd had almost more than I could take. She was nearly as upset as I was, and I knew if I said or did anything in that moment, I would regret it later. I took a deep breath and sent her up to her room, saying she could come down once she'd calmed down.

I sank into the sofa, took a few moments to settle my frayed nerves, then came in prayer to the One who had the answers I needed.

"What shall I do, Father?" I asked, almost in tears. "How do I handle this situation?"

A deep calm settled over me as I prayed. The answer, when it came, was profound in its simplicity: *Forgive her.*

When she came downstairs about 15 minutes later, I sat her down on the sofa beside me, and we discussed what had happened.

"Sweetheart," I said, "what you did to your brother was wrong. Jesus wants us to treat everyone with kindness, no matter how much they annoy us; and He also wants us to forgive each other when we make mistakes. I want you to know that Jesus forgives you, and so do I."

The look of incredulity that crossed her face spoke loudly. That one act of forgiveness was a greater lesson to her than any time-out could have been.

Heavenly Father, thank You for Your lessons in forgiveness. Teach us to be more like You, slow to anger and quick to forgive.

Carey Pearson

All the Same in the Dark

This is My commandment,
that you love one another as I have loved you. John 15:12, NKJV.

I have always endeavored to instill in my son the importance of valuing others in the same way God values us. As parents, we're sometimes unsure how well our words are heard or whether they've fallen on deaf ears. Little did I know how beautifully this principle would manifest itself in my son's life.

Curtis has always been loyal, almost to a fault. He and Charles had been friends since both were a few months old. They were day-care buddies and had been together, almost daily, for three years when a terrible tragedy struck. One night, the house in which Charles lived exploded and caught fire. Charles had most of his body severely burned in the awful accident. At the time, I sat down with my son and explained that even though Charles's looks may have been dramatically changed, he was still Charles inside. Always a deep thinker, Curtis seemed to absorb what I'd said. Time went by during which Charles underwent extensive medical procedures. His healing would be long and painful.

A year and a half passed before Charles was able to return to school. Since I had no clue when his first day back would be, I didn't get to have a final talk with Curtis beforehand. This is how their kindergarten teacher described it.

On Charles's first day back Curtis was there to welcome him as he entered the classroom. Many of the other kids were new and didn't know Charles or anything about the tragedy he'd gone through. They immediately asked what was wrong with him, but before the teacher could intervene, my son became Charles's defender. True friendship does not see scars or faults. Curtis said, "This is my friend, Charles. He may look different, but that's OK, because when we turn out the lights God sees only our hearts and how we act and treat each other." There was silence in the room as the teacher stood choking back her tears. Moments passed, and then the other kids began to greet Charles, and welcomed him into their group.

May we see with Your eyes, Lord, not the differences but the common cords
that bind us all together as brothers and sisters in Christ.

Lori Colwell

Teach Them of His Love

Jesus called the children to him and said,
"Let the little children come to me, . . .
for the kingdom of God belongs to such as these." Luke 18:16.

I've always thought Jesus was referring to the trust and innocence of children in this verse. And while I believe that's true, I think if we look at it from a parental standpoint, we'll see something more. He tells us, "Lead them to Me. Don't get in their way."

Our mission as parents is to help our children fall in love with Jesus. Now, before you think I'm throwing out the important role of daily worship, Sabbath school and church, memory verses, treating our bodies well, and training our minds to think on honorable things, think again. I am totally aware that this lifestyle is beneficial in raising our children. However, I have encountered too many instances of friends who grew up doing all the "right" things, keeping all the "rules," but who ultimately left God completely.

In his excellent book *It's All About Him* Lee Venden shares that if a person falls in love with Jesus, everything else will "take care of itself." If a child is raised to love Jesus, they will want to do everything that pleases Him, because they love Him so much.

In Matthew 7: 21-23 Jesus states that some will lose out on eternity. He says, "Depart from Me, I never knew you." Now note, He doesn't say, "depart because you didn't memorize all your memory verses, or because you made poor choices in your diet, or because you skipped church too often." He says, "You do not know Me." That's our mandate as parents: we are to teach our children to know Jesus. Making them follow all the rules without developing their relationship with Him will eventually result in rebellion, against us and against God. I think that the most important task for childhood is to see that our children fall deeply and completely in love with Jesus.

Don't be discouraged. God is on your side. As much as we love our children, God loves them even more. Amazingly, He allows us the privilege of introducing them to Him.

Dear Father, may we live in such a way that our children see our love for You, and follow on to know You too.

Mary Nell Rosenboom

Lost and Found

In the same way, it is not my heavenly Father's will
that even one of these little ones should perish. Matt. 18:14, NLT.

When we were young, we went to school one day, and someone had brought in a box with eight brown-and-white bunny rabbits. A Holland lop caught our eye. We fell in love with her long, floppy ears. She had a shiny tan and a white tip on her tail. We took the Holland lop home with us, carefully placed between us in the back seat. We played with the rabbit every day, fed her, took care of her, and loved her

One day we came home from school to find our little rabbit was gone. We were heartbroken, and through our tears we wondered why she had run away. We lived near a golf course and spent hours looking for her. We put up flyers all around the neighborhood. And we prayed and prayed for our rabbit to come home safely.

Then one day our mother told us she'd received a phone call to say that one of the golfers had seen the rabbit and had taken her with him to his home in the mountains. Can you imagine our joy? Mother drove all the way out to his house, where she found our beloved pet and brought her home to us.

This experience has always reminded me of the story Jesus told about a shepherd who owned 100 sheep. When one of his sheep was lost, the shepherd left them all to go and search for the missing one. He did not stop looking until he had found his beloved sheep. Our heavenly Shepherd knows each one of us by name. He knows and loves each of our children. They are His precious lambs. He has entrusted them to our care and keeping, and He is not willing that even one of them should be lost.

Dear Jesus, thank You for being the good shepherd and for loving us. Help us to be faithful in tending the little lambs You have placed in our care, and may not one be missing on the day You return to claim Your own.

Chidi, Lissie, and Tyreke Wilson

Teaching Children That God Is Love

You can't go wrong when you love others. When you add up everything in the law code, the sum total is *love*. Rom. 13:10, Message.

When our daughter was about 2 years old, she began to have what doctors referred to as "night terrors." I knew what they were because her older brother had had them for years. During night terrors a child wakes in the middle of the night with a dream so frightening that they scream, yell, even throw fits, but remain asleep through it all.

Night terrors became a part of our nightly ritual. Several times a week we'd be up half the night trying to gently wake her up during these screaming fits, then settle her back down to sleep. Sometimes it would take hours. We didn't understand why she was having them until we found out that her older brothers, who were in their teens, would sometimes chase her though the house wearing a scary mask.

God does not give us a spirit of fear. Fear is driven by the prince of darkness, who builds walls in our lives to prevent us from living in the light of God's love and grace.

One day I asked her if she wanted to get rid of her night terrors, and she said yes. I explained where fear comes from and how we needed to remove it from her life permanently. I asked her to repeat after me, "Jesus, I don't want fear in my life anymore. I want Your love to rock me to sleep. Thank You for the angels who stay around my bed, and for those who love me." With the trust of a child she repeated the prayer and never had another night terror again.

Why hadn't I thought about it before? I had been dealing with my own subtle fears and doubt. I wasn't sure that my own prayers were good enough to keep her free from having the terrors again. And so it is—when we're faced with a scary decision or something that we believe takes our power of choice away, we shrink back in fear. God seems far from us. But when we step out in faith, just as my little girl did, we can face it head-on, knowing that God's love will be there for us every step of the way. There is no fear so great that God's peace cannot calm every situation through His love.

Dear God, thank You for hearing and answering the prayer of faith.

Kellie Frazier

Nighttime Talks

Let the children alone, don't prevent them from coming to me.
God's kingdom is made up of people like these. Matt. 19:14, Message.

One of my favorite times each day comes at the end of the day as we tuck our little ones into bed and whisper, "Good night and sweet dreams." I know there have been times, as a busy parent, I have done this with a sigh of relief, thinking, *OK, now I can get something done.* After a busy day, I often look forward to having a moment to myself. I've learned, though, that there is a special window of time when we can listen, really listen to our children.

When the stillness of night comes, something special happens. Without the visual distractions, their little hearts are more open to share. They are relaxed and know they are safe at home with Mom and Dad. This is the time to catch up on all the events of their day. What do they have on their minds? A friend who was mean, something funny that happened, a serious question, or something they want you to join them in praising God for?

I have always encouraged my boys to share their thoughts and feelings. I see it as training them how to communicate well as husbands and fathers one day. This little extra effort to lie beside them and listen is so important to them. As they open their hearts, trust is built, and confidence comes with their knowing they are loved. During these moments a strong foundation of trust is built that will stand you in good stead through the turbulent years ahead.

Isn't that how we feel when we come to our heavenly Father? God wants to communicate with us too—to hear the funny events of the day that unfolded, or something that weighs heavy on our heart. Nothing that matters to us is unimportant to God.

After our night talks, I whisper to my children, "It is OK. God is with you. Mommy and Daddy are here." And they smile, close their eyes, and nod off to sleep.

Heavenly Father, thank You for always taking time to listen to my heart. May I not rush through these precious moments with my children, but may I love them with a listening heart.

Tami Faudi

Stuck in the Mud

With God all things are possible. Matt. 19:26, NKJV.

It was the end of summer and the fall breezes brought cooler days. The garden had produced her last crop, and the children wanted to be sure we'd gathered every last bit of it. We rented a garden plot a few miles from where we lived, so I loaded the four children into the car and drove to the garden. As we drove, I wondered how much mud we would find in the garden. The night before had brought a flood of rain. The garden plots were located in a big field, and ours was toward the middle.

When we arrived, I could see my concerns were valid. The garden appeared very wet. When I turned in, I could hear the slosh of mud splashing everywhere. I continued slowly and carefully toward our plot and after stopping the car, the children jumped out. I could hear their shoes tracking through the mud. The pickings were slim. One found two tomatoes. Another migrated to a green pepper and some withered collard greens.

After a few minutes we all climbed back into the car, leaving muddy footprints everywhere. I started the engine and put my foot on the gas. I heard the wheels spinning and watched as mud sprayed all over the car. After a few spins I decided to get out and take a look. Low and behold, the car just sat there, stuck in the mud! I told the children we were stuck. Actually, Stuck, with a capital S. I explained, "Someone will have to push us out of the mud. We have to get some help." To my amazement, they chorused in unison, "Jesus can get us out!"

Oh, the faith of children, I thought. One child prayed, "Jesus, You know we are stuck; pleeeaase help us get out of the mud." While we waited for help I thought I would try again. I pushed down on the gas and the car surged backward out of the mud. Yes. Backward! The children screamed and started to chant, "Jesus got us out of the mud! Jesus got us out of the mud!" As I drove home I thanked the Lord many times for answering a child's prayer of faith.

Dear Lord, may I have childlike faith and trust You. I know that with You all things are possible.

Edwina Grice Neely

Start With Jesus

Steep your life in God-reality, God-initiative, God-provisions.
Don't worry about missing out. You'll find
all your everyday human concerns will be met. Matt. 6:33, Message.

Someone once said, "The best thing a dad can do for his kids is to love their mother." And of course, the spillover of that affection will create a precious home environment for the children, but the saying speaks even more to the establishing of priorities. A father who chooses care and nurture of his bride over NFL viewing or fishing has engineered a well-ordered life.

It's an even greater truth that our paramount task as parents is to be rooted and anchored in Jesus. How else would we be able to teach them that God is love? Every other decision, task, objective, or success will flow from the health of our walk with the Lord.

All the New Testament counsel about godly parenting has a transitive-property flavor to it: we are right with God; we lead in our homes; the love and wisdom of Christ flow through to our children. Decisions about family values, discipline, entertainment, worship, rules—will all be blessed and guided when we journey to Calvary.

We needn't fear that our devotional time with Christ will lead to energy outages elsewhere in the home. Jesus sometimes would spend the entire night in prayer, then return to the hurly-burly of daily life and the ministry chore of "parenting" 12 slow-to-learn disciples.

In *Mere Christianity* C. S. Lewis offers an exceptional essay in which he writes about the calm, settled, dynamic life of people who are comfortably rooted in their Christian identity. "Their very voices and faces are different from ours; stronger, quieter, happier, more radiant. . . . They will usually seem to have a lot of time: you will wonder where it comes from." Well, it comes from a well-ordered life that puts Jesus first. "And all these things shall be added unto you. Allelu, Alleluia."

Father God, I pray that You would bring home to each of us the importance of steeping our lives in You. May we set aside our concerns each day as we come into Your presence, knowing You will meet all our needs. Fill us with Your peace, a peace the rest of the world will take note of, and may they be drawn to inquire of us from whence it comes.

David B. Smith

Making the Right Choice

Though it cost all you have, get understanding. Prov. 4:7.

During my career in engineering, I landed a very exciting, cutting-edge job with a corporation that did a lot of work for the Navy Department. Specific missile systems were being upgraded from the old analog systems to solid state. This was the beginning of the digital age. The changes were dramatic, and the opportunities for advancement were enormous. In agreement with my wife, I jumped into the arena and seized every chance to learn, grow, and further advance my career.

I traveled a lot, mostly at sea, which meant leaving home on Sunday or Monday, to return only for the weekend, or perhaps two weeks later. It was an exciting time. I was learning, gaining tremendous experience that included increased responsibilities. And I have to say that the pay was good.

On one of my weekend visits home, I held our 1-year-old son, Bill G., on my knee and spoke to him about my delight in being home, when I noticed him shift his head to one side and look at me with an intense, almost piercing gaze. As I considered what he must be thinking, it was clear to me that he was saying, nonverbally, "I know I've seen this guy somewhere before, but I can't remember where." A red flag waved at me.

I told my wife that I didn't think Bill knew who I was. She said, in a gentle tone, "Well, you're always gone." Right then I decided it was time for me to find another job. How could I keep working a job that would result in my son not knowing I was his father?

Shortly afterward I left that exciting, cutting-edge job. In doing so, I made a statement to each of us, that I valued being present in the life of my family more than prestige, position, or money. It's a decision I have never regretted.

Dear Lord, giver of the gift of children, thank You for this precious gift, and for the privilege of being in their lives.

Bill Neely

Tell Them of His Love

From a child thou hast known the holy scriptures, which are able to make thee wise unto salvation through faith which is in Christ Jesus. 2 Tim. 3:15, KJV.

One of my fondest childhood memories is of Aunt Metha reading to us from *The Golden Treasury of Bible Stories, Our Little Friend,* and *Primary Treasure.* She had three children of her own, and together we'd gather around her big, overstuffed chair in the living room for evening worship. Here is where the foundation for my religious upbringing was laid, as I learned about those Bible heroes who were honored for their service to the Lord and forgiven for their mistakes. True Christian stories I could relate to whether I succeeded or failed.

Aunt Metha was the reason we all faithfully gathered for prayer meeting, Sabbath school and church, Pathfinders, fellowship dinners, evangelistic meetings, and Saturday night socials. We didn't have time to get into trouble! We knew our Sabbath school teachers and Pathfinder leaders loved us and willingly sacrificed their time and money to make sure we were learning more than just our ABCs.

It's been my privilege, as an adult, to carry on the legacy so freely given to me: teaching God's little ones in Sabbath school from cradle roll to earliteen. VBS is definitely a challenge but has always been worth it. And all aspects of Pathfinder Clubs hold meaning for the leaders as well as the members. Who gets to visit Sergeant Alvin York in his home if Pathfinder leaders don't step up? My ultimate goal as a leader is to pass on what I learned as a child at the feet of loving people who answered yes when asked to fill a position at church.

As a parent, you already know the task God has set before you. Show your children His love. Hold them close as you read to them of Jesus; sing of Him; share His promises out loud so that they resound in the hearts and minds of your little ones. Prepare them for the world before they ever leave home. Tell them of His love.

Thank You, Lord, for surrounding me with adults who showed me Your love. May I be faithful to the legacy as I show Your love to the little ones around me.

Carol Wiggins Gigante

The God Who So Loves Us

For God so loved the world, that he gave his only Son, that whoever believes in him should not perish but have eternal life. John 3:16, ESV.

Do we understand what John meant when He wrote that God so loved the world? The best way for me to understand that phrase is to think of my experience as a parent. My firstborn son, the middle child in our family, had a little game he loved to play with me. When he was about 4 or 5 years old, I would ask, "Leslie, how much do you love me?" And he would reply, "I love you two million and two million and lots more." That was the biggest number he knew. Then I would tease him a little and ask, "Show me how much you love me!" He would stand on his toes and stretch out his little arms as far as he could and say, "Mommy, I love you soooooooooo much!" Of course, the game always ended with him in my arms, as we hugged each other.

When I taught in Korea, I often used this story of Leslie as I tried to explain the love of God to my students. I would tell them that the picture of Jesus on the cross, His arms outstretched, was really Him telling us, "I love you this much."

Four days before his thirty-second birthday, Leslie was killed in a car accident. I was still teaching in South Korea at the time and had to fly home for the funeral. On that long flight the refrain that played over and over in my head was "I loved you so much! Did you ever really know it?" At the church service I shared the story of the little game we played and the application I had learned. With my heart breaking, I invited the congregation to join me at the foot of the cross, where we'd always find a God who knows what it feels like to have a son whom you *so love* die! My son died because an overtired truck driver fell asleep in the middle of the day, but God's Son died because He *so loved* you and me!

As parents we need to be sure our children know that we love them; but, more important, we need to be sure that we introduce them to the God that *so loves* the world.

Father God, today we thank You with all our hearts, that You so loved us that You gave the most precious gift—Your Son—so we can have eternal life with You.

Joy Hank

Remind Me, Mommy

And these words which I command you this day shall be upon your heart; and you shall teach them diligently to your children, and shall talk of them when you sit in your house, and when you walk by the way, and when you lie down, and when you rise. Deut. 6:6, 7, RSV.

One beautiful Sunday afternoon Jenny was driving her little girl Ashley to the birthday party of a friend, and Jenny's sister-in-law, Mandy, came along for the drive. Jenny was a single mom who lived with her brother and Mandy in a good Christian home. God was the unseen guest who had been invited to live with them, and family worship was the most important time each day. Mandy had two teen boys, and Ashley was a smart little 4-year-old, growing up surrounded by a family who loved her and did not miss any opportunity to teach her of God's love.

As they drove to the party, Mandy poured her heart out to Jenny, sharing that her sons were doing things they shouldn't be doing. As they spoke, tears fell down her cheeks. Little Ashley had a very tender heart and noticed her aunt's tears. She said, "Mommy, Auntie Mandy, when I am big, if I do what my cousins are doing, you must say, 'Ashley, remember Jesus loves you. He wants the best for you. Don't make us cry like your cousins have done.'" The little girl paused before adding, "You'll do that, Mommy, right?"

Jenny and Mandy were stunned. They hadn't realized Ashley was listening to their conversation. And she seemed to have understood the scope of what they were talking about and the pain the boys were causing. Oh, how careful we need to be while speaking in front of children. They are like sponges absorbing every word we speak.

We must never underestimate the importance of teaching our little ones about Jesus and His love. Ashley had been taught from babyhood how much Jesus loved her, and she wanted to do the things that would bring joy to His heart. She knew the choices of her cousins brought Him pain, and she wanted to ensure that she would never forget how much Jesus loves her.

Heavenly Father, help me to be mindful of all I say and do in front of my child. Help me to live in such a way that Your love will shine through me, touching my child for eternity.

Z. Kathy Cameron

Finding His Love All Around

Let us run the race that we have to run with patience, our eyes
fixed on Jesus the source and the goal of our faith. Heb. 12:1, 2, Phillips.

Parents of little children are the busiest people in the world. Amid all the
demands of life, they must constantly decide how best to nurture, train,
and create joyful moments with their children. In the passage above, Paul
teaches the importance of keeping our eyes fixed on Jesus.

Looking back at the ways my parents showed us how to do this, one
activity stands out clearly as an example of living this principle. On Sabbath afternoons they organized an adventure. Often it would be a drive to a
secluded pond tucked behind a hill and surrounded by wispy weeping wil-
lows. In preparation for the outing, Dad helped us collect containers and
small nets. The goal was to collect something we could share and discuss
together.

What fun we had searching for the perfect thing to share. Sometimes
it was a new kind of flower, or a pollywog, or an insect. After we'd each
found something, Mom would spread out a blanket for us to sit on and
Dad would start the discussion. Beginning with our littlest sister, he'd ask,
"What does your flower tell you about Jesus?" As she held her flower out
for each of us to smell, she'd shout, "Jesus is bea-uuu-ti-ful! Just like His
flower!"

Then the next sister would point out, "This pollywog will turn into a
frog, because Jesus makes miracles happen." Then my oldest sister would
pronounce, "I think this caterpillar will become a monarch butterfly because it has the right kind of stripes and because Jesus wants us to learn
about how He can change our hearts."

The outing would only end once we were home and had carefully put
our specimens on a poster board, or on our dresser to care for during the
next week. Dad and Mom would ask us to look at them every day to remind us about Jesus all week long.

*Dear Savior and Friend, please help me to see You in the busy world around
me. Help me to create fun moments with my children in which they can find
You in the beauty all around.*

Lynn Ripley

As a Child

So he went back to Nazareth with them, and lived obediently with them.
His mother held these things dearly, deep within herself.
And Jesus matured, growing up in both body and spirit,
blessed by both God and people. Luke 2:51, 52, Message.

Jesus didn't grow up in a wealthy home or attend an elite school. His childhood was spent in the little mountain village of Nazareth. In the sunlight of His Father's smile, Jesus grew taller, stronger, and wiser. He was a child that people liked, and His actions and attitude pleased God. Like every other child, His mind and body developed gradually as the years went by.

Mary watched carefully as Jesus grew and developed. She saw the perfection in His character, His attitude, and behavior. It was a joy to encourage His learning and thinking. Through the Holy Spirit, she was given wisdom to cooperate with heaven in her boy's development, her boy who could claim only God as His Father.

As a child, Jesus was not taught in the synagogue schools. His mother was His first teacher. He learned of God and of heaven from her words and from the words of Scripture, including the very words that He had spoken to Moses for Israel. Even as a teenager, Jesus did not turn to the rabbis for His education. He did not need their instruction, for God was His teacher.

From His earliest years Jesus had one purpose: He lived to bless others. His studies of nature helped Him in doing this. New ideas flashed into His mind as He studied plants and animals. In life around Him, He was constantly searching for illustrations that would make it easier to share the truth about God. The parables He used later in His ministry show how open He was to nature and how its study can open a person to spiritual truths.

Heavenly Father, may we learn from the example that Jesus left us, to seek to know Your heart of love and to share that knowledge with others. May we not be too busy to come aside and meet with You in the beauty of nature and in Your Word.

Jerry D. Thomas

Trusting My Father's Love

Ask [for love], and it will be given to you; seek [for love], and you will find; knock [for love], and it will be opened to you. For every one who asks [for love] receives, and he who seeks [for love] finds, and to him who knocks [for love] it will be opened. Matt. 7:7, 8, NKJV.

When I was 6 years old, I needed surgery to repair an inguinal hernia. My father was the only surgeon in our rural county, and as it happened many years ago, he would be the one to perform the procedure. On the day of surgery, before I woke, Daddy came in and picked me up, wrapped me in a blanket, and took me to the hospital with him. I always felt safe in my daddy's arms.

He left me with the nurse and went to scrub for surgery. The nurse began to prepare me, and as she took out a needle I started to cry. I could see my dad across the hall and I said to her, "Please let my daddy do that." She went and got my dad. He immediately stopped what he was doing and came and placed the needle in my arm. I did not cry or squirm. I knew my daddy loved me and he would be with me even if it hurt. While he could not save me from the pain, he stayed close by my side.

Now as an adult, I have the greatest appreciation for what my parents gave me, a love for God and the knowledge that God is love. I have no doubt that my love for God and my firm commitment to remain in a loving and saving relationship with Him were profoundly impacted by the godly life of my parents and their unconditional love. It has taken me through the challenges that life inevitably brings: illness and death of loved ones, the loss of possessions or position, failings and fallings, and personal illness. Whatever the threat, I know I am in the loving arms of my heavenly Father.

If we want our children to know that God is love, then we must love the Lord. We can only give them what we have. If our children see our relationship with our Father God, as evidenced by our prayer life and time spent in God's Word, we will show them they can trust God's unconditional love.

Father, I claim Your promise and ask for love, that I may show my children they can trust You. May their love for You grow, even as they see my love for You grow.

Marilyn Armayor

Love From My Baby's Heart

Whoever does not love does not know God, because God is love. 1 John 4:8.

I watch as she tenderly tucks her baby into the cradle. She gently pulls the blanket up to cover him with warmth. She smiles, then bows her head in prayer. When she is finished, and I have wiped a tear or two from my eye, I hear her rise and turn toward me.

"Mommy, what's for lunch?" My sweet, precious 5-year-old is done with parenting for now. Her baby doll will lie in its cradle until the next time she decides its needs must be met.

I cook lunch and bring it to the table to share. We bow our heads, and I patiently wait as she adds many requests to our prayer, little things that matter to her, and because they do, they matter to her heavenly Father. We dig in and start to chat.

"Mommy, did Jesus cry when He was a baby?"

"Yes, honey. I'm sure He did. All babies cry to tell their mother they need something."

"Did Jesus fall down when He ran and get hurt like I did last week?"

"Yes, sweetie. I'm sure he scraped His knee, just like you."

"Did Jesus get picked on when He went to school?"

This one breaks my heart. Just last week she had been teased about her dolly, and it had hurt my baby's heart, and mine in turn.

"I'm sure at some time there were bullies in His life, too. I'm sure it hurt His mother, Mary, just as it hurts me to see you so sad."

"Was Jesus ever lonely?" I look down into her brown eyes and see the wheels turning.

"Yes, honey. Jesus was lonely at times."

"God must love us an awful lot, huh, Mommy!"

"Yes, honey." I swipe at the tears. "Yes, God is love itself."

She smiles at me. A knowing smile. Her brown eyes shine—God's love in my baby's heart.

Thank You, Father, that my children can see Your love. Thank You that they love You in response to Your love.

Kimberley Tagert-Paul

God Is Love

Whoever does not love does not know God, because God is love. 1 John 4:8.

I will never forget the day our youngest boy, James, refused to pray at bedtime. I wasn't sure what to do. I couldn't force him to pray, but I wanted him to realize the importance of prayer. I sent a quick prayer heavenward asking the Lord what to do. A few moments later I gently told him I would wait for him to pray. Silence. He had the covers over his head. I reminded him I was still there waiting for him. Praying was something we'd done every night, so it wasn't something new. Then the Lord impressed me to ask, "Would you like me to help you pray?" To my surprise, he said, "Yes." I prayed a short prayer and James repeated it. I was thrilled.

One thing I learned from that evening is that children don't always understand prayer the way we do. James viewed prayer very differently from the way I did. His young mind had a hard time understanding how we can pray to someone we can't see, about things he wasn't sure God even cared about. In time he came to understand what John 3:16 meant when it said, "For God so loved the world that he gave his one and only Son, that whoever believes in him shall not perish but have eternal life."

I'm so thankful that our boys have an earthly father who loves them and models God's love for them. It's unfortunate that so many of our young people, and some older ones too, view their heavenly Father as an unkind earthly father, just waiting and watching for them to do something wrong before striking out in anger.

As a freshman in high school I received the greatest gift when someone taught me that God wanted to be my best friend. Then I could understand that He cared about everything going on with me. He wanted me to be His friend too. How do we convey that truth to our children? By knowing His love for ourselves and modeling it for them in the way we live.

Lord, thank You for dying on the cross for my sins and for being my best friend. May the beauty of Your love shine through in all I do as a mom, and may my boys be drawn to Your love.

Tamara Michalenko Terry

Our Heavenly Father's Love

Jesus answered: "Don't you know me, Philip, even after I have been among you such a long time? Anyone who has seen me has seen the Father. How can you say, 'Show us the Father'?" John 14:9.

My son Sanghyun, who is now in middle school, was once asked while in kindergarten, "Sanghyun, what is your daddy like?" Everyone expected him to answer, "My daddy is a pastor." Instead, he smiled and answered, "He is a funny dad. He makes me laugh." Sanghyun saw his daddy as more than the pastor who stood in front of hundreds of people each week. As a son, he knew his daddy was funny and loved entertaining him.

Last week my daughter Hanna was a little bored during Tuesday prayer meeting, so she wrote her daddy a short message. One sentence especially touched our hearts: "I think of you, Daddy, whenever things are difficult. It makes me happy again." Her daddy's loving and tender care was a healing balm for Hanna's little heart. Their sweet relationship reminds me of our Father God. His love is far bigger than any earthly father's love.

The Bible tells us who our God really is. "The Lord, the Lord, the compassionate and gracious God, slow to anger, abounding in love and faithfulness" (Ex. 34:6). Jesus came to earth to show us the Father, and He demonstrated the Father's love as He went about doing good. The poor and humble were not afraid of approaching Him. Even the small children loved to be with Him and were drawn to His side.

In *Steps to Christ* we read that "even little children were attracted to Him. They loved to climb upon His knees and gaze into the pensive face, benignant with love" (p. 12). How wonderful and kind He was, that children loved to gaze into His face. Imagine how those parents felt to see Jesus respond with such love toward their children. One day we will meet Jesus in heaven, our Friend who loves us more than we can understand or measure. Oh, how I long for that day, when we can all be with Him.

Father in heaven, let us love our children as Jesus does. Let Your love flow through us and touch their hearts and lives. May we demonstrate Your love to our children.

Nami Kim

Live Every Day in Love

Jesus said unto him, Thou shalt love the Lord thy God with all thy heart, and with all thy soul, and with all thy mind. Matt. 22:37, KJV.

I had always wanted to be a parent and was thrilled when I was finally blessed with the birth of my son, Curtis. I took the parenting role very seriously, and my greatest desire was to raise my son in a loving, Christian home.

When I first looked at his face after a very difficult delivery, I caught, for a nanosecond, a glimpse of God's true love for us, His children. It stunned me. I felt overwhelmed, humbled, and renewed. It shaped the way I parent. So, instead of raising my son with the typical "do this, and don't do that" type of environment, I wanted to show him God's love. Every day, I took time to let him know God loved him and that I loved him. Over time we developed a sweet ritual. I would ask Curtis, "Who loves you?" to which he would reply, "You do, Mommy." And when I asked, "How much does Mommy love you?" he would reply, "With all your heart."

One morning while I was taking Curtis to day care, we were enjoying our morning ritual, but when I asked him, "How much does Mommy love you?" he grew quiet. After thinking for a moment, he responded, "Mommy, you love me so much that instead of dying for me, you want to live for me, every single day."

I fought the tears and a lump in my throat all the way to day care as I silently praised God that I had chosen to raise my boy with Christ in our home. As I reflected on his words, I realized that we'd been talking for the past couple days about God's love for us, and how Jesus chose to leave heaven to live among us, love us, and eventually die for our sins. I thought my heart would burst when I realized he'd understood our conversation and had applied that definition of love to my love for him.

Parents, are you ready to live for Christ, every single day? Are you ready to demonstrate God's love to your children? How else will they come to know God is love, unless we show them by our love?

Live out Your love within me today, and every day, Lord.

Lori Colwell

Hide-and-Seek

He replied, "I heard you walking in the garden, so I hid." Gen. 3:10, NLT.

Two versions of hide-and-seek are played in our home. The first version is fun and happens when my daughters ask me to count as they run and hide from me. Before I've opened my eyes, my ears have already picked up their sound of their excitement. There's not much mystery to it. The girls usually hide in the closet, under the bed, or under a blanket. What fascinates me is once I've found them and we begin another round they sometimes run to the very same place they'd hidden just a moment before.

The second version of hide-and-seek is not that much fun. It starts at the sound of something breaking, crashing, or when one of them yells out, "Stop it!" In predictable fashion I call out their full names. Silence responds. The guilty parties have found a way to make themselves disappear. As I begin the investigation I eventually find glum-looking little girls in the closet, under the table, or behind the couch. "Why did you hide?" is a question I already know the answer to. The heavy sense of dread that comes with being in trouble and the anticipation of my response have caused them to seek cover. Can you see the futility? Where could my little girls possibly hide in the house where I wouldn't be able to find them?

Now imagine the first two children of God playing the second version of this game. The heaviness they feel at the thought of being in trouble and the anticipation of the Father's response have moved them to cover themselves. They hear God calling their names, but they can't face coming before Him. Can you see the futility of it all? In the garden the Father had spoken into existence they tried to hide. Where could they possibly go to escape the presence of God?

My daughters are learning that life is much better when they admit they've done wrong. Hiding makes things complicated. Hiding makes it harder to receive help. Hiding can delay the application of grace. I would prefer for my children to run to me when they make mistakes. God would prefer that I run to Him when I make my own. Why would we hide from love?

God, help us to run to You when we've done wrong. Help us teach our children the same.

Pierre Quinn

Jesus Is Always With Me!

And surely I am with you always. Matt. 28:20.

I was a student in the seminary at Andrews University in Berrien Springs, Michigan, with my wife and three children. We lived at Maplewood Court B-71. Along with my studies, I delighted in sharing the care, responsibilities, duties, and training of the children with my wife.

One summer the university upgraded the children's playground at the apartment complex. Once the new equipment and landscaping had been completed I took my 2-year-old daughter to the playground. After carefully showing her everything and explaining how to safely enjoy them, I spoke to her in my most fatherly voice. In expressing my concern for her well-being and safety, I said, "Never come out here by yourself."

To my utter amazement, my 2-year-old responded, "Daddy, Jesus is always with me." A paradigm shift occurred in that moment. We had been intentionally teaching the children about God's loving presence and the fact that He'd promised to always be with us. We played and replayed Bible stories that taught of His love and often discussed God's provisions in the Bible and in the lives of contemporary people. We shared many events in our lives and the lives of our family with gratitude and confidence. Yet, that day my daughter heard me speak as though I thought God would leave her, contrary to all I'd been teaching her.

Her words caused me to examine my beliefs and how I expressed those beliefs about God's presence being with us at all times, in all places, in all circumstances and situations. That experience challenged me to examine the many passages of Scripture that address the presence of God. I came to realize that if I truly believed God would be with me always, then I did not need to be fearful. Nor did I need to invite God to be where He already is—with me always.

To the ever-present One, thank You for Your abiding love in our lives and for teaching us through the words of our children.

Bill Neely

April

The Art of Discipline

John the Baptist

The little boy greatly loved God and when he grew up he lived out in the lonely wilderness until he began his public ministry to Israel. Luke 1:80, TLB.

God had given John the most important work ever given to a human. He was to share a message that would change people's lives. He was to give them a glimpse of God's holiness, an understanding of what God expects.

To carry this message, he would need to be holy. He would need to be strong physically, mentally, and spiritually. He must be so strong, so much in control of himself, including his appetite and passions, that no matter what happened he could stand as firm as the rocks and mountains of the desert he grew up in.

John was to be a reformer. This is why the angel gave his parents such specific instructions. By his simple life and plain clothes, by refusing to drink wine or other alcoholic drinks, he spoke against the lifestyle of the day.

Self-control and self-discipline are important lessons to learn during childhood and the teen years. More than any personality or talents, the habits formed during those early years will determine whether a person will succeed or fail at the battle of life. The seeds sown during childhood will determine the harvest a person reaps—both in adult life and for eternity.

John prepared people for Jesus' first appearance. He is an example of those who will work to prepare people for Jesus' second coming. Today's world is filled with errors and lies. Satan's traps for destroying souls are everywhere. All who choose to pursue holiness, obedience, and respect for God must learn self-control. This kind of discipline gives the mental strength and spiritual power to understand and obey God's Word.

Father, help me to instill a spirit of self-control and discipline in my children while they are yet young. May I never underestimate the important role discipline plays in the life of a disciple: a Christ follower. That is what I want my children to be. Help me to this end, I pray.

Jerry D. Thomas

The Meanest Mother in the World

For the Holy Spirit will teach you at that time what you should say. Luke 12:12.

Before I became a parent I dreamed of being the perfect parent. Determined not to repeat my parent's mistakes, I attended child development classes and read parenting books. I thought I was ready when my adopted children arrived with their unique personalities and strong wills.

When Tina was 7, she invited her friend Kathy to spend the night. The house rule was clear: you must first obtain parental permission before inviting your friend over. On this particular day I had come home from work with an extra-strength migraine headache.

"Mom, Kathy is going to sleep over tonight."

"I'm sorry. Kathy won't be able to stay over tonight. You didn't ask permission first. Besides, I have a terrible headache. It just isn't a good day."

Tina stomped to her room. "You are the meanest mother in the whole world!" She reached her room, slammed the door, and jumped on her bed. I heard the headboard slam against the wall. The verbal venting continued. "Why can't you be nice like everybody else's mother?"

Three times she launched off her bed, reslammed the door, and vaulted back onto the bed. Each time the slamming, pounding, and jarring of the door and headboard against the structural framework of her room sent vibrations through the entire house and my throbbing head. I did not want to discipline her in my pain, anger, and frustration.

Then the Lord seemed to speak to me. "She loves her privacy. Remove her door."

I dragged myself off the sofa, took a screwdriver from the junk drawer and without uttering a word, popped Tina's bedroom door off its hinges and leaned it against the wall in the hallway.

Silence emanated from the bedroom.

Later, when my head felt better, I went into Tina's room. We talked calmly. I told her that when she had time to think about her behavior I would have her dad replace the door. Seven days with no privacy did the trick. We never had another door slam or an unapproved overnight guest.

God doesn't expect perfection. He wants parents who are willing to be led by His Spirit.

Father, thank You for using imperfect people to accomplish Your perfect will.

Karen R. Hessen

Respect

*Teach them his decrees and instructions, and show them
the way they are to live and how they are to behave. Ex. 18:20.*

It was Monday, and just a few hours before his piano lesson. I sat on a chair beside him as he made his way quickly and carelessly through his piece, eager to get his practice over with.

"Let's play it again, sweetheart," I said. "This time, don't rush it. Take it slowly so you can get your notes right."

He raised his eyes to the ceiling and sighed melodramatically.

"I know that!" he said scornfully. "Doesn't anybody in this house have any brains?"

I sat there, slightly stunned by his words, trying to decide how best to respond to the disrespectful remark from a boy normally so sensitive and gentle.

"H'mmm," I said softly, "that was a very rude and hurtful thing to say."

He turned and looked at me as if for the first time, eyes wide, he nodded to show the message was received. I was relieved at how quickly the lesson had been absorbed, grateful at how little effort it had taken on my part.

Years ago I might have responded with anger. I almost did so then. If I had allowed my temper to control the situation, he would have learned a completely different lesson that day. I would have taught him that anger is an appropriate answer to rudeness. Instead, I allowed God to soften my reply, and answered disrespect with love. As a result, he learned a better way to respond to insult.

I also learned an important lesson that day: Sometimes the only discipline required is respect and patience, especially when you are receiving exactly the opposite. Our attitudes are far more effective instructors than our words will ever be, and when we practice patience and self-control, we teach our children to do the same.

Father, thank You for Your lessons in mercy and grace. Grant us patience when our own is depleted, and may we never allow ourselves to stand in the way of the lessons You wish to teach our children through us.

Carey Pearson

I Will Lead Slowly

Please let my lord go on ahead before his servant. I will lead on slowly at a pace . . . the children . . . are able to endure. Gen. 33:14, NKJV.

What is it about the fast-paced life that has made our world so obsessed with it? It almost feels as though the world is stuck in fast-forward mode. We try to cram in more and more activities in less and less time. Remember when we used to dial? Now we speed dial. We used to read, now we speed read. We used to walk, now we speed walk.

How does this obsession with speed interfere in the way we raise our children? I believe it makes us forget that growing up takes time, maturing takes years, and perfection of character takes a lifetime.

I remember one summer when I tried to be the perfect dad by teaching my children how to make good use of their free time. I diligently prepared a schedule that started at 8:00 a.m. and ended at 8:00 p.m., and I crammed in as many activities as possible. I didn't want to waste a moment! It took just two days for everyone to object and complain about the regime. It was only when my son told me, "Dad, we are kids, not grown-ups," that I realized what I was doing and that I needed to slow down and adjust my teaching technique to a pace my children were able to endure.

In today's scripture we find that Jacob modeled empathy with his family. After he had that emotional encounter with his brother, Esau offered to walk ahead of him and his large family, to guide the way back to their father. Jacob could easily have said to his family, "OK, everyone, pick up the pace; let's hurry. My father is waiting for me. Hurry up!" Instead, Jacob controlled himself, and even though he was anxious to get home to see his father, he recognized the limitations of his children and chose to lead slowly at a pace they could endure.

Father, thank You for the opportunity we have to lead our children in this life. Please help us to be patient with them and to place their needs above our own. We trust in Your promise for wisdom for this day, and each day.

Ruber J. Leal

Trusting God

*I will say of the Lord, "He is my refuge
and my fortress, my God, in whom I trust." Ps. 91:2*

HIT IT!" I heard my son cry out from his position in the water behind the boat. I sat in the driver's seat awaiting his command to let me know when he was ready, and now his young voice indicated that he was ready to try this new adventure. As I steered the boat, I tried to see if he would manage to come up out of the water.

Last summer my son Seth asked to learn to water-ski. However, he showed some anxiety at the thought of being behind the boat by himself. My husband decided to wakeboard beside him so that just in case Seth was not able to get up, my husband would be there to grab him. Sure enough, on his first time out, Seth was not going to make it.

As I sat in the driver's seat looking in my rearview mirror I noticed two things. The first was Seth's face. There was no sign of stress. Not a worry appeared. He looked about as relaxed as a kid eating cereal on a Sunday morning while watching TV. With his father right beside him, he knew he had nothing to worry about. He had every confidence his father would hold him—and even hold him up out of the water, if necessary—until I was able to turn the boat around to pick him up.

The second thing I noticed was my husband's face—pure happiness was written across it. He had his boy, he had his family in the boat, and he was out on the water enjoying every moment teaching his son to water-ski. My husband was there to hold, to protect, and to love.

This scenario reminds me so much of our heavenly Father. Before my son even had a chance to think about falling, his father was there to grab him and hold him. My son was not stressed at all, because he had trust that his father was right beside him. Oh, to have that depth of trust! Let us trust that our heavenly Father will be there to hold us and to protect us, as well as take joy in our adventures.

Dear Lord, please help us to remember that You are there to hold us and protect us, as well as rejoice with us in our happy moments. Thank You for Your amazing love.

Lisseth Davis

How Big Is Your Aquarium?

Show me your ways, Lord, teach me your paths.
Guide me in your truth and teach me, for you are God my Savior,
and my hope is in you all day long. Ps. 25:4, 5.

We were shopping for fish. Not the kind you eat, but the kind you put into an aquarium and clean up after at least once a week. Our son was sure he was ready to assist with that task after successfully keeping a goldfish in a bowl for a year. I wasn't so sure. I loved the idea of an aquarium with multicolored fish. I relished the thought of watching them swim peacefully under a blue light and listening to the sound of the bubbles the pump would make.

Wandering down the aisle at the pet store made it seem easy to keep an aquarium looking attractive. There were dozens of pristine tanks with hundreds of beautiful fish swimming blissfully along in the clean water. They made it look easy. Almost like child's play.

But I knew better.

We'd experimented with guppies many years before. We started with four. And then the babies came. Dozens of them. We watched them disappear into the plastic grass seeking refuge from their hungry mothers. Soon, what started as four became too many to count, and the pristine effect happened only after regular and thorough cleaning. Keeping fish was work. Hard work!

I watched the clerk explain all of this to our son. He listened intently to her instructions. Then she said something I will never forget. It came like the whisper of God's voice.

"Fish grow according to the size of their environment."

I stood there staring at my young son. He too was like a young fish. He would only grow according to the size of his environment. We wanted him to grow well, strong and sturdy. We wanted him to be all that his Father had created him to be.

What a great reminder of our need to truly focus on what we were feeding him spiritually, the environment that we were raising him in. After all, we wanted to grow a big fish for God! Was it hard work? Oh, yes! Was it worth the effort? Definitely!

Father, help us as parents of Your young gifts, to raise them in an environment in which they can not only grow, but thrive in their relationship with You.

Kimberely Tagert-Paul

Think on These Things

Finally, brethren, whatsoever things are true, whatsoever things are honest, whatsoever things are just, whatsoever things are pure, whatsoever things are lovely, whatsoever things are of good report; if there be any virtue, and if there be any praise, think on these things. Phil. 4:8, KJV.

As parents we have the opportunity to train our children right from birth. We have the opportunity to determine what their developing minds will be exposed to. We have the responsibility for what they will hear, taste, see, and feel.

Not long ago a friend bought our little girl some beautiful animal books and cards at a garage sale. They were part of a set with accompanying DVDs. As she was showing them to us she suddenly realized that what she'd bought was very different from what she thought she'd bought. The books were filled with pictures of predators in their natural habitat! My friend was horrified and apologized repeatedly.

The situation gave us an opportunity to talk about how important it is for us to be diligent in guarding the hearts and minds of our children. Instead of focusing on the realities of the "natural" world, we should be teaching our children that cruelty and dying are not natural. God never intended for animals to hunt and kill each other. Nor did He intend for His children to die.

The apostle Paul wrote these words to help us keep our focus heavenward: "Whatsoever things are true, whatsoever things are honest, whatsoever things are just, whatsoever things are pure, whatsoever things are lovely, whatsoever things are of good report; if there be any virtue, and if there be any praise, think on these things."

Someday, when this old earth is made new, there will be no more suffering, no more dying, no more sadness. Someday, in heaven, there will be perfect peace, perfect harmony, perfect love. These are the things on which we should allow our minds, and our children's minds, to dwell.

Dear Lord, giver of life, help us to train the minds of our children to think of all that is true, pure, and lovely. And may we be diligent in guarding what we set before them.

Christine Gillan Byrne

Changing My Focus

And looking around, they suddenly no longer saw anyone . . .
except Jesus only. Mark 9:8, Amplified.

As the first-time parent of a 1-year-old, I sometimes feel more adept at disciplining the feral cat that recently moved, uninvited, into our home than my toddler.

How do I explain to this tiny person that it's not OK to drink the dog's water or pull everything out of the kitchen cabinets? How do I stop the violent tantrum when my little angel is sprawled on the floor, kicking her feet and swinging her arms while screaming at the top of her tiny (but efficient) lungs?

Before becoming a parent, back when I was a pro and knew all the answers, I promised myself I'd apply my training in psychology when it came time to discipline my future, naturally compliant children. You know what I'm talking about. Positive reinforcement. Finding replacement behaviors, etc., etc. It all sounds great, doesn't it? Don't get me wrong. I'm still a huge proponent of these practices, but in the heat of the moment they aren't the first tools I pull from my bag of tricks. Far too often, I find myself responding with "Stop it!" or "No!" or "Don't pile-drive the cat!"

When it comes to discipline, I've learned that it's good to step back and take a moment to readjust my focus. When I do, I realize it's often more helpful to look at myself rather than the antics of my daughter. No matter how good a parent I learn to be, Katie will still have meltdowns and misbehave from time to time. She's not yet able to understand the world in the same way I can. My best bet? Be disciplined enough to handle these annoying—and often embarrassing—situations.

It amazes me how often Katie mimics my actions. What if, instead of focusing on her behaviors, I focus on providing an example of what a disciplined woman looks like? After all, it's by beholding that we are changed, right?

Father, I want my child to be changed by looking at my example. Help me, first, to be changed by looking to You.

Beth Helm

The Blessing of Discipline

The road to life is a disciplined life. Prov. 10:17, Message.

One of the most important lessons a child needs to learn is discipline. This is easier said than done. Here are several tips you may find helpful.

Establishing a fixed schedule can go a long way to help maintain discipline. There should be a set time for family worship, bedtime, meals, play, etc. Of course, children should also learn to be flexible, as circumstances sometimes disrupt the steadiest routines.

Consistency is vital if discipline is to be effective. How else will children know where the boundaries lie? Consistency between parents must also be in place. If one parent is lenient and the other strict, the children will take advantage of it. They are adept at manipulation. If rules are broken, it should be followed up with consequences. This helps a child to prepare for living in society.

A simple diet of plant-based foods, nuts, and grains also helps with discipline. It enables optimum brain function, increases a child's attention span, and promotes good behavior. Sugar intake should be kept to a minimum.

Clearly defined, appropriate rules should be enforced and followed up consistently with a set of consequences if broken. Teach children to respect themselves, as well as the rights and property of others. Show them how to be good stewards of their time and money. Encourage them to set high goals and standards for themselves. Develop responsibility by giving them chores to do at home. This helps promote self-discipline. Look for opportunities to praise your child for a job well done.

Finally, treat children with respect and dignity. Never discipline in anger. Seek ways to enhance their self-worth by showing them God's great love for them.

Lord, please help me to raise my children with heavenly wisdom, a healthy dose of common sense, sprinkled generously with kindness and served with laughter.

Desiree Julies

Thinking Time

God disciplines us for our good, in order that we may share
in his holiness. No discipline seems pleasant at the time, but painful.
Later on, however, it produces a harvest of righteousness
and peace for those who have been trained by it. Heb. 12:10, 11.

Aaron! Stop taking your friend's toys!" I rubbed my forehead. Aaron, a strong-willed 2-year-old in my preschool class, had been disciplined repeatedly for snatching others' things. "You know what happens when you take toys." I walked the boy to Thinking Time, explained yet again why he was going there, and retreated to take a deep breath.

Why won't you obey? I yanked my drooping ponytail tighter. *Don't you understand how much fun you could be having?*

In my own spiritual life, I wasn't having much fun either. The Lord was asking me to eat a buffet of crow: seeking forgiveness from many, offering forgiveness to others, releasing poor habits, and forsaking old pleasures. Where was the abundant life I kept hearing about? True, God had brought me out of a difficult season of unemployment and depression, but my existence still seemed a half-life. Not the rich journey described by Scripture.

I watched Aaron squirm, then looked around the noisy room. Blocks for building. Puppets for imaginary play. Shaving cream for sensory stimulation. *You're only letting me show my disciplinary side, Aaron. I have so much more to share with you, if we could just move beyond Thinking Time.*

As I talked with Aaron and released him to go play, I wondered, was there more my heavenly Teacher wanted to share with *me*? Was my need for discipline preventing Him from displaying His playful nature? Perhaps I had to learn obedience first.

Across the room, Aaron picked up a toy vacuum no one was using. I straightened and smiled. Hope for Aaron, hope for me. I realized God was preparing me for the joyful "playtime" to come.

Father, even though I am grown, I am still Your child. I ask for an open spirit to accept Your correction, and I praise You for what You have planned for me.

Jaclyn S. Miller

Just Do It

Discipline your son, and he will give you rest;
he will give delight to your heart. Prov. 29:17, RSV.

I did it.

I made the decision to unplug our TV, allowing only one night on the weekend to watch a movie. It was not the easiest thing to do, since we enjoy sitting watching shows together, but I noticed that it was quickly becoming our main source of entertainment. I have to admit, it was even a source for a free babysitter at times. My kids were becoming bored and seemed to enjoy their toys and books less and less.

Our devotional time was being impacted. That, too, was becoming more and more mundane to my kids. I had to do something. Desperate times call for desperate measures.

After a few days I noticed something really interesting. My kids starting picking up their old habits. My son started reading his books again. Maddie began to entertain herself with her coloring books and toys. I noticed they both were being obedient without complaining. I have to say, the change was astounding.

I would say it's been a wonderful transformation. My life has been made easier instead of harder. It is a shock to discover the impact television and the media can have on us and our kids.

If stepping away from media consumption can have such a huge impact on our family time, what kind of impact does it also have on our relationship with our Father?

It's a daily struggle to be a good parent and role model. A daily challenge to fight against being distracted with this world and the things the devil throws in our path. A daily fight to raise our children in the right direction. I want to do all that I can to ensure that Christ is at the forefront of their lives. Even if that means I have to be the bad guy every once in a while and say no. Even if it means unplugging the TV. Isn't that what our Father does for us? Sometimes He says no when it is in our best interest.

Help me to remember, Father, that correction and discipline impart wisdom to a child, but a child left to itself will bring shame to its mother (Prov. 29:15).

Jill Simpson

Respect and Courtesy

Train up a child in the way he should go;
even when he is old he will not depart from it. Prov. 22:6, ESV.

Among the most important things we can teach our children are respect and courtesy.

When my three boys were very young, I remember sitting around the supper table with them. Each evening we would pray before we ate, asking God to bless the food. We also practiced good manners, using phrases such as "Please pass the vegetables" and "Thank you." After they were done eating, the boys were taught to carry their dishes to the sink and rinse them. Finally, we taught them to say "Thank you" for a good meal. They are teenagers now, yet they still carry their dishes to the sink and thank me for a good meal.

Teaching children to show respect toward others brings much joy to the home. It also goes a long way in soothing many of life's irritations, making life easier for everyone. It is also good training for them on how to treat their mates and children once they are grown and have families of their own.

I've received many compliments from other parents when my kids have gone to parties or sleepovers on how respectful and polite they are. I can look back with pride on how respectful my boys are to me and to others. Respect and courtesy exercised in the home is carried over into all aspects of life. My boys hold doors open for women at church or a restaurant, they offer to help out if they are at someone else's house, and they speak respectfully to anyone and everyone they meet.

But most important of all, my boys respect God, and when children have respect for God, it shines through in their behavior and manners. Teaching respect has made a huge difference in the way my kids have turned out. It is very sad for me to see so many children today who talk back to their parents, or have total disrespect and disregard for others.

Lord, please help us to raise our children to have respect and courtesy for others, and, most of all, for You.

Shirley Jones

Strong and Mighty

[That you may be] strengthened with all might,
according to His glorious power. Col. 1:11, NKJV.

Strong-willed children are often mistaken for being uncooperative or defiant. The definition of a strong-willed child is a child who has a mind of their own and who seems to want to run in the opposite direction of where their parents want them to go. A dictionary definition might be obstinate, or stubborn, both of which have negative connotations.

But there are many positive aspects to being strong-willed. A strong-willed child has a powerful will, desire, and drive to accomplish their goals. That's a good thing! The strong-willed child doesn't give up easily and is typically persistent and determined, not easily dissuaded or discouraged. It is important to teach the strong-willed child to pursue worthwhile projects. Rightly trained, the strong-willed child will grow to be a person of strong convictions who can stand up against the crowd and remain steadfast, not swayed by their peers.

But if not directed well, a strong-willed child will struggle to get their own way. For instance, a child who insists on going outside in the rain and throws a temper tantrum unless they get their way is strong-willed in a stubborn, negative way.

Dallas Cowboys coach Tom Landry used to say, "Don't pray for an easy life. Pray to be a strong person." This is exactly what Scripture is admonishing here. Pray each day that your family will be able to make tough decisions based on God's principles and will be able to remain strong and mighty.

Instead of praying that your child have a soft, easy, mellow personality, pray that they will be strong in their convictions, mighty in their beliefs, powerful in their conscience, and grow to become young men and women of valor for God.

Father, while it might be easier to raise a child who is compliant, I pray that my child will be strong in the face of temptation and sin, mighty as they speak and live for You, and courageous even when the consequences may be painful for them.

Claudio and Pamela Consuegra

Character Building 101

*Not only so, but we also glory in our sufferings,
because we know that suffering produces perseverance;
perseverance, character; and character, hope. Rom. 5:3, 4.*

Nothing builds character like having children. Perhaps that's how God intended it to be all along. While we're focused on doing all the right things to help build and shape the character of our children, the Lord works to shape and mold our characters—keeping us humble and pliable in His hands.

I love this quote by Walter Anderson: "Bad things do happen; how I respond to them defines my character and the quality of my life. I can choose to sit in perpetual sadness, immobilized by the gravity of my loss, or I can choose to rise from the pain and treasure the most precious gift I have—life itself." What a great way to keep things in perspective.

My husband and I have three children, all boys. It is both humbling and humorous to reflect on all the character-building moments we have experienced: From leaving a grocery store before we'd finished shopping so the other patrons didn't have to hear our child anymore, to leaving church early so everyone could actually hear the sermon.

What were our choices? One option was to never take the child to the store or church until he was older. That might seem to be the easiest, but would fail to teach the child appropriate behavior. Instead, we chose not to be "immobilized by the gravity" of the situation. We kept trying different solutions until we found one that worked best for our son.

The longer I'm a parent, the less I feel the need to have all the answers. As 1 Peter 5:6 says: "Humble yourselves, therefore, under God's mighty hand, that he may lift you up in due time." Keep everything in perspective. Let God build your character. Trust Him to give you the wisdom, perseverance, and the sense of humor you will need to help shape and develop your children's character.

Lord, thank You for continuing to mold my character so that I can be the person You would like me to be. Help me to trust in You through all situations.

Tamara Michalenko Terry

Character Counts

*We do not want you to become lazy, but to imitate those
who through faith and patience inherit what has been promised. Heb. 6:12.*

A parent always sees their child in a unique light. We see their strengths, the miracle of their existence, the beauty of their abilities, and the cuteness of their antics. Sending our little miracles out into the big wide world of school can be the hardest thing we ever do, because we know that others will never see them quite the way we do.

My son is bright. He learned to read before he was 3 and could count to 100 forward and backward before kindergarten. As his mother, I was filled with pride at his small accomplishments, and I sent him off to school, hopeful that his teacher would see the same things I did, namely, his intelligence.

His teacher didn't seem much concerned with his ability to read and write. Instead, I was called repeatedly into the school for the same issue— he kept tuning out when the teacher talked, and didn't want to do the assignments. He was bored, I thought. He needed more challenge.

Then I started to notice the same behavior at home. He didn't want to help me with chores because it was "too boring." He didn't want to do his coloring homework from school because coloring was "too boring." Suddenly I realized that it wasn't his intelligence that was holding him back, but a point in his character that needed some work.

It doesn't matter how bright my son is if he doesn't learn to work hard. It doesn't matter how intelligent he may be if he doesn't apply himself to the little jobs, the daily chores that combine into something much bigger—a well-formed character.

It is their character that will ultimately determine their happiness. A hardworking man of average intelligence will go further than a lazy genius. A kind woman with average ability will be appreciated far more than a self-centered overachiever. Our children will learn how to read and write, but will their character be polished and ready for the challenges life will bring?

Father, help me to raise my child to have strength of character so that others will see You in my little one's heart.

Patty Froese Ntihemuka

Absolute Limits and Consequences

Chasten thy son while there is hope,
and let not thy soul spare for his crying. Prov. 19:18, KJV.

Standing precariously on one shaky leg, my almost-2-year-old son was testing his absolute limits. He knew the floor-level bricks of our fireplace hearth were off-limits, but they were so tempting to march across. Having previously tested his finger with subsequent penalty, he had to confirm that all parts of his body were subject to the same rule. Dangling his foot over the bricks, he lowered his toe, and then raised his eyes to look at me. He lost his balance at that point and set his foot solidly on the bricks beneath. The look on his face told me that he already knew his actions would have consequences. Sadly, I knew I had to enforce the rule for his safety, and because discipline and correction at an early age is critical to character development and ultimately to his salvation according to Proverbs 19:18.

How often do we test our absolute limits with God, perhaps even risking our own salvation? Probably more often than we care to admit. We want to know our boundaries yet try to get away with as much as we can. Maybe because we want to do what we want to do; or maybe because we think we know what will make us happiest. Whatever the reason, our imperfect human nature is a lot like that of our children.

Just as our family rule for staying off the hearth was put in place for safety, God has given rules to keep us from our own demise. How sad He must feel when having to deliver the penalty when we test our absolute limits and make choices leading us away from Him and His gift of salvation, a gift for which He paid the ultimate price.

Heavenly Father, please grace me today with contentment for Your rules, trusting that You know what is best for me. Help me not to push the limits and guide me in delivering correction to my child with discernment, love, and the goal of leading my child to You. Thank You for hearing my prayer.

Karen Barnett

Listening Versus Obeying

*For the moment all discipline seems painful rather than pleasant,
but later it yields the peaceful fruit of righteousness
to those who have been trained by it. Heb. 12:11, ESV.*

How many times have you heard yourself say to your children, "You're not listening!"

We parents tend to say it often. The truth is, our kids are listening to us. What they're not doing is obeying us. Listening and obeying are two entirely different things.

One day our 6-year-old middle son put a 12-inch two by four on our sidewalk. Next to it he put a soda can he found in the garage. Then he deposited a large rock next to the can. As I visited with my neighbor in our driveway, my peripheral vision was on my son. I watched him methodically maneuver his treasures while attempting to create something out them. Caught up in conversation with my neighbor, I wasn't entirely sure what he was doing. I thought I saw him bend over, put the wood on top of the can like a teeter-totter, then place the rock on one end of the board.

I felt it in my bones—this was an accident waiting to happen. I interrupted my neighbor in time to see my little boy's foot in the air as he bent over the top of the board.

"No, son, wait!" I cried. He looked at me and looked back down. "Don't step on that board," I continued, "or it will . . ." The next thing I heard was *bam!* Down went his foot hard on the end of the board, sending the rock straight up and into his forehead. He hit the ground and started to wail as a large egg began to appear on his tender little forehead.

The egg was consequence enough for him that day. I didn't need to discipline him for not "listening" to me. He told me later that night that he had heard me. What he didn't do was obey me. His mind couldn't register something he wasn't willing to obey.

"No, child, don't do it or it will hurt." This is what our loving Savior says to us, and yet our minds don't register what we're not ready to hear. Natural consequences feel like the heavy hand of discipline at times, but it truly is the best disciplinary action that parents can use to show their deepest love for their children.

O Lord, give me a heart willing to listen and obey. Thank You for loving me!

Kellie Frazier

Discipline With Love

For the moment all discipline seems painful rather than pleasant, but later it yields the peaceful fruit of righteousness to those who have been trained by it. Heb. 12:11, ESV.

Women put their careers on hold and go through the pain of pregnancy and childbirth in order to have a child. Jesus said, "When a woman is giving birth, she has sorrow because her hour has come, but when she has delivered the baby, she no longer remembers the anguish, for joy that a human being has been born into the world" (John 16:21, ESV).

Chelsey was our joy. Our gift from heaven! A wonderful baby and a great toddler—we knew we were blessed. Developmentally she was off the charts. She started walking at 8 months, and at the age of 1 she was running and talking up a storm.

With her increased mobility came an upswing in curiosity, and it often got the best of her. This is when I learned how difficult it was to enforce the rules we had put in place for her safety. Discipline is tough—and not just for our children. But because I loved Chelsey, I had to discipline her. Each time my little girl disobeyed, she was sent to the corner to consider her actions. That's where she learned to count from one through 10.

As small as she was, I would explain to her that what she had done was wrong, and that because I loved her so much, I had to punish her. As she cried, I cried too. Because I loved her my heart was hurting with hers. I would stay beside her during her time-out, and we'd both count together. She knew I was with her, even though I had not done anything wrong. While we waited together, I would remind her each time about God and His love.

As parents, we shouldn't miss any opportunity, even while punishing them, to talk to our children and teach them about God's amazing love and sacrifice for them. That is something that will be engraved in their memories forever.

O Father, give me wisdom to discipline and help me show Your love to our little one. Thank You!

Z. Kathy Cameron

The Alternative

A gentle answer turns away wrath, but a harsh word stirs up anger. Prov. 15:1.

You aren't doing what I asked you to do! Get busy! NOW!" The words tumbled out of my mouth. *I hate Fridays!* I thought. *The kids take forever to do their chores. They're too easily distracted. I feel like a slave driver whipping them all day long!* The whip I was using was my tongue. Then something else popped into my head. Something a good friend had recently shared.

"Parents, never speak hastily. If your children do wrong, correct them, but let your words be full of tenderness and love. Every time you scold, you lose a precious opportunity of giving a lesson in forbearance and patience. Let love be the most prominent feature in your correction of wrong" (*The Adventist Home*, p. 440).

"Require obedience, and do not allow yourself to speak carelessly to your children, because your manners and your words are their lesson book. Help them gently, tenderly over this period of their life. Let the sunshine of your presence make sunshine in their hearts. These growing boys and girls feel very sensitive, and by roughness you may mar their whole life. Be careful, mothers; *never scold*, for that *never* helps" (*Child Guidance*, p. 216; italics supplied).

Never scold? Seriously? How would anything get done? I grew up in an environment in which scolding was par for the course. I had never thought of it being *wrong*. I thought it was *necessary*! But now the Lord had convicted me of my harsh spirit. Whipping my kids with words was neither kind nor loving. "Lord," I asked, "what is my alternative?"

Later, as I worked in the kitchen, I saw my son sauntering around the corner, clearly distracted from the chore he was supposed to be doing.

"OK, Lord, I'm about to scold him right now! But what do You *want me to say?"*

The words, when they came, were sweet: "Justin, are you doing what Mommy asked you to do?" This time I felt calm—much to the surprise of both of us.

My little boy smiled, then quickly turned around and started to work again. "Yes, Mommy," he answered cheerfully.

Thanks, Lord, I breathed. Your way works so much better.

Cheryl Kronner Wiley

Dumber Than a Dog?

Train up a child in the way he should go,
and when he is old he will not depart from it.   Prov. 22:6, NKJV.

M y son was almost 2 when we were visiting some friends who also had toddlers. While we were in the family room I saw my son climb up four steps to a landing and prepare to jump into the room below. I called, "Stop," rushed over to him and told him with words and gestures that if he jumped, he would hurt himself—ouch, and cry—waaaa! He solemnly took my hand and let me lead him back down the stairs.

After one of the parents questioned whether I was trying to train him before he was old enough to understand, I decided to make it a matter of study. Medical science tells us that a fetus is impacted by what a mother eats, her mood or emotional state, and even what music she exposes her unborn child to.

I also discovered that puppies can begin training even as you bring them into your home. By walking through the door in front of the puppy and letting it follow you, it learns this is its new home and that it belongs to you. The recommended age for obedience training is 6 to 8 weeks. I figured my child was a lot smarter than a dog, so I should be able to train him from birth, right?

A great biblical example of diligent, godly parental training is the child Samuel, who by the approximate age of 3 was given by his mother to serve God with Eli the priest. Even at such a tender age he revealed a noble, godly character. The Bible records, "The boy served the Lord by assisting Eli the priest" (1 Sam. 2:11, NLT). A beautiful description of this is found in chapter 55 of *Patriarchs and Prophets*.

To those who think you can't train a child until they are 3 or 4, let me say, "Your child is not dumber than a dog either. We were created in God's image—so train them early—you won't regret it!"

Marilyn Armayor

Coming Clean

Like living stones be yourselves built into a spiritual house. 1 Peter 2:5, RSV.

Around our house you could always tell when Mom was on a mission. I would grab a couple big, green garbage bags and head for our daughter's room. She collected every paper she ever wrote on, every book she ever read—which is considerable and probably numerous enough to set up a small library—and every trinket she could get her hands on. I'm sure you get the picture.

She and I had different ideas on what the words "tidy" and "organized" meant, so about once a quarter we did what was referred to as "the deep cleanse." Once I crossed the threshold into her room, there was no going back. My husband remembers coming in through the back door from work to be greeted by huge bags of stuff in the music room. While I was busy taking them out of Katie's room, Katie was frantically trying to save her treasures and carrying them back into her room. It was never pleasant, but we were all relieved when the ordeal was over.

It made me think of Hezekiah's cleansing of the Temple. Scripture tells us he used a three-step cleaning process that was both simple and effective. First, he had the Temple doors opened so the light could show where all the garbage was. Second, he and his cleaning team cleaned all the garbage out. And third, they took the garbage to the Kidron Valley and had it burned. After that, they removed the garbage from the land all around them—not just from the Temple.

Coming clean is a good thing! First, we need to open the doors of our hearts and let the light shine in. The Holy Spirit will show us what needs cleaning. Then we need to give all the garbage to God and ask Him to destroy it. But we can't stop there. Next, we must cleanse the land around us if we want to make sure our cleaning wasn't in vain. Coming clean isn't always easy—but it's always worth it!

Father, please take away the garbage I've hoarded in the mistaken belief it was treasure: Anger that I can easily justify; resentment at being treated unfairly. Everything that's cluttering up my life and keeping Your presence from shining Your love to everyone around me.

Tawny Sportsman

An Angel in Seattle

Foolishness is bound up in the heart of a child;
The rod of discipline will remove it far from him. Prov. 22:15, NASB.

While visiting friends in Seattle, we were introduced to a young Christian family with a 2-year-old son. He was the sweetest, best-behaved, most respectful child we had ever met. The friend who introduced us to this family described the boy as an angel. Appropriately, his name is Seraph, which is short for Seraphim. Though we were still newlyweds and had no children at the time, we never forgot how impressive this little "angel" was.

Two years later our daughter Eden entered our lives, and we quickly realized that parenting is filled with challenges. The hardest period began as she began to crawl and then walk. She was so excited at being able to get around on her own that she began to fight sleep at all costs. Although exhausted, she refused to take naps or sleep, even at night. This made for a very sleep-deprived, grumpy family.

Remembering our experience with Seraph, we contacted his mother and asked for her advice on parenting. She told us about some Christian parenting books they had based their whole parenting philosophy on. We ordered them, and oh how we wished we'd read them sooner! The first was an entirely Bible-based book on the use of the rod. We began putting its principles into practice to teach Eden to sleep when she was tired. Within a week, she went to bed without a fuss and began taking longer naps and sleeping through the night. We all became more cheerful.

Before we were parents, we knew about the concept of the rod as presented in Scripture. Although neither of us had negative experiences with physical discipline, the controversy over the issue made us apprehensive to even try it. Just as the cross appears foolish to some, our culture regards the practical teachings of God's Word as irrelevant. We learned through this experience that God's ways truly are higher than our own.

Father, thank You for Your Word. Give us a correct understanding of it and the faith, courage, and love to follow Your guidance wherever it leads us.

Nick and Deanne Snell

The Purpose of Discipline

No discipline seems pleasant at the time, but painful. Later on, however, it produces a harvest of righteousness and peace for those who have been trained by it. Heb. 12:11.

G randma, I don't think your father would like the way you are acting!" he said.

My heart stopped for a moment. He never knew my dad; his words were from the Lord. I had been yelling—on a rant about something or the other.

"Oh, Tommy," I said. "I'm so sorry. What should I do?"

"Time-out!" he said matter-of-factly. I went to the bottom of the stairs and sat thinking while he played in the tub. After about 10 minutes I called up the stairs and asked, "Can I leave time-out now?" "No, not yet!" he answered. Then he came down and sat by me. He was the adult.

"Have you learned anything, Grandma?"

"Yes; yelling does not please my heavenly Father."

"OK, good," he said as he hugged me.

Tommy understood this method of correction. His parents had taught him well, so he used it on me. It worked, too.

The key to correction is love, because "the Lord disciplines the one he loves" (Heb. 12:6). God's definition of love is simply this—"Love is patient, love is kind. It does not envy, it does not boast, it is not proud. It does not dishonor others, it is not self-seeking, it is not easily angered, it keeps no record of wrongs. . . . It always protects, always trusts, always hopes, always perseveres" (1 Cor. 13:4-7).

The word "discipline" means "instruction given to a learner." In the Greek it means "instruction for children." To "chasten" means "to educate to correct." The word "punish" comes from the word "scourge," which is a penalty for criminals, "to flog."

Our goal is to instruct, not punish; to teach our children right from wrong. God's love for His children is not permissive but instructive. As Christians we want our kids to grow up and follow Jesus. Correction is a powerful way to reveal our love—and our Lord's love—to our children.

Father, You continue to teach Your children, no matter how old we are. Help us to train our little ones the way You do us.

Claudia LeCoure

Discipline—an Act of Love

The Lord disciplines those he loves,
as a father the son he delights in. Prov. 3:12.

Walk with me through the local supermarket. As we pass the produce section, a mother scolds her son for taking a bite out of an apple. Do you hear the whispers of the passersby? We continue to meander through the snack aisle while a toddler stamps her foot and screams for her favorite treat. Do you see the disapproving frowns?

Few areas of parenting are as vulnerable to judgment as that of discipline. What one parent considers fair, another thinks too harsh—or too lenient. What's a parent to do?

King Solomon, the wisest man who ever lived, compared parental discipline to God's discipline. What can we learn from this comparison?

Discipline displays love. Solomon says that God disciplines "those he loves" and a father disciplines the child he "delights in." A popular saying expresses a similar thought: "God loves us just the way we are, but He loves us too much to let us stay that way."

Discipline sets boundaries. Just as railings on a balcony keep us from falling off the edge, God's boundaries keep us safe from harm. In the same way, the boundaries we set for our children keep them safe and guide them as they grow to maturity.

Discipline gives correction. The *New Living Translation* renders Proverbs 3:12 as "The Lord corrects those he loves." If one of our children nears a safety boundary, love prompts us to bring that child back to safety. If they cross a behavior boundary, love prompts us to act to correct that behavior and explain God's standards.

Discipline encourages maturity. As distant in the future as it may seem now, our children will one day be independent adults, responsible for their own decisions. How much better it will be for them if they have learned healthy boundaries from a loving parent rather than from costly mistakes in adulthood.

While discipline differs from family to family and child to child, love for our children should lead us to provide appropriate, godly boundaries and firm, loving correction.

Heavenly Father, thank You for loving me enough to correct me when I stray from Your ways. I ask for Your wisdom in disciplining my child, whom I love.

Cheryl Faith Tarr

God's Not Finished Yet

God is the one who began this good work in you,
and I am certain that he won't stop before it is complete
on the day that Christ Jesus returns. Phil. 1:6, CEV.

Growth takes time and yet, as parents we often expect perfection in our children overnight. Is it possible that our expectations—and demands—regarding our children are higher than those we ask of ourselves? While it's easy to forget that God is not finished with us yet, it may be even easier to forget He's not yet finished working with our children either.

As adults we struggle with certain behaviors and continue to grow and mature spiritually throughout our lifetime. Remember, the text for today tells us that the work God is doing in my life will not be complete until the day that Jesus returns to take me home with Him. Why should we demand anything other than that for our children? Why do we want them to overcome their challenges *now*?

Don't be impatient with your child. Focus on the positives. Look for areas in which you see growth, and take the time to affirm that in your child. If your child only hears about their faults, they will become discouraged, develop poor self-esteem, and not be motivated to attempt new things for fear of failure. It is through failures that we all learn. It is only in falling that we learn how to get up.

I'm thankful that I serve a God who never gives up on me. And, we should never give up on our children. Paul reminds us in Philippians that "He won't stop." Christ keeps working on my heart and my attitudes day after day. Ever patient and always gracious, He loves me and continually forgives me and allows me to start anew. His mercies are new every morning. Now, that's great news for us and for our children.

Dear Lord, please help me to exercise patience with my child. As I trust You to finish the work that You have started in me, may I be gracious with their shortcomings and immaturity. You're not done with any of us yet! Thank You, Lord.

Claudio and Pamela Consuegra

Gardens Take Time to Grow

Train up a child in the way he should go,
and when he is old he will not depart from it. Prov. 22:6, NKJV.

When I was a child, the drive-through window was still a mystery and the Golden Arches hadn't yet wrapped their arms around every neighborhood. "Grandmother's Pies" and "Mother's Bakery" meant your grandmother and mother were really in the kitchen up to their necks in flour dough. Spring began with the arrival of *Gurney's Seed and Nursery Catalog,* and most families tended gardens.

A while ago, driving with my children down the Columbia Gorge, we stopped for some McQuick pies. Less than 10 minutes later I looked back to see the pies among the sappy, happy bags barely nibbled. How strange, I reflected. Nothing in mother's garden ever went to waste. It seems my boys have yet to understand pies are grown.

In the microwave age, where even our lawns are rolled out, our fast-food society seems only to have given us more calories with less in them. Our four-minute-marriage mentality has given us bigger but emptier homes. Prime-time parenting has entrenched our children with fast-action icons, yet left them strangers to Bible characters.

Perhaps what we need is less drive-throughs and a few more gardens; fewer products named "Grandma," and more real-life grandmas in our homes; slower cars and slower foods. But perhaps what we need most of all is the realization that anything worthwhile takes time to grow.

If husbands and wives took time to cultivate gardens together, would they cultivate better marriages? And what would happen if families sat on garden swings each night counting real stars instead of television stars? In our plastic-fork world, we're tempted to want drive-through results even in our homes. Yet, anything of quality takes time to plan and prune. Gardens take time to tend. Children take time to train. And real pies take hard work.

I believe God placed Adam and Eve in the garden for a plethora of reasons, but mostly to remind us: What matters most is not ordered but tended. And so, I have decided the next pie my boys eat is the one they bake!

Dear Lord, help me take time to tend what matters most.

Cindy R. Chamberlin

Who's the Boss?

Children, obey your parents in the Lord, for this is right. Eph. 6:1, NKJV.

In this simple verse, the Bible sets up a secure framework for successful parenting. Discipline is sometimes messy, but parents have a divine challenge to give their kids the security of knowing they have a loving but determined set of parents at the helm.

My cousin, the late Morris Venden, describes it this way: A hapless mom calls out into the backyard: "Please come inside; it's about to rain."

Kid: "How come?"

"Well, uh, those clouds look bad; I don't want you to get wet."

"How come?"

"Because you have school tomorrow. If you catch cold, I don't have anyone to babysit."

"How come?"

"Well, because the precipitation in the air . . . and my work schedule . . . and why am I explaining all of this to you?"

Meanwhile, both of them are soaked through, Mom feels foolish, and the frustrated child is thinking, *I need a grown-up, but there's no one in charge around here.*

By contrast, in a second home, Mom calls out: "Honey, please come in. I think it's going to rain."

"How come?"

"Because I said so."

"Oh. OK." And the child understands that God gave her parents as protectors.

The family framework needs to be simple, clear, and understood. Most of all, it needs to be bathed in love. Graciously explain to your children that they are your God-given charges, that you feel fortunate to have the blessing of this role. And because of your love for them, you simply will not allow them to slip away from the path of safety. You may not choose to be a proverbial tiger mom, but out in the jungle you will always be their guide and fierce protector.

Thank You, Lord, for helping me provide a strong framework of protection for my child.

David B. Smith

First Things First

Train up a child in the way he should go:
and when he is old, he will not depart from it.   Prov. 22:6, KJV.

In our home we had dessert only on special occasions or when we had company, and Katie knew that she had to eat her "body-building foods" before she could have dessert. One evening when we had company, Katie didn't particularly like what we were having and was just picking at her food. When I reminded her that if she didn't eat there would be no dessert, she didn't seem too upset, which was surprising because she normally ate her dinner with no problem—especially when dessert was in sight.

I cleared the plates from the table and saw that she hadn't finished her dinner. Then I dished up dessert and served it to everyone, but Katie. She looked alarmed and asked where hers was. I reminded her that because she hadn't eaten her "body-building foods" she couldn't have dessert. She looked a little bewildered, and then I could see the lightbulb come on and she said, "But Mom, the body-building section is full, but the dessert section is empty." Oh, how I wanted to give her that dessert! But I couldn't. As difficult as it was to keep a straight face and to stick to the rule, I did, and she still remembers that experience to this day! It made quite an impact.

How long do you think you or your children could live a healthy life just eating dessert? You're probably thinking, *not very long*. Then I wonder why some of us think we can maintain a healthy prayer life by investing only "snack time" in prayer and time with God.

If we will invest some "body-building" time in prayer, God will equip us as we parent. If we invest only "snack" time in prayer, He won't be able to give us what we need to be the kind of parent our child deserves and needs.

It's difficult to discipline ourselves to spend quality time with the Lord in our already hectic world; but we are called by God to do just that. By putting Him first, He can work through us to touch the hearts of our children, and that will make an impact for heaven.

Thank You for calling me to live a disciplined life, Lord. Help me to demonstrate that consistently each day.

Tawny Sportsman

Weary Disobedience

But now it comes upon you, and you are weary;
it touches you, and you are troubled. Job 4:5, NKJV.

It was like any other day at home with my son, Michael. He was learning to crawl, and I was learning how to be a parent. For some reason, though, on this day Michael seemed intent on reaching the trash can that he might explore its contents. Not on my watch, little buddy! More than once I removed him from the area and told him quite plainly he was not to get into the trash. Nothing worked. He just kept being drawn back to that trash can like a magnet.

Glancing at a clock, I realized what was going on. It was time for a nap. I was pretty certain that Michael's repeated disobedience was being triggered by his exhaustion. He needed to nap, but he didn't know how to tell me. So I let him know that I was onto him.

"Just because you're tired doesn't mean you can disobey," I told him.

Then the Lord stepped in to parent me. In that instant He repeated my own words back to me. As they echoed around in my ears, I finally got the message loud and clear. I had my own *trash cans* that I was continually being drawn toward. I was tired and weary of several things that had been really frustrating me. It was starting to show. I was stocking up on junk food for comfort eating, even though I knew it wasn't good for me, especially with my Crohn's disease. I had become quick-tempered, especially with my husband. And I found myself coming up with at least 10 reasons to avoid Bible studies and fellowship with my church family. I was tired and it was showing. But just because I was tired, the Lord whispered, didn't excuse the poor choices I was making.

I decided I needed to take a nap with Michael that day. While we both woke up refreshed and happy, I also woke up determined to surrender my frustrations to God so they didn't continue to wear me down.

Father, thank You for the teaching moments that come unexpectedly through the day. Thank You, too, for calling me to rest, even when I don't always realize that I need it.

Sharon Leukert

Christ-infused Discipline

*For the moment all discipline seems painful rather than pleasant,
but later it yields the peaceful fruit of righteousness
to those who have been trained by it. Heb. 12:11, ESV.*

You've got to be more stern with her. Stand your ground. You give in too easily."

I gave Michelle's bottom a quick smack, picked her up, and put her back in the queen-size bed. I was at a friend's house, trying to get my child to go to bed so I could join the adults in the living room. We had been at this for more than 30 minutes. I'd put her in bed, begging her to stay put, reminding her that if she didn't she'd be punished. But she would have none of it!

My friends were adamant I was doing the wrong thing, but after 45 minutes of this routine I bundled Michelle up, and the two of us went home, where she immediately fell asleep in her own bed. I was exhausted, but couldn't sleep because I was so bothered by the incident.

The next morning when I changed her diaper I saw marks on her bottom from the spanking. I was devastated. Discipline is a tricky subject. There is absolutely no one-size-fits-all answer, but here are a few guidelines that might help in moments of indecision.

Never, ever discipline in anger. Sometimes behavior calls for drastic measures, but those measures can be meted out with a calm and nonjudgmental manner. Keep your own emotions in check at all times.

Listen to counsel from others, but remember that you are the parent and know your child better than others do. Had I not been pressured, I never would have spanked my child as many times that night. Responsibility for the behavior is mine; however, I wish I had taken that responsibility before being motivated by my friends.

Love covers a multitude of sins. When we have to discipline, remember to follow it with unflagging love. These lessons are learned best when followed by loving actions.

To this day I regret that night, but it made me realize that God holds me accountable for the children He has blessed me with. I answer to Him, and Him alone. He has forgiven my transgressions—so has Michelle.

One last bit of advice—the hand that molds a child is more effective when it is tucked in the hand of Christ. It's amazing how effective Christ-infused discipline can be.

Help me keep my hand in Yours, Lord!

Candy Graves DeVore

May

Parenting Through Tough Times

Tomorrow Has Its Own Worries

So don't worry about tomorrow, because tomorrow will have its own worries.
Each day has enough trouble of its own. Matt. 6:34, NCV.

If we give ourselves to God and commit ourselves to do His work, then we don't need to worry about tomorrow. God knows the end from the beginning. We cannot see what will happen tomorrow, but He can.

When we take control of our own lives and depend on our own wisdom for success, we are doing something God hasn't asked us to do and are trying to do it without His help. We have taken to ourselves the responsibility that should be God's. We have put ourselves in His place. This will, indeed, create anxiety about possible danger and failure, because we are on a sure path to disaster.

But when we really believe that God loves us and wants us to succeed, we'll stop worrying over the future. We'll trust God the way a child trusts a loving parent. Then our troubles and problems will disappear because we will want only what God wants.

Jesus didn't promise to help us carry tomorrow's burdens today. He says, "My grace is enough for you" (2 Cor. 12:9, NCV), but, like the manna the Israelites received in the wilderness, His grace is given daily, for each day's problems. Like the Israelites on their long journey, we will discover the "bread" we need each day.

We are given only one day at a time, and for that one day we can live for God. We can place our one day in Jesus' hands, giving Him both our plans and our worries. "'I say this because I know what I am planning for you,' says the Lord. 'I have good plans for you, not plans to hurt you. I will give you hope and a good future'" (Jer. 29:11, NCV).

If we commit ourselves to the Lord each day, choosing to be free and happy as we obey and serve Him, all our worries will be stilled, all our issues settled, all our confusing problems solved.

Thank You, Lord—I can trust You with all my tomorrows, as I leave today in Your hands.

Jerry D. Thomas

Breaking the Rules

To those who have sorrow in Zion I will give them a crown of beauty instead of ashes. I will give them the oil of joy instead of sorrow, and a spirit of praise instead of a spirit of no hope. Isa. 61:3, NLV.

There are moments in the life of every parent when things are not all peaches and cream. Sometimes you have to walk across a field of thumbtacks instead.

The boys and I had spent weeks in a field of thumbtacks, and it was wearing on us all. The eldest was preparing for standardized tests by attending tutoring every day after school for several hours. Additionally, he was going through a growth spurt and spent his free time taking out his aggression on his brother. Nothing I did or said seemed to help, and I was about ready to run screaming from the house.

In the middle of the second week I parked the car and tried to convince the 7-year-old that he needed to go in to tutoring. Instead of the usual angry protests, he burst into tears.

"I just need a day off," he said. "Just one day. That's all I want."

My heart broke as I realized how burned out he was. Turning on the engine, I drove away from tutoring class, because sometimes you need to break the rules. Sometimes children need a break. And sometimes their parents do too.

After tutoring the next day, I took the boys out for dinner.

"If we can have a good evening together, a fun evening with no fighting," I said, "then I will take you both out for ice cream after dinner."

The joy on their faces as we walked into that ice-cream shop, the uncontainable delight that erupted in screams of elation, completely eclipsed the struggles of the past weeks. It was exactly what we needed, and I went to bed that night encouraged. We'd left the thumbtacks behind, at least for a time, and found there was more to life than the difficult times. There are also peaches and ice cream!

Father, thank You for Your grace, which carries us through the difficult times.

Carey Pearson

The Least of These

The King will reply, "Truly I tell you,
whatever you did for one of the least of these brothers and sisters of mine,
you did for me." Matt. 25:40.

One of my biggest frustrations as a new mom was how little time I had for myself. Our first child had terrible colic during the first four months of his life. He never slept for more than two hours at a time. Often it was even less than that. To get him to sleep my husband and I would take turns holding and bouncing him for nearly an hour. It was exhausting, to say the least.

The conversations with my husband during this time were often confusing and frustrating because of our sleep-deprived brains. My conversations with God were nearly nonexistent. I was filled with guilt that, when life got a little tough, I couldn't make the time to connect with Him.

One day after I'd had all I could take, I was sharing with a friend how difficult my life had become, how tired my husband and I were, and how guilty I felt for not having the time or energy for prayer or worship. He listened quietly for a moment, then said something really insightful. "You know, when Jesus spoke about 'the least of these,' I have always imagined He was talking to the parents of young children. He knows what's going on in your life right now. He's right there beside you." I felt flooded by such a sense of relief. *Of course He knew,* I thought. What a revelation!

It's so easy to forget in those first bewildering and exhausting steps into parenthood that the Creator of the precious babe you're rocking to sleep truly cares and understands what is happening in your life. Even on days—or nights—when all you can muster is a weary "Help me!" He hears and answers. He is right there beside you, holding you close through every sleepless night.

Dear Lord, thank You for creating this baby. Thank You for thinking of me—even when I'm too weary to string together two intelligent sentences. Strengthen me, I pray, and thank You for caring for us all.

Kristin Breiner

Three Important Words

In him we have redemption through his blood, the forgiveness of sins, in accordance with the riches of God's grace. Eph. 1:7.

So many times in the early days of learning to be a parent, I got things very wrong. I still do. Parents aren't perfect. In fact they are quite fallible. The sooner you figure this out, the easier things will be for you and your children.

One of the most important lessons I learned as a mother was to be able to say these three little magic words: "I am sorry." They are important for your children to hear. As God's first representative on this earth you are His model, the first teacher of God's character. And, as we are forgiven, we must freely forgive.

Saying "I'm sorry" doesn't make you less of a parent; in fact, it makes you a more godly parent. It shows your children that God freely forgives us as we come to Him with our mistakes. It is a powerful way to teach children of God's love.

Some parents feel that saying "I'm sorry" undermines their authority. It doesn't. It strengthens it. Say "I am sorry" often, and without fear. You are setting an example that will live long in your children's memories and will forever impact their lives.

In the same manner, when they do something wrong, teach them to say, "I am sorry." And let them know you forgive them. Did they break something in their play? Remember, it's just a thing. Should they be careful? Yes. But still, it is just a thing. As we forgive them, we teach that God forgives them too. Without knowing about this trait of God's character, they won't want to have a relationship with God. They will fear Him instead.

An ancient Chinese proverb states, "He who cannot forgive burns the bridge over which he himself must pass." Instead of burning bridges, build a bridge. Forgiveness can build a bridge that will lead your children to the throne of God.

Lord, You have freely forgiven us at a great cost. Help us to forgive, and in so doing may we lead our little ones to You.

Kimberely Tagert-Paul

When Strength Is Gone

God is our refuge and strength, a very present help in trouble. Ps. 46:1, KJV.

My oldest daughter, Briana, missed half of the first day of kindergarten. Passing out on the playground will do that to you. That day I received the phone call no parent wants to get. On the other end of the phone the kindergarten teacher asked me if Briana had a history of fainting. I almost dropped the phone as questions flooded through my head. Thankful that the school was literally around the corner, we hopped in our van and raced there.

Arriving at the school, my wife, youngest daughter, and I quickly made our way to the office. There we met a severely weakened version of the bright and energetic little girl we had dropped off just hours before. Briana's teacher told us she'd had a normal morning and after lunch the class went outside for recess. Just before recess was over, Briana walked over to her teacher and said she wanted to go home. Immediately after that she fainted.

"How could this have happened?" I asked myself. We retraced the day. Briana had been too excited to eat breakfast that morning. Her full lunch bag indicated she'd been too excited for lunch as well. On her first day of school she probably felt overwhelmed and nervous. When her body couldn't take it anymore, she found her strength was gone. I picked up my little girl and fought back tears as I carried her to the van and drove toward the doctor's office. In her weakest moment when she could do nothing for herself, she had to rely on my strength. Thankfully in the days since, there have been no major issues with Briana's health. Not willing to take any chances, I still pray for her health and safety every day before school.

This incident reminds me of my own limitations. No matter how much I pretend, I am not a superdad. At times life leaves me overwhelmed and nervous. When my strength is gone, I have no choice but to depend on God. Even when I'm unable to express it, God knows when He needs to carry me, just as no words are needed for me to know when I need to carry my little ones.

Thank You, God, for carrying us in our weakest moments as parents. Help us to trust in Your strength and not our own.

Pierre Quinn

He Will Answer When We Call

The Lord hears his people when they call to him for help.
He rescues them from all their troubles. Ps. 34:17, NLT.

Last year I wasn't sure if my son would pass first grade. We had moved
twice since he started kindergarten, and it had taken its toll on him,
putting him behind in school both socially and academically. As an only
child, and a shy one at that, he found it difficult to make new friends. To
make things worse, he'd struggled harder than the other kids when it came
to learning how to read. He hated school because it was so hard for him.
Many times when I picked him up after class, he climbed into the car and
started to cry. This happened almost every school day.

As a mother, watching my tenderhearted 6-year-old suffering was agony. I often wanted to cry with him. We worked so hard, for so long, on his
reading and still weren't sure if he would pass. Some nights, after making
sure he'd fallen asleep, I would cry. My heart was breaking for my sweet
boy, and as hard as I tried to come up with ways to help him, I kept coming
back to one thing: pray! And we did. Every morning on the way to school,
he and I would ask Jesus to help him in school that day. I prayed for him
throughout the day, and each evening we'd pray again as I tucked him into
bed.

One evening, at the women's Bible study group, I asked for prayer. After I shared our situation with the group, we prayed together. When the
study was done that evening, one of the women approached me. She shared
that she was a teacher whose specialty was in pinpointing exactly where
a student struggled in learning to read. She offered to work with my son
and help him learn to read. We started the process right away. In fact, I
started taking him to her house that same week. In working with her, and
continuing to work hard at home, my little guy improved his ability to read.
What an answer to prayer. And what joy we shared when he passed the first
grade.

*Thank You for feeling the heartache in every parent's heart as they suffer with
their children, Lord. Thank You for helping us find solutions in answer to our
prayers.*

Bonnie Nyachae

Love in Meltdown Mode

Love is patient, love is kind.... It always protects,
always trusts, always hopes, always perseveres. Love never fails. 1 Cor. 13:4-8.

I sit with him in my lap facing away from me. I hold his tiny arms in front of him and embrace him with my whole body. No form of discipline is suitable for this situation. He kicks; screams; cries and thrashes. My shins, bruised; my lip, swollen; my tears and prayers hang silently in the air. Long minutes crawl by as I restrain my son during another overload meltdown. We sit together, alone, in a room adjacent to onlookers at a family gathering. My stomach is tied in knots once more.

As a parent I want to make all the right decisions in shaping the character of this precious gift entrusted to me by God—even when clarity grows muddled during the heat of battle. Still, this time I feel relatively certain it has not been a war of his will against mine.

Nothing calms him except, eventually, his own exhaustion and the weight of my love. I know this is not about rebellion. Instead, the challenges of a long day have him tired, hungry, and completely overstimulated. The load is more than he can bear. Finally, he fully surrenders and slumps against me. When all is quiet, except for his hiccups, he whispers, "I'm sorry. I love you, Mommy."

I cannot help being reminded of the unfailing love and patience our heavenly Father lavishes on us, His children, when life causes us to melt down. We become exhausted by sickness or financial burdens; we hunger for peace and goodness; and long for moments when we can unplug from the overstimulation of this crazy world. He gently holds us close, His arms firm and strong, until we calm down and fully surrender to His protection, grateful for the hope He generously and humbly offers.

Father in heaven, thank You for Your unfailing love. Please help us to remember Your beautiful, unchanging example. Give us strength to hold our children close and protect them through the frustrations of life so that they may see You in all we do.

Karen Barnett

The Lord Gives and the Lord Takes

The Lord gave and the Lord has taken away;
may the name of the Lord be praised. Job 1:21.

My husband and I looked forward to expecting our first baby. We were certain I'd become pregnant easily, but after two years went by I began to get worried. I noted with concern that none of my husband's siblings had been able to conceive. We decided to bring the matter before the Lord.

We set aside time for personal prayer, and each Sabbath at 5:00 p.m. we went to our special place of prayer—the prayer garden at AIIAS. We prayed for a baby for another three years before I conceived. I'll never forget our excitement as we waited for the results of the pregnancy test. We were overjoyed and praised the Lord for giving us such a gift. That little gift is now 7 years old—a cute and talented little girl.

Two years later we were blessed when I became pregnant with a baby boy. My husband worked hard to save for the new addition to our family. At the time, he was working on his thesis and dedicated it to our son. A few months into the pregnancy I went for my routine checkup and was devastated to learn that I had a blighted ovum pregnancy. This happens when a fertilized egg implants in the uterus but fails to develop into an embryo. When I returned home and told my husband, we both wept in each other's arms and cried out to the Lord in our grief.

My first pregnancy reminds me of the many couples in the Bible, such as Abraham and Sarah, Isaac and Rebecca, Jacob and Rachel, who had children after several years of asking the Lord. He heard their prayers and provided the answer they longed for. However, my second pregnancy served to remind me that my children are not my own. These precious jewels belong to the Lord, and as parents, we are only stewards. Like Job, I have learned to say, "The Lord gives and the Lord takes away. Blessed be the name of the Lord."

Lord, grant me the grace to receive Your answer to my prayers, whatever it brings. May I never forget that You have entrusted these little ones to me. Help me to love and treasure them and to trust their lives to Your care and keeping.

Leonora O. Carado

Sleepless Nights

*The nights of crying your eyes out
give way to days of laughter. Ps. 30:5, Message.*

Two years after Karen and Paul were married they had a beautiful baby girl. Karen got home from the hospital, and baby Annie turned into an inconsolable bundle of distress! She had a case of colic that caused her to cry for days on end. They didn't know what to do. They had followed all their physician's advice—different baby milk, tummy rubs, buggy rides, even chamomile tea, but nothing helped. This was unbearable for Karen and Paul, and it nearly cost them their family.

They experienced many sleepless nights, and mom felt like the worst mother in the world. She couldn't stop her baby from crying! She was exhausted and felt guilty for getting angry. Her patience was being tried. Couldn't they enjoy their first weeks as other parents do?

"I feel awful saying this, and I would never do it, but I can see why some moms are driven to shake their babies. You are sleep-deprived and desperate," Karen said with tears rolling down her cheeks. There were many times she found herself having to walk away from Annie just to get herself back together. When Annie slept, Karen dreaded the moment she would awake, because she knew the crying would resume.

Karen's relationship with Paul quickly deteriorated; they had no time for each other. "We took the stress out on each other. After falling out over a bag of chips, the last thing I wanted to do was sit down and talk things through. I just wanted to have my tea, then go to sleep."

Karen told me they didn't know what else to do. I suggested that they try praying nonstop during those sleepless nights. From then on, each time Annie cried they wrapped their arms around her and each other and prayed. This helped them in their relationship. Paul said, "That baby became the most prayed-for child of this generation. We believe that God will use Annie in mighty ways." They remembered those were some of their longest and most boring prayers, but they recently told me, "We wouldn't change those sleepless nights for anything in this world. We are seeing those prayers answered in the life of our teenage daughter."

Thank You, O God, for being a faithful Father who hears our cry and keeps His promises to His children! Indeed, joy comes in the morning.

Z. Kathy Cameron

A Letter to My Daughter

I am marvelously made! . . . You know me inside and out, you know every bone in my body; You know exactly how I was made, bit by bit, how I was sculpted from nothing into something. Like an open book, you watched me grow from conception to birth; all the stages of my life were spread out before you . . . before I'd even lived one day. Ps. 139:14-16, Message.

You came into this world too early. At only 28 weeks, you weighed in at nearly two pounds. Your tiny body rested perfectly in your daddy's hand, and your cry was that of the tiniest kitten. My joy was unspeakable when the nurse said I could take you out of the incubator and hold you. You were almost 24 hours old.

I looked at the feeding tube in your nose and whispered, "I'm so sorry." My guilt overwhelmed me. I had let you down when you were at your most vulnerable. My body was incapable of carrying you to full term. I was your mother and I had failed you even before you were born. Though you had 10 toes and 10 little fingers, you had been registered a miscarriage. How would that trauma affect you? Would I keep apologizing forever? I was so aware of your frailty. How could I ever make it up to you? I wondered. Yet you seemed content in my hands.

We brought you home at 6 weeks. You weighed three pounds. Your big sister could hardly wait to meet you. She was such an energetic, carefree child. Would you be as free as she? Or would you be held back because my body had let you down? We dressed you in baby doll clothes for six months. You were our precious little doll.

For the next three years I refused to cry. I would not allow myself to be real. If I broke down and became vulnerable, would something inside you break too? I determined to be strong for you. No matter the cost.

The day you went to preschool I was so happy. You were going to be OK! You had no hidden disability to hold you back. That was the day I finally gave myself permission to cry. Through my tears I released the years of guilt I had borne. I could smile again.

Your body grew strong and perfect. No longer fragile, you danced with joy and confidence. You stepped onto the stage and claimed your world. Though you don't know it, you have given me the sweetest gift: forgiveness. My heart overflows!

Debby Botes

Growing Garlic

For thou shalt eat the labour of thine hands. Ps. 128:2, KJV.

I once planted a row of garlic bulbs in my vegetable garden. I watered the row faithfully, but saw no sign of life from the bulbs. I vaguely remembered that garlic takes a long time to grow, so I determinedly continued watering, hoping that I would get them to start growing. After a while I gave up, thinking there must have been something wrong with the bulbs, or perhaps I didn't know enough about growing garlic. I did continue to water them, just in case. And one day I saw the fresh green tops peeping through the ground! All this time, under the ground where I couldn't see it, that garlic had been putting down roots, preparing to grow. Soon my garlic plants were a good six inches high, and I looked forward to eating the fruit of my labors.

Sometimes parenting is like growing garlic. You put in a tremendous amount of effort, and yet see no results. At times you find yourself hopeless, discouraged, and disheartened. You put so much of yourself into your children, and yet don't see the change in their behavior, attitudes, and characters that you would like to see. You see only the negatives and wonder if you really are getting anywhere with them.

What looks like no progress is not necessarily so. Believe that there is something going on inside that you can't see. It will manifest itself in good time. Your job is to prepare the soil of the heart, making sure there is no rebellion, creating the right environment for spiritual growth, and giving your children genuine affection. Then you are to plant the seeds—training them in right habits and giving words of encouragement. You are to keep the weeds out—giving consequences for bad choices and not allowing negative behaviors, attitudes, and character traits to develop. God will cooperate with your efforts and bless them. You *will* eat the labor of your hands.

While you cannot expect a harvest without some effort on your part, the responsibility to get those seeds growing is not yours. Only God can give life.

Lord, help me to do my part faithfully so that You can do Your part. Please give life to the seeds I plant in my children's hearts.

Jenny Lovemore

Dealing With Tough Issues

For the Spirit that God has given us does not make us timid; instead, his Spirit fills us with power, love, and self-control. 2 Tim. 1:7, TEV.

I don't want to be a princess. I want to be a boy, like my brothers," 5-year-old Jean yelled from her bedroom as she heard her mother's footsteps approaching.

Mother became curious and raced into Jean's bedroom, asking, "What's up with my little princess?"

"I tell you, I don't want to be a princess," Jean screamed. With tears rolling down her chocolate cheeks, she added, "I told you this before, but you won't listen."

"OK, baby. Mother is listening now."

"My brothers get to go outside and play basketball. They say that I can't play, that I should do girls stuff. Look at me!" she continued through her sobs while tossing her dolls and tea set across the room. "This is boring!"

"But Jean, you do get to play basketball with your brothers sometimes," Mother tried to encourage her daughter.

"No, no, I play only when they don't have friends. I want to play all the time. I don't want to be a girl."

Mother held Jean close to her, and trying to comfort her, she promised her that she would get to play with her brothers more often.

Everyone struggles with their sexuality. Today, more than ever, Christian parents are concerned about their children's sexuality. When is the right time to talk to your children about gender differences and roles? How much should you say to your young children in order not to rob them of their innocence, nor to prejudice their thoughts about their sexuality?

Our Creator cares about everything concerning our lives. If He knew us before we were formed (Ps. 139:13), then we can trust Him to guide us and our children with their sexuality.

Lord, please help me to trust You to lead in every aspect of our children's lives, including their sexuality.

Sandra Fletcher

Food From the Raven

God will meet all your needs
according to the riches of his glory in Christ Jesus. Phil. 4:19.

When my husband felt a call from God to be a pastor, he quit his job in engineering, and we moved to Michigan. While he was in seminary, we did not have any sponsorship or financial help of any kind. We were just living off his retirement. We had three children at the time, and we were able to get a two-bedroom apartment. Close quarters did not bother us, because we were so excited about the call to ministry. God told me before we were married that my husband was going to be a pastor. I had been waiting for 10 years.

The three years in Michigan passed quickly, and in the final quarter he was offered a job. But the money ran out before his first check was due. We had to wait until the end of the month. We had no money to buy food. Every day we looked in the mail for the check, but it didn't show up. But we didn't worry. We remembered that God knew we had three children to feed.

One morning we gathered for family worship, the children stood by as my husband played the piano. We were singing praise to God, when all of a sudden we heard a loud knock at the door. I was sitting about four feet from the door, so I quickly ran over. I opened the door and looked to the right, then to the left. No one was there. I looked down and right in front of the door were two bags of groceries. In the bag, we found peanut butter, bread, lots of veggies and fruit, and one more tiny gift. In the tie between the two loaves of bread was a dollar bill—just enough money for the Laundromat! We had plenty of food until the check came at the end of the month and clean clothes too! We continued to praise God and thanked Him for supplying our needs. That was a worship we will always remember. We continue to share our story of how God left food on our doorstep.

Dear Lord, thank You for always being there to supply our needs. We are truly grateful for all of Your provisions.

Edwina Grice Neely

Making a New Friend

Friends come and friends go,
but a true friend sticks by you like family. Prov. 18:24, Message.

It didn't take long after the birth of our first son to realize that life had changed in more ways than we'd thought possible. Leaving my job as communication director to be home with our son full-time was a no-brainer for us, but the changes in friendships were totally unexpected.

In her article "Friendships Will Change as You Age Whether You Like It or Not," Ashley Samsa writes, "Many of my married friends started having babies, which pulled them further away from the active social lives they once had. My groups of friends were now split into three categories: unmarried, married without kids, and married with kids. Trying to get the unmarried girls' schedules with their still-active social calendars to match up with the new moms' schedules, which were now filled with diapers and bedtime stories, was next to impossible."

The silver lining, once embraced, is that the great friendships made during those years can last a lifetime. Sharing life with other new parents enriches a day full of diaper changes, fussy babies, and endless cleaning. We get together to study Scripture, do a favorite hobby, exercise or play a sport, or even read books that aren't about parenting.

Thankfully, we all have one friend who will never change no matter what happens in our lives. That is our best friend, Jesus Christ. He is willing to listen to whatever we need to share and is available at any time for counsel of any kind. That is very helpful during midnight feedings, when one can feel all alone. Claim the words in Isaiah 41:10: "So do not fear, for I am with you; do not be dismayed, for I am your God. I will strengthen you and help you; I will uphold you with my righteous right hand." As with any friendship, it is important to nurture it. Once a parent, your schedule is not your own, and finding devotional time can be tough. We need to be more creative with fitting it into our day. After all, isn't our Best Friend worth the time?

Lord, thank You for being a consistent friend when those around me may be changing. Help me to be open to the new possibility of friendships.

Tamara Michalenko Terry

God's Bathroom Door Is Always Open

Have you never heard? Have you never understood? The Lord is the everlasting God, the Creator of all the earth. He never grows weak or weary. No one can measure the depths of his understanding. Isa. 40:28, NLT.

I remember those moments. Those mounting pockets of stress that grabbed hold of me, urging me to steal away to a place of refuge. I needed a break from Toddlerville. No doubt I had been holding my breath far too long, draining my mental stability and parenting skills. Kicking into survival mode, I'd attempt to occupy my kids using one of my top three distraction tools—cartoons, fruit snacks, or naptime. Then I slipped away to my "happy place" and closed the bathroom door.

Alone at last. Rest. Breathe. Gather my sanity. Compose my appearance—at least somewhat. After all, once I opened that door I would jump back into the trenches again.

Rarely did I get very far with my plan of renewal. Before I could ever reach the "gather my sanity" stage, there'd be a little voice calling from outside the door.

Just a few minutes, Lord. That's all I need!

But I was their comfort zone. They longed to talk to me. To be with me. To share with me. And they needed me to take care of them, protect them, and comfort them. I loved that, despite needing a break now and again.

Our heavenly Father is like that. Except that He doesn't barricade Himself in a bathroom. Unlike me, He does not lose His sanity or need to rest. He is always ready to embrace His crazy kids at a moment's notice. There is a warm, fuzzy factor in knowing that no matter what, God's door is always open.

Lord, thank You for assigning me the important role of raising these beautiful children. Give me strength and wisdom so I can be the best mother possible. Help me to keep the door open and point to You as the true source of all that is good and comforting.

Cindy Lynn Jacobs

When Your Heart Breaks

Can a mother forget the baby at her breast and have no compassion on the child she has borne? Though she may forget, I will not forget you! Isa. 49:15.

When I started working as assistant chaplain, I was particularly excited over the fact that I would be visiting patients with newborn babies in the obstetrics unit. My excitement grew all the more when I saw baby gifts and cute stickers I would be delivering to my little patients.

As my daily visits continued, I became perplexed over what I observed: Some mothers with their newborn babies looked very grave and confused. I wondered why they were not happy on that joyous day. After talking with them I realized that their babies had serious physical issues for which recovery was not guaranteed. My heart ached for those mothers who poured out tears of sorrow and despair over their babies. They did not seem to care about their condition or pain during labor and delivery. Their one and only concern was their suffering babies.

It was the same in the pediatric unit. Mothers and fathers were ever concerned with their little children under great pain. Their eyes were fixed on their children whether they talked with doctors, nurses, or chaplains. I could immediately sense that most of them had not slept that night, but they didn't care. They were only happy and able to laugh when their kids were recovering, but were in tears and despair when they were going through a tough time.

As a mother of one son, I immediately felt for them, recalling the times when he was sick. I just could not sleep or concentrate on my work as my heart broke for him. I am sure those parents I met have gone through the same thing. Their love and concern for their children were the same, regardless of nationality, race, age, and religion.

As I recall my visits to those parents, I cannot help thinking about our God who watches over His children day and night. If we parents with a sinful nature can pour all our hearts and souls on our sick and suffering children, how much more would God remember and care for His children suffering from sin and cares?

May we be reminded of Your marvelous love every time our hearts break for the precious gifts You have granted us—our children.

Heidi Ok Kyung Ha

Happy Times With Jesus

Fix these words of mine in your hearts. Deut. 11:18.

The dreadful memory remains. A Bible and lesson book under my arm, I marched down the hall toward our daughters' room. "Come now!" I called. "We're going to study your Sabbath school lesson." My voice sounded shrill and stressed, even to me. No wonder my girls wanted none of it.

But I felt responsible, for nothing in my husband's childhood had equipped him to spiritually guide our children. And I loved the Lord. I depended on Jesus every day, and I wanted our children to love Him too. But my method? Wrong! Eventually I learned that the best way to help your child love Jesus is to make knowing Him an intricate, happy part of their daily lives.

Make conversation about Jesus as natural and ordinary as playing. Guide your little ones to feel the softness of a pet's fur. Show them how some flowers turn to face the sun. Talk about the cushion of grass God made to cover the dirt, and remind them that when sin entered the world so did stickers and biting insects. Take them outside to see sunsets and the phases of the moon. As they help you cook, retell the story of Jesus feeding thousands with so little. Day after day, let the small things of life remind them how much God loves us.

Pray! Pray for them and with them. Take their prayer requests seriously. Share your requests and rejoice with them when they're answered. Some families keep a booklet with dated reminders that here (on this day, on this spot) God helped them. What a treasure that becomes.

Make Bible time a cozy time with your child snuggled nearby. Yes, I know that the reality may be different, but strive to make it a happy time. Let them ask questions. Older kids will love acting out the stories, and that helps anchor it in their minds.

Written Bible stories—for the very young that means three or four sentences, read daily. Review memory verses daily but don't stress if they don't memorize easily. Share your personal and family stories of times God led. That makes an impression like nothing else does.

Father, thank You for showing us how best to share Your love and loveliness with our little ones.

Penny Estes Wheeler

A Spoonful of Sugar

*We are troubled on every side, yet not distressed;
we are perplexed, but not in despair; persecuted, but not forsaken;
cast down, but not destroyed. 2 Cor. 4:8, 9, KJV.*

Slim pickings" was too generous. Her cupboards were almost bare. The story of the widow of Zarephath came to mind. In the cupboard was a little white sugar, a cup of lentils, and a cup of rice that was for the evening meal for her family of six. Her family had fallen on challenging times, and their faith was being tested. All future meals were in question.

She had laundry to do, and she had to walk past the pantry to get to the washer and dryer, where she would use plain hot water because there was no detergent. As she passed, she heard shuffling and noticed movement through the crack in the door. Opening it, her heart broke. Her daughters each had a spoon and were quietly eating sugar straight from the container. Their eyes were wide with concern, as they thought a punishment was certain. Her eyes welled with tears and she grabbed them, hugging them close. She told them it was OK and promised them God would not let them down if they were faithful. They cried and prayed together. Late afternoon came and she prepared the meal of lentils and rice. The family sat down to their evening meal with smiles and a positive attitude. During the meal her husband's phone rang. He stepped away from the table to answer. Returning after a few minutes, he quietly finished his meal.

After the meal, when the kids were tucked into bed, her husband slipped away. However, before leaving, he shared with her that a friend had put $100 into their bank account. Together they thanked God for the blessing. Morning came with the smell of delicious food wafting into the kids' rooms. They awoke to a vivid faith-building moment—one they would not soon forget. God had filled their cupboards, and their tummies.

Dear heavenly Father, as we share difficult times with our children may we pull together and look to You to provide all our needs. May we teach them that no matter what trouble may come, we do not need to be distressed; if we don't understand why challenges befall us, we do not need to despair; when we feel persecuted, we have not been forsaken; though we may be cast down, we are not destroyed. Thanks. In Jesus' name, amen.

Karen Barnett

Count Your Many Blessings

The children born to a man when he is young are like arrows in the hand of a warrior. Blessed is the man who has filled his quiver with them. Ps. 127:4, 5, GW.

We intended to have two children. When our second child was 5 months old, we found out I was pregnant with a third. As I dragged myself through the exhausting days of pregnancy with a 2-year-old and a baby, it seemed every stranger I met—and everyone else—had the same thing to say: "Boy, are you going to have your hands full!"

Call it hormones, but some days it was almost more than I could do not to snap at them. "No! Really? I thought the third would be a charm."

"Why do they keep saying it?" I'd tearfully ask my husband. "Don't they know I'm already overwhelmed?"

In the midst of it all, one thoughtful woman made a world of difference. Seeing me battling one child into a high chair one day, while another one howled beside me in the stroller, she came over to talk.

"When my two were this age," she began, "we thought about having a third. But I was so overwhelmed that I said I just couldn't handle any more." She smiled ruefully. "But now, my two are teenagers and I really wish we'd had that third one!"

She went on, "I know it's hard now, and it'll be really hard for a while. But just wait. You'll be so glad you did it."

Eyes brimming with tears, I thanked her. And for the next two years, I can't tell you how many times I clung to the hope of her words. I won't deny it. We ate a lot of ramen noodles for a few months there. Our house was a disaster. But now my youngest is 6. We get into the car to go places, and it's amazing! They can all go potty unassisted, put on their shoes, and strap themselves into their seats! I love having three children, and having them all so close together has turned into a huge blessing. I know it can be overwhelming, but hang in there. And if you're past those tough times . . . remember to pass on the hope to someone else.

Thanks, Lord, for the encouragement of a stranger and for Your grace, which pulled me through some really tough days. It's been so worth it!

Nicole Crosier Parker

Cry Out to Jesus

I waited patiently for the Lord to help me, and he turned to me
and heard my cry. He lifted me out of the pit of despair . . .
He set my feet on solid ground and steadied me as I walked along.
He has given me a new song to sing,
a hymn of praise to our God. Ps. 40:1-3, NLT.

M ommy, is TD home now? Can I play with her?"
"No, Kelley. Remember, your sister is not coming back. We cannot play with her anymore." How do you explain death to a 3-year-old? How do you help a little girl grieve the loss of her sister and constant companion?

Our happy home was now torn apart; my husband and I were struggling to deal with the loss of our eldest daughter while trying to help our youngest comprehend the unimaginable: Kimberley was not coming back. Kelley, a naturally happy child, became sullen, afraid, and angry. All our parenting skills seemed to vanish, and the confusion was overwhelming.

But God is so amazing. Through the intensity of our questions and troubles, He came through for us. I did not always wait patiently, but God fulfilled His promises and gave me the wisdom and patience to comfort and love my girl through her anxiety. There were many nights I had to hold on to His promises. "For our present troubles are small and won't last long. . . . Don't look at the troubles we can see now; rather, we fix our gaze on things that cannot be seen" (2 Cor. 4:17, 18, NLT). And this one: "God is our refuge and strength, always ready to help in times of trouble" (Ps. 46:1, NLT).

Parenting through tough times can cause huge valleys of despair, mountains of distrust and unsolicited anger. It can pull a family apart or bring them closer together. The choice—though not easy—is ours. It is up to us as the parents to choose to cry out to Him, claiming the promise that "the Lord is close to the brokenhearted; he rescues those who are crushed in spirit" (Ps. 34:18, NLT).

Dear Father, I put myself and my children in Your care. Please fill the gaps I leave behind on my parenting journey. Thank You for the blessing of having these little ones in my life.

Darla L. McCarty

When They Push Your Buttons

*Fathers, do not exasperate your children; instead,
bring them up in the training and instruction of the Lord. Eph. 6:4.*

Do you think the Lord has this counsel in the Bible to remind us that we are not always right? Otherwise we could start quoting the other parenting Bible verses to our children: "Honor your father and your mother, so that you may live long in the land the Lord your God is giving you" (Ex. 20:12). "Children, obey your parents in everything, for this pleases the Lord" (Col. 3:20). "Listen, my son, to your father's instruction and do not forsake your mother's teaching" (Prov. 1:8).

My favorite quote to give our older children is "You may not like the rule, but you do have to follow it." If they argue, I just add, "When you are 18, you can live on your own and have your own rules. Of course, I would prefer you to be in college, but that would be your choice." To which they roll their eyes and leave. Yes, they've heard it a few times.

Something to remember is that it takes two to argue. If your child wants to argue a point (which for some is their favorite thing to do), it may be best not to respond. If you have already stated the rule, simply walk away. If your child follows you, grabbing on to you and throwing a tantrum (yes, I've been there), simply get down to their level, look at them eye to eye, and say, "I am not going to discuss this with you any further. If you are going to continue this behavior, you will need to have a time-out." If you are consistent, the child will learn that you mean what you say.

Most children have an amazing gift: They know how to push our buttons. The key is to not let them. That requires a lot of prayer, deep breathing, and sometimes hiding in a closet! Through it all just remember Proverbs 22:6: "Start children off on the way they should go, and even when they are old they will not turn from it."

Lord, please give me patience to deal with my children during the tough times. I love them dearly, but sometimes they can get frustrating. Help me not to exasperate them, but to train them in Your ways.

Tamara Michalenko Terry

Keeper of the Waves

He gave the sea its boundary
so the waters would not overstep his command. Prov. 8:29.

He was such a little guy, no more than 3, with blond curls that danced in the wind. He had everyone's attention at the beach that day. While building a lopsided sand castle, he laughed—it was the laugh of innocence, a peal of total delight.

We were at the beach hoping for a few hours of respite from the turmoil that had become our lives. This was the same beach where my new husband had put his arm around me for the first time, while pretending to point out a sailboat. It was here he first told me he loved me. Those days of endless dreaming had come crashing down. Difficulties with jobs, money, and illness marked our days, along with the relentless intrusion of death into our barely begun world.

A tiny squeal brought me back from my deep thoughts. The lad was now joined by his father, who dangled his toes over the waves that crashed upon the shore. Oh, those waves! Crashing, crashing against the shore. The pain of loss and hardship reminded me again of the waves that pounded in our lives. The ebbs barely allowed us time to catch our breath before the next wave crashed over us.

I turned back to the little guy and watched as he edged closer to the shoreline. His baby steps sent the water tickling over his feet, and he jumped back in surprise. Then timidly he edged forward again. Finally, fear conquered, he stood firm as the fringes of the waves swirled gently around his ankles. He had realized the crashing waves could come only so far. His bright grin said it all.

I was reminded of a promise for our own lives. "God is faithful, who will not suffer you to be tempted above that ye are able" (1 Cor. 10:13, KJV). The Keeper of the waves was our Abba, watching over the waves. He wouldn't let the waves consume us in their press.

Thank You, Father, though we experience dark days and sad ways on this earth, You hold us carefully, allowing us to grow but not be harmed. Thank You, my Keeper of the waves.

Kimberley Tagert-Paul

No More Fix-It Lists

Being confident of this very thing, that he who began a good work in you will perfect it until the day of Jesus Christ. Phil. 1:6, ASV.

Do you see your child as a gift from God? He has entrusted you with one of the greatest treasures you will ever have. Yet, do our words and our actions show that we regard them as such? If we were to take an inventory, perhaps we would be surprised at how often we speak in ways that would show otherwise.

Focusing on the negative is an easy trap to fall into. Complaining and griping is one of Satan's tactics that all too often works. Do you find yourself speaking negatively about your child, whether to your spouse or to God? It is easy to make our daily prayers look more like a fix-it list.

That list becomes long as we spend our prayer time asking God to "fix" our children and our spouse. We gladly hand God His to-do list every day, and our prayers ascend to the heavenly throne sounding something like this: "Lord, fix John's grumbling, make Katie quit fighting with her little sister, help Michael study harder and make better grades, and please let Susie sleep through the night."

When was the last time you devoted your prayer time exclusively to thanking God for each member of your family instead of complaining about them? Bring them to Him, mentioning them each by name, and thank God for specific things about each one. Why don't you consider telling them, too? Knowing you have been a praise on someone's prayer list can be a powerful thing.

By focusing on the positives, our daily fix-it lists to God can become times of thanksgiving and praise. "Lord, thank You for John's ability to see things that need changing, thank You that little Katie can stand up for herself when she sees injustice, thank You that Michael enjoys being out in Your creation, and thank You for little Susie's energy."

Dear Lord, thank You for my children. Thank You for the awesome privilege of being their parent. Help me not to get so caught up in the negatives that I forget to thank You for the positives.

Claudio and Pamela Consuegra

So Much More

Go and sell all you possess . . . and come, follow Me. Mark 10:21, NASB.

Recently I made the decision to be a stay-at-home mom. It was quite a mental struggle adjusting from working full-time to being a homemaker. I felt I was giving up a career I had spent 14 years developing. What had been the point of all the hard work and all the student loans if I was just going to stay home raising children? What about my dreams of getting a Ph.D. and being a groundbreaking neuropsychologist? How could I give it all up?

When I get stuck thinking about what I have given up, I say I'm in an "Alexander the Great funk." I call it that because I walk around feeling that I should be out conquering the world á la Alexander the Great. Instead, I am at home entertaining a toddler and washing dishes. Rather than working on my doctoral thesis, I'm waging war against my to-do list and the laundry monster. It doesn't help that people keep asking me when I'm going to get a real job.

However, I have discovered something awesome. I now have time for my family. I no longer have to spend hours writing papers or worrying about finding someone to take my older kids to school in the morning so I can run out the door to work.

In Mark 10 a rich young ruler asked Jesus what he needed to do to inherit eternal life. Christ informed him that he had to sell all his possessions and follow Him. The ruler left sad. He couldn't imagine giving up everything he had. If he could have seen into the future, he would have realized that Jesus was offering so much more than worldly wealth.

We might not be rich young rulers, but we all have something we struggle to give up. For me it was the career I had worked at for half my life. Yet, in choosing to follow God's leading, I have discovered a better life than I could have ever imagined. What might you gain if you were to let go of your "possessions" and make the choice to follow wherever God takes you?

God, You offer us so much. Thank You for the invitation to follow the plans You have made for us. Help us be brave enough to step out in faith.

Asheley Woodruff

In His Time

I have told you these things, so that in me you may have peace.
In this world you will have trouble. But take heart!
I have overcome the world. John 16:33.

Nichole and Greg married young. They were busy, young professionals who worked hard and traveled often. Having a family was not on their radar. After seven years they decided it was the right time to start a family. They were overjoyed when Nichole became pregnant right away. They were ready to embrace parenthood! But at the end of her first trimester, Nichole had a miscarriage. They were devastated and struggled to understand why. They had slowed down; they were still young and healthy. Their faith was strong. So where had they gone wrong?

The doctor advised them to wait another year before trying again. They did, and when Nichole became pregnant a second time, they were happy but nervous. At five months their baby was stillborn. They weren't sure they'd be able to get through the mountain of grief, and they decided not to try for a family ever again. A few years went by, and they slowly began to put their lives back together. They could see how God was at work in their lives, and they began to heal from their loss. Their heartache helped them draw closer to each other, and to God.

Quite unexpectedly, Nichole found out she was pregnant—again. They were beyond scared. All the memories of losing two babies flooded their minds. The emotional pain was almost unbearable. But God's timing was perfect. They had settled into their jobs and were not traveling as much; their relationship with the Lord had strengthened. At eight months my friend gave birth to a healthy baby girl and boy! They named the little girl Jaasiel, "made by God," and the little boy they called Jonathan, "given of God." They were doubly blessed!

Sometimes God is silent when we pray. We are left wondering why tragedy rips us apart. Heartache doesn't necessarily happen because we've done wrong, but simply because we live in a broken world. In these moments we need to cling to the Word—"My grace is sufficient for you" (2 Cor. 12:9, NKJV).

Father, in spite of the pain we experience, I thank You for reminding us that Your timing is always perfect, and Your grace is sufficient!

Z. Kathy Cameron

Just Love Them!

Dear friends, let us love one another, because love comes from God. Whoever loves is a child of God and knows God. 1 John 4:7, TEV.

When I was pregnant with my first child, I was given lots of advice. I know many new moms complain about this, but I felt so overwhelmed and uncertain about becoming a mom that I was actually seeking advice, or at least reassurance. A stranger would ask when I was due, and I would blurt out something like "I'm not ready!"

Some people told me to sleep as much as possible because once the baby arrived I would never sleep again. The cynics told me to enjoy life today because I'd soon be tired and poor. The optimists told me I was embarking on the greatest journey imaginable. They were all right!

I received one piece of advice from several people whom I admired as parents, and it became my favorite because it was so simple. They told me, "Just love them. Love your children and they will be fine."

I think this is so important, not just because loving a child affects the way you teach, nurture, and discipline them, but as a parent you are demonstrating God's love. A child will learn about God and develop their picture of Him based on how you love them.

When Jesus was on earth, He was also asked for advice. A teacher of the law asked, "If you had to choose the most important commandment, which would it be?" Jesus answered, "Love the Lord your God with all your heart and with all your soul and with all your mind and with all your strength" (Mark 12:30).

My baby is now 2 years old, and our days are filled with laughter, tantrums, potty training, and a few more tantrums. It is easy to feel overwhelmed. What kind of person will she become if we can't curb the tantrums? What if she never learns to use the toilet? During these times of uncertainty I remember the wisdom of others and remind myself, "Just love her."

O Lord—help me to survive the tears, the tantrums, and the training. And when I feel overwhelmed, comfort me with Your love—even as You show me how to love this little person You've entrusted to my care. Thank You, Lord.

Dena King

Slow-moving Trains

We know that all things work together for the good of those who love God—those whom he has called according to his plan. Rom. 8:28, GW.

You're running behind schedule to get 7-year-old Elsie to her violin lesson, but you're nearly there. Just cross the tracks and there it is. But wouldn't you know it, just as you approach the crossing the bell starts to clang, the lights begin to flash, and that long striped arm descends. Should you floor it? Nope; it isn't worth it. So you punch the brakes. And wait.

While the slowest-moving line of freight cars in recorded history ambles past. Decision time. Fuss about the cars—or enjoy them? Chastise yourself for not leaving home 15 seconds earlier, or count the cars with Elsie.

Much is at stake in your decision. Not only will it affect your stress level for the rest of the day, but Elsie will learn how adults handle unplanned disappointments. Will it ratchet up your anxiety—or provide a precious nine-and-a-half-minute recess with your beautiful second grader? What a teaching moment, this.

Life is full of slow-moving trains. A downpour on the day of the much anticipated picnic. The unwanted report from the doctor. The kids choose up sides, and Elsie isn't chosen to be captain. Life is like that. And it is in these circumstances that Elsie gets the Lemons-to-Lemonade 101 class from Mom and Dad.

Parents get to hand off some crucial life lessons during these times. We can choose . . . to have the picnic in the garage . . . or, be glad we had that doctor's exam when we did . . . or, I know you're disappointed not to be captain, but you got to play and your team won.

So keep a smile on your face, Mom and Dad; acknowledge her frustration, and assure her there's a brighter day ahead. God is, after all, in control.

Teach us, Lord, to accept the slow-moving trains in life as Your invitation for us to slow down and enjoy the moment.

Don Jacobsen

When I Am Afraid—I Will Trust

Casting all your care upon Him, for He cares for you. 1 Peter 5:6, 7, NKJV.

She sat in the tub pulling her little legs up to her chest as tightly as she could. The sobs racked her body, and the intakes of breath after each sob were ragged. "But Mo-m-m-y, I m-is-s Dad-dy so m-m-uch."

Kayla's daddy had been gone for six months—he had another six left to complete his tour of duty before he could even think of coming home.

"Here, let me wash your back." They had been through this before. Kayla's mom knew the warm water would calm her little girl and help her gain control of her emotions. How it hurt to see her cry. It's tough for an adult to deal with absence, but for a child it can be spirit-crushing.

Parenting is tough enough without adding in the bitterly sad times—temporary absence or permanent absence because of death is a blow. How do we as parents pull our kids up when the very thing that is breaking their heart weighs heavy in our chest as well?

While it may sound trite, the truth is that we can't bear these burdens alone. Quiet, reflective time is imperative—and often we have to physically distance ourselves for a few minutes in order to make any progress forward.

Once Kayla was dried off, dressed, and in bed, Mom said her prayers with her and kissed her good night. With a gentle "I love you, Kayla," Mommy turned off the light and quietly stepped out of the room. Before the boys could call her, or the dishes distract her, she slipped into her bedroom and closed the door. Down on her knees, she poured out her heartache to her Lord.

When we are overwhelmed with life and our days seem tough at best and unmanageable at worst, we must pull away from the vortex and find Jesus. He can be there with us in the maelstrom, but we will feel His presence best if we have tied ourselves to Him spiritually in our alone time. All it requires is a simple "Help me, Jesus." He will honor our call.

When you find yourself sucked into the intensity of the moment grasping for a lifeline, grab for Jesus. Call His name. Bind yourself to Him. He will see you through the maelstrom and give you strength to do the same for your children.

Thank You for Your promises and plans, Lord, to give us a future and a hope.

Candy Graves DeVore

The Way Mark

*Do not let the floodwaters engulf me or the depths swallow me up
or the pit close its mouth over me. Ps. 69:15.*

The waves crashed over us, tumbling us in its foamy depths. We dug our feet firmly into the sand and grabbed a quick breath before the next wave caught up to us. I gulped a mouthful of air and crashed upward through the next wave.

"This is fun," I shouted back to my husband, who was struggling to keep upright.

"I told you," he managed to choke out before the next wave crashed over his head. Our young son smiled, safely riding the waves in his life jacket. We were wave jumping in the cool waters of Lake Michigan. While others chose to sunbathe, we headed straight for the water.

This beach had a strong undertow, and so we prepared ahead of time, placing our bright beach towel in a heap far from where the undertow began—a way mark to keep us protected from the undertow's power. As long as we made sure we didn't drift far from the way mark, we could enjoy the water without succumbing to its danger.

After a delightful picnic under the shade of our beach umbrella, we plunged back into the water, forgetting about the way mark in our haste for fun. Four giant waves thrust us under the water, and this time the sandy bottom was gone.

"Don't panic," my son said. Looking around, I saw him floating safely near my husband, who, like me, was struggling in the grasp of the waves. Regaining his footing, he called for help, but the crashing waves swallowed his voice. We were in danger of drowning.

"Lord, save us, please," I pleaded under the water.

I felt a strong push, and there it was, the feel of sand between my toes. I crawled out of the water as my husband pushed our son onto the beach. We collapsed in exhaustion, then prayed in thankfulness to the Lord. We had almost drowned because we had forgotten our way mark.

Lord, You have set up a way mark for us to follow. Help us not to lose our way by taking our eyes off of Your Word, for it is the road map for our lives as we parent our children.

Kimberley Tagert-Paul

Peer Pressure

*But with me it is a very small thing that I should be judged
by you or by a human court. In fact, I do not even judge myself.
For I know of nothing against myself, yet I am not justified by this;
but He who judges me is the Lord. 1 Cor. 4:3, 4, NKJV.*

Bullying and peer pressure are very real problems facing our children today. While it may be easy for us as adults to say things like "Just ignore it" or "Pay no attention to them," it is not an easy thing that our children face. In fact, our glib response will tell them we have minimized the problem and will end up making it harder for them to cope with the issue.

There is increasing pressure on our children from their peers. Considerably more than we faced as children. They are judged by how they dress, what they eat, who they associate with, and what they look like. Our children want to measure up to the expectations of their classmates. They want to fit in and be part of the in-crowd. It is human nature to want to be accepted and have friends. However, oftentimes this pressure and the inability to be accepted have led too many young people to suffer deep depression and can even lead some to commit suicide. How can we as parents counteract this peer pressure?

As parents we need to openly discuss bullying and peer pressure with our children. Role-play various situations in family worships and discuss how to deal with them. Have your children come up with some scenarios. They may be the very situations your child is currently dealing with. This will give your child the tools they need to respond to these challenges when they arise.

Have you talked with your child about how to deal with peer pressure and bullying? Are they currently facing these issues? Do they know that they have a safe place to go to seek help? Are you aware of the resources available to parents struggling to help their children in this situation?

O Lord, this world is such a different place to grow up in compared to when I was a child. Please give me a sensitive and wise spirit to know how best to help my child deal with these issues. May home always be a safe place and Your love be a strong tower.

Claudio and Pamela Consuegra

Let It Rain, Let It Rain!

Unto You do I lift up my eyes,
O You Who are enthroned in heaven. Ps. 123:1, Amplified.

This morning I went running in a very light and gentle rain. I wouldn't run outside if it were pouring with rain—I don't like getting my running shoes wet. This felt more like a thick mist, and it was highly invigorating. It had been raining all night, and the air smelled wonderfully pine-fresh. The morning was hushed, and it was just me and the wide expanse of dark sky stretched out high above, with a hint of the dawn in the east.

I lifted my face to the sky and suddenly had to smile. Ever since I was a little girl of about 6, I remember my mom telling me to lift my face to the sky whenever it rained, for rain makes your face beautiful, or so she said. I believed her and dutifully lifted my face to the rain to wash it whenever I had the opportunity. More than 30 years later I'm still doing it! What's more, I'm teaching my children to do it as well.

It has become a kind of family tradition—something we do when it rains and we're outside. It has been passed on from one generation to another. What may have begun as one of those mom-inspired moments has turned into a wonderful lifelong memory and source of encouragement.

Speaking encouragement to our children reminds them of God's continual love, even in the face of the pounding rainstorms that will surely come our way. While I still don't like rainy days, when they come I think of my mom and smile. I go outside and look up, holding my face high as I encourage my boys to do the same.

Forget the dark clouds and hold your face into the rain. Turn the apparent obstacles into opportunities. Lift your face to the sky—the rain will make it beautiful! Let it rain, let it rain!

O Lord, I lift my eyes to You and my heart is filled with praise! You send the rain and thread the skies with rainbows. Help me to teach my children to keep their eyes lifted to You—whether it rains or shines!

Thandi Klingbeil

June

Encouragement for Parents

God Is Searching for You

*Even though you are bad, you know how to give good gifts to your children.
How much more your heavenly Father will give good things
to those who ask him! Matt. 7:9-11, NCV.*

Jesus looked out at the people who had gathered to hear His words. More than anything, He wanted them to understand the mercy and loving-kindness of God. To illustrate their need and God's willingness to give, Jesus talked to them about hungry children asking their parents for food. He said, "If your children ask for bread, which of you would give them a stone?"

He appealed to the deep, natural love parents have for their children. No parent with a heart could turn away a child who is hungry. What would others think of parents who would tease their children with a promise of food and then disappoint them? So how can we dishonor God by imagining that He won't respond to the needs of His children? While it may be possible for a parent to ignore a hungry child, God can never ignore the cry of a needy heart. That is such a tender description of His love!

This is the message from the Father's heart to those who feel that God has forgotten them in their darkest times: "Can a woman forget the baby she nurses? Can she feel no kindness for the child to which she gave birth? Even if she could forget her children, I will not forget you. See, I have written your name on my hand" (Isa. 49:15, 16, NCV).

Every promise in God's Word gives us a reason to pray, knowing that He has promised to answer. With the simple words and the faith of a child, we can tell the Lord exactly what we need. We can tell Him about our situation, asking for food and clothing, as well as for spiritual blessings and the assurance of salvation. Our heavenly Father knows that we need all these things, and He invites us to ask Him for them. God will honor every request for our necessities made through the name of Jesus.

The gifts of the One who controls heaven and earth are available to His children. These precious gifts come to us through the Savior's sacrifice; gifts that will meet the deepest needs of the heart; gifts that will last forever; all given to be enjoyed by those who come to God.

May I always remember that You have written my name in the palm of Your hand.

Jerry D. Thomas

Learning to Say No

So Moses' father-in-law said to him, "The thing that you do is not good. Both you and these people who are with you will surely wear yourselves out. For this thing is too much for you; you are not able to perform it by yourself." Ex. 18:17, 18, NKJV.

Moses was going to work every day as the sole judge over all the tribes of Israel. The number of people demanding his time was so great he worked from dawn until dusk without making a dent in the workload. His wise father-in-law, Jethro, saw this and immediately recognized a man who could not say no to requests for his time.

He suggested Moses focus on only two things: representing the people before God, and handling the most difficult of the disputes. The rest of the work could be delegated to other capable men. Moses listened, delegated, and soon found himself doing far more than he had ever done before, but in much less time. If this advice worked for Moses, will it not also work for us?

In order to fulfill our God-given responsibilities as parents, we must set appropriate boundaries. We have the responsibility to set limits for ourselves and for our children. Satan's main focus is to distract us as parents from being the primary disciple makers for our children. And he accomplishes this very easily.

By causing us to be incessantly busy, he robs us of the energy and time that should be devoted to parenting. Busyness is one of the greatest challenges facing parents today. Perhaps it is time for us to consider the wise advice given to Moses by his father-in-law. We must learn to identify and focus on what is important instead of allowing ourselves to become frazzled by the many mundane tasks that can consume our day.

Why not take some time today to review your to-do list. Are you too busy to have quality time with your children? What actions do you need to take to ensure that your career or other "stuff" does not push your children to the end of your priority list?

Lord, help me to see the busyness in my life for what it is: a destructive distraction that will keep me from being the parent I long to be. Help me to reorganize my priorities around Your will for me and for my family. Thank You, Lord.

Claudio and Pamela Consuegra

JUNE 3

My Snow Angel

He has put his angels in charge of you. Ps. 91:11, NCV.

During one of the worst winters we experienced in Maryland, it started to snow and did not stop until a foot of the white stuff coated the ground. The snow plows were kept busy trying to keep the roads clear, and the piles of cleared snow grew like ski slopes along the side of the roads. I watched in amazement as the mountains got bigger and bigger.

One evening my daughter had a field trip to the observatory to view the planets through a telescope. It was supposed to be a perfect night for viewing the stars. The weather report on the radio said the roads were clear, but warned travelers to watch out for black ice. I hated to drive at night even when the weather was good, and besides, I was pregnant. There was nothing else to do but suit up in hats, gloves, coats, scarves, and boots. It was freezing outside and we wanted to be warm! We climbed into the car and carefully drove to the observatory.

After viewing the glorious display in the night skies, we boarded the car to return home. Less than a quarter mile from home, while driving downhill, I hit a sheet of black ice. The car swerved across the road, and I imagined us crashing in the dark. We came to a screeching halt, and after whispering a prayer of thanks, we looked through the windows and to our amazement we were stuck in one of the "snow mountains" on the side of the road. The door wouldn't budge. We were close enough to walk home, but we couldn't get out of the car.

We looked up just then and saw a man walking down the road. He didn't have on a coat or gloves, but he had a shovel in his hands. He walked right up to our car and exclaimed, "You need to get out of here! Another car could come and slide right on top of you." That hadn't even crossed my mind.

He began digging us out of the snow. He moved so fast, it seemed as if he had a mechanical shovel. Then he said, "When I tell you it's clear, go!" We thanked him, and as he pointed to go, we eased out as easily as if we'd never been stuck. We turned back to wave and *he was gone!*

Dear Lord, You are always there. Thank You for sending Your angels in times of need.

Edwina Grice Neely

164

Trust Him Always

The Lord is good, a refuge in times of trouble.
He cares for those who trust in him. Nahum 1:7.

Our daughter weighed 10 pounds and was 22 inches long at birth, the epitome of health, until the unexpected happened. At 8 months she started to throw up. The ER doctor said a stomach virus was going around and sent us home. But as we celebrated the beginning of another year, thanking God for His blessings, we realized that New Year's Day was not going to be much fun.

Chelsey was sick. The throwing-up continued. Our happy, healthy baby was slowly slipping away. She stopped laughing and became still, and we knew we were in trouble. On New Year's Day her pediatrician sent us to the children's hospital for tests.

On arriving at the ER, we found the staff waiting for us. The doctor had made arrangements with the top child radiologist and surgeon of the hospital. Our baby was quickly rushed to radiology. Three gallons of water were pumped into her tiny, dying body. She never moved or even blinked.

I remember standing with my husband, looking at her, as tears rolled down our cheeks. All I could say was "God, You gave her to us as a gift. She is Yours, however. I trust You. If You need to let her sleep, Your will be done, but You'll have a lot of work to do with me. If You decide to allow her to live, may she be an instrument in Your hands. Thank You, Father."

As I ended that prayer the doctor told us they would need to perform surgery to see if anything else could be done. Though we received reports often, that was the longest time of waiting time we had ever experienced. Our world had turned upside down. Our only hope was to trust Him. Three hours later our prayers were answered. The doctor came by and told us the surgery had been successful!

How sweet it is to trust in Jesus. When we surrender everything to Him, the peace that He gives in the midst of the storm is beyond all understanding. No matter the circumstances you may be going through right now, give it to the Lord in prayer and trust Him.

Lord, thank You for being my refuge in the storm! Thank You for Your love, care, and protection. Help us to always look to You and trust You, no matter what the outcome may be.

Z. Kathy Cameron

Bumps in the Road

Can a woman forget her sucking child,
that she should have no compassion on the son of her womb?
Even these may forget, yet I will not forget you. Isa. 49:15, RSV.

After all the hoping for and dreaming of the new baby, there may come a sickening realization once you take the baby home, that parenthood is much harder than you ever thought possible. Parents of newborns sometimes ask themselves silently, "Why did we do this?" They typically don't express these thoughts out loud for fear they'll be thought of as bad parents.

You might liken it to "buyer's remorse," but you can't return the baby for a refund, and you know you can't run away. You find yourself trapped in a bittersweet world of exhaustion with little reward. The only thing to do is to keep on keeping on, wondering each night, "Will this be the night that I sleep for five hours straight?" You're not asking for much—just five hours' sleep. That's the amount of sleep pediatricians refer to when they say the baby will sleep "through the night." This is the side of parenting that nobody talks about, yet it is very real.

Although you might wonder if these feelings indicate you're not parent material, take heart: this is not an indication that you are a poor parent. These thoughts simply indicate that you're an exhausted human being.

Based on the Bible verse above, it seems Isaiah saw regret and exhaustion in the community of mothers around him so many years ago. Feelings aren't sinful. Acting on feelings can sometimes be sinful, but feelings are simply chemical changes within the brain. Wistfully remembering prebaby days when life was carefree and wondering why you thought having a baby was a good idea is not sinful.

Knowing women's hearts through the ages, God is aware of the despair that exhaustion can bring. Be kind to yourself. God knows how you feel. Perhaps God allows babies to cry so we don't regret, so deeply, their growing up, since babyhood is otherwise so very sweet.

Lord, give me the strength to get through the night. Thank You for Your understanding about how tough this is. Thank You that tomorrow is another day, and eventually this will be just a sweet memory.

Nancy Beck Irland

Finding Satisfaction

Pay careful attention to your own work,
for then you will get the satisfaction of a job well done,
and you won't need to compare yourself to anyone else. Gal. 6:4, NLT.

All right, I admit it. I want to be Supermom. But there's always that one mom that seems to do it better than I do.

You know the one. Her house is spotless. Her kids have amazing manners. They know the alphabet by the time they are 2 years old. They give out homemade valentines. She scrapbooks every week and teaches the preschool class at church. Her hair looks as if she just stepped out of a salon. And, of course, she's the one who points out that I've worn my shirt inside out to storytime at the library . . . again.

It's overwhelming. I question whether I will ever be enough. So I take classes on parenting in hopes of doing it bigger and better. But then I compare myself to the instructor. And once again I feel like a failure.

"Angela," a friend comforted me recently, "you know the Proverbs 31 woman didn't do it all in a day. That chapter is a list of the achievements she accomplished over her lifetime. What verse do you need to focus on for today? What is God calling you to do right now?"

Let's face it, I'm never going to be Supermom. There will always be that one mom who seems to do it better than I do. But I can still be a supermom.

I can focus on my own strengths and appreciate the work God gives me. My house might not be spotless, but my kids know that spending time with them is more important to me than taking care of our possessions. I throw great surprise parties and take the most pictures at sporting events and rewrite well-known songs to personalize them for my kids. That's what I am called to do. And hey, if I wear my shirt inside out again, we will just get a good laugh out of it.

These are the jobs I can do well. That's the satisfaction God wants me to find.

Lord, help me to keep from comparing myself to others. Thank You for the strengths You've given me and the work You've prepared for me. I will do my best so that I can live a life of satisfaction.

Angela Ruth Strong

The Lord Is My Rock

The Lord is my rock, my fortress and my deliverer;
my God is my rock, in whom I take refuge. Ps. 18:2.

I spent the better part of two months holding a 1-year-old child as she struggled to adjust to life at day care away from her mom and dad. Her parents listened to me every day as I explained how children need time, some more than others, to understand and trust their world away from home. I assured them that I would always communicate with them on her progress and that if things became too stressful for her I would call them.

As the days went by, Heather slowly began to adjust and to trust me. Gradually I could leave her for a few minutes at a time in her day-care room along with her caregivers and peers. She began to eat and sleep better, and to play on her own, as she felt secure in her environment. This past Christmas I received a beautiful note from her parents in which they wrote, "Thank you for being Heather's 'go to place' away from home."

As parents we also need a "go to place." We need someone to turn to, knowing they will never fail us. God wants to be that place of safety for us. He created us in His image and loves us with an everlasting love. Being a parent is an awesome and sometimes fearful responsibility. But we do not have to do it alone. God knows the way and He will guide us.

Jeremiah 29:11 states, " 'For I know the plans I have for you,' declares the Lord, 'plans to prosper you and not to harm you, plans to give you hope and a future.' " Romans 8:35 asks, "Who shall separate us from the love of Christ? Shall trouble or hardship or persecution or famine or nakedness or danger or sword?"

Keep your communication open with God, and He will help you understand and trust Him until you gradually let go of the stress and feel secure in His environment, in which all things are possible. Open your heart to Him and let Him take care of everything. You will find, as did Heather, you will sleep better, eat better, and enjoy life to its fullest.

Dear Father, I need a "go to place." Help me build trust in You, my fortress and rock. Thank You for the safety and peace that Your everlasting love brings me.

Darla L. McCarty

God's Great Love

Nothing in all creation will ever be able to separate us from the love of God that is revealed in Christ Jesus our Lord. Rom. 8:39, NLT.

Before I became a mom I had no idea the kind of love I would have for my child. When I saw his little face for the first time, my heart ached with an intensity I'd never known before, until I thought it would burst. As he grew, there were times I thought that I couldn't possibly love him more than I did at that moment, and yet I felt my love for him deepen with each passing day.

I would relish the sound of his giggle, memorize the contours of his face for hours, and spend immeasurable amounts of time trying to make him smile. Excitedly, I shared every new movement and sound with my husband at night, and many nights we would race each other into his room to kiss his sweet face and just watch him sleep. He was, and continues to be, my world.

Since becoming a parent, I can now understand God's love for me in ways I could not have imagined before. I am a child of God. He loves me more than I can possibly imagine. He excitedly watches over me and gently guides and trains me. Romans 8:38, 39 says nothing can separate us from God's love. Ever. It is completely unconditional. Though I'd always known that God loved me, I had never pictured His love as that of a parent, because I'd never experienced firsthand a parent's unconditional love.

I had never pictured God being excited about me, smiling over me, His heart swelling with love and pride over me. Seeing God in that way changes my whole perspective of Him. Now I know that when He trains and disciplines me, it's out of His great love for me: the love of a father. His love is deep and wide and can't be separated by anything—not angels, or demons, or earthly powers, or height, or depth. I am a dearly-loved child of God. He gets excited with me, He cries with me, He cares about the little things in my day. He loves me more than I can comprehend. What a God! What a Father!

Lord, thank You for giving me the privilege and gift of parenthood. I can now better understand Your great love for me.

Jenny Trubey

I'll Be So Happy When . . .

This is the day the Lord has made.
We will rejoice and be glad in it. Ps. 118:24, TLB.

Greg was born in 1957, and our daughter Gail was born in 1959. This was before disposable diapers, so before washing the cloth diapers, they had to be rinsed out. Although I didn't have to do it that much, I hated doing it and I remember saying, "I'll be so happy when the kids don't need diapers anymore." I also thought, *I'll be so happy when they can walk and feed themselves.* Then we were blessed with three more beautiful children, Curt, Rob, and Chris.

With five active children in the house, there were times we were tired and wanted to rest, but there was always someone who needed attention. I thought, *It will be so much easier once they're in school.* And of course, they all did go to school. And it was a bittersweet time when each started first grade. At that time we didn't stop to cherish each day because there were always more days ahead. Life was busy, and they went to academy and college and got married. And we didn't stop to appreciate each day because there were always plenty of days ahead.

Then they started bringing our grandchildren home. Jamie, Jenny, Jason, Jody, Tana, Lynee, Michael, Ben, Cody, and more. Although my wife, Pat, loves babies, I prefer them when they can walk, talk, play, and ride horses and bikes. So I said, "I'll be so happy when they can ride on the tractor and play in the barn. I can tell them stories and teach them things." And they did grow, and we did have lots of fun doing all of those things. And then they were gone.

They grew up and went to college and got married and now they are bringing their babies to see us. They are all adorable, active, and difficult at times. And it would be easy for their parents to say "I will be so happy when . . ." But if they're like me, there will come a day they'll say, "I wish I could hold them and cuddle them and kiss their hurts away." But that won't be possible, because they will have grown up and those days will be just a memory.

I don't want to rinse diapers again, but I would gladly do it if I could have our children and grandchildren back in my arms again. I would be more present in the moment and cherish each day, whatever that day contained, knowing there might not be many more.

Thank You for this day, Father. You have given it to me and I'm thankful.

Neal J. VanderWaal

Friends and Advice

But if any of you lacks wisdom, let him ask of God, who gives to all generously and without reproach, and it will be given to him. James 1:5, NASB.

A few months ago I joined an online support group for moms and noticed most of the women who participate are mothers of infants or toddlers. It made me wonder, Is this because they have figured everything out? Or do they feel as though they should have it all together and feel self-conscious about asking for the opinions of others? Perhaps.

My children are entering the middle stage of childhood, and I find it is just as important for them to have support and friendship as it was when they were infants and toddlers. Parents need it too. We need to be reminded that we are not alone in this. We need to know that other parents struggle with similar behavior in their children, whether it's lying, sibling rivalry, destructive behavior, or bad attitudes. It's important for me to hear how other parents are handling these behaviors. This gives me fresh ideas on how to manage them.

At times we may feel that others are judging us, but we parents know our kids better than anyone else does. We know what makes them tick. I would encourage you not to let the nit-picking of others get under your skin. Take the good advice and toss the rest. Most people are well intentioned, but not everyone can word things well. I would also encourage you not to be the nitpicker. The golden rule applies to moms and dads, too.

It is so important for us as parents to pray for wisdom, both in raising our own children and in giving worthy advice to others. Last time I checked, no one is perfect, not even the mom at your play group who seems to have it all together. We must make every effort to do all things in love both for our children and others. We will accomplish the most good when we are considerate of the struggles of those around us.

I challenge you to encourage another mom or dad this week. Encouragement is like a smile—easy to share and wonderfully contagious.

Dear Lord, please send Your Spirit to be present in my life today so that what others see and hear is straight from You.

Kirsten Holloway

Food Fight

*Don't do any work—not you, nor your son, nor your daughter,
nor your servant, nor your maid, nor your animals,
not even the foreign guest visiting in your town. Ex. 20:10, Message.*

With four kids you might expect that I would have at least one picky eater. I have had three. I have tried everything, including "that's fine if you don't eat it; it will be there for your next meal." I've told them, "You have to try at least one bite or no dessert." I've even done the airplane, and the train. Sometimes it worked. Sometimes it didn't. It was at a church potluck that this exasperated mother finally learned how to find a true Sabbath rest.

As usual, I had gone through the line balancing my plate as well as one for my 6-year-old daughter, who was known for being picky. We sat down and got ready to start the ritual bargaining we'd become accustomed to each mealtime.

Just then I felt eyes on me from across the table. As the pastor's wife, I would probably hear about this again. One more thing I probably wasn't doing right as a mom. My daughter dropped her fork, and I told her to go get another one. As she walked away, the woman across from me spoke in a very soft, calm voice.

"You know, I had that same problem with my kids. And one day God showed me that arguing with my kids was taking away our Sabbath blessing and if I would just let it go for one meal, we would all experience Sabbath rest. From then on, I let them eat what they wanted. If we were at potluck and they ended up eating chips and cake—it was just for one meal. If we were home and they wanted noodles with no spaghetti sauce and pie, oh well. I knew they wouldn't do it forever. But, in this way, we all enjoyed Sabbath." She smiled and added, "For whatever it's worth."

I can't tell you how freeing that was for me. For one meal we all got a Sabbath rest. And I'm happy to tell you, two of the picky children have grown into healthy eaters. They eat vegetables without being asked! Even on *Sabbath!* The fourth child is only 4 years old, so the jury is still out, but I have hope!

Lord, thank You for the parents that have gone before and for the times they lovingly share their wisdom with us.

Michelle Yeager

Climb to the Top

The things which are impossible with men
are possible with God. Luke 18:27, NKJV.

It was a beautiful, fresh spring day. A group of us were taking a 30-minute hike up a steep hill. Would our 4-year-old make it? We wanted her to. I understand that even a 3-year-old can walk as far as an adult, just not as fast. As we slowly made our way over the rough terrain, she held my hand. She asked to be carried, but I let her keep walking, directing her attention to the things around her. After a rest, we tackled the steepest part of the climb. It was slow going and she said her legs didn't feel good, but we kept encouraging her and she made it to the top!

What hill are you climbing today? What challenge is staring you in the face? Are you wondering if you can make it? Jesus encourages you that He will hold your hand. "I, the Lord, have called You in righteousness, and will hold Your hand" (Isa. 42:6, NKJV). With your hand in His, you will make it. Think of the situation that feels impossible to handle right now. Then take a moment to give it to Jesus. Completely.

Perhaps it seems as though no one else is struggling with steep hills to climb, and you are tempted to give up or to think God can't help you on this one. Remember, we seldom know of the internal struggles others face. The tears they cry in silence. But God is faithful. He has promised not to leave us alone as we face our mountains.

"The Father's presence encircled Christ, and nothing befell Him but that which infinite love permitted for the blessing of the world. Here was His source of comfort, and it is for us. He who is imbued with the Spirit of Christ abides in Christ. Whatever comes to him comes from the Savior, who surrounds him with His presence. Nothing can touch him except by the Lord's permission. All our sufferings and sorrows, all our temptations and trials, all our sadness and griefs, all our persecutions and privations, in short, all things work together for our good. All experiences and circumstances are God's workmen whereby good is brought to us" (*The Ministry of Healing,* pp. 488, 489).

Dear God, thank You for the hills I get to climb today. Forgive my lack of faith. I put my hand in Yours and know You can and will do what I've thought was impossible.

Heather Krick

A Miracle on Wheels

God can do much,
much more than anything we can ask or imagine. Eph. 3:20, NCV.

Our old car had 180,000 miles on it and was showing its age. The heater had stopped working, and we had to wrap our three children in blankets to keep them warm during the long, cold Michigan winters. The defroster was broken too, and while my husband drove, I scraped ice off the windows so he could see the road. We didn't go out much, but we faithfully attended Wednesday night prayer meetings and Sabbath services.

One day my husband prayed, "Lord, if You'd just give me enough time and money to fix up this car, I could make it like new." He planned to go to the junkyard to find parts to mend the dilapidated ceiling and broken heater. A year passed with no time or money in sight.

The next summer my husband took an extra job as a census taker. One sunny day he went to a house located on a fruit farm. He knocked on the door, and an elderly woman opened the door and invited him in. She had workers on the farm living in small houses on the property. She explained that he'd have to go and talk to the foreman for an accurate count. When he returned, she'd placed a bushel of apples and a quarter bushel of tomatoes in his car. He was so grateful for the kind gesture. She invited him to come back with his family.

We went to visit many times. He'd play the piano, and we'd sing songs and pray with her. Often as we left she'd hand us an envelope with some money in it. We were so grateful.

Time passed, and the crisp fall started to roll in again. The car still had not been repaired. One evening the kind woman called and asked us to come over. We loaded up the children, and when we arrived she told us to pile into her car. She drove us through the fruit orchards toward a car dealer's lot. Once there, she pointed to a brand-new Buick LeSabre and told us to get inside. The plush seats felt so good. Then she reached into her purse and pulled out a certified check. She said, "If you like this car, it is yours!" We didn't waste any time accepting it.

When we remembered my husband's prayer, we thought God must have chuckled to hear it, because He had something far better in mind for us all along. How like our God!

Lord, You're amazing! Help me remember that You can do more than I can imagine.

Edwina Grice Neely

A Stuffed Animal

Everyone who had blue, purple or scarlet yarn or fine linen, or goat hair, ram skins dyed red or the other durable leather brought them. Ex. 35:23.

When our daughter Tina was 3 years old, her father and I opted for a simpler lifestyle—one that would allow me to be a stay-at-home mom and give us a better chance at adopting a second child. Our decision required a move from fast-paced southern California to a country environment in Placerville, California. We sold our home, loaded the truck, and headed north.

The first Easter, as a single-income family, we realized how different our existence had become. This year, like always, I made Tina a new dress to wear to church. There would be colored eggs to hide, but there was not enough money to buy the customary stuffed animal for Tina's Easter basket. Traditions were important to me. I was not willing to abandon this one.

I found what I was looking for in my sewing supplies—a pattern for a stuffed dog. A scan through my box of fabric scraps came up with two small pieces of faux fur, giraffe cloth leftovers from a costume, and a small square of imitation sheepskin. If I had enough small scraps I could sew them together and make a dog. A phone call to my mother and an announcement at my women's Bible study yielded remnants of imitation zebra, poodle, cow, elephant hide, bear, leopard, and lion. I cut and stitched and carefully planned each section of the dog. With leftover felt I shaped eyes and a red tongue. Embroidery thread stitched his nose and mouth in place.

Tina's father brought home a large square of foam used for packing around furniture during shipping. With scissors we cut it into popcorn-sized pieces, which I stuffed inside the dog until his sides were tight. When I sewed him shut, he was the most handsome scrap dog ever. Best of all, Tina loved him. She named him Scrappy-doo. He is still her all-time favorite toy.

Giving through others is just one way God provides. Whether it is collecting materials to build a tabernacle in the desert 3,500 years ago or a child's toy in northern California in 1979, He can inspire His people to give generously. God is so faithful.

Father, thank You for Your example of giving and for the generosity of friends, neighbors, and even strangers that so often helps us through difficult times.

Karen R. Hessen

The Tyranny of the To-do List

But the Lord said to her, "My dear Martha, you are worried and upset over all these details! There is only one thing worth being concerned about. Mary has discovered it, and it will not be taken away from her." Luke 10:41, 42, NLT.

L aundry! So much laundry! And where's my shopping list?"

"OK! I'm up, I'm up!"

"My child . . ."

"Yes, Lord. I'm listening. I'll do it right away!"

"And call Jenny! You should have called her yesterday!"

"Yes, Lord. I'll write that down too. Oh, the baby's starting to fuss."

"My dear child, that wasn't Me. I just want to tell you how much I love you."

"You mean it's not You yelling at me to get everything done?"

"No, My child. But I do want you to come spend some time with Me."

"Can I bring the baby? He's really fussing now."

"Of course, My child. Come as you are. I'm always here."

When Jesus went to visit Martha and Mary in Bethany, Martha longed to be a good hostess. There was so much to do to prepare a dinner fit for the Messiah. How I can relate to her flurry and fluster! The daily tasks of life fill my to-do list quickly, and oh, how it shouts at me!

Jesus never intends for my to-do list to be my tyrant, though. As good and right as it is to serve my family or perform my duties well at work, none of those is the most important thing. Jesus told Martha that only one thing is worthy of our focus—the thing that Mary chose, sitting at His feet. When I choose to take time in my day to sit at the feet of Jesus, hearing from Him through His Word and pouring out my heart to Him, He reassures me of His presence and love. He renews my mind for the challenges of the day, so I can see them without hearing them shout.

Lord Jesus, thank You for calling me into Your presence and reminding me of Your love. Please help me to keep my mind attuned to You throughout the day.

Cheryl Faith Tarr

Children Are a Blessing

Your wife will be like a fruitful vine within your house;
your children will be like olive shoots around your table.
Yes, this will be the blessing for the man who fears the Lord. Ps. 128:3, 4.

It struck me as odd that God felt the need to mention in His Word that children are a blessing. Why state the obvious? It never made any sense to me until I had children of my own. Now I know why. He needs to remind us because we have a tendency to forget. Let me elaborate.

It's naptime for 10-month-old Markus. His almost-3-year-old brother, Lukas, graciously agrees to quiet time in Mommy and Daddy's bedroom. I sit at my computer and click my way through diverse mommy blogs on the Internet. The world is a happy place. Between clicks and thoughts about mommy things, I notice Lukas has stopped singing to himself. *He must be asleep*, I think as I click onto the next link. This peace and quiet is wonderful. *Click.* I am surprised Lukas is asleep. *Click.* He rarely takes a nap anymore. *Click.* He must be tired. *Click.* I miss these moments of peace and quiet so much. *Click.* I should go and see if he really is sleeping. *Click.* Oh, maybe just one more story, then I'll check. *Click. Click. Click.*

Parents everywhere, even the extroverts among us, can relate to the desire for a few minutes of alone time. Well, you know what happens next. I slowly open the door to make sure I won't wake my little man, and I'm greeted by a bright-eyed boy with a toothy grin and all the enthusiasm only a toddler can muster. "Look, Mama, I have cream," he squeals. Not only does he have cream from head to toe, the bedroom furniture, bedding, and floor also have cream. I don't know whether to laugh or cry. The sheer joy plastered all over his face makes me feel guilty for wanting to throttle the little guy. Slowly I groan myself into cleaning mode.

And that is why God needs to remind me that my children are a blessing. When the diapers malfunction, the porridge lands on the floor for the third time that morning, and both kids are screaming because one wants to build the house and the other wants to tear it down, you tend to forget. But, they really are a blessing!

Thank You, Lord, for the reminder that my children are a blessing. Help me to remember Your words when the unexpected happens today.

Maike Stepanek

When to Call the Doctor

"For I know the plans I have for you," declares the Lord, "plans to prosper you and not to harm you, plans to give you hope and a future." Jer. 29:11.

Perhaps, like me, you have rocked a sick toddler in your arms and worried. You took her temperature and it was high, but not too high. Maybe it's an ear infection, or maybe it's just a little bug that will soon pass. You give her Tylenol, rock her a little more, and keep worrying. Should I take her to the doctor? Your thoughts go back and forth, until you're certain that whatever you decide will be wrong. You worry, worry, and worry some more!

Worry is such a natural part of being a parent. We love the little beings in our care desperately and want only the best for them. Each parent seems to have their own unique worry list. Social awkwardness, physical handicaps, stubborn personalities, and even life-threatening disease.

Worry has plagued many of my days and nights, but I have found in recent years that there is a doctor with a prescription for that: God, the Great Physician. Jeremiah 29:11 has helped me turn my worries over to God and let Him take care of them. I have written this promise on the back of an old photo of my girls and keep it tucked inside my Bible. What a wonderful comfort!

It also reminds me that He created my children for a purpose. He has a wonderful plan for their future, and part of His plan was to have Shawn and me raise them. I cling to this promise in Jeremiah and the knowledge that He has a plan for a hope and a future for each of us.

Worry may continue to plague us all from time to time in our parenting experience, but it doesn't need to overwhelm us. We are all erring humans making our way through our parenting experience as best as we know how. There is one worry that we can lay to rest right now, and that is when to see the doctor. Jesus, the Great Physician, is on call 24/7, and He loves to hear our concerns, our disappointments, and our joys. All of them! His door is open and His payment is easy—He'll take our worries in return for His peace.

Thank You, Jesus, for being our Great Physician!

Jean Boonstra

Baby Makes Three

You make known to me the path of life; you will fill me with joy in your presence, with eternal pleasures at your right hand. Ps. 16:11.

Thinking *we* rather than *me* is a challenging task for young couples. Once the baby arrives, that calls for thinking *three!* The changes a new baby will bring can cause many marriages to become less satisfying and even more vulnerable to divorce. While a new baby brings wonder and joy, it also sets off a number of discoveries that can profoundly impact a marriage.

Some couples say their marital happiness dropped after childbirth, as they hadn't thoroughly understood the immense responsibilities of parenting. There are fewer shared activities, and communication decreases in proportion to the increased demands of parenting.

Other challenges may include increased conflict and less affection from each other. Moms say they don't feel emotionally supported by their husbands or receive help with household tasks. Men say that what they try to do is often met with dissatisfaction.

So should couples stop having children? Definitely not. But recognize that having a baby will change things. Choosing to make your relationship a priority after childbirth will strengthen your marriage. Change, good or bad, can be stressful to your relationship. Commit to working on your marriage relationship, even when there's little time or energy to do so. Accept that you will face marital challenges. Avoid the tendency to turn away from each other. Your baby shouldn't be more important than your relationship as husband and wife.

Assess the atmosphere of your home. Is it one of criticism or one of acceptance? Find ways to regularly have fun together. Be involved in your spouse's life and activities. Set up some "time off" opportunities for each parent, each week. Trust other people to care for your child. Remember that when you take good care of yourself, which should not be confused with being selfish, you can better care for your baby and your marital relationship.

Lord, we determine to stay committed to experiencing Your faithfulness in our marriage. May we experience freedom and fulfillment in this grand adventure called parenting.

Susan Murray

Rooms Filled With Hope

*David was greatly distressed because the men were talking of stoning him;
each one was bitter in spirit because of his sons and daughters.
But David found strength in the Lord his God. 1 Sam. 30:6.*

James Whistler was an American-born artist with quite an imagination. When he first married, he couldn't afford any furniture, except for a bed. He didn't let that stop him. No, he knew that someday in the future he would have the things he needed for his family.

So what did Whistler do that set him apart?

He took chalk and drew detailed inscriptions on the floor of the furniture that he desired and believed he would one day own. He planned, and in planning, chose to believe that his dreams would come true. Then he got busy and set about to make it happen.

How often, as parents just starting out, we become discouraged because we don't have the things we need. It might be literal things such as furniture, or even the knowledge on how to parent well and discipline correctly. It might even be the faith to believe that God has a future and a plan for you and your precious children.

Whatever the needs we have, God has promised that if we come to Him, asking for His help, He will be faithful to provide us the things we need to serve Him and be good parents. They will come in the perfect timing of a loving God. He promises to provide for us. He asks us to trust Him.

James Whistler didn't have all he needed when he started out. But he creatively dreamed of the future. Then he went about knowing that it would work out. He didn't wait around for it to happen; he took action to make it happen.

As parents we can learn from Whistler. Is it time for you to develop a plan of action, and with God's help and guidance, get up and do it? We don't need to be afraid. We have a God who delights to give His people their heart's desire.

Thank You, Lord, that You tell us in Psalm 31:24 to "be strong and take heart, all you who hope in the Lord." Please strengthen us as we hope, and plan, and work for our families.

Kimberley Tagert-Paul

Raising a Godly Generation

Praise the Lord! How joyful are those who fear the Lord and delight in obeying his commands. Their children will be successful everywhere; an entire generation of godly people will be blessed. Ps. 112:1, 2, NLT.

Stepping into parenthood was, for me, more like coming to realize the fact that my life was no longer my own. When my newborn was 2 weeks old, I found myself in the emergency room hooked up to an EKG. The doctor informed me I'd had a minor heart attack. More tests were run that revealed a blocked artery, and soon I was rushed in for an angioplasty. After a week of recovery in the hospital, I arrived home once again to care for my newborn.

Facing this health issue with newfound motherhood quickly taught me not to get stressed about daily tasks. All I could do every day was the best I could manage. Sometimes the simple act of taking a shower took so much energy that I had to rest afterward. Dishes and laundry often had to wait until the next day. There were times I didn't accomplish much of anything, but no matter what happened daily, my child's needs came first.

Being a mother became such a joy for me. Seeing that beautiful little face every day blessed my heart. When I had days of sorrow and I questioned my worth, God reminded me of the very special task He had assigned to me as a parent. Through reading the Bible, I understood it was my duty to help raise up a godly generation, that even in praying over my child and fulfilling the simple, daily tasks required to care for him, I was accomplishing this.

After my child became a toddler, there were so many days I was grateful for having learned this lesson early. By then my heart had healed and I had more energy, but still, any parent knows a toddler can resemble a tornado blowing through your house. That little tornado, however, will someday help build a godly nation.

Loving Father, I thank You for the responsibility you have given me as a parent. Thank You for teaching me that the most important part of parenting is training up my child to become a part of a godly generation that will lead others to You.

Bonnie Nyachae

Making a New Friend

ADONAI will make you the head and not the tail;
and you will be only above, never below—if you will listen to,
observe and obey the mitzvot of ADONAI your God. Deut. 28:13, CJB.

Over the years I have learned that as men, God has called us to be the head and not the tail: We are the head in our families, and when we stand before Yeshua Messiah to give an account of our lives, we will be held accountable for our families. When this realization struck me, its magnitude shook me to the core.

As men we must take 100 percent responsibility for our lives. It is a great responsibility that the Lord has bestowed upon us. Our homes are our sanctuaries; our home is our personal church. We are the protectors, providers, disciplinarians, and priests of our families. Our children watch our every move; they look to us for wisdom, guidance, support, and love.

Our actions or inactions will greatly influence our children. Do they witness us studying the Word? Do they beam with joy as we pray over them? Do our children see how we conduct ourselves at home and in the world? Do we humble ourselves before them and seek their forgiveness when we are wrong? Do we express our love and adoration toward them on the good days as well as the hard days?

Brothers, we must always remember that our children are not ours; they are God's first. We have the great privilege and responsibility to take care of what is His. Yes, one day we will stand before Yeshua and give an account. It is my hope He will say to all of us, "Well done, My faithful servant, well done, My son."

Abba, Father, may the great and mighty power of Your love, wisdom, and understanding flow out to all men today. Teach them to be good stewards of what is Yours. In the great and mighty name of Yeshua Messiah.

John Gold

One Little, Two Little, Three Little Sick Ones

He tends his flock like a shepherd:
He gathers the lambs in his arms and carries them close to his heart;
he gently leads those that have young. Isa. 40:11.

I hate it when one of the children is sick. I worry and fret and form knotted muscles in my back. My husband reassured me the other night, as he was attempting to karate-chop the knots into submission, that our sick child would be OK and I needn't worry. I knew he was right, but what really filled me with dread was the thought of the others catching ill too. One sick child is no fun, but I wouldn't wish three sick children on my worst enemy.

We had already been stuck in this cycle of illness for the past three weeks. It would've been bad enough if it were just one bug they were fighting, but no, it had been multiple bugs. As soon as one got over the first bug, he would catch another. This most recent bug had my little guys running fevers of 103° to 104°F for five days, and I spent Sabbath morning at the walk-in clinic, with doctors trying to figure out if my 6-year-old had pneumonia or bronchitis.

His coughing had even begun to worry our landlady. She called my husband to make sure he was OK. The children's room is right below hers, and the coughing, which sounded like a large goose honking, was keeping her awake at night. Oops. After treatment to help his breathing, and a chest X-ray, it turned out to be bronchitis, so we were sent home with meds and an inhaler. Eventually their fevers broke, as the medication did its work.

My husband doesn't understand how I manage it, and sometimes neither do I. Have you noticed how often we mothers are able to push ourselves to do things we never thought possible—all for the sake of our children? And while I dislike being stuck in the house for days and weeks on end, I'd dislike it even more if I had to go to work and leave them with a babysitter when they felt miserable. There is nothing like a mother's comfort to a small child, and as a mother, there is nothing like God's comfort during difficult times.

Thank You, Lord, for being there to calm us when the stresses in life are closing in. Help us to remember to rest on Your able arms.

Kirsten Holloway

God's Comfort in Loss

Cast thy burden upon the Lord, and he shall sustain thee:
he shall never suffer the righteous to be moved. Ps. 55:22, KJV.

I was scared and extremely disappointed as I lay in a hospital bed awaiting emergency surgery. For a year we'd anticipated adding another child to our family, and finally tests showed I was pregnant. However, in the third month my joy was snatched away with cramping pain and hemorrhaging. I needed the bleeding to stop, but I feared going under anesthesia. "Father," I cried, "please be with me. Give me comfort."

Immediately 1 Peter 5:7 came to mind: "Cast all your cares upon Me because I care about you." I sensed my Father's presence all around me and was able to relax. By the time I was wheeled into surgery my heart was no longer anxious.

The following days were difficult. The doctor could not explain what had happened. There was no fetal tissue. Would I have my baby in heaven someday? I wondered. I longed for answers that never came. Yet through my tears I knew my Father cared.

A few months later I was blessed with another pregnancy, which I carried to term, giving birth to a healthy son. I enjoyed our two children, watching them grow and learn. Then I became pregnant again, but something went awry and for the second time I had to undergo another emergency D & C. Once again, the loss was devastating. I truly wanted another child. Eventually my husband agreed to try again. After months of waiting, I finally conceived and we welcomed a beautiful little daughter eight and a half months later.

Each child has filled our lives with joy. I feel truly blessed. Our son is gifted musically, while both our daughters have a creative bent. I don't know whether or not I'll have my other babies in heaven. I trust God's understanding heart. Today I thank Him for seeing me through those difficult experiences of loss.

When my heart aches, thank You for Your comfort, Father. Thank You for caring. Help me to trust Your heart even with my loss.

Barbara Ann Kay

His Face Lights Up

The Lord your God in your midst, The Mighty One, will save;
He will rejoice over you with gladness, He will quiet you with His love,
He will rejoice over you with singing. Zeph. 3:17, NKJV.

The morning's hustle causes me step to away just briefly, yet the moment I enter the door and our eyes meet, joy radiates visibly from his sweet face. His smile could light the world. Immediately he starts to run toward me in his wobbly toddly way, his hands outstretched, his eyes aglow. He babbles ecstatically, and even though he can't yet articulate the word "Mommy!" I know he is delighted to see me.

As he draws closer, God gives me a glimpse of myself, and I see the layers of reserve I hold tight around my heart. As I look at my son's innocent adoration, these layers drop to the earth and a new picture of God's love peeks out at me through the love of my little boy.

Who is this God whose eyes light up at the sight of me wobbling toward Him? How long has it been since my face last lit up with God's presence? Can I accept the reality of a God that rejoices over me with singing? I'm so disappointed at the way I haven't lived up to my own expectations, let alone the standard of God's holiness, that it has kept me from receiving the love that comes from the father-heart of God. That is, until this moment when all I see is joy.

My deepest need is to allow that love to infiltrate my heart. O God, who set the stars in place and yet still finds joy in me and in you. Amazing love! He loves us as a daddy loves his child. He loves to watch each bumbling attempt at growth and development.

Today, as we let our minds think on our heavenly Father, let us remember the joy and gladness etched upon His face when He looks at us. As we paint a picture of who He is for others to see—may they see only His love.

Abba, Papa, please quiet me in Your love today. Help me interact with my children, my spouse, and the circle we come in contact with, from that place of singing—Your singing—over me. Thank You for loving me in spite of my weaknesses and insufficiency. Make me a conduit of Your grace today.

Kristen Hoover

Through the Eyes of a Child

And He took them up in His arms, laid His hands on them,
and blessed them. Mark 10:16, NKJV.

Tonight, dear son, while shopping for groceries, with next week's menu planned according to what was on sale and which coupons we had, there were a few cents left over from our tight budget. The smile on your face as we put the bottle of bubbles in the grocery cart was priceless. You couldn't wait to get home and see what that little bottle held.

We put away the groceries and reached for your treasure. Daddy got on the floor with you and opened the seal. He pulled out the wand and showed how the circle on the end must contain a clear film of liquid before the bubbles could appear. Then he held it up to his carefully pursed lips, and gently blew. The results were pure magic.

You squealed at the sight of the first clear orbs. You clapped your hands and grinned for all you were worth. You turned a full circle by scooting around, then looked expectantly at your father for more magic.

He blew again, and this time some of the bubbles were picked up by the wind from the box fan and they danced around the room, transforming it instantly into a wonder world of glistening rainbows. You climbed to your feet and wobbled around chasing them. You caught one in your tiny hands and it popped. Your surprise tore at my heart.

You quickly recovered and chased more in your upwardly mobile way, toddling after each burst of bubbles that came from the wand your daddy held. Your joy was contagious. We forgot for a moment how hard things in life were as we saw the world through your precious eyes. Those few minutes will stay with me forever. A sweet reminder that we, too, have a Father who wants to bless us with His wonder. Only, we get so caught up with the problems in our lives, we forget to see the simple joy each day holds. Those God-given moments of joy that dance through our lives, transforming us and giving us the hope and promise of a kingdom home filled with wonder.

Thank You, Father, for reminding us of Your love, Your joy, Your wonder as seen through the eyes of a child.

Kimberley Tagert-Paul

Where You Are?

Look at the birds. They don't plant or harvest or store food in barns, for your heavenly Father feeds them. And aren't you far more valuable to him than they are? Matt. 6:26, NLT.

Somehow no one warns you or maybe I just didn't want to listen. I wanted to be a mom. I wanted to have kids and hear them call me "Mom." But then, as I stepped on Cheerios and Barbie shoes (boy, do those things hurt), trying to get to the toddler who'd had another accident because she just "fuhgots 'bout that," I realized I was exhausted.

I still loved being a mom, but I hadn't had hot food in years, and come to think of it I didn't usually go to the restroom without an audience. I knew that God had given me these kids to raise and I loved them, but I felt like I was being swallowed up and in danger of disappearing. I wasn't even really sure who I was anymore. The lack of sleep each night made it pretty hard to think clearly.

Back before I had kids I knew that in dry times such as these I would need to connect to God. Plug into a Bible study group, surround myself with people who understood, and most important, get into the Word. But how do you do that with a baby that is colicky and a toddler who doesn't have an inside voice? That's when God said to me, *What's that in your hand?* Um. "What, Lord? Do You mean my smartphone?"

In a whirlwind God sent me to YouTube, where I found sermons from my pastor and some of my favorite speakers; to my own church's Web page, where all the sermons were archived! What genius thought that up?

I can't tell you how amazing it is to put headphones on and hear an entire sermon! To be *fed!* Even while making the kids lunch, or driving the car pool, or wiping up syrup, or putting your child on the potty. Where you are, is where God wants you. But where you are, is where He can feed you because He values you.

God, thank You, thank You, for feeding us where we are. And for loving us too much to just leave us there hungry. Thank You for feeding us and for raising us up to be where You are. And thank You for Cheerios and sweet, sticky, syrup kisses.

Michelle Yeager

Summertime!

Whatsoever thy hand findeth to do, do it with thy might. Eccl. 9:10, KJV.

W hen driving, I often listen to radio WGN in Chicago. One of the hosts recently told about a trip he took with his family. On Sunday they got on the train, rode to a stop some miles from home, got off, bought hot dogs at a nearby stand, hopped back on the train and rode it back home. Later, they took the train to another destination and had a grand time—all for about $12. His point was that it doesn't have to cost a lot to do something as a family.

This experience reminds me that with summer upon us, this is a great time to make plans for when school is out. One of the best things you can do for your children is to view summer as a time to expand their world and make memories. The little ones who aren't in school yet will also benefit. So why not plan some family activity each week? Activities need to last at least 30 minutes, but they can last much longer. Don't wait for a financial windfall. Find things to do that you can afford.

When home, show your children how to operate appliances appropriate to their age. They can assist in cooking and housekeeping. Remember that home should be a safe place to learn and practice many new skills. A child who learns to concentrate on activities often becomes very competent, and constructive activities increase self-confidence and raise self-image. The child with interesting, challenging, constructive and planned fun doesn't have time for, or as much interest in, negative activities. Children benefit from a balance of free time and organized activities. Some keep children so busy with lessons and excursions that they don't have quiet time, or time to spend alone.

A child who has fun in a wholesome, productive way is a happier child. And happier children are more receptive to their parents. Your whole family will benefit when you put together plans for summertime learning and adventures together. Try it and see!

Lord, help me to be creative in finding things to do with my family that are fun and affordable. Please come through this day with us and infuse it with Your sweet Spirit.

Susan Murray

A Gift From God

Children are a gift from God. Ps. 127:3, TLB.

I quit my job as a speech pathologist to be at home with my son. He was 7 months old. One morning I lay in bed thinking to myself, *This baby is only 7 months old. I have four years and five months to go before he will be old enough to go to kindergarten. What in the world am I going to do with him?*

A little of the excitement of having a newborn baby had worn off and was replaced with feelings of loneliness, helplessness, and worry. My thoughts continued. I can bathe the baby and keep him clean, I can play with him, feed him, and give him something to drink. I can clean the house, cook the meals, wash the clothes . . . O Lord, is this my job description for the next four years? Heaven help me! I'm tired of this routine already!

Then one day it happened. During my devotions I turned to Psalm 127 and the Lord spoke to me loud and clear. *"Children are a gift from God!"* After that moment I began to look at my child differently. I realized how richly I'd been blessed with this gift and that God had a plan for his life. I changed my perspective and started to thank God for giving me the opportunity to work with Him to train up this child in the way God wanted me to.

I realized I had chosen one of the most important jobs of a lifetime. Every day I had the opportunity to lead my child to the source of all understanding, meaning, wonder, knowledge, and wisdom: to God.

I could show my child the goodness of God every day. The God who created the water I bathed him in, the food I fed him. The only God to worship, the God of the home he lives in. I had the opportunity to give my child a spiritual foundation that will remain with him for a lifetime. I stayed at home with my child until he was old enough for kindergarten, and I have never regretted it.

Dear Lord, thank You for making me a parent. Help me to remember my child is a gift from You, for me to love unconditionally, just as You love me.

Edwina Grice Neely

I Blinked

This is the day which the Lord hath made;
we will rejoice and be glad in it. Ps. 118:24, KJV.

Nearly 30 years ago I found myself in a state of shock when the doctor administering a prenatal ultrasound found not one healthy heartbeat, but two. I was expecting twins! I vividly remember the not-so-pleasant particulars of the pregnancy: the morning sickness, the shrinking maternity clothes, the swollen feet. The list goes on, but the details aren't much fun to rehearse.

By the time my beautiful daughters entered this world I was exhausted. I had endured a full day of intense labor. This was before the days of the epidural. But finally the twins made their debut. When my mother arrived in the hospital room a few hours later, she observed that I looked "half dead." I felt completely dead, so I took her words as a compliment.

After the girls were cleaned, assessed, and wrapped snugly in hospital blankets, my husband perched them, one at each of my shoulders, for a birthday picture. Just as the picture was taken, I blinked.

When I opened my eyes, I found myself in a strange place. I was posing for another picture. Each of my babies was again beside me. Instead of swaddling blankets, however, they were donned in college regalia. And they weren't babies anymore! They stood at the edge of their own adult world that would include graduate school, marriage, and babies of their own.

It is so easy, especially in the first few years of our children's lives, to get caught up in the "business" of parenting. It's a continual round of feeding, changing, and soothing. When the babies were up all night with ear infections, it wasn't easy to say, "This is the day the Lord has made," and even more difficult to "rejoice." But God's Word admonishes us: "Don't blink!" Enjoy every moment. Praise God for each new day and each moment of life. Praise the Lord for the special times and for the challenges through which He shapes our characters. Each moment is a gift. I'm now more determined than ever to relish every step along the way.

Thank You, Lord for THIS day. The day You have made. Whatever challenges may come my way, help me to rejoice in this moment, in this day.

Rene Drumm

Emotional Support

Husbands, love your wives,
as Christ loved the church and gave Himself up for her. Eph. 5:25, Amplified.

There is an old saying, "The best thing a father can do for his children is to love their mother." When children see an outward expression of love between parents, they feel a deep sense of security.

One weekend my husband and I went to a small café. It was a comfortable place, more of a "come as you are place," rather than fancy. We found a table next to a young couple who sat close beside each other. The back of my chair touched the back of the young woman's chair, and my husband and I sat facing each other.

The young man's arm was around the young woman's shoulder as they spoke softly. I overheard them talking about different types of wood, oak and cherry, but I didn't hear the context of what they were sharing. As they continued to speak intimately, I heard a few words about their kids. When we got up to leave, I noticed the wife was leaning back on her husband's chest, contentment written on her face. The closeness of their emotional support seemed unusual in this setting. This man knew what his wife needed, and it was more than just taking her out for breakfast.

As women we long to be listened to, considered, and understood; we want our husbands to care about us and to support us emotionally. When moms and dads treat each other with love and kind consideration, we are teaching our little ones to do the same.

It may seem selfish to spend time together without the children. But when we love and care for each other's needs, we are ensuring a happy home for our children, one that will stay intact regardless of the storms of life that may beat against it. Though it may not always be easy or convenient, it is necessary for the health of the family.

O Father, we need Your love in us to help us show love toward our spouses and to care for their emotional needs. Please help us to protect the security of our little ones.

Claudia LeCoure

July

Single Parenting, Stepparenting,
and Parenting Through Divorce

We Never Walk Alone

God has said, "I will never fail you. I will never forsake you." Heb. 13:5, NLT.

Dear Daughter,

I cannot begin to imagine the pain you are going through. It must seem like the end of the world, and I imagine you have asked yourself many times, "Why try?" I cannot imagine the hurt you feel when you see your children on Facebook at your ex-husband's house pasting on smiles for the camera with their dad's new, younger, model wife. I cannot imagine the loneliness of having no one to cuddle and hold when it's his weekend or the excruciating feeling of abandonment. I wish I lived closer and could wipe away the lonely tears as I did when you were younger and would scrape your knee or fall off your bicycle. Raising children in homes where those children have both parents is challenging enough. Raising them to believe in a Father who under no circumstances would forsake them is a daunting challenge when they have seen their earthly father cast their mother aside for someone else. So how does a divorced, single mother raise her children in the face of such adversity?

First, remember you have an everlasting friend in Jesus who will never fail you or trade you in. Even though we are all sinners who have turned our backs on Him at times, He is always faithful to us. He will supply the wisdom that you need to meet the challenges of single parenthood. Second, remember that your children need you. No one can take your place in their hearts, and they will need your strength to deal with the hurt and loss that they are feeling. The plastic smiles they wear for the camera only mask the confusion they feel inside now that their family has fallen apart. The new wife will never replace you as their mother. Finally, live today as a daughter of the King of the universe, because that is exactly what you are. The hardest part may be forgiving as the King forgives; but always remember, you "can do all things through Christ who strengthens" you (Phil. 4:13, NKJV), even forgive.

Father, be close to me today so that through my lonely feelings I can still know with certainty that You are here. Give me Your strength, wisdom, and even Your forgiveness.

Dan Solis

God Hears

But the Lord stood with me and strengthened me. 2 Tim. 4:17, NKJV.

I'm tired. A 3-year-old and a newborn. How did I get to this place? I had told myself this would never happen. I had promised myself that the D word would never be part of my vocabulary. Ever. Yet here I am in the middle of the night with a newborn whose scream could rival a dentist's drill whether I'm holding her or not and a 3-year-old who's had one too many pieces of candy.

Lord, I don't want a divorce. I adore my children, but I don't want to do the single-parent thing. Do You care? Can You hear me? Please. If You can hear me, can we all just go to sleep in this recliner? There's no way I can call in sick. That's not a luxury we single moms get.

And that's the last thing I remembered that night as I heard my morning alarm ring in my bedroom. God had granted sweet sleep for all three of us, and I was grateful.

As I scrambled to pack diaper bags with formula, extra clothes, and diapers my phone rang. It was my daughters' father, my unhappy husband. He was with his new girlfriend, and he was angry at me. I can't remember what I had done, or why he was so angry. I was so tired. I just listened. And the tears began to roll. It was the weary, ugly cry wrung from a ragged heart. You know the one—when you are just so done. Done with it all. You have no fight left. When he was through with his rant, I said, "I'm so sorry you feel that way," and I hung up the phone.

"Lord," I cried, "You have to help me! I can't do this! It hurts too much! God! Help me!" As the words came out of my mouth, I looked up and saw one of those infamous God billboards to my right. It said, "I love you. I love you. I love you.—God."

The most beautiful sign I have ever seen. If I hadn't been driving, I would have fallen to my knees as the God of the universe stooped down and wrapped His arms around me and told me He loved me.

Lord, thank You that You answer us when we need You, that You will use anything at any time to let us know You love us and adore us.

Michelle Yeager

Homeward-bound

Don't let your hearts be troubled. Trust in God, and trust also in me.
There is more than enough room in my Father's home. . . .
When everything is ready, I will come and get you,
so that you will always be with me where I am. John 14:1-3, NLT.

Being a single mom was wearing on me. There was never enough time for everything. Leaving work late added to my frustration. I'd be late picking up my 5- and 7-year-old children from school. They would be hungry, and I didn't have anything at home to cook. "God, are You kidding me? I'm doing my best down here! Just help me get home!"

"Mommy, can we stop at Taco Bell?" *Great idea,* I thought, so we headed to H Street. As I approached the light, it turned red. I slowed, then quickly turned right. I glanced in the rearview mirror, only to see flashing lights. I was getting pulled over!

The officer approached my door. "May I see your license and registration?"

I handed him my papers.

"Ma'am," he asked, "do you know why I pulled you over?"

"I ran a red light."

"Where are you going in such a hurry?"

"I'm trying to get home," I responded.

"Do you realize everyone out here is trying to get home? If everyone disobeyed the traffic rules, no one would make it home."

God, I prayed silently, *I know You won't give me anything I can't handle. Perhaps I'm trying to carry too much on my own. Please help me to trust in You more.*

"I'm not going to give you a ticket," the officer continued, "but I am going to ask that you remember what I said and pay attention to the rules of the road so you can get home safely."

Instead of feeling overwhelmed, I felt blessed. Blessed to have two beautiful children, to have a God who loves and cares for me. It was going to be a good evening.

Lord, help us to trust You more, especially when our lives seem overwhelming.

Rebecca Swinyar Neff

Honoring the Father

For God does not show favoritism. Rom. 2:11.

Often when I look at my husband's two sons I see their mother—her likeness, a facial expression, a mannerism or personality trait. They are constant reminders that my husband has a past that did not include me. I, of course, had a past that did not include him. I'm sure my two children prompt similar thoughts in his mind. I love his sons, but sometimes I feel regret and resentment because I missed parts of their lives I cannot ever reclaim.

My husband and I are careful to treat our children equally. There will be an identical division of our resources when we leave this earthly life. We try not to compare the children—they have different gene pools, challenges, and opportunities. We believe we show honor to each other by respecting and caring for the other's children. Our extended families, however, make huge obvious differences in the way they behave toward and gift our respective children, making it difficult for us to celebrate birthdays and holidays together. The favoritism they show is hurtful and unacceptable.

As I have contemplated this situation in our family and have worked through it with my husband, I have often thought about Joseph, Jesus' stepfather. The Bible doesn't tell us anything about Joseph after Jesus reached the age of 12. It doesn't give us many clues to his parenting style. Did Joseph resent abandoning his carpentry business and living as a refugee in a foreign country because of threats to Mary's child? Did he compare his birth children to Jesus? Did Joseph show favoritism to his biological children and treat Jesus in demeaning ways because Jesus was his Stepson? I'm sure God would not have chosen Joseph for the task if he had not been the right man for the job. The Bible does make it clear that Joseph was honoring God. That is what I do when I commit to a loving and nurturing relationship with my husband's children.

Heavenly Father, thank You for loving adults who nurture, support, and lead by example. Give them an abundance of kindness, compassion, and mercy that they in turn can bestow on those You have given into their care.

Karen R. Hessen

Within Reach

*These commandments that I give you today
are to be on your hearts. Impress them on your children.
Talk about them when you sit at home and when you walk along the road,
when you lie down and when you get up. Deut. 6:6, 7.*

Binoculars in hand, my stepson Addison sat quietly on our wraparound porch in anticipation of spotting new species of our feathered friends. Feeders hung in the pine trees nearby.

Addison had taken a liking to bird-watching, and I was delighted to share the experience with him. After a few minutes the birds began to dine at the feeders. He looked up his discoveries in the book I gave him and jotted down his findings during our whispered conversation. Then he turned the binoculars around to look through them backward. With a chuckle, he encouraged me to do the same. Curious to see what fascinated and humored him at the same time, I did it.

I had a clear view, but the lenses made objects seem much farther away than they were. I knew I could take a step toward what I focused on and touch it, but the little tunnel I peered through kept the scenery at a distance.

For me, stepparenting sometimes feels like the backward view through binoculars—looking at something that seems far away. Addison and his parents share a bond I will never have with him. I can touch his life and love him, but I remain outside that bond even though we are close. Challenging as this dynamic is, I look to Jesus to affirm my ability to lead this child.

I believe He has given me the privilege of taking part in the command "Train up a child in the way he should go" (Prov. 22:6, KJV). I could easily become caught up in feelings of inadequacy, knowing I am not his birth mother, but despite my parental status, I am learning to focus on this responsibility. No matter how this relationship appears to me at times, Addison and I share our own unique closeness that Jesus has placed within reach.

Thanks, Father, for the opportunity to love and guide one of Your little ones as my own.

Kelli Haines

When Anger Serves No Purpose

Good sense makes one slow to anger,
and it is his glory to overlook an offense. Prov. 19:11, ESV.

It was Sunday evening. Pickup time according to the divorce papers was 5:00 p.m. To my ex-husband, this was merely a suggestion. I called ahead and was told it would be 6:00 before they finished their dinner. Since arguing never achieved anything, I conceded.

Arriving at 6:00, I phoned from the car. No answer. I called again. After repeated attempts, my son picked up the phone. "Mommy, we are eating dinner. Can you come in and eat with us?"

"No," I said. "We need to get home." When his father took the phone, I heard my son crying in the background. I knew he was tired, and this was just too much for him. It was too much for me.

It was now 6:35, and it would take 20 minutes to drive back home. The anger began to rise. Controlling my tongue had become increasingly hard to do. For a fleeting moment I considered calling the police, but I knew that would only upset my son further. Instead I put the car in reverse and backed out of the driveway, wondering how long it would take before they noticed I was no longer waiting.

My ex-husband called a short time later to ask where I'd gone. "Home," I said. "When you finish your dinner, you can bring him to my house. If you would like to keep him until the morning, you will need to take him to school. I'm sure you miss each other."

I hung up the phone. I'd kept my cool and refrained from responding in anger, deciding instead to focus on my son's feelings and his well-being in the moment. Despite my anger and frustration at the situation, I found a way to defuse the situation. Many times, retreating from a tense situation is the best course of action when a child is caught in the middle.

Thank You, God, for helping me to focus my attentions on my innocent child rather than on my own emotions. Please give me strength and the good sense to control my anger in this turbulent time when my emotions are raw.

Shirley Troilo

Show No Favoritism

*My brothers and sisters, believers in our glorious Lord Jesus Christ
must not show favoritism. . . . But if you show favoritism,
you sin and are convicted by the law as lawbreakers. James 2:1-9.*

Everything was great until Mom had a new baby," Sabrina said as she told the story of her painful childhood.

"It all started after a major hurricane hit the small island on which we lived. My real mother's home was blown away by the storm. My siblings and I were forced to find shelter at the neighbor's house. It felt safe there. After three days my two sisters and one brother went with our mother to some unknown place. In my childhood innocence I begged to stay with the family that would later adopt me as their daughter.

"My new mother was kind to me. She gave me many pretty clothes, toys, and good food. Dad was my best friend. As their only child, I went everywhere they went and was loved.

"Then, shortly before my sixth birthday, Mom had a new baby. He was cute, and I was happy to have a brother, but I began to feel jealous. He was getting all of Mom's love and attention. I cried often because I felt neglected, and this made my mother angry. She began to beat me and spoke harshly to me. At the age of 10 I ran away from home.

"Dad tried to be my best friend when my mother was not around. When she was, she cursed at him and spoke evil of the two of us. Within eight years I had three siblings, and as we grew up, things got worse. I became everybody's servant. To put an end to the emotional and physical abuse, I left home.

"I eventually recovered from my depression and anger, and was able to forgive my mother for being so awful to me. I am glad I did, because she died soon after."

In God's sight everyone is equal and deserves to be loved. It is unacceptable for parents to show favoritism.

Dear Lord, thank You for the privilege to open our homes to children who are less fortunate. May we show Your kindness and love, equally, toward each one of them.

Sandra E. Fletcher

The Virtual Babysitter

*Whatsoever things are true, whatsoever things are honest,
whatsoever things are just, whatsoever things are pure, whatsoever things are
lovely, whatsoever things are of good report; if there be any virtue,
and if there be any praise, think on these things. Phil. 4:8, KJV.*

Raising my daughter on my own is definitely challenging at times, and I have to admit that at times I've allowed YouTube to babysit her while I hurry to finish my chores. From an early age, however, I've taught her that programs involving violence, or other unwholesome activities, were completely off-limits. *Curious George, Leap Frog,* and *Octonauts* have become some of her favorite programs, and, if allowed, she'd be happy to watch unattended for hours.

I have noticed, though, that we do not screen many of the Bible stories before allowing our children to watch them. Scenes with violence appear so frequently, and as a parent I cringe to think that some of the negative messages we would like to protect them from are embedded within the same stories we use to instruct them about God and the Bible. A friend shared how a young boy was seen chasing his little sister around the room with a "sword," calling her a "Philistine" and issuing threats in the process. While many Bible stories include some type of violence, let us be sensitive in how this is shared with our little ones.

Though technology has many positives to offer to our children, let us guard carefully the avenues to their minds by paying special attention to the stories they watch or even listen to. As parents, it is our responsibility to protect them from the subtle tricks of the evil one, whose desire is to destroy them from an early age. Paul reminds us in Philippians 4:8 to think on things that are true, honest, just, pure, and lovely. Let us apply these same principles to the things we allow them to watch. May God help us to instill within them the discipline to watch only the programs that will edify both the physical and the spiritual. Christ, while He was on earth, demonstrated that children are an important part of His kingdom. May we seek daily to follow His lead and train them accordingly.

Dear Lord, continue to strengthen us as we parent and grant us a double portion of patience as we care for the little ones with whom You have blessed us.

Louise T. Brown

A Quiet Place? In My House?

*Very early in the morning, while it was still dark, Jesus got up,
left the house and went off to a solitary place, where he prayed. Mark 1:35.*

I grew up as a pastor's daughter and have heard that verse my entire life. All through growing up and through church school, all through academy and beyond. I didn't really think of it much until I had children. For a while I would hear it in church and would make an almost irreverent response: What do you mean when you say I should be like Jesus and find a quiet, solitary place to pray? I haven't been able to go to the restroom by myself in years!

Don't get me wrong. I want the early-morning-peaceful-dark-by-myself time, but either the extra sleep calls, or I think, *If I'm going to be up, shouldn't I work on getting organized before the herd wakes up?* Oh, wait. What? That's part of organization?

One day I decided to try taking the above verse literally. I got up before everyone else and decided nothing else mattered but spending a little time with God. I got a notebook and started writing what I wanted to tell Him as if He were sitting with me, sharing the early morning with me. The amount I wrote didn't matter, as long as I said what I wanted to say.

Wouldn't you know it? That was the key. That was the key to "psycho-mommy" not coming to visit! I was more patient and organized somehow. It was the strangest thing! I was at peace.

Just recently I've added one more thing. I sit for one minute before I race out the door. One minute to just be with God. One minute to see if He wants to say something to me. One minute, no matter if I'm already late. That one minute has calmed me down, refocused me. It has reminded me to whom I belong. That one minute is me mentally going away to a quiet place and being with God. I may have to increase it, I'm liking it so much!

Thanks for pointing me back to You, God. Spending time with You is truly the best part of my day. Thanks for these precious minutes!

Michelle Yeager

JULY 10

Sheltering Arms

For He has not despised nor abhorred the affliction of the afflicted;
nor has He hidden His face from Him;
but when He cried to Him, He heard. Ps. 22:24, NKJV.

I was just a little girl when my mother found out that her husband of 22 years had been abusing my older adopted sister. As soon as she knew, she packed her bags and with me in tow scurried away from him. This was back in the 1970s and early 1980s when such abuse was not talked about, nor were the signs as clearly known as they are today.

It was a heart-wrenching and emotional time for both of us. For those first few months Mom found a place to live in a small camping trailer in a park. All we had to our name was one car and a few belongings. It didn't matter to my mom where we lived or where we'd find out next meal—all that mattered was keeping me away from a man that could harm me. There were even a few times when both of us landed in the hospital. I would often suffer from asthma and pneumonia. My mother got terrible migraines and caught various flu bugs that came along. I believe the biggest reason we got so sick was because of the emotional stress and the toll it took on our bodies.

With help from God, my mom was able to find an apartment where we could live and where both of us could have our own rooms. By the time I was 7 I had a personal relationship with Jesus and gratefully accepted the comfort and care He offered me. I would often talk to God about the pain I could see my mother going through, and I would do my best to give her comfort. Sadly, because of the stigma we endured and the constant gossip, my mom quit going to church. As time went on she would listen to sermons and encourage me in my continued belief of God's care for us. In spite of our anger and pain, His arms were always there to comfort us.

Being in a single-parent family is incredibly tough, but never underestimate the power of a parent's love. I never doubted my mother's love—even in the deepest pain her love, and God's comforting arms, saw me through those difficult years.

Dearest Father, please continue to hold those of us that are hurting and let us feel the comfort of Your strong arms.

Wanda L. Davis

202

Children by Marriage

Anyone who welcomes a little child like this on my behalf is welcoming me. Matt. 18:5, NLT.

Stepparents. Stepchildren. It is possible for both words to have negative connotations, but I like to look at the positives. I introduce my children by marriage as "my children." It has been almost 16 years now, and I've never once not considered both of these girls as gifts to me, even during the difficult years.

What the three of us had in common 16 years ago was that we all loved their dad. For me, I knew I was not their mom. They already had one. I only asked to be respected because they lived in our home. On their own, they titled me "Mom number two." When I am introduced, however, this title is shortened to "Mom." Each time I hear that, my heart grows larger with love.

I have many friends and acquaintances who are in blended families. Most have survived the difficult years and are now reaping, like me, the rewards of friendship with their adult children. I think parenting, as in marriage, takes commitment, and when all else fails, one must be true to that commitment. I also know that love is a choice. I am told to "love my neighbor as I love myself." My neighbors definitely include my husband's children.

I have been accepted into God's family. The Father and I love the same person: Jesus. God loves me with His agape love—selfless, sacrificial, and unconditional. It is the purest and highest form of love mentioned in the Bible. If God chooses to love me so, how can I deny loving another person—especially a child—in that way?

Is it always easy? Of course it's not. It is possible, however. I had a team of prayer warriors on my side. I read tons of books and research on "stepparenting." We went to a Christian counselor. Like God, you will do whatever it takes in your child's life to have them open their heart to you and love you back. It's not easy, but the rewards are worth the effort.

Dear Father, You love us with agape love. Help us to love our children by marriage as You love us. Thank You for placing these precious people in our lives.

Mary Nell Rosenboom

A Child's Request

Fear not, for I am with you; be not dismayed, for I am your God.
I will strengthen you, yes, I will help you,
I will uphold you with My righteous right hand. Isa. 41:10, NKJV.

The words of a child can strike a chord in your heart like none other. Their simple, yet honest words can have more impact than many elaborate ones. You see, I learned this past weekend that my dear little Maddie, who is 5, has been secretly praying that her momma will get married. That she wants a daddy to play with her. When we heard this, we joked and teased, but inside I crumbled. My heart ached to give my child what she desired, but because of how I had fallen in sin, she came into this world fatherless.

This world has become so accepting of single parenthood to the point that it is as much a norm as parenthood within marriage. What are we thinking? It seems God really did have our best interest at heart when He told us to wait until marriage. He knew what the child needed. For a daughter needs her mother, yes, but she needs her daddy, too.

I have fond memories of my dad reading to me on Sunday mornings from the newspaper, his voice changing comically to imitate each character. I remember blowing kisses to him, thinking it was the funniest thing as he staggered about as each kiss landed. Now I watch each of my children blow kisses to their papa, and hear them laugh as he staggers with each kiss that reaches his cheek. While it is true that no father is perfect, my father is good.

When he heard the longing in my daughter's voice for a daddy, he said to her, "Maddie, I know I can't be your daddy, but your papa loves you a lot."

I told Maddie that even though she doesn't have a daddy, she does have a heavenly Father. Even though she can't see Him yet, He will never fail her. He will always love her just the way she is. He will guide her. Mold her to be the most beautiful person ever. Her Dad is a Father to the fatherless. What a blessing!

Heavenly Father, thank You for hearing the longing in a little girl's voice and understanding her need for a daddy. Thank You that in Jesus You have made provision for our every need!

Jill Simpson

Jesus Is My Daddy-O

Behold, what manner of love the Father hath bestowed upon us, that we should be called the sons of God. 1 John 3:1, KJV.

As a single mother I have always sought to help my toddler understand that though she has an earthly father, God is her divine Father. One day, when she was 3 years old, I was sharing with her the magnitude of God's love for me in that I was chosen to be her caregiver until Jesus returns to claim her at His second coming. I wanted her to know how much I treasured being her mommy. This line of reasoning did not sit well with her at all, and because of her limited understanding of life on this earth, she quickly exclaimed, "Mommy, I don't want Jesus to come back for me. I want to stay here with you!"

How often do we as parents behave in a similar fashion? We tend to forget that this world is not our home. We tend to lose sight of the reason we were selected to take care of God's children until His return. We often feel overwhelmed with caring for our precious gems, but today I want to encourage you to keep trusting God to fill the gap. We have been tasked with the awesome responsibility to nurture and train our little jewels not only for this life but for the life to come. Their little minds are like wet sponges soaking up everything we do and say. If, as parents, we heed the admonition to "train up a child in the way he should go" (Prov. 22:6, KJV), we will always be mindful of our words and actions toward them.

God is ever available to assist us with this great responsibility. Why not trust Him today to be that Father in your child's life? My prayer for parents is for us to teach our children from an early age to share everything with Jesus. He is constantly by our sides and always willing to come to our aid. May our heavenly Father continue to abide in your homes and in the lives of your children today and every day.

Lord, help us to keep our eyes fixed on You rather than the things of this world, that we may not become distracted from our walk with You.

Louise T. Brown

God Knows Us Best

For your Father knows what you need before you ask him. Matt. 6:8.

A single parent's life is not always easy. Especially if you've been a dependent, insecure person like me. I married young and thought it would be forever. The divorce came as a shock to me. I was a Christian and had not thought I would become one of the divorce statistics. God blessed me with a lively, outgoing bundle of love that kept me going through the tough times. He was always there to kiss the tears from my cheeks, give me a hug, and show me his love was unconditional. He did not mind that I was not supermom or that I was insecure and did not know how to go about this thing they call life.

As the years passed, I met a wonderful man and remarried. My son loved him, but soon realized that life would no longer be the same as before. He now had to share me, and he wasn't sure he liked the idea. One day he asked why I'd remarried when we had been so happy by ourselves. I explained that I'd had some really sad times and some tough financial times. God had sent someone wonderful to love us and to help us. Like the time when the car would break down, or something went wrong in the house, and I had no clue how to fix it. Now we knew we had someone to help us.

I also pointed out that one day he would leave home and I would be alone. He was not totally convinced and at the age of 9 argued that when he got married he would tell his wife that his mother was going to live with them.

My son is 21 years old now and understands life so much better. At the age of 16 he approached his stepdad and thanked him for all he had done for him. He is also very glad, as close as we are, that he does not have to live with me for the rest of his life.

Sometimes shortsightedness makes us lose the bigger picture. Like little children, we want things to stay the same. But we have a wonderful God that we can trust. He knows our needs before we do.

Thank You, Father, for knowing us so well that we can leave our whole life in Your hands and not worry about a thing.

Elaine Koen

Squelching the Inner Critic

For you created my inmost being; you knit me together in my mother's womb. I praise you because I am fearfully and wonderfully made; your works are wonderful, I know that full well. Ps. 139:13, 14.

Putt-putt golf on a warm August afternoon usually leads to fun, but this particular outing led to frustration. My husband, Mark, and I took Addison, my stepson, to play a couple games of putt-putt. We carefully chose our clubs and ball colors before we began, then walked down to the green. The challenge to hit the ball into the hole started fairly easy, but increased in difficulty, each shot trickier than the next.

Addison, already a well-practiced golfer at his young age, was determined to beat us. When he made a few mistakes, he became irritated to the point of willfully missing the hole. Mark and I asked him why he was doing this, and he said, "I'm no good at golf."

We continued to play, encouraging him to keep trying, but he insisted on losing, so determined he even began to lie about his score. Mark and I both told him to stop, but he persisted. His attitude wore on us because we knew Addison was better at golf than this, yet he'd convinced himself he was not. He had given up.

As I strained to hold on to every last bit of patience I possessed, God reminded me of the times I tell myself I am not good enough. If I am this troubled about Addison tearing himself down, how must my heavenly Father feel when He sees His children doing the same?

God's Word says we are "fearfully and wonderfully made" by Him. When we grasp this reality, we squelch all the negative self-talk, and we begin to see ourselves the way our heavenly Father sees us. I believe God gave me this insight through our game of putt-putt in order to direct Addison's thoughts and my own during our self-defeating moments toward our Master Crafter and the value He places on us.

Dear Lord, everything You create is wonderful. Help us to remember this includes ourselves.

Kelli Haines

I Choose

A thief is only there to steal and kill and destroy.
I came so they can have real and eternal life,
more and better life than they ever dreamed of. John 10:10, Message.

Being a single parent isn't for wimps. There are times when repeating even the easiest of chores becomes overwhelming. No one comes in to help with the dishes. If the baby gets a bath, it's because I gave it to her. I have clean clothes because I put them in the washer. I do it, but it is exhausting, and all the while, my girls' dad is off somewhere else, laughing and enjoying his new life with his new family.

I'd told Gabbi not to stand on the arm of the couch several times. She'd moved on to torturing her baby sister. Maybe if I quickly threw some food into the oven and cut up carrots and apples, I could get back to my girls before the 3-year-old did more damage.

If I could make it until 6:00, when the kids' dad came to pick them up, then I could get a break for a couple of hours. Ugh! I didn't want to be *that* mom. But, God, I am *so tired*.

The phone rang. It was my girls' father saying he couldn't come and get the girls. I don't remember everything that was said, but it made me question my abilities as a mom. I just started to cry.

Three-year-olds are very intuitive. At least mine was. Gabbi came over to me and put her tiny hand on my back and hugged me. She patted my back and said, "Mommy, why are you crying? Are you sad? Did my daddy make you sad?"

That was my moment. Through the words of my child I came to realize something that would transform my life. No more. No more was I going to let this man, or any person, decide what mood I was going to have. I was Jesus' girl, and it was time I started living like it. My girls' father did not get to decide who I was or how I acted. I would live with joy. From that moment on I would laugh because I chose joy and laughter. Sometimes the laughter comes through tears, but that's OK. It's the laughter that counts in the end.

Lord, thank You for showing me joy and laughter. It has made everything more bearable.

Michelle Yeager

Remember the Sabbath Day

Remember the Sabbath day, to keep it holy. Ex. 20:8, NKJV.

Friday night was a special time in our home—we'd make soup and bread in the bread maker, then grab blankets and sleeping bags, throw them out on the family room floor, light the gas fireplace, and watch *Veggie Tales* or Bible Story movies until Jennifer (7) and Nick (3) fell asleep. Their dad would carry them to bed and tuck them in.

Life changed dramatically after the divorce, and everything related to family activities became painful and difficult. The kids were at their dad's every other Friday night, so our long-standing tradition went by the wayside.

"Lord," I prayed, "how can I make Friday night special in spite of these difficult circumstances? Please help me to see beyond my own pain and help my children see You in all of this. I know you have a plan for us [Jer. 29:11], so help me to trust in it and in You. Help me make Friday night special once again, something the kids will look forward to and cherish."

A few weeks later I tripped over our backpacking tent in the garage. It must have fallen from the shelf onto the floor. The thought hit me: *What if we put the tent up in the family room and pretended we're camping?*

Friday night, that's exactly what we did. It wasn't easy, but we sure had fun working together to get it pitched. The kids loaded their blankets, pillows, and favorite stuffed animals into the tent. After we ate, we watched *Veggie Tales* and Bible Story movies until Jennifer and Nick fell asleep. Instead of carrying them up to their beds, as before, they slept in the tent.

As Sabbath morning dawned, I started a new tradition. We made monkey bread together before we headed out the door for church. Our evening was the talk of Sabbath school. God had heard and answered my prayer. Even though Jennifer and Nick are in college now and we've outgrown the tent, we still gather on Friday nights when we can, watch *Veggie Tales*, and eat monkey bread on Sabbath mornings.

Lord, thank You for the gift of the Sabbath. Thank You for giving us the opportunity to delight in You. Help us to honor You in all we do and say.

Rebecca Swinyar Neff

When I Am Weak

That is why, for Christ's sake, I delight in weaknesses,
in insults, in hardships, in persecutions, in difficulties.
For when I am weak, then I am strong. 2 Cor. 12:10.

I didn't want to get a divorce. Only people who were flawed and who hadn't tried hard enough got divorces. People who were quitters. People who only cared for themselves, and not about their children's futures. It was a horrible thing to finally make that decision and classify myself and my family in the camp of the bent and broken.

There was no explaining this brokenness to the children. They weren't broken, but our family was, and it was obvious to them that I didn't have all the answers. At 11, 9, 7, and 5 years of age, they were tossed out on the ice of reality, to slip and slide around what was out there, and figure out how to decide for themselves what was true, what they would believe, and how they would respond.

There are so many things we can't do for our children. We can't keep them from being hurt. We can't save them from fear, from sorrow, from feelings of betrayal. The only One who can keep them safe, who can protect their hearts through all the devastating experiences we can't prevent, is God.

During the weakest time of my life, I could only commit my children to God's care. I could only point them to the Savior. God was my only hope, and He was the only one I could recommend to my children. I could not forge this relationship for them; I could only lift Him up.

As I look back on those dark days, that is what I believe brought us through. When the children couldn't depend on me, they found they could depend on God.

Father in heaven, I praise You for Your love and for Your faithfulness to Your children. Thank You for being our strength when we are weak, for holding us together when we are broken, and for loving us when we feel forsaken. Thank You that in our darkest times You are there for us. You will never leave us to battle through on our own, and for that we thank You.

Cheryl Woolsey Des Jarlais

Rush Hour

*Now, all discipline, while it is happening, does indeed seem painful,
not enjoyable; but for those who have been trained by it,
it later produces its peaceful fruit, which is righteousness. Heb. 12:11, CJB.*

As a single dad, the Lord has taught me how to discipline in love. Some things require only a swat on the behind and some things do not. When my daughter was young I lived out in the country. There was a road about 100 yards from the front of the house, and our mailbox was across the street.

As I was mowing the lawn one day, my daughter wanted to do something nice for me and retrieve the mail. Out the corner of my eye I saw her cross the street toward the mailbox, oblivious to danger. With the speed of a bionic man I ran toward her and told her to stop just as she pulled down the mailbox door. When I reached her, I guided her back across the street to the safety of our yard.

After correcting her in a firm voice, I sent her to the old wooden chair on the front porch to think about what had just occurred, tears running down her precious little cheeks. About 15 minutes later the Lord told me, "Now love her through it." I shut off the mower, took a deep breath, and walked toward her.

Picking her up off the chair, I gave her a big hug and told her I loved her very much. I explained how important it was to look both ways before crossing the street, then led her back to the road to teach her how to do it properly. I reinforced how much I loved her, and we spent time playing in the yard as the sun began to set.

About a week later she and I were working in the yard, and she asked if she could get the mail. I told her of course she could—I had to trust her. She completed the journey successfully and came running toward me with the biggest smile on her beautiful face. "I did it! I did it, Daddy!" I hugged her and told her how proud I was of her. She never forgot that lesson, and neither did I.

Abba, Father, thank You for disciplining us in love.

John Gold

A Birthday Wish

I will answer them before they even call to me. While they are still talking to me about their needs, I will go ahead and answer their prayers! Isa. 65:24, NLT.

I remember my twenty-sixth birthday all too well. It was a time of bitterness, not happiness. My family wanted to take me out to dinner to celebrate, but I canceled, tears running down my face, an empty feeling inside me. My dreams, all I had hoped for—and this was where I was.

You see, I was pregnant with my second child, Maddie.

An unwed, single mother. It wasn't by choice. After eight years I was back in the same boat. It was even worse, though, the second time. Living with the knowledge that I was having to do it all alone again. Feeling like the world was judging me. There's that girl again, pregnant. Doesn't she learn? I had plans. I had dreams. This wasn't where I thought I would be at 26. What I missed was how God was looking out for me. He saved me from a terrible relationship, a destructive life, and blessed me with a good job and good friends.

Those friendships and that job carried me through for five years. They made me grow up and discover myself. My church never questioned or judged me, just opened their arms to me, and loved Maddie like their own.

God blessed me with the most supportive, wonderful family. My daughter, though unplanned, has been a wonderful, joyous addition to my family. Life would be so dull without my chatty Maddie. You see, before I even really had God in my life, He was already at work. Little did I know, He was answering my prayers before I even prayed.

Now, instead of feeling down or depressed about how I'm not where I'd wanted to be in life, I can see how far He has taken me: from nothing to everything. Yes, I would say He's watching out for me. Life may not be working out how I'd planned, but God is working it out the way He has planned.

Loving God, I praise You, for You are so good to Your children! Thank You for hearing our prayers and for providing for us.

Jill Simpson

Save Your Children

I will contend with those who contend with you,
and your children I will save. Isa. 49:25.

My 3-year-old daughter ran back across the yard and up the porch steps to where her father stood in the partially open door. She tugged on her father's hand. "Please, Daddy. Please come to church with us." He refused. It was the first time in her life he had stayed behind.

Both of us cried all the way to church. Sabbath had changed forever. I hoped it would be temporary, but it was not. I sat in church silently praying, "God, how am I going to raise her? How can I give her spiritual direction without her father? She is his child too. How, God? How?"

I talked about my concern with my small group, and they prayed.

The next Sabbath the pastor conducted a baptism. Watching intently, my daughter turned to me and said, "Mommy, I want to be baptized."

I looked at her. We had never talked about baptism. I wondered if she understood what it meant. Tears came to my eyes as I absorbed the message God had just sent me through my child. He would lead her to Himself. He would put the desire for spiritual things in her heart.

Sometime later, I watched as she colored during church, apparently unaware of the sermon being preached. On the way home she accurately recounted the themes of the sermon. At times she would ask me to explain the sermon to her. I was happy to put the concepts into simpler language, ignoring the standard of not talking in church. Later, while driving her to school, I would tell her Bible stories. Amazingly, God often touched my own heart with insights that seemed to pop into mind during the telling. Throughout her childhood, she never lost the desire to be baptized.

Father God, You are love. You are the Creator of our children's hearts and understand their yearning for love. Teach us to love like You do. When circumstances, our own personalities or difficulties remove that love, please take over. Please keep Your promise and save our children. Thank You for working out the details.

Lynn Meadows

Hold Fast

This day I call the heavens and the earth as witnesses against you that I have set before you life and death, blessings and curses. Now choose life, so that you and your children may live and that you may love the Lord your God, listen to his voice, and hold fast to him. For the Lord is your life. Deut. 30:19, 20.

As a parent, you know that safety pins come in handy for many things. For me, the safety pin took on a whole new meaning on August 30, 2007, when my baby boy came into this world. I arrived at the hospital at 8:00 a.m. to start the exciting process of bringing my little boy, Nathaniel, into the world. I was only 39 weeks along, but my precious boy was getting too big, so the doctors felt it necessary to start the labor early.

As the nurses began hooking up the heart monitors, they searched and searched for his little heartbeat. My heartbeat began to elevate as 10 long minutes passed, and still there was no sign of life. They wheeled in an ultrasound machine to confirm the devastating news. "I'm so sorry, but your son is no longer alive."

My heart just broke. I would give birth to a nine-pound-10-ounce perfect yet lifeless baby boy. My new yellow car seat would go home empty. I felt alone, but knew I wasn't. Looking back now, I was far from being alone. Besides family and friends, God never left my side. He put people into my life that had a similar experience, and our stories helped each other. He strengthened me and lifted me when my heart hurt so badly.

At Nathaniel's funeral, I chose the theme of a safety pin. I wanted people to remember my baby Nathaniel, but more so to remember to "hold fast" to Jesus. Clasp on to Him and don't let go. If you have lost a child in any way, you know the deep pain that exists. I encourage you to keep your safety pin clipped to Jesus. He will get you through.

Lord, help us to hold fast to You daily. Help us to love our children as You love us. Thank You for the gift of Your Son and the promise of seeing our children in heaven soon.

Kimberly Spare

Love Your Neighbor

You shall love your neighbor as yourself. Matt. 22:39, NKJV.

Each day was long until Daddy got home. Baby and I would play, nap, clean the house, and at day's end walk as far as we could until we could see his car coming. As my sweet little girl grew and we added a sister, it seemed that nothing changed. I was not a little-people person, and even though I adored my girls, my cup as a young wife was empty.

We only had those brief moments with Daddy when he came home, before he hurried off to study for his master's and then Ph.D. degrees. I was married yet I lived the life of a single parent. I felt so isolated. Everything to do with home life was mine to take care of. I was sinking and had to learn to swim fast.

I started living for the weekends at church and often had Saturday evening get-togethers at our home. I gathered a group of little girls and would take them to ballet after school, or swimming, or horseback riding. We found places to go and things to do to keep us busy, busy, busy. Anything that would help shut out the devastating loneliness that gripped me.

After years of teaching kindergarten and primary at church, I turned to youth ministry, then women's ministry. I served Jesus with all my passion and used all my gifts in serving Him. He was my joy. He filled my cup until I no longer felt so alone.

I enjoyed strong, Christ-filled friendships with many of my girl friends. We encouraged one another, prayed together, and shared the challenges of parenthood. It wasn't quite the same as sharing with my husband, but the Lord used it to help ease the sense of loss I felt at his lack of connection with me and our daughters.

I wish I could say that I made it work. I didn't always make good choices. There were days when I took my eyes off Jesus, and the consequences took years to heal. Loneliness—whether single or within a marriage—can leave a person vulnerable in many areas. How important, then, that we learn to hold fast to His hand. He is more than enough!

Father, walk with us through the journey of single parenting, whether in a marriage or not. May we be strengthened with this truth: You, O Lord, are enough.

Emra Wagener Smith

Dealing With Anger

A person's wisdom yields patience. Prov. 19:11.

Someone once said, "Control your anger. It is one letter away from Danger." We are counseled to be slow to anger, yet in the midst of a great storm brewing between you and your little one, if there is not wisdom stored in the heart, the result can end with parental guilt and rebellion planted in the child's heart. Here are some prevention steps to take before an emotional tornado blows through your homes and leaves a path of destruction:

1. Pray and have devotions daily. As a young mother of two, I have been greatly blessed with the reminder that the biblical day starts in the evening. So after the little ones fall asleep, I sit and talk to my heavenly Father, who brings me peace from His love letter.

2. Paste sticky notes all around the house, stating: "When I am angry I will whisper" or "When I am angry I will give hugs." In the midst of great emotion we aren't using our frontal lobes (thinking/judgment), so it's best to wait until we are calm so we can model to our kids how to handle conflict in a Christlike way—with love, wisdom, and patience.

3. Exercise! I have joined a health club that includes child care for up to two hours per day, so I can do group exercises, run on a treadmill, lift weights, or go swimming while the kids play with other kids under adult supervision. Experts say exercising three to four times a week gets the stress out, helps with cognitive fog, releases endorphins, and keeps us in shape. Even if you're not crazy about exercising, I encourage you to find something you enjoy doing, and then stick with it.

4. Practice keeping your emotions under control by reminding yourself of how Jesus works—and how He does not. He desires to reason with us (Isa. 1:18), He leads His flock gently (Isa. 40:11), He speaks tenderly (Hosea 2:14), and He prays without ceasing (1 Thess. 5:17).

Dear Father, help us to control our anger; we know that how we react to stressful situations is how our children will react. Give us Your peace like honey: smooth and sweet.

Katie Miller

Just as I Am

No one will be able to stand against you all the days of your life.
As I was with Moses, so I will be with you;
I will never leave you nor forsake you. Joshua 1:5.

Ever felt that everything you have done as a single and divorced parent left you feeling poor and wretched? Have some of the decisions you've made created conflict and doubt? I have felt that way since I became a single parent who is now divorced.

The old favorite hymn "Just as I Am" is the theme song of my life, especially when the enemy attacks everything and everyone precious to me. I struggle with the idea that it is not supposed to be this hard raising two children and that I should not be alone. Emotions overwhelm me on some days. On other days, the weight of my financial struggles threatens to drown me, and I am tempted to lose hope.

"Poor" and "wretched" are the words that describe my darkest moments when the ones I depend on cannot make a break with the past to allow growth and healing. Those who claim to help me the most are often the ones who bring the most conflict. Single parenting is not easy and is often filled with people who are looking to turn your Christ-given duty into an unbearable cross.

Hagar and her son were turned away by the only people they knew. Hagar must have been scared and mad at the people who ruled their lives. She was miles and miles away from home with a small child and no idea of how to get back. However, God had a plan in mind for them.

In Genesis 21:17, 18, God heard Hagar's cries. He opened her eyes and showed her He still cared, even after she had given up hope. I strongly believe God was with her constantly throughout her journey through the Beersheba Desert. Just as He was with Hagar, who was forced to leave all she knew, God will stay with you throughout your journey. Do not give up hope, no matter how lonely you feel, because God still wants you just as you are.

God, I thank You for Your goodness to us. When life leads us to places we never thought we'd go, when all goes wrong, You are there, walking beside us. Thank You for Your love.

Maurette Saint Fleur

A Friend Indeed

Lord, you alone are my inheritance, my cup of blessing.
You guard all that is mine. . . . You will show me the way of life,
granting me the joy of your presence
and the pleasures of living with you forever. Ps. 16:5-11, NLT.

Dear Daughter,

W e cannot remake history. We must learn to make the best of our present situation, and we are not alone. You spent many years and your earnings buying your home and its furnishings, and paying off your ex-husband's loans, only to be tossed out empty-handed while his new wife enjoys the fruits of your labor. This is not fair, but it is a reality that is repeated often in a society in which men and their lawyers still hold the upper hand. Despite this, God has good news for us!

First, God is your inheritance. He supplies your needs because He is your cup of blessing. He guards the most importance treasure that you have—your children. You may think that vengeance would be sweet or that it would be nice if the world saw your ex-husband for who he really is; but if he were exposed today and even if lightning struck him, it would bring you neither joy nor pleasure. Real joy and pleasure come as we let Jesus show us the way to abundant life and realize that this is only found as we live in His presence. Living in His presence is not hard. It comes as we open our hearts to Him in prayer and as we listen to Him speaking to us in Scripture. If this is not your daily routine, you will never find genuine satisfaction with life regardless of what happens to your former husband.

By living in God's presence and entrusting your treasured children to His care, your children will learn from your example how they, too, can have the real pleasure in life that only comes from following Jesus. Though your means are meager, God, your inheritance, will supply your needs according to His riches. Your children will learn that God's inheritance is better than the gifts they receive to win affection. They will know God's joy through your example.

God, be my inheritance today. Supply my needs. Guard my children. Let me live with You now and forever.

Dan Solis

Jehovah-jireh

My God will supply every need of yours. Phil. 4:19, ASV.

Kristy and Tony married soon after graduation and moved to Kansas. They looked like the perfect couple, but after a while Kristy noticed that Tony didn't seem to like to work. He changed jobs frequently and said it was always someone else's fault. Kristy was the sole provider when she found out she was pregnant with twin boys. She felt devastated when Tony showed no excitement.

Tony was a no-show at the delivery when Kristy gave birth to two healthy boys. She never heard from Tony, and so she moved in with her family to raise the boys. She had a roof over her head and food on the table, and was able to stay home and earn some money while babysitting the neighbor's kids. She struggled to go back to her home church as a single mom, which she never thought would happen to her.

Jonathan and Eleazar grew up with love and attention, in a family environment with aunts, uncles, grandparents, but they missed having a dad. It was hard going to school and watching the other dads pick up their kids. There were many times Kristy would fall asleep crying. But God provided good male role models for Jonathan and Eleazar.

Though it was very difficult to raise the boys on her own, three things have encouraged Kristy. First, prayer; she knew she had a Father that she could come to. A Father that was not deaf. Second, she trusted God to take care of her and provide her needs. She had already seen Him bless her in so many ways in the past, that she didn't believe He would abandon her now! Third, God surrounded her with a supportive family and friends.

Today, Kristy thanks God for providing for her and her boys! She gives witness to the truth that Jehovah-jireh is her provider and He is more than enough for her and her boys.

Father, thank You for Your promise that You will be a father to the fatherless. I hold on to that promise today. Thank You for meeting all our needs.

Z. Kathy Cameron

A Lesson in Trust

Cause me to hear thy lovingkindness in the morning;
for in thee do I trust: cause me to know the way wherein I should walk;
for I lift up my soul unto thee. Ps. 143:8, KJV.

As a single mom working full-time to support my family, I was always second-guessing myself. Maybe I was being too strict; maybe I wasn't strict enough. Was I worrying too much? Or not enough? Was I doing enough to support my two boys emotionally? financially? spiritually? I agonized in prayer over every decision, so afraid I would do something that would traumatize them for life! This went on for many months, until I was nearly paralyzed by fear and anxiety. I knew I couldn't go on like that—not for my own sake, or my boys'. Gradually, I came to realize that these children were not my own, but were bought with a price. My job was to trust them into the care of their Lord and Savior; to turn them over to Him, every moment of every day.

My oldest son suffered from severe asthma attacks, and it wasn't unusual for us to spend two or three nights a month in the emergency room. Often I would stand out in the hall listening to him breathe, making sure he was all right before turning in for the night. Not long after I began giving my boys to the Lord every morning, I was standing in the hall one evening listening, when I heard a burst of laughter from both my boys. I stepped into their bedroom, sure they must be up to some mischief, only to find them both fast asleep.

As I knelt by my own bed that night, I sent up a prayer: "Father, thank You for showing me that when I place complete trust in You, my children dream happy dreams." I won't say things always went smoothly for us, but after that night, whenever I recognized the old signs of stress and anxiety, I would remember their laughter-filled sleep. It was like a special promise to me that I could trust my children completely to Him, and everything would be all right.

Father, as we strive to be godly parents to our children, help us to remember our first responsibility is to trust them completely into Your care and keeping.

Beverly Thorp Logan

Motives

Create in me a pure heart, O God,
and renew a steadfast spirit within me. Ps. 51:10.

It was one of those mornings. If you're parents with kids still living at home, you will know exactly what I'm talking about. My son was just acting bad. He took every opportunity to test the boundaries. Imagine it— this is the morning rush—the scramble to get out the door and off to work and school on time!

After an extremely long week, I had to go downstairs and cry. I was overwhelmed, and just needed to cry. My daughter came downstairs and found me crying. She immediately marched back upstairs and told her brother that he'd better apologize.

We finally left the house, but I was fed up. I had reached that point where you just don't want to hear any more "I'm sorry"s. Well, we had to run to the store, and while we were there my son kept trying to hug me and apologize. He'd remembered his sister's words and was trying to make good on it. He tried again and again. I was so not ready and asked him to stop. Then he said, "Well, Jordyn told me I should tell you I am sorry." Now, that almost made me mad, but God immediately gave me the following insight.

We do this to God every day. What is our motive when we ask God for forgiveness? True repentance comes when we have a relationship with God. Unless we have a relationship, how can we truly understand the impact of our sinfulness on others? Personally, I have to ask to be convicted of the sin. I don't want to ask for forgiveness just because the Bible says it's wrong or because someone told me that I had to apologize to God. I don't think that's what God desires from us. He desires that we ask for forgiveness because we are sorry. Just as with my son, his apology was not meaningful, since he was apologizing because someone told him to.

Have you noticed how some of our deepest spiritual lessons are learned from our kids? Single parenting is tough for everyone. I'm just so grateful for a heavenly Father who steps in at the right moment—and takes my breath away with His grace.

Thank You, Father, for teaching me through the lives of my children how much I need to come to You in true repentance. Thank You for loving tired and worn-out parents everywhere.

Robyn Logan Williams

How Dare You?

God's loyal love couldn't have run out, his merciful love
couldn't have dried up. They're created new every morning.
How great your faithfulness! Lam. 3:22, 23, Message.

Taking our family camping was one of our favorite vacations. We had
been doing it for years, and this particular year the stress our jobs had
put us under made this especially sweet.

Early one morning as I read my book and drank my hot chocolate, my
pj-clad baby dug in the dirt while everyone else slept in. I couldn't help
looking out at the crystal-clear lake and thanking God for such a beautiful
place. The sun shone in all the right places.

My cell phone beeped with a message. Strange. We hadn't had much
reception in our little paradise. "Did you see the e-mail?" I immediately
went and downloaded the worst news imaginable. Our best friends' grandson had passed away in the night, gone at 16 months. The tears. I didn't
know that many were humanly possible.

Then, the anger. I was staring out at the lake, and it just built up in me
and exploded. I was furious at Him. I got so angry I yelled at God. I said,
"How dare You? How dare You let the sun shine on such a horrible day?"

He answered me. And the answer took my breath away. He didn't yell
back, as He rightly should have. I recognized the voice as His because it was
filled with love and comfort. He said, "I have to. If I don't, everything I've
told you your entire life would have been a lie."

As people, we are so wishy-washy. We're friends one day, enemies the
next. I'm happy with God one moment, angry at Him the next. God doesn't
do that. He is faithful regardless of our mood. God doesn't pick and choose
which times to be there for you. When you aren't sure you can trust that He
is there, the proof of it is in the sun, which rises every morning. Because He
is faithful, we can trust that we will see our little buddy again.

*Thank You for Your faithfulness, God. There are so many times we may not
understand, but You are always right there to put Your arms around us and
be there for us regardless. Thank You.*

Michelle Yeager

A Praiseworthy Example

Whatever is true, whatever is noble, whatever is right,
whatever is pure, whatever is lovely, whatever is admirable—
if anything is excellent or praiseworthy—think about such things. Phil. 4:8.

Parenting is scary. It is an awesome yet daunting responsibility. Children don't come with an operating manual, as does a smartphone or a late-model car, or upgrades that you can check on your computer. Sometimes children seem smarter than their parents—and sometimes they are—or they have innumerable operating parts. No two children in a family are the same, even if they are identical twins or of the same gender.

Children need an example. Being a disciple of Christ is one function of a parent. Be a role model, someone whose words, deeds, and actions can be emulated with confidence. When children see that you follow in Christ's footsteps it makes it easier for them to follow, and the reminder to "train up a child in the way he should go, and when he is old he will not depart from it" (Prov. 22:6, NKJV) is a positive thought to keep in mind. When children do not find you to be overbearing and unreasonable, they will consider God in a positive light. When our children are given this type of example, they will grow "in wisdom and stature, and in favor with God and man" (Luke 2:52)—just as Jesus did.

Let your life—your kindness, your patience, the way you treat your spouse, their friends, and others—be to your children an example of how God deals with us as individuals. Your actions will have a positive effect on them that will last throughout their lives and may encourage them to choose to do the right things when they become adults. "If we wish our children to possess the tender spirit of Jesus, and the sympathy that angels manifest for us, we must encourage the generous, loving impulses of childhood" (*The Desire of Ages*, p. 516).

Discipling must begin while your children are small. Don't wait until they are teenagers or you will lose the game. Be involved in their lives from the start. Treasure your moments together. Pray for them every day. You will reap great rewards later.

Dear Lord, You have given us children to bring up as a little flock to present to You when You return. May we be an example to them in our words and actions and be Your true disciples.

Beverly Henry

August

Parents Are Called to Be Disciple Makers

Lover of Little Children

Then were there brought unto him little children, that he should put his hands on them, and pray: and the disciples rebuked them. But Jesus said, Suffer little children, and forbid them not, to come unto me: for of such is the kingdom of heaven. And he laid his hands on them. Matt. 19:13-15, KJV.

Children are the Lord's heritage. The soul of the little child that believes in Christ is as precious in His sight as are the angels about His throne. They are to be brought to Christ, and trained for Christ. They are to be guided in the path of obedience, not indulged in appetite or vanity.

"When the disciples sought to send away the mothers who were bringing their little ones to Christ, He rebuked their narrow faith, saying, 'Suffer little children, and forbid them not, to come unto me: for of such is the kingdom of heaven.'

"He was grieved that the disciples should rebuke the mothers for bringing their children to Him; that His followers should say, by word or action, that His grace was limited, and that children should be kept away from Him. . . .

"A great responsibility rests upon parents, for the education and training which shape the eternal destiny of children and youth are received in their early childhood. The parents' work is to sow the good seed diligently and untiringly in the hearts of their children, occupying their hearts with seed which will bring forth a harvest of right habits, of truthfulness and willing obedience.

"Correct, virtuous habits formed in youth will generally mark the course of the individual through life. In most cases those who reverence God and honor the right will be found to have learned this lesson before the world could stamp its image of sin upon the soul. . . .

"Oh that parents were truly the sons and daughters of God! Their lives would then be fragrant with good works. A holy atmosphere would surround their souls. Their earnest supplications for grace and for the guidance of the Holy Spirit would ascend to heaven, and religion would be diffused through their homes as the bright, warming rays of the sun are diffused through the earth" (*That I May Know Him*, p. 40).

Ellen G. White

Parents as Disciple Makers

And these words which I command you today shall be in your heart.
You shall teach them diligently to your children, and shall talk of them
when you sit in your house, when you walk by the way, when you lie down,
and when you rise up. You shall bind them as a sign on your hand, and they
shall be as frontlets between your eyes. You shall write them on the doorposts
of your house and on your gates. Deut. 6:6-9, NKJV.

As a parent, one of the most important decisions you will make is in regard to the education of your child. You will need to consider the school to which you will send your child. What environment will they be exposed to for those hours during the day? Is it one that will mirror the same values that you want your child to emulate? It may be stating the obvious, but it is important to point out that the school atmosphere should support and reinforce the values that we as parents are practicing in the home.

In essence, parents must assume the role as the primary disciple makers for their child. This job is not to be left up to the Adventist teacher, the Sabbath school teacher, or the pastor. While the school and the church indeed support, encourage, and reinforce the home values, it is also true that you, as the parent, will be the single most influential person in your child's life.

This wise counsel in Deuteronomy reminds me that parenting is a full-time responsibility that I cannot pass off to someone else. It happens 24 hours a day, 365 days a year. It happens when I sit and when I stand, when I lie down and when I rise up. Parenting is a verb and not a noun. It is defined by the life I lead and by the example that I set.

Have you relied too much on others to disciple and train your children? Are we too willing as parents to pass the torch that is given us to carry? What steps do you need to take to make sure you take hold of those reins of parenthood today?

Lord, I am weary and overwhelmed right now. Will You please help me carry this load? I'm looking to You for wisdom. Please increase my strength. And my faith. I love You, Lord.

Claudio and Pamela Consuegra

Hey, Mom, I Get It!

Train up a child in the way he should go,
even when he is old he will not depart from it. Prov. 22:6, NASB.

Will Rogers, one of my favorite theologians, once said, "There ain't nothin' basically wrong with all of us, except we're selfish." That doesn't apply to you and me, of course, but have you noticed that it sure does fit a lot of folk? Including our kids. Well, not our kids, but most of the neighbor kids.

Truth is, we're all born crying to have our wishes met, and unless something happens to sweeten that mind-set it's likely to stay with us to the grave. And the thing that "sweetens that mind-set" is called parents. And the strategy used by those loving parents begins when the youngster reaches the age of about 2. The technical term for it is chores. You want your kids to learn respect and good manners? Here is where it begins.

I'm not a fanatic about much regarding parenting issues, but I come close when I talk about chores. Beginning between the second and third birthdays the little ankle biter, Kevin Leman's term, needs to experience a growing awareness that life is no longer a free ride. They are part of a family, and being part of anything means that you help pull the load.

Understand, kids don't just wake up one morning and say, "Hey, Mom, I get it!" It's gradually impressed on them as they see their chore list on the refrigerator, as they see Dad and Mom helping each other, and others, and as they are taught to look for ways they can be helpful to others. It takes a while to "unselfish" the human heart. You and I didn't catch it by the age of 3, either. But we live it before them and wear them down. It's both caught and taught.

Did you see the TV commercial in which a soccer coach comes into a motel with a bunch of middle school soccer players? The students are each carrying their own little bag and the coach is carrying all the sports equipment. They may win soccer games but they're not learning about life. If I were the principal, I'd have a chat with that coach; he's missing the big stuff.

Father, may I show, by my example, the joy found in carrying my share of the load and thus lightening the load of others.

Don Jacobsen

Leaving a Family Heritage

But store up for yourselves treasures in heaven, where moths and vermin do not destroy, and where thieves do not break in and steal. Matt. 6:20.

I watched my young adopted children as they rapidly outgrew their clothes and toys. I wondered what they would take from their childhood into their adult lives. Their DNA came from their biological parents, so they would not have my stature, curly hair, or quirky sense of humor to pass on to children of their own. Sure, there would be family recipes and holiday traditions that they would cherish forever. Certainly, we were making memories to last a lifetime.

Perhaps I would be able to leave each of them a small financial inheritance, but that is so dependent on circumstances. No matter how diligent I might be in setting money aside to provide for their futures, an illness or economic setback could use up all those hard-earned savings. Besides, I wanted them to know how to be self-sufficient—to be able to provide for themselves through working and wise living—with anything I might be able to leave for them being an added bonus.

During a visit with my aunt Francie, my mother's sister, she shared with me one of her most precious childhood memories. When Francie was a very young girl she walked into her parents' (my grandparents') bedroom and saw them kneeling in prayer beside their bed. The vision has remained with her for more than 80 years. Now, that's a legacy I would like to leave for my children.

I hope to follow my family's tradition and leave for my children the example of a faithful parent—one who spends time in prayer, who treasures the Scripture, practices forgiveness, honors God, expresses love and compassion, and makes time to worship. It will not only be my heritage handed down to my children, but the same one handed down to me from my mother and my aunt. It is the same legacy my mother and her sister received from their parents eight decades ago. It is an inheritance safe from illness and economic turmoil; even moths, vermin, and thieves cannot steal it—because it is stored in the treasuries of my children's hearts.

Lord, thank You for the example of faithful parents and grandparents.

Karen R. Hessen

The Lord Works Upstream

"For I know the plans I have for you," declares the Lord, "plans to prosper you and not to harm you, plans to give you hope and a future." Jer. 29:11.

I stood in Israel on the bank of the Jordan River, with my 16-year-old son and my mother beside me, at a site just east of Jericho where it is believed the Israelites crossed into the Promised Land. As we stood together, soldiers with machine guns patrolled the riverbank, and minefields stretched in the distance to protect Israel from its neighbor, Jordan.

I couldn't help thinking back to a story in which the river served as a different border, between the Israelites and the Promised Land. As the Israelites finally approached the Promised Land the river did not divide the way the Red Sea had. Instead, when the priests carried the ark to the middle of the river, it simply stopped flowing. God had stopped the river upstream near Zarethan, quite a distance away from where the Israelites were crossing. The river then continued to flow to the Dead Sea until the riverbed was dry. God knew the exact moment the Israelites would be crossing the Jordan, and before they even reached the bank God had already performed a miracle to provide a dry riverbed.

God leads each of us and has promised to have good plans for us. When I held my beautiful son and daughter for the first time I was humbled by the responsibility God had given me. I chose to dedicate my children to God and tried to do my best to provide them with every opportunity to learn and grow closer to Jesus. While I know that I made mistakes as they grew, I found comfort in the promise found in Jeremiah 29:11. God planned ahead to stop the river for the children of Israel, and I know that He has a plan already worked out for my life and the lives of my children. All I need to do is be like the priests, step out in faith and trust God to make the path for my family.

Father God, You provided for me when I did not even know I was in need. Help me, Lord, to trust You with my life and the lives of my children. Thank You for Your promises and for entrusting Your children into my care.

Lisa O'Connor Clarke

Watch Me!

*But Esau ran to meet him, and embraced him,
and fell on his neck and kissed him, and they wept. Gen. 33:4, NKJV.*

You have probably heard the expression "Do as I say, not as I do," but that does not work when it comes to parenting. Whether we like it or not, our children are created to learn by watching us as we live our daily lives.

One of the amazing facts about eagles is that they learn to fly and hunt by observing their parents. These skills are not instinctive like those of some of God's creatures. However, eagles are born with a different instinct called imprinting. Bird shelters that rescue eagle eggs must hand-feed them with an eagle puppet so the eagles do not imprint on their human caregivers and end up rejecting their own kind. And when it comes to parenting, our children don't fall too far from the "imprinting" model found in nature.

Today's scripture shares what is considered one of the most moving family reunions in the Bible. Jacob's children had seen their father agonize over the encounter with their uncle Esau, and had also seen their father's desire for reconciliation. When the moment of truth arrived, Genesis 33:4 tells us that the brothers embraced, kissed each other, and wept as Jacob's wives and children watched.

Years later one of the children who had watched his father and uncle reconcile and forgive each other imitated the same behavior in another moving family reunion. In Genesis 45:14, 15, we see Joseph graciously kissing and weeping over his brothers as he freely offered them all forgiveness, and set in motion a plan for reconciliation.

As we pause and think about the power our modeling has over the lives of our children, may we have the grace to live our lives in such a way that our children learn to "do as we do."

Father, what a privilege we have to imprint on the minds of our children Your own love and character. Please give us the strength and the consistency we need all the days of our lives.

Ketty R. Leal

Discipleship and Discipline

Fathers, do not provoke your children to anger, but bring them up in the discipline and instruction of the Lord. Eph. 6:4, NASB.

Mom always said that the best medicine for Denise after she had misbehaved was to ground her from watching TV. On the other hand, a good old-fashioned spanking worked wonders for the rest of us. This was back in the 1970s when spanking was an accepted form of discipline. We were pretty well-behaved kids.

Twenty-five years later, when I had children of my own, new techniques on discipline abounded: time-outs and positive reward systems were the new buzzwords. I read all the books and attended workshops on how to raise my strong-willed children.

As parents, our mission should be to raise our children so they will transition easily toward responsible adulthood. With life as crazy as it is today, more and more parents are desperate and feel overwhelmed in the struggle to get their kids under control.

We can make life so complicated by trying to do the best for our children. Let's face it—we're human, and we will make mistakes. I have found that when I look to the Lord for wisdom it becomes a whole lot simpler. Following Jesus' example, let us make disciples of our children. Look at it this way: A disciple is a follower, or student, of a mentor, or teacher. As our little ones observe and mimic every move we make, they learn from us, how we react and handle various situations. Through following our example they live and learn each day.

Parenthood is an awesome responsibility. We have been called by God to carry out a sacred mission. Let us seek His instruction and make disciples of our children, and lead them in such a way that they become confident, responsible, generous men and women committed to God.

Lord, guide me and give me the strength and patience to be the best example I can be to my children. May they know I am connected to You, see Your reflection in me to grow up as men and women of God.

Linda Wolfaardt

Communion Whispers

*And he said unto them, This is my blood of the new testament,
which is shed for many. Mark 14:24, KJV.*

It is Communion again. "Do you remember what the bread is for?" I ask my 6-year-old.

"It's not bread, Mommy; it's a cracker," corrects my know-it-all 4-year-old.

"The bread is the body of Christ. Does that mean you are eating His real body?" answers the 6-year-old with a question of his own.

"No, dear; it's a symbol," I reply.

"What's a symbol?"

"It's something we use to remind us of something we don't want to forget," I improvise.

"The broken bread, or cracker," I look meaningfully at my know-it-all, "reminds us that Jesus' body was broken. That means He died so we could have eternal life," I whisper.

"Can I have some?"

I break the square symbol into one half and two quarters and show them how to hold it without breaking it. The 4-year-old starts to nibble at hers.

"You have to wait till everyone has been served and the pastor says, 'Take, eat; this is My body.' Remember to chew slowly. I'll explain later," I add as the eyes of one member reprimands our stage whispers.

The testimonies begin. A mother talks about her daughter who is battling cancer. She starts to cry, setting off sniffles across the whole church. At the pastor's prompting to eat, I eat, still tearful, because it dawns on me in a new way that it is for pain like this that Christ's body was broken.

"Next is the wine," I whisper softly. "It reminds us of Jesus' blood that was shed for us."

The children want some. To keep the peace, I promise each a sip and eyeball them into silence. We listen to a few more testimonies from people who feel safe enough in this rather large congregation to bare their hearts as two sets of eyes from cute small faces watch it all.

Dear God, help me to model You to them. Let the words of my mouth and the deeds I do be truly representative of You.

Yvonne Rodney

Killing the Snake

Be sober, be vigilant; because your adversary the devil walks about like a roaring lion, seeking whom he may devour. 1 Peter 5:8, NKJV.

Mommy, there's a snake!" an urgent voice called. My heart sank as I looked out of the window and saw a rattlesnake coiled up under a plant near the front door of our country home. My husband wasn't home, and wouldn't be for some time. This was his job! Praying hard, I told the children to stay inside and went to get the flat-blade shovel from the shed. Adrenaline pumped through my veins as I faced the snake and tried to think of the best way to kill it before it struck me. I went for the head and then gave a few extra blows just to be sure it was really dead.

There's another snake we should be even more afraid of than a rattler, one that will always harm when he gets the chance. This makes me think: How intensely am I doing battle with the devil? Does my heart beat faster as I work with my child to get the victory over selfishness, shrieking, appetite, vanity, disobedience? Do I put all my energy and focus into defeating Satan in my home and family? He wants to ruin our day every day. Do we sit back and say, "Whatever," or do we arm ourselves with the Word of God and do hand-to-hand combat for the sake of our children? Do we consistently work with our children until we know the victory is completely won?

One of my children loves to be in charge. I had spoken with her about the importance of not being controlling and not making others do what she wanted. At bedtime she told me she can't stop wanting what she wants. We talked about choosing Jesus first thing in the morning and praying throughout the day. I made a chart so she could put up a star any time she chose not to be controlling. When I would see her win over self and let someone else have their way, I would say: "You can get a star; Jesus is helping you." I began to see her make the effort to listen to the Holy Spirit, and to choose to give in to others. What a victory for both of us!

Father God, help me to do whatever it takes to help my children have victory over sin and Satan today. Please give me grace to consistently help them find the joy of making right choices.

Heather Krick

Lilies and Sparrows

O Lord, how manifold are thy works! In wisdom hast thou made them all: the earth is full of thy riches. Ps. 104:24, KJV.

How many blue toys do we have?"
"Four!"
"How many red toys do we have?"
"Three!"
"How many green toys do we have?"
"One!"
"Great! Now how many do we have all together?" I quizzed.

A furrowed brow and a huge smile later she shouted a gleeful, "Eight!"

As we placed our colorful treasures into the toy box, my daughter received reminders about her colors and the principles of basic addition. She, however, thought she was playing a game and was simply overjoyed with my undivided attention. Teaching our children the basic building blocks of what they need to learn can be a fun and interactive experience—one in which they do not even know they are learning.

Our heavenly Father does the same thing with us while we play and spend quality time with Him. Through tiny green inchworms and purple-orange sunsets, fantastically structured spiderwebs and mist-spraying waterfalls, brightly colored autumn leaves and luscious rich spring grasses, He has given us information about His playful and artistic side. He has taught us that not only will He care for us, but we will have a fun and enjoyable experience when we spend time in His stunning and marvelous creation. His very character is revealed in how tenderly He cares for lilies and sparrows; and He wants us to know that in all things He cares for us, too.

Heavenly Father, please help me to have fun and enjoy these precious, short years as I train my children. Help me to turn their hearts and thoughts to You as I show them Your beauty.

Karen Barnett

Words Fitly Spoken

A word fitly spoken is like apples of gold in pictures of silver. Prov. 25:11, KJV.

We first met Jan Doward and his family when we taught together in Washington State. Jan visited us in Pennsylvania several years later, and three of us enjoyed a long after-dinner conversation around our kitchen table. The children were generally within hearing range, although not part of that conversation.

Before we left the table, Jan quietly cautioned us, saying that conversations within our children's hearing could possibly cause them to question those in leadership. Those were helpful words, spoken in love and concern. Even though this was already a value for us, we had evidently relaxed a bit and said more than we should have. After that we made extra effort to discuss information and opinions we had issues with only when we were alone and had our own privacy. It wasn't always easy or convenient!

In this tell-all world, with time and energy constraints, children often overhear things they don't need to hear or know at their developmental stage. Long ago I learned that children are excellent recorders, but they are often poor interpreters.

It's not that we should shield them from the realities of living in this world, but we would do well to ask ourselves why we are sharing certain information in front of our children.

Consider the blessings of taking Proverbs 25:11 to heart. Instead of airing our frustrations about others in front of our children, we can fill our conversation with the positives in our life. We can share positive things about our pastors and work colleagues and pray for them and their families. We can speak well of our spouse, relatives, neighbors, and the teachers and staff at school. Show appreciation to store clerks and deliverypersons. Let your children know how much you appreciate the many people in your life, including them. These will be words fitly spoken, and perhaps those around you will better understand how the church remains a storehouse of the riches of God's grace!

Lord, may my words never leave a bitter taste in another's heart.

Susan Murray

A Day With My Toddler

Behold, God is my helper. Ps. 54:4, NKJV.

One beautiful Friday morning I carried the basket of wet linens outside with my 2-year-old daughter following behind me. I watched her out of the corner of my eye as I hung the sheets. As I reached for the last one I saw her heading toward the wooded path. "Come back," I called.

No reply. I quickly pegged the sheet, then started after her. Calling her name, I hurried down the trail toward the creek. How could little legs outdistance mine and disappear so quickly?

After frantically hunting all over the woods and along the creek for half an hour, a prayer for Irytta's safety upon my lips, I finally found her. Or maybe she found me. We met in the woods halfway between the creek and our house. Her little tennis shoes were wet. I scooped her up in my arms, tears of relief flooding my eyes. "I've looked for you everywhere. Why didn't you answer Mommy?" I asked.

"I went to creek," she replied simply. "I not lost."

"You must never go again without me," I scolded gently. "And when I call, you need to come. Now, stay in the yard and play while I cook for Sabbath."

A few minutes later I glanced out the kitchen window to see my darling dipping a week-old kitten up and down in a bucket of water. Sprinting out the door, I rescued the mewing baby.

"I giving kitty bath," my daughter stated.

"Let's dry the baby and put him back with his sisters. Their mama bathes them with her tongue," I instructed. "Come inside now and play with your dollies."

The remainder of the day I kept my toddler by my side.

As a young mother I want to guide her in learning appropriate behavior, and keep her and the pets safe. This is often a wearing and interruptive job, and no matter how hard I try to be a good mother I need God's help. I am so thankful for guardian angels.

Heavenly Father, I cannot parent without Your help. Guide me today, and please be the extra set of eyes I need.

Barbara Ann Kay

Teach Them to Love the Lord

*You shall teach them diligently to your children,
and shall talk of them when you sit in your house,
when you walk by the way, when you lie down,
and when you rise up. Deut. 6:7, NKJV.*

The immediate context in Deuteronomy 6 is the giving of the Ten Commandments by God Himself in chapter 5. So when it says to teach "these words" (Deut. 6:6) most certainly the Ten Commandments would be in mind. It is easy to focus on teaching our children the Ten Commandments because they are outwardly observable behaviors. But let us not overlook the importance of teaching our children to love the Lord with all their hearts, souls, and strength (verse 5; Matt. 22:37, 38). The two are directly connected. If we teach our children to love God with all their hearts, then obeying the Ten Commandments will be a demonstration of their love. But if we teach them to obey the Ten Commandments without teaching them to love God, we're in danger of raising legalistic children, who may rebel against the commandments because they don't love the One who wrote them. Love for God will lead our children to obey God's ten commandments.

If we're going to teach our children to obey God's law, we ought to be obeying it ourselves. If we try teaching our kids to obey God's law by telling them "Do as I say, not as I do"—we will fail in teaching them to obey God. Our example in spiritual things is huge in the eyes of our children. If they see us being spiritually lazy, not going to church, not reading our Bibles or praying, and breaking God's law—they will wonder why they should go to church, why they should read their Bibles and pray, and why they should keep God's law.

The text says we need to teach them more than a short family worship in the morning and evening—we need to teach them to love Him and obey Him throughout the daily routines of life, at work, at play, at meals. God and His Word should influence us all throughout the day.

Father, please help us teach our children to love You, and because they love You, they will want to keep Your commandments.

Jared Miller

No Fear

For I am the Lord your God who takes hold of your right hand and says to you, Do not fear; I will help you. Isa. 41:13.

I woke startled, my heart beating fast. Looking around, I realized I was only dreaming. I fell back on my pillow, my heart still pounding with fear. A few days earlier I had happened to look out my window and saw two sets of footprints in the snow that covered the icy pond. I looked again, not wanting to believe what I saw. My heart stopped as I realized those footprints were made by my two little boys. I ran outside calling their names, and heard them reply, "We're over here, Mommy." I saw them peek around the huge maple tree. My first reaction was to yell, "What were you thinking? You could have died!" But I quickly asked God to give me wisdom to deal wisely with the situation.

My boys have always lived on water. They know the rules, and they're usually really careful to obey them. I was shocked by their disobedience. I called them inside and quietly asked them to explain why they had gone out on the ice. As they explained, the sight of their sweet faces tore at my heart. They'd seen our dog walk on the ice and thought they weighed less than the dog and figured it would be OK for them to follow him. I shuddered to think how it could have turned out, and realized how much our little ones need us.

I sat them down and through tears told them how serious the situation was, and that I needed to trust them to obey. They got the message and felt sincere remorse. How I thanked God for their guardian angels and for sparing their lives that day. That walk across the frozen pond could well have been their last one.

As parents we can do the same thing with the Lord. He has our best interest at heart. The boundaries and rules He has given are to help preserve us. He set them in place because He loves us. Just as our children need us, we need the Lord.

Dear Lord, may I not forget that I need You as much as my children need me. Thank You for watching over them and keeping them safe.

Tami Faudi

Flying Kites

The earth is the Lord's, and everything in it, the world,
and all who live in it. Ps. 24:1.

Words often fail to express the joy a mother feels as she holds her newborn in her arms for the first time. It has been almost 40 years since I had this experience, and I still remember how my heart was filled to bursting with love for this little creation of God—His gift to us!

For many parents, having a child brings a heavy sense of responsibility as well as an awesome opportunity to shape the child into what God wants them to be. Unfortunately, many parents attempt to shape their children to fulfill their own unfulfilled dreams. This was never God's intention for parenting.

Children are entrusted to their parents for a small window of time—parents are God's stewards. The responsibility lies with the parents to bring up their children to know and love God as their heavenly Father.

I liken parenting to flying a kite. God hands us the kite that represents our children. He says to us, "Help Me fly this kite just for a while." So we help to launch the kite, holding the string close to us. The younger the child, the closer parents need to hold them, keeping in mind that they are His stewards to disciple the little ones for Jesus. As they grow older, like a kite flying higher and higher—catching the wind—we have to keep letting out more and more string so that the kite can reach greater heights.

Then one day God says, "Hand Me back the string; the kite is Mine, and I will now fly it." When that happens, parents have to learn to let go, step aside, and let God take over. This is not an easy task; it may be painful, but children come to a point in life when they need to launch out on their own. That is when we need to remind ourselves that God loves our children far more than we love them. When the time comes for children to leave the nest, parents need to respect their privacy and independence while staying available should they need our help. From then on, they return to God's safe hands; our role is to intercede for them each and every day.

Father, while my children are still so young, help me hold them close and teach them of Your love. Give me wisdom to know when to let the kite fly higher, trusting always that they are in Your hands.

Sally Lam-Phoon

Look to the Rock

Listen to me, you who look for righteousness,
you who seek the Lord: Look to the rock from which you
were cut and to the quarry where you were dug. Isa. 51:1, CEB.

Not very long ago I decided I wanted to write a story about my ancestors who came to America from Sweden. I wanted to tell about how they lived their lives and how they carved out a future for themselves and their descendants in the New Country. I had grown up hearing how upright, moral, and sincere they were in their behavior, long before they even became Seventh-day Adventists.

One of my favorite stories was about the trans-Atlantic crossing my great-great-grandmother embarked on when she was only 17 years old. All the lower-class immigrants were jammed together in one of the cargo holds of the ship. There was no division of men and women—which meant no privacy. In order to maintain her modesty, my great-great-grandmother would pin a sheet around her bunk when changing her clothes. My great-great-grandfather was on the same ship, and even though they'd never met, he took notice of her modesty and determined that he wanted to be married to the young woman who had such a virtuous character.

In today's world, raising our children to have high standards of morality and virtue can seem an impossible challenge for parents. This becomes even more challenging if we grew up with less-than-stellar examples to follow. That's why I love Isaiah's counsel to look to "the rock" from which we are cut. God Himself formed us and placed His laws in our hearts. If we follow His example, and teach our children to do the same, even those who do not know Christ will take notice.

Father, thank You for giving us Jesus—the perfect example to follow. Please help us to be remember the Rock from which we were cut—to be imitators of You and to teach our children to be the same. In Your strength may we be good examples for our children to follow.

Asheley Woodruff

Learning to Love

*My dear friends, we must love each other. Love comes from God,
and when we love each other, it shows that we have been given new life.
We are now God's children, and we know him. 1 John 4:7, CEV.*

I stepped out onto the porch of our quaint holiday cottage. The sun was just rising above the lake, and a sense of peace came over my soul as I looked at the majestic mountains in the distance. Slipping back to bed, I hoped to catch a few extra minutes of sleep, but soon my two preschoolers jumped into bed and began to argue about who was going to snuggle closest to Mommy. A minute later their daddy dived under the blankets, and squeals of laughter filled the air.

Unfortunately it soon turned sour. A simple conversation somehow turned into an argument. Jaws were clenched, eyebrows creased in anger, as our voices grew louder and louder. We had forgotten there were two little ones in our bed. They looked puzzled when their father charged out of the room in a fury and left to watch TV in the other room.

Two interesting things happened shortly after our ridiculous squabble. Our children immediately started to fight with each other. And then my stubborn husband came into the bedroom, with our two screaming children, as his stubborn wife gave him an icy glare. But ever so gently, he spoke to our children, and explained to them that we'd done wrong. As he held my hands while speaking, my heart softened. We were sorry for what we'd done and said, and apologized to each other and to our children.

In *Child Guidance* we read how "children imitate their parents, hence great care should be taken to give them correct models" (p. 215). "Fathers and mothers, you are teachers; your children are the pupils. Your tones of voice, your deportment, your spirit, are copied by your little ones" *(ibid.).* As parents, we demonstrate to our children what it means to be a disciple. With God's help, let's commit to being the best disciple makers possible.

Dear Lord, thank You for forgiving us when we mess up. Please help us show our children what it means to follow You. Thank You, Lord.

Olivia Bomester

Inquiring Minds Want to Know

After three days they found him in the temple courts,
sitting among the teachers, listening to them
and asking them questions. Luke 2:46.

He was born asking questions," I sighed to my husband. We'd just answered another set of imaginative questions from our 7-year-old son, Donnie. We weren't sure if he was just a creative thinker, or bent on exasperating us. "Why" wasn't his first word, but it quickly followed "Mama" and "Dada." Most of the time his questions were an attempt at gaining knowledge.

One winter day Donnie lay back in a dental chair, having his teeth cleaned for the first time. We sat in the waiting room, listening as he pelted the student hygienist with questions. The dentist was a close friend. He came into the waiting room, grinning.

"He's really testing Kristie's knowledge." Buddy laughed. I sighed and stood up to quiet Donnie, but was stopped by my friend. "Leave him alone. He's just doing his job."

His job? Yes, questions helped children learn and acquire knowledge, but I had never looked at it as a "job" before.

There have been hard questions along the way, some that were not answerable because of age appropriateness. One day, while I was cleaning, one of those questions came up. I prayed silently, asking for an appropriate answer. I stopped cleaning and called Donnie to me.

"Would you push the piano over a few feet so I can vacuum under it?" His 7-year-old body didn't contain the strength needed for the job. He tried. He pushed with all his might.

"It's too heavy for me, Mommy!" He looked up at me with the saddest brown eyes. I scooped him up and tossed him on the couch, then settled in beside him.

"I know, honey. And sometimes the answers to certain questions are too hard for us to understand. We have to wait until we are bigger. Then the answers will make sense." Those brown eyes lit with understanding. The questions never stopped. But neither did his learning.

Please give us the patience we need, Lord, to help teach our precious children so they can learn about their world, and about You.

Kimberley Tagert-Paul

The Importance of Godly Parenting

Her children rise up and call her blessed;
her husband also, and he praises her. Prov. 31:28, NKJV.

Parents play a critical role in shaping the characters of their children. Mothers play an especially important role in the spiritual lives of their children. Having a godly mother makes all the difference in a child's life. The Bible reminds us often of the important role of a mother. Jesus was always loving and tender with Mary, His earthly mother. God chose her to be the mother of His Son, knowing that she was a godly woman who would raise Him with Holy Spirit guidance. Even when He was in excruciating pain, hanging on a cross, Jesus thought about the needs of His mother. Being a good mother is often a difficult job and requires an extra measure of unselfishness. The expression "a mother's work is never done" is so true, because a child never outgrows the need for their mother. The needs may change, but even adults benefit from a mother's unconditional love.

Fathers also play a critical role in the lives of their children. God has given them the sobering responsibility of being the spiritual leader and head of the home. Boys as well as girls need the love of their father. Just as Christ taught by example, so should earthly fathers lead by example. The apostle Paul says in Ephesians 6:4, "Fathers, do not irritate and provoke your children to anger [do not exasperate them to resentment], but rear them [tenderly] in training and discipline and the counsel *and* admonition of the Lord" (Amplified).

God expects parents to lovingly train their children and prepare their hearts for heaven. There is no other job on earth more important or more rewarding. Parents should set aside special prayer time each day specifically to ask God for wisdom, discernment, and Holy Spirit guidance so they may teach their children to love Jesus as their personal Savior and share with others the good news of Jesus' soon return.

Dear Lord, please be with parents who may feel overwhelmed by the responsibilities that come with parenthood. May they turn to You for strength, courage, and joy as they seek to lead their little ones to You.

Brenda Walsh

Leading by Example

Follow my example, as I follow the example of Christ. 1 Cor. 11:1.

I've always been amused by the relative ease I feel in witnessing to a stranger far from my home. The closer I get to home, the harder it is to share my Christian experience with others. My neighbors have a better chance of finding out if there is a mismatch between my words and my actions than does someone I will never meet again.

I still might be able to fool the neighbors, but I can't be a fake Christian in my own house. My kids will see through me in a minute. And as uncomfortable and humbling as it is to have them up in my business all the time, I am grateful for the call to authenticity. Having children definitely drives me to Christ!

When my wife was pregnant with our first child, I was sharing my apprehensions about becoming a parent with a friend. My friend gave me some profound advice: You can count on making mistakes as a parent. You will not be able to prevent your children from getting hurt, and sometimes you will be the cause of the hurt. The best thing you can do for your children is give them tools for dealing with hurt. Show them how a Christian handles problems. Model for them humility, show them how to say "I'm sorry," and teach them how to lovingly confront someone who has wronged them.

I want to be the best parent I can be. Unfortunately I am not perfect. But, by God's grace, I am able to talk with my children about my mistakes. I tell them that Daddy is supposed to be obedient to God, just like they are supposed to be obedient to me. Sometimes I am disobedient even though I love God and want to please Him. When I do wrong I tell God I am sorry and ask Him for help. And then I get to model for them the most important lesson I hope to teach my children. They get to see firsthand that God really does help. Jesus changes lives.

Lord Jesus, please help my children to see and learn about You from the way I live my life.

Ryan Ashlock

The Little Missionary

And there were many in Israel with leprosy in the time of Elisha the prophet, yet not one of them was cleansed—only Naaman the Syrian. Luke 4:27.

Naaman was commander of the Syrian army, which had defeated Israel. They captured a little girl, who became the servant of Naaman's wife—far from home, she had no contact with her anguished parents. But they had taught her well.

Naaman developed leprosy, but, highly regarded by the king, he kept his position. He was also humble enough to accept his servants' advice. Even this child could tell him, through his wife, of Elisha the prophet. She could have said, "He deserves this," but she was filled with God's love, and knew that His blessings were not limited to Israel.

With no idea where God might use her, this girl's parents had taught her to love, trust, and obey them and God—and that nothing is impossible with God. They had prepared her well.

Her testimony reached King Benhadad. Her confidence in Elisha's God led him to send Naaman to the prophet. He gave Naaman a letter to Israel's king, probably Ahab's son Joram, apparently assuming he controlled the gods and prophets in his kingdom. Naaman also took gold and silver worth about $6 million today, indicating the intensity of his desire for healing.

The girl's faith had inspired faith in Naaman and Benhadad, but the Israelite king showed none. He assumed evil motives and became angry. But Elisha heard of it and sent his servant with instructions to wash in the Jordan River seven times. Naaman's faith wavered at this point, but again he listened to his servants, humbled himself, and obeyed—and was healed. Returning to Elisha, he said, "Now I know that there is no God in all the world except in Israel."

This little girl started a chain response that led to Naaman's healing and brought knowledge of God to Syria's highest leaders. And if we instill the gospel commission in our children, we have no idea how far their influence may reach.

Dear heavenly Parent, who has promised to guide all of us earthly parents, help us to rightly represent You to our children, to teach them early to follow Your principles, and to lead them into a personal relationship with You.

Madeline Steele Johnson

Our Children Can Call Us Blessed

*She speaks with wisdom, and on her tongue there is tender instruction.
She keeps a close eye on the conduct of her family,
and she does not eat the bread of idleness. Her children and her husband
stand up and bless her. Prov. 31:26-28, GW.*

I love the following quote from *Sons and Daughters of God*: "In rightly training and molding the minds of her children, mothers are entrusted with the greatest mission ever given to mortals" (p. 252).

In training my children, I often felt like the odd man out when I would make a decision not to do some of the things my friends and church family seemed to do with ease. Because I wrestled with a desperate addiction with watching movies, I never felt comfortable introducing my children to something that I had struggled so hard to overcome. I didn't want to introduce them to harmful—or even distracting—things that would stay in their minds for a lifetime.

Today I praise the Lord when I see them now, as young adults who love to read their Bibles. It is something they are naturally drawn toward. It forms the foundation of their lives.

Great was my joy when just the other day I received flowers through Netflorist. It was a beautiful arrangement of sunflower buds, not quite unopened. When I read the card my heart was filled with praise to the Lord. My youngest son, who had a birthday the following day, had sent it me. The card read, "I just want to thank you from the bottom of my heart for the way you reared me, with the life skills, values, principles, and everything else, but most of all, thank you for teaching us about God. I chose sunflowers because of the sunshine I am able to bring to others because of you, Mom."

This was the best bouquet I had ever held in my hands! The sunshine we bring into our children's lives can truly return unto us after many years. "Train up a child in the way he should go, and when he is old he will not depart from it" (Prov. 22:6, NKJV).

Thank You, Lord, for the guidance You give us as parents when we diligently seek it. We praise You for the blessings our children become as a result of their upbringing. You, Lord, are the perfect parent!

Elario Belita Coombs Fortune

The Fire of the Spirit

Behold, God works all these things, twice,
in fact, three times with a man, to bring back his soul from the Pit,
that he may be enlightened with the light of life. Job 33:29, 30, NKJV.

I find life is like splitting wood. Sometimes we are perfectly shaped logs on the outside, but God must teach us how, through His transforming grace, to split off the sinful layers so He can ignite the fire of His Spirit within us.

I recently ordered three cords of wood that didn't come sufficiently split. They came in rounds that were the right length for the stove, but without being properly split they would not burn or ignite easily.

My dad is quite experienced at chopping wood and enjoys splitting it, but I figured three cords were a bit much for him to chop and split by himself at the tender age of 87. I asked him to teach me the best technique for splitting wood. It didn't start well. I struggled to find the rhythm of the motion and had to adjust to the strength it takes to split a round block of wood. After a while the rhythm and strength started to flow, and I was able to work with more precision and accuracy.

It works the same way with children. The more persistent they are in learning a task, the easier it will become for them. Children learn best when parents guide them through the mistakes and encourage them to get back up and try again.

Too often, because of the barriers we've put in place because of past mistakes, we struggle to let God's Spirit shine through us. Once we turn to Him with a willing, teachable heart, God will come with a sharp ax and start removing the outer layers of our selfish and sinful nature. It may hurt; in fact, it usually does. But He is a tender craftsman. As the layers come off, we become soft enough to be ignited by the fire of the Holy Spirit, sharing the light of His love with the world around us.

Thank You, Father, for not giving up on Your children and persistently seeking to teach us how to shine for You.

Wanda L. Davis

Seeing His Face in the Stars

So all of us who have had that veil removed can see and reflect the glory of the Lord. And the Lord—who is the Spirit—makes us more and more like him as we are changed into his glorious image. 2 Cor. 3:18, NLT.

My middle child and I lay with our heads pressed together on the pillow cherishing the rare, uninterrupted time. Our hearts reached out to each other as we talked of God. The Milky Way sparkled above us, the Big Dipper was trying to catch the sun that had disappeared over the mountain, and a shooting star darted by.

This creative child asked question after question regarding the Lord and our lives. Many times I had to say, "I don't know; we'll have to ask when we get to heaven." After another round of questions I could not answer, she gazed silently upward, then cuddling closer, she said, "Oh, never mind; I'll ask God when I get there." I felt grateful my little 7-year-old worrier felt confident of her heavenly destination.

"Actually," she interrupted my thoughts, "I sometimes think I won't have to ask God anything . . ." another star-loaded pause, ". . . sometimes I think that when I see His face I will understand sooo much! I think when I look at Him, I will be able to see so many things and I'll just, you know, see the answers."

My stunned mind regarded the wonder of that statement. Who in the world could come up with a thought like that? How did she decide that God's face was so full of information?

Her little starlit sermon continued. "I mean, really, Mommy, remember that lady that was so sick and all she had to do was touch His robe? I mean, if just touching His robe could do so much, can you imagine what looking on His face will do for us?"

Again silence reigned. For her, the silence was about snuggling and stargazing. For me, it was about wonder, love, and the absolute knowledge that we do, indeed, need to become as little children to understand the complete awesomeness of God.

Father God, help us to seek Your face and to trust You with all the answers.

Carol Bovee

My Example

And you yourself must be an example to them
by doing good works of every kind. Titus 2:7, NLT.

I have always known the example I set to my children is very important. It's been said that we should be like the person we want our children to become. Sometimes this idea hits home more strongly than others. Just this morning my son, in a very simple yet profound way, helped me to realize again that my children are watching me and will tend to become like me.

We were just sitting down for breakfast. Being an oatmeal-loving family, we don't venture off that menu too often. This morning, however, we were having biscuits and gravy. My daughter wasn't quite sure if she should leave the biscuits whole and put the gravy over them, or if she should first break them into pieces. After voicing her dilemma, my 7-year-old son came to the rescue and said, "Just do what Mama does." And that's exactly what all three of my children did—just as Mama did.

Silently I contemplated that idea for a moment. My example was helpful when it came to choosing whether or not to break up biscuits, but even more important, my example serves as their guide to becoming like Jesus. They are watching me even when I don't realize it—even when they don't realize it. By observing my behavior, they are learning what to do, what to say, how to react, and how to treat others. What example will I give them? Only God can give me the strength and the wisdom to be the kind of godly example I want to be for my children. Only God can fill me daily with His Spirit and enable me to walk as Jesus walked so that my children can have that chance as well.

Lord, help me to be the example I should be so that my children will become who You've created them to be. Help them to see You in my actions, hear You in my words, and learn by my example just how much they are loved by You. May they in turn become examples to those around them of Your love and grace.

Amy Austin

Raising Little Princes and Princesses

*I have known him, in order that he may command his children
and his household after him, that they keep the way of the Lord,
to do righteousness and justice, that the Lord may bring to Abraham
what He has spoken to him. Gen. 18:19, NKJV.*

God calls every parent to command their children in the way of the Lord. It is a fact: parents cannot train their child's every step, but they can set their feet in the right direction. We help our children shape their characters, instilling in them the moral values by which they shall live, even in the most adverse circumstances. We must teach our children of the honor they have in belonging to the King of kings, train them to conduct themselves as little princes and princesses awaiting their introduction into the kingdom one day.

We need to learn the art of turning the hearts of our children toward the heavenly kingdom, that they may have a greater motivation to resist the temptations of this world. We must instill in our children's hearts the everlasting principles of heaven, repeating to them again and again that their citizenship is in heaven, where Jesus lives. Their character is the only thing they will take to heaven with them.

In France Louis XVI was dethroned and imprisoned. His son, the little prince, was exposed to every vile and filthy thing. His jailers used dirty language and crude ways to debase him, trying to coerce him into shaping his life according to these influences. But the little lad did not yield to these temptations. When he was asked why he would not enjoy all the amusements that were offered to him, his simple yet resolute reply was: "I cannot do what you ask. I was born to be a king."

Parents, we are all journeying toward the heavenly kingdom—princes and princesses, charged with the duty to prepare our little princes and princesses for the kingdom of God. Let the King of kings continue to empower us as we faithfully fulfill our parenting duty.

Father God, we thank You for the blessing of parenthood. Teach us how to fulfill our duty. Help us to teach our children to keep Your way even in the most adverse circumstances.

Nephtaly Dorzilme

The Hermit Crab

*In all your ways acknowledge Him,
and He shall direct your paths. Prov. 3:6, NKJV.*

When my children were small our neighbor gave them a hermit crab to thank them for watching over her garden while she was on vacation. Its shell had been painted with yellow and orange flames over a coat of dark blue. They left the crab in a box on the floor in front of the air conditioner. I was afraid it would be too cold for the hermit crab, so I set the box on our front porch before I went to bed. The next day was Sabbath, and when we woke, it was to discover that the hermit crab had escaped its box.

We searched the porch and couldn't find it. Truthfully, it could have been anywhere. We have a flower garden in front of our porch. In front of flowers big rocks lead toward a huge grassy area that slopes down to the road. The crab could have fallen between the rocks or be headed toward the road, for all we knew.

All day long we looked for the hermit crab, praying we would find it. Toward evening my daughter was sitting on our back steps looking sad. I asked her if she wanted me to pray with her again, and she said yes. I asked God to show us His glory by showing us where the hermit crab was. When we finished praying, she said she was going back into the house. I went in also to get a flashlight and started searching the front yard with my son. He eventually got tired of looking and began walking back to the house, and I followed him, still shining the flashlight back and forth.

All of a sudden, in the beam of the flashlight, I noticed something under the grass, something dark blue with orange and yellow flames. What a miracle! In the dark of the night, in the beam of a flashlight, under the grass, on a big front lawn, the Lord directed my path and helped me find a tiny hermit crab.

Thank You, Lord, for the knowledge that You love my children as much as I do, for caring about the little things that mean so much to them. Thank You for showing them Your love.

Deborah Marschner

Gentle Instruction

Fathers, do not irritate and provoke your children to anger
[do not exasperate them to resentment], but rear them
[tenderly] in the training and discipline and the counsel
and admonition of the Lord. Eph. 6:4, Amplified.

When a father heeds this verse concerning his children, it means a lot. One thing a father should not do is tease his children to the point that they become angry and exasperated, which may cause them to become resentful. Instead, he needs to rear them tenderly.

According to Webster's dictionary, to "rear" means "to erect by building, construct, to raise upright; to bring to maturity or self-sufficiency usually through nurturing." Some men may see this kind of warmth as a weakness, yet Jesus gave us the perfect example of what it means to be a man: patient and gentle. As we allow, He tenderly trains and builds our character.

While shopping one day, I turned down an aisle to see a dad supervising his young son and daughter as they did push-ups. I thought this was a creative way to discipline kids in the store instead of yelling at them in front of other shoppers. The kids didn't seem to mind, and they got the point that their behavior wasn't acceptable.

In her book *In My Father's House* Corrie ten Boom tells the story of when she was young and touched the cold hand of a baby who had died in a neighbor's home. Fear filled her, and she thought the adults would think she was being silly if she told them of her fear. That night her papa read from Psalm 46:2: "Therefore we will not fear" (NKJV). She went on to say, "My faith in Papa, and in the words he read from the Bible, was absolute. If they said not to fear, then God would take care of it. I felt secure again."

Life is full of opportunities to train and teach in tenderness. Remember that kids struggle and need encouragement as much as we do. Jesus taught us to respect children, and to become like them—"trusting, lowly, loving, forgiving"—not childish but childlike (Matt. 18:3, Amplified).

The way we treat our children will help train them to be tender and thoughtful with others, not only while they are young, but also in the years that lie ahead.

Father God, help us to be tender and gentle in training and correcting our children.

Claudia LeCoure

I Will Make You Fishers of Men

"Come, follow me," Jesus said, "
and I will send you out to fish for people." Matt. 4:19.

We're all familiar with the Chinese proverb "Give a man a fish, and you feed him for a day. Teach a man how to fish, and you'll feed him for a lifetime." It is a concept that teaches the value of training someone to be self-sufficient rather than being continually reliant on others. But how do you teach a person to become a "fisher of men," resulting in blessings not only for the here and now but also for eternity?

When we teach our children how to be disciples for Jesus it is natural for them to want to "go and tell" others about Jesus. Children love to run and tell others about something that excites them. They can naturally become our sweet bearers of good news, and as parents, we should be diligent to cultivate this tendency and encourage our children to love and serve humanity—as Jesus did.

Of course, it's easier to do this if we are modeling the "fisher-of-men" principle in our own lives. In our talk and by our example we can daily demonstrate to our children the importance of sharing Jesus with others. If it's something that excites us, it will excite them also; sharing Jesus can become contagious. When we turn our children's gaze upon their Creator they will instinctively run to share their excitement about their Friend Jesus with others. There are few more powerful or compelling ways to share the gospel than to hear the story of Jesus from little ones who love Him with such purity.

The more closely we follow Christ, the more closely our children will pattern their behavior after ours. By our example we will have furthered the kingdom by forming little followers for Jesus.

Dear Father, thank You for choosing me to help lead my children to You. Please help me to teach my children to follow my example, as I follow the example of Christ.

Jocelyn D. Zvosechz

Sweeter Than Honey

Sweeter also than honey and the drippings of the honeycomb. Ps. 19:10, ASV.

As parents, as Christians, we talk about getting into the Word and the importance of reading our Bibles. But how do your children see this acted out in your life? Is it just talk? Or do they see you with your Bible, absorbed with reading God's Word? More important, what is their perception of His Word as it relates to them? Do they know that the Bible is for them too, or is it just for the grown-ups?

For Christmas my five children received brand-new Bibles from their grandparents. For the younger ones, it was their very first real Bible, and they were all extremely excited. Personal devotional time is something we value and put on our daily schedule for our children, and they had been reading Bible story books, since those are easier for them to understand. After receiving their own Bibles, though, there was only one question from five different voices. "Mommy, can we read our new Bibles?"

I'll be honest. My first reaction was to say no. After all, if they were to get the Bibles out every evening, they would probably get worn and torn and wrinkled very quickly. We want to teach our children to respect the Word, right? That it is holy, special, and to be treated with respect and reverence. But if that is all we are teaching them, will they inadvertently learn that the Bible shouldn't be touched?

Thankfully God spoke to me in that moment. I didn't want my children to be afraid of getting into the Word and making it their own because they wanted to keep the Book itself from getting ruined. So I told them yes. The excitement was palpable. They got out their Bibles with such joy and anticipation that it made me want to get mine out too. So I did. And we read together. There is nothing like eating up the Word with your children and watching them devour it. What joy to watch them discover that God's Word is sweeter than honey.

Lord, may I teach my children that Your Word exists for building a living relationship with You. That it is sweeter than honey.

Elizabeth Fresse

Better Than Gold

They are more desirable than gold, yes, than much fine gold. Ps. 19:10, NASB.

My children were so excited about reading their new Bibles. Even my 4-year-old was trying to sound out words so he could read verses along with his siblings. Knowing that guidance would help it become more meaningful, I got out my Bible and we turned to different passages together. That was when then they noticed that my Bible contained some very colorful sections. They were fascinated and wanted to know what it meant.

"What's that, Mommy? Why is that red?" I explained that I had highlighted passages special to me, promises, or reminders of how to follow God. They were intrigued. Since I had received a brand-new set of Bible-marking pens not that long before, I had a few extra. I gave each child one marking pen and showed them how to use it. You would have thought I'd handed them a brick of gold!

That was the beginning. While much parental guidance is still required, I love seeing my children search for gems to highlight in the Word of God. Each night I'll show them one or two that I have chosen, and we discuss what the verses mean and how we can each apply them to our lives. I let them decide if they want to highlight a verse or not—I want it to be personal for them. They are also welcome to come to me at any point and ask if it is all right for them to highlight a verse they found. Their whole Bible would be highlighted if I didn't require this from my little ones!

The increased level of excitement has been amazing. They have been claiming promises and highlighting and applying verses to their lives like I've never seen children do before. It is a pattern and a habit I hope to nurture in them so that it will continue to grow and never die.

God, thank You for the inspiration to get our children excited about Your Word. We pray that You would help them, and us as well, to really understand and internalize the truth that Your Word really is sweeter than honey, more precious than gold, and a priceless treasure worth digging into.

Elizabeth Fresse

September

The Fruit of the Spirit

Crazy Discipling

Go to the people of all nations and make them my disciples. Matt. 28:19, CEV.

Have you heard of it? It's the place millions go for a hot drink and good fellowship. It's called Starbucks, and it's popular because it provides a warm place in a cold world. Starbucks CEO Howard Schultz said, "What's gratifying is that we were determined not to allow the outside world to define the company's future." The apostle Paul said something similar: "Don't let the world around you squeeze you into its own mould" (Rom. 12:2, Phillips). So there's the world's mold and there's the Christian's mold. Ellen White says, "The world is crazy after show and fashion and pleasure" (*Testimonies for the Church*, vol. 4, p. 646). Christian parents have a different crazy. We are commissioned to make disciples—and to start with our own family.

First, that means we must bear the fruit of the Spirit. Parents are called to be disciplined models. Our single-minded goal must be to reproduce the character of Jesus in ourselves, so we can lead by example.

Second, it means to make disciples for Jesus. This means that parents are called to be disciple makers. As a toddler, Kristle would sit faithfully during potty training. After 10 minutes she would stand up, point to the empty potty, and triumphantly declare, "Nuffin' in there." When Jesus came looking at a certain fig tree for fruit, He found "nothing but leaves" (Mark 11:13). In other words, nuffin' in there. Our singular focus must be to reproduce the image of Jesus in our children, because God is looking for something. He's looking for children He can recognize, because they look like His Son.

So does your son look like His Son? What about your daughter? It's not too late. Through prayer, you can "still bring forth fruit in old age" (Ps. 92:14, KJV). Just remember, whatever character you want them to have—first model it yourself.

Dear Lord, parenting is crazy—and we love it. Thank You for the assurance that if You've called us to it, You'll see us through it.

Jeffrey O. Brown

Someone Spilled the Beans

Then our mouth was filled with laughter and
our tongue with joyful shouting; then they said among the nations,
"The Lord has done great things for them." Ps. 126:2, NASB.

One summer, when our sons were still young, we were enjoying dinner at my parents' place when someone passed a large dish of green beans to my dad. He didn't have a good hold of it, and it slipped out of his hands, upside down, into his lap. The beans were hot. I had no idea my dad could dance like that!

As Mom got towels and started mopping up the juice, someone came with a dustpan and began scooping up the beans, while Dad did the hokey pokey, dribbling bean juice down the hall to change clothes.

When everyone returned to the table to resume the meal, our youngest boy broke the silence with an insightful comment. "I'm glad it wasn't me who dropped the beans," he observed, "or I would sure have got in trouble." Unfortunately, he was probably right. But that event helped remind me how important it is to distinguish between an accident and a rebellious spirit in dealing with my kids. Accidents are part of being human; that reality needs to temper my response.

Is it always going to be deliriously happy around your house? As the kids say, "Whatever!" Actually, I prefer the word "joyous" to "happy," anyway. "Happy" is related to "happen," and it most accurately describes the attitude of one who is affected by what happens around them. True joy, on the other hand, is not affected by circumstances. Not by wealth or poverty, not by sickness or health. Not even by spilled beans.

Our kids are helped as much by watching their parents' joyous, unflappable attitude as they are by about anything we do. Remember, joy is contagious.

O Lord, help us to see the funny side of life and not be weighed down by unnecessary burdens. May Your joy in us be contagious, not only within our families, but within our churches and our communities.

Don Jacobsen

Patience for the Road

Be patient with each other, making allowance for each other's faults because of your love. Eph. 4:2, NLT.

I often ask God for more patience. Instead of answering the way I want Him to, with an instant injection of this virtue, He simply provides more opportunities to exercise patience. This often happens during the drive to Grandma's house. Imagine three and a half hours on the road with a 3-year-old, an 18-month-old, and a wife who is not fond of the interstate.

Things usually go well until the last hour of the trip. By this time the kids are tired of songs and imagination games. My wife is tired of the monotonous scenery. I'm tired of not being there yet. It only goes downhill after that: the van is too hot, the kids are hungry, the traffic is too slow—Murphy's Law gone wild! At this point I can scream, or I can grip the steering wheel and whisper a prayer. I choose the latter.

No matter how difficult things get, I can't turn around. The destination is Grandma's house. Nothing else will do. So amid the temperature issues, fatigue, and family irritation I must press on. By the time we arrive and get settled no one talks about how long or tiring the trip was. The only thing that matters is that we made it.

When I ask God to take the wheel of my life, I wonder how much I put Him through. How often do I complain that the journey is too hot, or not exciting enough, or that I want a different scene? There's always something to irritate me or to make me wish I hadn't chosen to commit to the journey. In spite of it all, God is patient with me. He knows that anything less than the destination He has for me will not do. He drives. I do my best to trust and believe. I try hard not to ask, "Are we there yet?"

If God can be patient with me on my spiritual journey, at the very least, I can be more patient with my family on the road to Grandma's house. Or any other place that we travel together.

Lord, thank You for being patience with us on our journey with You. Grant us the willingness to extend patience to others.

Pierre Quinn

Love for the Least of These

*Truly I tell you, whatever you did
for one of the least of these . . . , you did for me. Matt. 25:40.*

My protective nature as a father is on display most with my children, especially for my daughters. I was spending some quality time with my daughter Gracie one afternoon. She was only 7 years old, and I was still the "man of her life."

As we drove, Gracie was sharing stories from school—she loved her friends, her teachers, and almost everything about her life. I asked her, "You like almost everything?" Gracie struggled to get her thoughts together, and she said, "Yes, Papa, except there is this one boy . . ."

Instantly I was on the defensive. My mind pictured a 7-year-old boy taking her attention away from me. No way! *Just wait until I give that little boy . . .* Before I could finish my thought Gracie brought me back to reality.

"His name is Jeffry, and he doesn't have any friends, and I try to be as nice to him as I can. I think he feels very lonely, Papa."

My heart melted that day. I was reminded that Jesus tells us to love "the least of these." At only 7, my child was able to have compassion for a boy who had no friends. Not only was I proud of her, but I knew Jesus would be proud, too.

How often do I pass by people who need a friend? Someone who might need a helping hand? Or someone who might need a smile? Most adults have learned to filter out the Jeffry's of this world. We look for people who are like us or who can offer something.

I stopped the car that day, choked back a few tears, and looked Gracie in the eye and said, "Gracie, you are a very good friend. Jesus is so happy when you reach out to people like Jeffry. Thank you for reminding me of that."

Father, thank You so much for loving me, even though I make many mistakes. I am grateful for Your love. Remind me to look for those who need to be loved the way You love me. Help me to teach this to my children and never to think that anyone is beyond the reach of Your love.

Jason Hanselman

Lead On Softly

In malice be ye children. 1 Cor. 14:20, KJV.

You can't watch giggling children without smiling—even laughing—yourself. Their happiness is contagious; it comes from deep within. Only when a problem comes does their joy dissipate; and yet, only for a short while. Pretty soon they're back to finding happiness.

Young children do not naturally hang on to anger. They don't harbor resentment. They are very forgiving. Even when their will has been crossed or when they have been disciplined, they easily forgive and love.

Perhaps this is why God tells us through the apostle Paul: "In malice be ye children." Malice is not natural to children. Malice is learned from others. It is that meanness, nastiness, cruelty, and hatred that they either witness or experience and, in turn, demonstrate toward others. No, malice is not natural in young children; those who are older and should be wiser teach it to them.

The apostle Paul instructs us to not "provoke" our "children to wrath" (Eph. 6:4, KJV), lest we cause them to become discouraged. Rather, we are to bring them up in the nurture and admonition of the Lord. We are to "lead on softly," such as the children are "able to endure" (Gen. 33:14, KJV).

Imagine a home filled with the laughter of children with parents who lead on softly. What a joyful home it would be; what a magnificent witness for Christ's kingdom. "The greatest evidence of the power of Christianity that can be presented to the world is a well-ordered, well-disciplined family" (*The Adventist Home,* p. 32). "The home then becomes as an Eden of bliss; the family, a beautiful symbol of the family in heaven" (*ibid.,* p. 28).

Father, help me to lead on softly, such as the children can endure, to not provoke my children to anger and to eliminate any hint of malice in my own behavior. May today be a sampling of heaven's joy.

Christine Gillan Byrne

Fear Not

*For God did not give us a Spirit of fear
but of power and love and self-control. 2 Tim. 1:7, NET.*

Parenting is full of challenges. One of the most difficult things parents must face is fear for their children's safety. The what-ifs can drive us crazy. It's hard to trust God with our little ones.

One year, when my daughters were 5, 3, and 1, my extended family met at a rented lake cabin in Wisconsin for a week of vacation. We were working to clean up the cabin on the last day of our trip while the youngest was napping. I sent the older two out of the house and down a short path from the patio, where my dad was cleaning the grill, to a small screen house to play. A moment later I spotted them rounding the path on their way back. I went out and repeated my instructions, ordering them back to the screen house. I didn't want them to be wandering around outside by the water. They went back down the wooded path, but returned again a moment later. Frustrated, I scolded them for not following directions and demanded they stay in the screen house until I came to get them.

They hesitantly started back up the path, but then stopped and turned. "But we are afraid of the snake," my oldest daughter said. My dad and I walked up the path with them and discovered a huge snake coiled on the doorstep of the screen house, hissing and poised to strike.

Hand me the mother-of-the-year award! Trying to keep my children safe, I ordered them into danger—three times! I accused them of disobedience without giving them the chance to explain themselves. I hate to think what could have happened if they hadn't been cautious.

As a parent, I could easily let worry consume me. Every day I must make a conscious choice to commit them into God's capable hands. Make a choice today to reject the fear and worry. Embrace the power, love, and self-control God freely offers through His Spirit in us.

Lord, today I commit my children into Your hands. Please help me to resist fear and show my children how to trust You with all things.

Andrea Michelle Wood

The Red Tractor

Except the Lord build the house, they labour in vain that build it. Ps. 127:1, KJV.

Our eldest son, Pedrito, used to play ball in a minor league. When we went to the games, our other son, Ariel, would not sit down to watch his brother play; he loved to go to one corner of the field where he said he had a car that was his. He used to invite us to visit his favorite corner, but my husband would say to him, "Not today, Ariel, some other day!" And so time went by.

One day, we arrived at the game a little late. My husband parked farther from the field but closer to the spot where Ariel's car was, so he went to see it. It turned out to be an old, abandoned tractor with no motor. It was red, and when the sun hit it, it shone. It was so thrilling for our 7-year-old son to make believe it was his car. He could not take it home because it was too big; he could not drive it because it had no motor. He was a child and even though he was asking his father for help, he could not make the tractor run. But it was entertaining for him to go spend time with "his" car, even for a little while. It was very important to our son that we paid attention and went to see something that was so special to him.

Could it be that when we spend time with our children, they demand less of us? I believe so. This is important in their development, because they feel secure, special, and appreciated.

To our Father in heaven, we are His precious jewels. He is always ready to take care of us whenever we need it. He is always prepared to help us in whichever problem we may have, even if at times He tells us, "Hold on a bit. Now is not the time." It is important that we realize things are better in the Lord's time and not our own.

The red tractor that our son thought so much about didn't have a motor, and so it didn't work. In much the same way, the family needs a motor so things can work well. God must be that motor, and the parents and children should do fine-tuning with God on a daily basis: fed by the Divine Word, daily prayer, understanding, kindness, love, gentleness, serenity, and the fruit of the Spirit. I will assure you, then, that your home will be a piece of heaven on earth.

Lord, be the motor of our homes. Help us to stay fine-tuned!

Alina Careaga

Choosing Priorities

See how very much our Father loves us,
for he calls us his children, and that is what we are! 1 John 3:1, NLT.

I was busy. I did not need interruptions. It had been raining all day and I was finally able to send the kids out to play. I focused on making my lesson plans for the next day. The doorbell rang.

Grrr.

I determined to ignore the sound, and kept typing. The doorbell rang again. I typed more. I had so much to do, and I figured it was the kids playing. No one else rings the doorbell with such frequency!

The bell rang twice more in rapid succession.

Oh! I was perturbed. I stomped to the door, ready to let the kids know I was busy with important things, ready to remind them of their inappropriateness.

There lay a bundle of flowers—no stems, broken, and lying in a beautiful and pathetic little lump on the front step.

Suddenly nothing I was doing was important. And nothing was more beautiful. I picked up the little bunch of mismatched flowers plucked in the prime of their beauty. I carried them inside and gently laid them on the counter, smiling the whole time.

I went back to the door and hollered, "Thank you!" and set off to find those giggling little blessings that were hiding around the corner, waiting to see what Mommy would say, waiting to remind me of my priorities.

O my precious Father, thank You for loving me, one of Your children, even when I'm busy. Thank You for my blessings. Help me to prioritize correctly. Help me to share Your love in such a way that others know *they are important, valued, and loved unconditionally—by me, and by You!*

Carol Bovee

Kindness Counts

*And be kind to one another, tenderhearted,
forgiving one another, even as God in Christ forgave you. Eph. 4:32, NKJV.*

Has kindness ever made your day? On my first international journey I landed in the U.S.A. with no dollars in my pocket, just traveler's checks. Those don't work for renting carts, and I hadn't been able to clear customs and exchange money yet. I was flabbergasted when a fellow traveler whipped out the cash and paid for a cart for me so I could easily move my oversized suitcase, carry-on, and guitar. Her kindness made my day and is remembered 20 years later.

I imagine that the spies never forgot the kindness of Rahab in housing and hiding them; or Elijah, the kindness of the woman of Zarephath who fed the prophet her last morsel; or Samuel, his mother's kindness in bringing him a new cloak every spring.

Jesus Himself took time to be kind to children. "Christ watched children at their play, and often expressed His approval when they gained an innocent victory over something they were determined to do. He sang to children in sweet and blessed words. They knew that He loved them. He never frowned on them. He shared their childish joys and sorrows. Often He would gather flowers, and after pointing out their beauties to the children, would leave them with them as a gift" (*Sermons and Talks*, vol. 2, p. 191).

We parents are just grown-up children, and if kindness means so much to us, how much more to our little ones who have such great needs and wants.

Notice that unkindness to children gets special mention in Mark 9:42: "But whoever causes one of these little ones who believe in Me to stumble, it would be better for him if a millstone were hung around his neck, and he were thrown into the sea" (NKJV). That's pretty serious.

Let God overwhelm you with His kindness today and you will have something to give to others. By God's grace, as you speak kindly to your children, even when you don't feel very kind, they will learn to be truly kind to others as well.

Dear Lord, please fill me up with You today. May I smile and not frown, may I speak kindly and not harshly, and may I show Your love wherever I go.

Heather Krick

Joy in Jogging Home

Therefore, since we are surrounded by so great a cloud of witnesses, let us also lay aside every weight and the sin that clings so closely, and let us run with perseverance the race that is set before us, looking to Jesus the pioneer and perfecter of our faith, who for the sake of the joy that was set before him endured the cross, disregarding its shame, and has taken his seat at the right hand of the throne of God. Heb. 12:1, 2, NRSV.

As my first pregnancy is progressing through the sixth month, my body is changing almost daily. Finding my balance thrown off by the increasing weight in the front, I've started waddling and using handrails! Everything from putting on my shoes to getting out of our little car seems to be a challenge worthy of grunting and puffing. But my midwife reminds me that the labor will be like running a marathon, and I need to continue training for it now. I decided to go to the park.

As I started down the trail listening to hymns through my earphones, I noticed the people around me jogging—but they were different. They were joyful! A family of three passed me running, and the youngest kept glancing back with a precious smile. The beginning of a gorgeous sunset had just started coloring the sky ahead, and the raw coastal beauty just north of San Francisco Bay surrounded us. I was caught up in the spirit and started jogging too! The joy of those around me pressing toward the same goal offset my extra weight, and I too could join in their joy and run freely—with maybe a bit of a waddle.

This is what God has intended Christ's followers to be to the world—an offer of irresistible joy to run home to Jesus! Some can only manage an awkward waddle, but our heart's joy can inspire our neighbors to cast aside their excuses and run for the joy set before them. All the way Jesus jogs before and beside us, our personal trainer ready to pick us up and even carry us when we fall. No matter how small my efforts, as long as I focus on the Light ahead and move forward, I am running with endurance. What an incredible encouragement! There is an end, and I, with God's grace, will get there. In just a few months I will be holding new life in my arms. And someday I will be a new creation in the arms of my Savior. What joy is that prize!

Dear Jesus, help me receive the encouragement You offer from the joy of those around me so that I too will run with endurance and inspire others to run home to You. Thank You.

Jessica Earl

She Touched My Heart by Touching My Face

As you know how we exhorted, and comforted, and charged every one of you, as a father does his own children, that you would walk worthy of God who calls you into His own kingdom and glory. 1 Thess. 2:11, 12, NKJV.

Becoming a parent radically revolutionized my spiritual life. I instantly felt different. Once my daughter London was born and they put her on my chest, my heart swelled. We don't really have a word in the English language to describe what it feels like to become a parent. I'd say "love" but it was something much more than that. It was like love, but mixed with responsibility, duty, and, most of all, anxiety. It was the sense that I had to protect her and provide for her needs. She was crying, so I tried my hardest to console her. I wasn't sure if she was cold, so I pressed her tightly to my chest. When she stopped crying and looked at me, I melted. I tried to sit a little taller, smile a little brighter. I wanted her to look at my face and feel peace.

A beautiful moment happened in my life when she was a month old. While I was nursing London, she put her hand out and touched my face. The rush of emotional energy that I felt was indescribable. For almost a year I had loved this tiny person. Before I even met her my heart grew three times the size just at the realization that she was going to exist. Since then I had been falling madly in love with her and finally, with one touch of her hand—which I understood as an acknowledgment of who I was on her behalf—she made me feel that she loved me back.

This is when it hit me, that this moment, right here, *this* must be what it's like to be Christ. When she touched me and acknowledged me for the first time after all the days, minutes, and hours I'd spent praying and worrying and loving her, I realized this is the closest to Christ I will ever be. I felt connected to Him because I knew that He too knows what it is like to spend all your energy loving someone; elated at the slightest sign and wonderstruck by the tiniest movement forward that could possibly suggest that just maybe, we like Him too.

Lord, thank You for loving me while You were still knitting me together. May I love my children the way my Father first loved me.

Heather Thompson Day

Enjoy the Journey

*At midday, O king, I saw in the way a light from heaven,
above the brightness of the sun, shining round about me
and them which journeyed with me. Acts 26:13, KJV.*

In the past few years my husband and I have been able to visit several Amish communities in Indiana, Ohio, and Pennsylvania. We aren't alone, as thousands of other "English" people (the Amish term for people who aren't Amish) visit these communities as well.

What draws people to spend their vacation time among the people of this unique culture? Could it be the sense of peace that is prevalent among the Amish people and communities? The rhythmic sounds of the horses' hooves pulling the buggies are definitely soothing. Traveling through the farmlands built on rolling hills may bring a sense of calm to weary visitors.

Since most Amish don't allow their pictures to be taken, tourists must be satisfied with the pictures in their memories. Some of my favorite pictures are remembering families slowly riding along in their buggies enjoying one another's company. The joy was evident on their faces as they laughed, smiled, and interacted with one another on their journey. Distractions are seen by the Amish as drawing them away from God and family. For this reason they choose to live their lives as simply as possible and stay close to home.

As we journey on this earth toward heaven we are sometimes overloaded with distractions. I remember as a young parent I sometimes craved a few moments of peace to myself. Certainly those peaceful moments are essential to parenthood. However, I wonder if it's possible to find peace and joy in the journey as we are surrounded by our children. What if we turned off our technology gadgets for just a little while each day and enjoyed the journey more with our children? God will travel with you as you find and treasure those moments with your children, listening to their hearts and laughter.

Lord, thank You for the beautiful blessing of my children. Help me find moments today that belong only to them—to savor their smiles, exclamations, questions, and unconditional love.

Verna Reinbold

God's Day

Fools give full vent to their rage,
but the wise bring calm in the end. Prov. 29:11.

First it was the vase. I had bought it for my mom and saved it as a reminder of loving her. A ball smacked it from the shelf, and it shattered into pieces too small to glue back together. After I reminded my boys that balls were meant for outside, and a time-out in their room, the day went forward.

Next came a call from the doctor. Tests had come back, and I needed to make an appointment. Not the words you want to hear over the phone on a busy day. Or any day.

"Mom!" The word was yelled from the front yard, somewhere up in the maple tree. My sons had been outside for only a minute. The oldest stood at the base of the tree, looking up at where his younger brother was caught on a branch in the middle of the tree.

"Can you help him down?" I asked full of hope and trepidation.

"Why? He did it. I told him not to. But he climbed up there anyways." I was out of words and courage.

Five minutes later, negotiations complete and rescue successful, we went back inside for a break. That's when I found the cat enjoying the lunch I had started preparing.

"What's for lunch?" Two sets of eyes appeared around the corner as the cat jumped down. I looked at the clock. It wasn't even noon. I settled the boys down with a quick lunch, then I took time to pray. What a day, and it had barely started.

"God?" He knew what the day was like. He knew how short my nerves were and how I was doing my best not to lose it and do what I wanted to do: yell at someone. I can't help it! I'm Irish. I love deeply and easily; but I have a quick temper, and this day was shaping up to be a test of my motherly patience. That's when it hit me. Maybe I hadn't asked the right question.

What was God's day like? What had He endured? What antics from His children had He had to deal with? Certainly more than a broken vase, a child stuck in a tree, and a naughty cat. The anger left me, and grace took its place.

Father, thank You that life is full of experiences, and You walk before each one of us. Help us to rein in our tempers as we are reminded that You treat us with Your wonderful grace.

Kimberley Tagert-Paul

When I Am Afraid

*I will always look to you, as you stand beside me and protect me from fear.
With all my heart, I will celebrate, and I can safely rest. Ps. 16:8, 9, CEV.*

Daddy, Daddy, please help me! I am afraid" came the whispered words from that side of our bed. "I had a bad dream."

Our children always went to Daddy's side of the bed for help in the middle of the night. They said, "Mommy always jumps and scares us more when we talk to her." So the tradition became firmly established. They would wake Daddy, and he would wake me.

Together we would cuddle our frightened little one. We would choose a praise song to sing to Jesus. Often it was "Jesus Loves Me" or "My God Loves Me." Then we would pray for God's peace to calm their heart. The next step was to spread a pallet made of a thick quilt next to the side of our bed. We tucked our children into this little bed, covering them with their favorite blanket—always assuring them that Jesus had sent His guardian angel to watch over them.

This same story might repeat itself for the same child more than once, but it never seemed to happen more than three times. Usually after the second time, our little one would come to Daddy's side of the bed and say, "I had a bad dream. Will you help me sing a praise song to Jesus? Let's go to my room."

We knew they had learned Jesus' answer to fear when as part of their conversation at breakfast they would share their experience from the night before: "Mommy, Daddy, I was afraid last night, so I sang to Jesus and prayed for Him to help me. He did, so I went to sleep."

Thinking back on those experiences reminds me of the lesson that I learned from a time when I thought I was teaching. No matter what makes me afraid—finances, a job challenge, or a child's illness—the answer is always in Jesus. Our psalm points us to Him and invites us to celebrate His power to protect us. In the simple acts of singing and prayer we find new assurance of His constant presence. Then we too can sleep as soundly as our babies.

Dear Jesus, help me find my voice of praise for You even in those most difficult moments. May my joy in You bring peace to my heart that reflects in security in my child's life.

Lynn Ripley

A Mother's Gift of Grace

"But where sin increased, grace increased all the more." Rom. 5:20.

One Sabbath afternoon, when I was 12 years old, my parents and I drove to Palouse Falls State Park in Washington. We had been there a few times before, and it was one of the favorite places that occupied our summer Sabbaths as I was growing up. Tables in the shade provided a welcome spot where we could devour the delicious picnic lunch that Mom had prepared. The thunderous roar of the massive falls was an impressive natural wonder to remind us of God's creative power, and there were hiking trails that would lead us to more adventures.

After lunch we set out on a hike leading down to the base of the falls. My feet were nimble and quick, and taking risks was a significant part of my youthful approach to life. On our return to where our car was parked, without considering the consequences, I blazed my own trail separate from the established path. Because I was ahead of my parents, when I accidentally dislodged a rock it went cartwheeling down the embankment toward my dear mother. There wasn't enough time to avoid the cascading rock and it struck her a glancing blow on her head.

What had I done? Blood streamed down her face, now ashen from shock. I could only imagine the pain caused by my impulsive and careless action. Dad removed his shirt, using it to apply pressure on the wound. Eventually, to my relief, the bleeding stopped.

Was I ready to face the consequences? What I deserved was a scolding—or worse. What I got instead was grace. No blame. No shame. Just grace. Did I deserve to be yelled at? I thought so. Was I truly sorry for what I had done? Yes! I squeezed out all the lessons about personal responsibility that my brain could absorb, and my learning was reinforced by my mother's grace and my father's mercy. I thought I deserved punishment, but what I got has been a lifelong lesson. Punishment may have taught me to be more careful, but grace . . . was . . . well . . . *amazing*, and it taught me an important lesson about love.

Dear Lord! I confess that my parenting is not always filled with grace. Teach me how to be more loving . . . more grace-filled . . . more like You . . . as I respond to my own children!

Don Murray

Parenting Requires Patience

I waited patiently and expectantly for the Lord;
and He inclined to me and heard my cry. Ps. 40:1, Amplified.

Being a good parent allows us many opportunities to understand the real definition of patience and endless chances to put what we learn into practice. Parenting has to be more than theory. If it is anything, it ought to be practical.

Sometime ago we asked our young daughter, "What does it mean for us to have patience with you?" She responded with silence. This made us really sit back and examine ourselves and our level of patience with her. Did we scream and yell to get her attention whenever we became anxious?

When anxiety takes over we have to recognize how we convey messages during tense situations. "Anxiety weighs down the heart, but a kind word cheers it up" (Prov. 12:25). Exercising patience helps prevent impulsive responses and places us in a more rational state to make good decisions. It is not easy to develop patience during intense encounters, especially if you have not practiced patience consistently.

It is important to establish goals to change negative behavior and produce positive outcomes. Any step to correct a difficult situation requires us to first recognize that there is a problem. Our daughter was concerned about the negative communication within the family, and so we realized that change was needed in order to redirect the family dynamics. After recognizing the problem, we had to implement action. It is important, and encouraging, to realize that we can learn how to improve our lives if we desire change.

As parents, we need to be mindful of any issue that prevents positive communication within our home. Let the family meeting be used as a tool to measure outcomes. Remember to focus on the objectives and concerns of the family.

O Lord, please give us wisdom in each decision regarding our children and may patience grace our home as we communicate in both the carefree and the anxious moments.

Arthur E. Nowlin and Kim Logan-Nowlin

A Happy Mess

A joyful heart makes a cheerful face. Prov. 15:13, NASB.

Have you noticed that laughter makes some people really nervous? If there is laughter in the classroom, some doubt whether much learning is going on. If there is laughter in the home, are the kids really getting the training they need? If there is laughter in the church, can there be all that much spirituality?

See, it's my belief that we ought to drive our kids bonkers with the joy they see in us. Joy is not only contagious; it's attractive. It's fun to be around people who are joyful!

One of the most convincing evidences that you're onto something big is when there is frequent, hardy laughter in your home. Parents learning to laugh at themselves. Turning assignments into games. Laughing your way through spilled milk and misplaced keys.

Quite often when I'm chatting with parents my first suggestion will be "Lighten up." Some moms and dads live in mortal dread that they are going to commit some single horrendous parenting gaffe and scar their kids for life. So they ratchet up the intensity, apply every rule they can remember, and go through the day as focused as a lifeguard at a busy pool.

I remember reading the story of a little boy, maybe 3 or 4, who was getting the milk out of the refrigerator door when he dropped the carton. It hit the floor, splashed all over the place, and lay on its side, gushing a puddle of milk beside the kitchen table.

What's a mom to do? What would *you* do? Here's what this mom did. She picked up the carton and then said something like "Well, that's one of the biggest messes I've seen for a long time. I think we ought to enjoy that mess before we clean it up, don't you? Take off your shoes and see how it feels to splash around in milk when you're barefooted. Then we'll clean it up."

We can leave our kids with few more valuable legacies than a childhood filled with happy memories.

O Lord, may our lives be so filled with Your joy, our lives so radiant with Your love, that our homes will resound with the sounds of happiness and laughter.

Don Jacobsen

Just Be Patient

Love is patient, love is kind. 1 Cor. 13:4.

It was a gorgeous day. When you live in Seattle, it is almost compulsory to get outside and enjoy the blue skies and fine weather while it lasts, because, inevitably, the rain will return. I had planned to take the little one down to the lake for a picnic and a walk and was eager to get going. Everything was ready. The food was prepped, the stroller was in the car. The only thing holding us up was naptime, and she was having trouble falling asleep.

I waited for what seemed like an eternity before turning to her.

"Go to sleep now," I said. "We can't go to the lake until you've had your nap, and I want to get there while the sun is still out."

She sat up and looked at me, resting her little hand on my knee, and said, "Just be patient."

Her words hit me like a soccer ball to the stomach, and I was instantly ashamed of losing it. Sometimes it takes being schooled by a toddler to open your eyes to flaws in your own character.

We made it to the lake with plenty of sunshine to spare, and had a wonderful day together. More important, I was reminded of the importance of patience. When I consider how many times I have made mistakes, how long I've struggled to conquer old habits and cultivate new ones, I am tremendously grateful to belong to a Father who is slow to anger, and who loves me unconditionally.

Father God, I thank You for not giving up on us. We try Your patience every day, yet somehow You never run out. There is always more to be had. Teach us to be more than merely receptors of Your grace, that Your patience would overflow the confines of our hearts to bless those around us. Teach us to be more like You.

Carey Pearson

Fruits of the Spirit

But the Holy Spirit produces this kind of fruit in our lives: love, joy, peace, patience, kindness, goodness, faithfulness, gentleness, and self-control. Gal. 5:22, 23, NLT.

Who can resist fresh-picked fruit? Blueberries, strawberries, raspberries, peaches, and apples may be found in numerous fruit stands around the country. Each fruit stand and orchard has its own charm and personality. There's always excitement in the air at harvesttime. Children love fruit. This connection makes the fruit of the Spirit a favorite topic in our Bible lessons.

Several years ago I prayed for a way to teach my students how to learn and remember the fruit of the Spirit. Memorizing them had always proved challenging to me, and each year I had to start from scratch to learn them. God answered my prayer, and the children and I are now able to remember them.

First, think of the number of syllables in each fruit. Did you notice that the first three, love, joy, and peace, have one syllable? Next, you will see that the second three, patience, kindness, and goodness, have two syllables. By now you have probably figured out the last three, faithfulness, gentleness, and self-control, have three syllables.

Now, clap the syllables as you say them with a quick pause in between each set of three. It's that simple and the children love reciting them. The enthusiasm is a perfect springboard for talking and praying about the Holy Spirit developing the fruit in their lives.

You will be amazed how often you can refer to the fruit of the Spirit as you teach your child to trust in Jesus. In day-to-day experiences, you as parents will see evidence of the Holy Spirit working in your child's heart in a specific instance or a long-term change. Teach your child to be aware of the gifts of the fruit of the Spirit in their hearts and actions as you lead them to Jesus. It's an exciting way to help Jesus seem real in their hearts.

Heavenly Father, please guide me as I teach my child about the gifts of the Holy Spirit. Bring awareness of the fruit of the Spirit in our lives as we continually strive to strengthen our relationship with You. I praise You for these marvelous gifts.

Verna Reinbold

His Bidding Is His Enabling

If we live in the Spirit, let us also walk in the Spirit. Gal. 5:25, NKJV.

It was a beautiful morning, and I was looking through recipes when I got the call. The sun was shining through my window right onto the phone as I answered.

"Hello, Ms. Horne. We are having a family meeting for your sister's children who are in state custody. We would appreciate your attendance."

My heart sank and my mind reeled as I recognized this not only as a call for help from the state and my sister, but as a call to action from God Himself. Four amazing but very-difficult-to-manage kids were in need of someone to care for them. I knew in my heart that I was the one God had chosen for this incredible task, but still the question *What do I do?* swam through my thoughts. With no children of my own, could I really handle such an important task? It wasn't long before I realized that I would have to rely on God at every moment if I were to help these kids and keep my sanity.

It is no mistake that the fruit of the Spirit is in the singular form. If you have love, you have them all. And you need them all to be successful in revealing Christ: love, joy, peace, longsuffering, kindness, goodness, faithfulness, gentleness, and self-control. I also recognized that I must first seek out these things for myself, before I could give to little ones who would try and test me every step of the way. Loving them in every moment and situation; purposely giving joy to each day; creating peace where there is none; being longsuffering through every trial by taking nothing personally and never giving up; acting in all gentleness with mercy and grace; seeking out goodness and trusting that God would provide; allowing my need for God to be completely transparent to each child; giving all my frustrations to the Lord only.

It has been 16 years since I took them in, and this is still the best recipe I have for sharing the love of God with my children. The best part is seeing the healing it has given to each of them.

Lord, teach me to love the way You love. Guide me in every step that I take, to reveal Your Spirit of love and light to those You have entrusted to my care.

Peggy Horne

Developing the Fruit of the Spirit

*I ask you to forgive your brothers the sins
and the wrongs they committed in treating you so badly. Gen. 50:17.*

The two sisters faced each other with deep frowns and searing glances. "Turn around in circles three times." The oldest girl rolled her eyes but did as she was told. "OK, now face each other and hold hands," their daddy said. They begrudgingly complied. "And repeat after me, 'Inky dinky doo, I love you." They knew it was coming—they had done this routine with their daddy many, many times. Before the words were spoken the giggles started. Within just seconds they were in a pile on the floor hugging and laughing that belly laugh only a carefree child could enjoy. They knew they were sisters forever and would love each other even longer if possible.

More often than not, as adults we model an unforgiving attitude toward our spouses, our children, and even those on the periphery of our lives. "I can't believe the electric company charged me a late fee again!" "Ugh! I *hate* all this dog hair on the couch." It is our ability to show forgiveness and forbearance when we think no one is looking that will teach the strongest message to our children. And it is our inability to show love that will be remembered as well. Admittedly, when we get to the end of our lives, we will regret the times we didn't forgive, we will mourn the loss of relationships because of a lack of forbearance, and we will ache over the opportunities to love that are lost. Teaching forgiveness, forbearance, and love can be difficult. It can be daunting. But the truth is forgiveness-teaching moments are with us every day. They begin with you as a mom or dad. When was the last time you had an argument with your spouse in front of the kids? Can you imagine what an impact it would make if you faced each other, turned around three times, said, "Inky dinky doo, I love you," and then hugged? It seems ridiculous to even conceive such an idea. But take a lesson from the little ones in your care—loving behavior is sweeter than the torture of not forgiving. Start modeling forgiveness today—it won't go unnoticed.

Father, give us hearts that forgive as readily and completely as Yours.

Candy Graves DeVore

Kindness

*Gracious words are like a honeycomb,
sweetness to the soul and health to the body. Prov. 16:24, ESV.*

My sister is a teacher. She recently told me about Carrie, a new student in her classroom who had been adopted. Carrie struggled to make friends with classmates and to understand some of the nuances of social interactions. These struggles led to ongoing boundary issues. One day Carrie behaved inappropriately, and my sister had to ask her to step outside the classroom for a few minutes of time-out. There had been so many complaints by parents and students about Carrie, and knowing this child's story made my sister long to change this negative situation. So she decided to stop class and remind her students that Carrie longed to belong. She reminded them of how many times Carrie had brought her adoption book to share with them during show-and-tell. She challenged her students to consider what it must be like for Carrie and asked them to go out of their way to be kind and understanding to their classmate.

My sister found out a few days later that Susie had gone home and shared her frustration about Carrie with her mother. She'd talked about the suggestion her teacher had made. Her mother had stopped what she was doing and explained Proverbs 25:22 to her child. She'd talked with her about how we are advised to "heap coals of fire" upon the head of our "enemy." She'd gently suggested her daughter try doing this with her classmate.

A few days later when Susie got into line, Carrie pushed herself in front of her. My sister moved to intervene, but before she could she heard Susie say, "There you are, Carrie; I've been holding this place for you." At that moment Carrie's eyes lit up, and she beamed; her demeanor changed, and her whole body relaxed. Incredibly, Carrie has not pushed her way in front of others in line since, and there has been a marked improvement in her interactions with other students.

How easy and human it is for us to want to get back at those who hurt or annoy us. But gracious words and one kind act can change the course of a life. What a blessing that these children had this mother and this teacher to guide them.

Father, help our first thought toward others be kind and gracious.

Colleen Duncan

Growing for the Good

Truly I tell you, whatever you did for one of the least of these
brothers and sisters of mine, you did for me. Matt. 25:40.

When I adopted and brought home a severely abused child, I naively expected everyone to embrace him as I did—seeing him for the special child he was. Most people did, of course—relatives and church family, neighbors, even strangers. In spite of his striking features, it was impossible not to see his disabilities. He wore heavy leg braces and eye patches, and functioned well below his age level. Both adults and children noticed.

His father and I were able to shelter him from most of the unkindness of people until he entered the school system. We found the schools did not do a very good job of protecting him from ridicule and bullying. If we had a birthday party for him, no one showed up. If there was a soccer game at school, he was chosen to be the goalie, because they thought it was fun to watch him fall down when the ball was kicked into his stomach. It was great sport to stick their foot out in the aisle of the bus and trip him as he walked by. There was no limit to name-calling. He so desperately wanted a friend that he was willing to trade new Christmas presents for a few moments of someone's time. We ached for him. If we could have bought him a genuine friendship, we would have.

We lived in a small rural community. It was clear the students who were the biggest offenders were from homes in which children like our son were referred to as "retards," "crips," "geeks," or "spazzes." The parents would see nothing wrong with their child's mean, hurtful, discriminating behavior. I made it my mission to encourage positive behavior by rewarding any act of kindness I saw in a child at school. Not only did I tell the child, I wrote a letter to the school and also to the child's parents commending their kindness. Kindness is a fruit of the Spirit. Young children need to have positive reinforcement for showing their good qualities, even in childish manners, and practicing the loving ways of Jesus. The rewards for kindness must outweigh the compensation for meanness if we want our children to grow for the good.

Abba, continue to bless the little children and guide them in Your loving and gentle ways.

Karen R. Hessen

Clean Hands and a Pure Heart

Who may ascend into the hill of the Lord?
Or who may stand in His holy place? He who has clean hands
and a pure heart.... He shall receive blessing from the Lord,
and righteousness from the God of his salvation. Ps. 24:3-5, NKJV.

Every Adventist mother knows how easily Fridays overflow. Expectations pile up: Clean the house, the children, the clothes. Shop for food. Prepare a special meal. Keep the kids in line.

One Friday things just would not come together. Pressure rose. My temper shortened. Instead of helping, the children made more messes. I started to get upset and was yelling. I frantically tried to push my kids into action, with no success.

Then came a clear message to my heart from God: "I desire clean hands and pure hearts."

I froze. Clean hands. Pure hearts. What did He mean? Wasn't my heart clean? No. It was filthy. I was yelling about getting ready for Sabbath. I was angry at my kids. I had a deadline that I wasn't going to meet. My house was a mess, but my heart was worse.

It was time for a change. Cleaning for Sabbath was not the most important thing. Letting God clean my heart was much more important than neatly arranged toys or fancy desserts.

As I pondered what to do, I wandered to the piano and began playing hymns. I started to sing, and the children came in to listen. The words touched my heart. Praying aloud, I asked God to forgive me, cleanse me from sin, and give me a clean heart. He gave me wisdom and guidance in how to prepare for the Sabbath. Relaxing, I let go of my expectations about how the house should look. We were getting ready for Sabbath the happy way, with singing. The floor wasn't mopped, but it didn't matter. When the sun went down, we were all calm and happy.

I started preparing for Sabbath differently. The lunch menu was simplified: haystacks, something in the Crock-Pot, or baked potatoes. If cleaning couldn't be done with a happy attitude, it was better not done. It helped to have some chores done before Friday so I didn't have to rush. I would stop to sing, pray, and remember why I was doing all of this, and our God of love.

Lord, thank You for teaching me the most important part of getting ready for Sabbath. Please give me the clean hands and a pure heart I need, to be ready to stand in Your holy place.

Barbara Frohne

Coming—Ready or Not

Therefore keep watch, because you do not know
on what day your Lord will come. Matt. 24:42.

We had just moved from the mission field to our new home. I was heavily pregnant, but with 40 days to go I thought I would be fine. Wanting to show ourselves friendly, we had invited people for Sabbath lunch. I spent Friday cleaning the house, making food, washing the dog, and doing a multitude of household chores. When I eventually got to bed that night my back was aching. Thinking it was the result of bending over the bath to wash the dog, I tried to settle down to sleep, but sleep did not want to come. Just as I would drift off, there would be a nagging pain that refused to be ignored. I woke my husband to complain about my inability to get comfortable, and he started timing my grunts and groans.

"Right," he said a little while later, sitting up in bed and switching on the light, "it is time for us to go to the hospital. You are in labor."

"Can't be," I wailed. "I still have a month to go; besides, I haven't read that part of the book yet!" But labor pains and babies wait for no woman. When the time for birth comes, no amount of bargaining or pleading will buy you time.

Our little baby daughter was born 11 hours later, and when I held her in my arms I knew that I could not have waited for her any longer. She was perfect and healthy and on time—it was her parents who did not know how to count. I remember, with great clarity, the strong emotions that flooded my heart while holding that tiny bundle of life. If anyone had tried to wrest her from my arms, I would have pursued them to the ends of the earth to get her back. I loved her fiercely, even though I had held her for only a few minutes. I knew I would give my life for hers, if needed. A pervasive sense of well-being settled upon me. This little person was flesh of my flesh and bone of my bone. And she had arrived, safely, even though her mommy had not read that part of the book yet.

O Lord, thank You for life and the experiences that shape us. Help me to be ready for Your coming and the start of that most wonderful adventure called heaven.

Deanna Pitchford

The Fruit of Patience

*And he passed in front of Moses, proclaiming,
"The Lord, the Lord, the compassionate and gracious God,
slow to anger, abounding in love and faithfulness." Ex. 34:6.*

I'm convinced that if Jesus were here today He wouldn't drive a car. This belief started when we first moved to our new city. We were moving from a rural town to a sprawling metropolis. From four stoplights, to too many to count, with highways and off-ramps weaving through town.

The first time I drove in the city, I was told which exit to take, and, white-knuckled, I turned onto the ramp. I looked for traffic to my left. Several cars were behind me, but catching up quickly. I expected them to move over into the empty lane to allow me to move into the proper lane. Instead, I was pushed off onto the side of the busy road as the ramp ended. I thought it was just first-time luck. Later I realized it was just the way the people in my new city drove: Fast, furious, and not willing to share the road with each other.

"What a crazy man!" I yelled.

"What, Mommy? Someone is crazy?" My son called from the back seat.

"Never mind, son." I prayed for patience and forgiveness. It was only later, when my son was telling his father that Mommy thought the people in our new town were crazy, idiots, and irresponsible, that I saw my need. I needed a heaping measure of the Spirit's fruit of patience.

The Greek term in Galatians 5:22 is the word *makrothumia*. It can be described as long-distance in time or space. The Bible tells us that patience is rewarded, that it comes from testing, and is a virtue to be taught. I clearly wasn't doing that with my son listening from the back seat.

In our fast-paced world, it's not the easiest fruit to obtain. Time doesn't just stretch before us; it makes demands. Yet, the Spirit longs to give us this precious gift that will make us not only better parents, but better people. Without it, our lives become chaotic and miserable. As the Spirit brings this precious fruit into our lives, we must exercise it as a living example to our children.

Father, some of the kinds of fruit of Your Spirit aren't as easy to accept as others. Patience takes time to develop. Please give us a special measure so we can be examples to our children.

Kimberley Tagert-Paul

Christ in Me

I am the vine; you are the branches. If you remain in me and I in you, you will bear much fruit. John 15:5.

A young anthropology student from Chicago, Illinois, decided to do a doctoral dissertation on the Navajo in Arizona. Early one October morning, dressed in blue jeans, cowboy boots, denim jacket, cowboy hat, he loaded up his shiny, new pickup truck and headed south to Arizona.

When he arrived at the hogon, the father of the family came out to meet him. Without a word he took him into the home and pointed to a space along the wall for him to place his belongings. With that the student spent a long night ignored by all. Hoping things would be different in the morning, the young man joined the family circle for breakfast. Not one person spoke to him. After several meals alone the student decided to serve the family any way he could.

He began to play with the children, swinging them around as their father would do. Then he began drawing five-gallon buckets of water from a nearby creek to save the mother some time and energy. Soon he began to notice a few more vegetables in his stew each evening. Within a couple of weeks the student and the father became good friends and colaborers in the family chores.

But good things must come to an end. Soon the day arrived when the young man would return to the university. As the family gathered together, the children were the first to say goodbye. They fastened themselves to his legs and began to cry. After assuring them that he would write letters, the young man turned to the mother of the family. She, for an entire year, had provided for his every meal. These two friends, along with the young brave, sadly bade each other farewell.

As the young student turned to get in his pickup, he was surprised to hear the voice of the grandmother. She had not spoken a word to him the entire year. Now, as he was about to leave, this little elderly woman took a step toward him and in broken English that she had obviously practiced many times came the words "I like . . . me best . . . when I'm . . . with . . . you."

O Lord, I like myself much better when You are living in me! Please fill me with Your Spirit so my children will grow in You as they grow up.

Garry Sudds

Something Bigger Than Ourselves

My help comes from the Lord, the Maker of heaven and earth. Ps. 121:2.

My husband had just come in from working in the garden. I was preparing dinner with my boys. While he took off his shoes, I glanced at him with a smile. I was suddenly surprised to see our four-wheeler out the window, slowly rolling by across the lawn. I realized it was rolling toward our pond! I couldn't speak. I just ran out the door in my flip-flops calling, "Carl, Carl!" I flew down our porch steps. I reached for the handlebars, but it was too late. It had gained momentum going down the hill. It slid right between two apple trees, and *splash!* Right into the pond.

My husband had realized what was happening and ran straight for our backhoe. The four-wheeler started to sink as air bubbles escaped. I jumped into the cold, deep water, trying to grab it before it got out of my reach. Grabbing the tow bar with one hand and a bush with the other, I looked back at my boys. They were running down to help me. I heard my oldest cry out, "God, please help us! Don't let it sink!" His sincerity struck me as I saw tears in his eyes. My child had immediately gone to God for help. My child had amazing faith. What a lesson I learned. I was just thinking, *This is crazy! Why am I doing this?* My child reminded me to go to God for help.

My husband successfully retrieved the beast out of the water. We stood there not believing what had just happened. Now we can laugh at our crazy experience. But we also reflect with our boys on the graciousness of God by letting me look up at the right time. Imagine if I had not looked outside at that moment. We would have wondered what had happened to our four-wheeler!

It is also good to remember that sometimes we need something bigger than ourselves to get out of a mess. My husband had a big machine to use, and my son remembered to go to God. We share these parallels with our children. They are learning from real-life situations. And my children teach me what I sometimes forget: In trouble go to God, who is our Creator and Helper.

Father, incline my heart to always turn to You first in every trouble. Open my mind to learn the lessons You teach me through my children.

Tami Faudi

The Fruit of Joy

But be glad and rejoice forever in what I will create,
for I will create Jerusalem to be a delight and its people a joy. Isa. 65:18.

You were created to be joy! Did you know that? The day you were born, the Lord Himself rejoiced over you with joy. You did the very same things with your little ones. No wonder a mother can forget the pain and exhaustion of labor. You hold your child close to your heart, and joy spills forth all over them.

Joy is a response to something or someone. It goes much deeper than pleasure. It radiates throughout us, and it can't be hidden. Joy is a living emotion. God calls us His joy, and He rejoices over us. No wonder God tells us that joy is a fruit of the Spirit.

Do you have pictures of your children in which the joy they feel is evident on their faces? When you celebrate with your children, whether a holiday or a birthday, joy just seems to radiate from their little faces. Where did they learn that joy? Where did it come from?

From you, of course! As you let God's love shine, the joy that follows is plainly visible. Raising your little ones to love God will bring out the second fruit of the Spirit: joy.

But where does joy go when things aren't running as well as you like? when parenting becomes a chore? Like an old basketball, you become deflated and can't do the job you were meant to do.

The gift of joy, God's joy, is different from ours. It doesn't disappear at the first sign of trouble. It's a fruit that grows in us as we yield to the Holy Spirit. The Bible tells us in Nehemiah 8:10: "Do not grieve, for the joy of the Lord is your strength." Joy comes from the Lord, taking a firm root in us as we grow—and indeed, it becomes our strength. Strength to parent the precious children that God has given us, even during the hard times.

Father, sometimes it is hard to feel the joy that should be within us, especially when parenting becomes a challenge. We ask this day and every day that we don't depend on feeling the joy to know that it is in us. We ask that You will nurture its fruit in us, and let it spill out for our children to see.

Kimberley Tagert-Paul

Patience

*But the fruit of the Spirit is love, joy, peace, forbearance,
kindness, goodness, faithfulness, gentleness and self-control. Gal. 5:22, 23.*

Being patient is a challenge for any household of today. In a world of "I must have it now," "Hurry up!" and "I can't wait," where tired and overworked parents give in to the whining of impatient children, forbearance is a much-needed virtue.

In a lesson about modern versus old technology, my kindergartener quickly learned that people of the "olden days" had a lot of patience. He bluntly asserted, "It must have taken forever to send a little note by the messenger guy on horseback!" Today, clicks of a button will deliver you an instant message or a package to your door. Let's not forget that the way we wash clothes or eat a meal has drastically changed over a century. It has changed how we view time.

But let's also look at our patience as parents and what our children observe in us. How many times have you asked your child to pick up after themselves and they "forget" time and time again? Are you short-tempered with them? Are you impatient in traffic? Better yet, how patient are you when enduring long lines or are put on hold for customer service? We are the appointed example to our children and bear the fruit of it, good or bad. But our saving grace is God, our divine example. And we, knowing all the forbearance He has had with us, would do well to follow His example and bear good fruit through those whom He has entrusted to us.

Whenever we experience a bout of being impatient, this song helps put it all into perspective:
"Have patience; Have patience.
Don't be in such a hurry.
If you don't have patience, you'll only start to worry.
Remember; Remember, that God is patient too.
Just look at all the times when others have to wait on you!"

Lord, give me a heart of patience that will exude in everything I say and do. Thank You for being my example.

Jocelyn D. Zvosechz

October

Special-Needs Parenting

Unexpected Outcomes

The Lord is my strength and my shield;
my heart trusts in him, and he helps me. Ps. 28:7.

We all long for a healthy baby. During a pregnancy the unknown about a baby encourages parents to hope and dream about what their child will be like. Often parents develop an idea or mental picture of this perfect child-to-be. The sad truth is that with all the medical interventions possible, some parents still experience miscarriages, stillbirths, neonatal deaths, or have babies with lifelong challenges.

When parents face any of the above challenges, there is always a cycle of grief and loss. For those who have a child born with disabilities, parents say it isn't so much about the severity of the condition as it is about mourning the loss of the healthy child they imagined. This cycle of grief and loss involves:

Shock and Panic: The first stage is one of disbelief and disorientation.

Searching: After the shock, parents begin to search for the hoped-for child. This may be evidenced through denial, searching for a diagnosis, or placing blame.

Experience of Nothingness: A time of strong emotions, parents must face the reality of the child's disability. Anger, guilt, and depression are some of the emotions felt at this stage.

Recovery: This is the time that the hoped-for child and the real child are integrated. Families begin to see the child's assets along with the disability.

Maintenance: This is a relatively stable state of equilibrium. Each parent must take their own journey, while using internal and external coping mechanisms to help deal with each new hurdle or obstacle.

Unexpected outcomes are just that—something we don't anticipate. If you are an expectant parent, consider making a "What if?" list. Anticipate the joys as well as the possibility of having to come to terms with the fact that sometimes pregnancy and childbirth experiences don't yield our desired outcomes. It is an essential and necessary step in becoming a parent.

Lord, You are our strength and our shield. May we be ever faithful.

Susan Murray

Beautifully and Wonderfully Made

I praise you because I am fearfully and wonderfully made. Ps. 139:14.

Ever since I was a little girl, I dreamed, like many little girls, of becoming a mother one day. I played with my baby dolls, and as I got older I loved to babysit just so I could hold and hug little babies. When I became pregnant, I was so excited. My heart was filled with plans and dreams for my little one. I prayed for my child. "Dear Father, please help my baby to be healthy, strong, and wise. Help him or her to inherit my wit and charm and my hubby's eyes and smile. I pray that my baby will grow to do great things—discover the cure for cancer and baptize hundreds—and I pray that my child will love You."

Just imagine learning your child has a disability or an illness that crushes all you had hoped and dreamed. One parent compared it to planning a vacation to Hawaii. You do your research—find out the best time of year to go, what to see and do. And you plan and prepare, shop for the most appropriate clothing, purchase your plane tickets. On the day of departure you are so excited. You board the plane, settle in, and with closed eyes you picture yourself walking along the beach at sunset. As you begin to soar through the sky, the flight attendant announces, "Good morning, ladies and gentlemen, and welcome aboard. Sit back and relax. We should be in Holland within 12 hours."

This is how it felt for me. Learning that my son had a disability felt like planning to go to Hawaii, only to end up in Holland. It has been quite a journey. Only through much prayer, and by God's grace, have I come to appreciate, love, and enjoy the experience of being in "Holland." I have learned that it isn't a bad place; it's just not where I'd planned to end up. The stresses and challenges of raising a child with a disability have made me stronger. Most important, I have learned to see my son as God sees him—a child who is beautifully and wonderfully made—a child who is made in the image of God.

Dear heavenly Father, teach me to see and appreciate my child as You do. Help me not to live by my fears but by my hope and trust in You.

Davenia Lea

He Answered My Prayer

This is the confidence that we have in Him,
that if we ask anything according to His will, He hears us. 1 John 5:14, NKJV.

Having empathy has always come naturally to me. As a young adult I felt that if I truly wanted to lighten the burdens of others, I needed to more fully enter the pain of those around me. I prayed, "Father, let me feel deeply what others feel." Little did I know where this prayer would lead.

It began with the birth of my second daughter. My husband was out of town, and my parents-in-law had come through to help take care of big sister. On the day I went into labor my mother-in-law had a heart attack and ended up in the hospital with me. The birth did not go well, and it took many hours and much struggle before I could hold the tiny, precious little girl in my arms and introduce her to her big sister.

Life felt overwhelming at times with a baby who fed every two hours night and day for two years. She was too quiet, and it became obvious that she was developmentally delayed. She was diagnosed with ataxic cerebral palsy and only began to walk at the age of 6. We seemed to live at one kind of therapy place or another.

A caring doctor friend urged us to see a geneticist and have her re-evaluated. We did, and I'll never forget the day we were given the diagnosis. He greeted us with the words "Your daughter is mentally challenged. She has Cornelia de Lange syndrome. Here is what you can expect." We left his office, and I stepped off the sidewalk and felt as if I'd fallen into a deep, dark vacuum.

Time passed, and I heard His gentle whisper, "Remember when you asked Me to help you feel another's pain?" He had answered my prayer, and through the many subsequent years, He has given me strength—and joy—for each stage of the journey. I have never asked, "Why me?" for not only did Jesus answer my prayer, He gave me a gift beyond measure.

Thank You, Jesus, for hearing my prayer and enabling me to walk this path. Thank You for the gift of Candi. Please give hope, strength, and courage to other parents, as they, too, are given these gifts beyond measure.

Emra Wagener Smith

Your Child Belongs

This kingdom of faith is now your home country.
You're no longer strangers or outsiders. You *belong* here,
with as much right to the name Christian as anyone. Eph. 2:19, Message.

Because we live in a windy valley, every spring I have "volunteer" flowers show up in some unusual places around our property. I have a soft spot for these misplaced flowers, and I never pull them up and toss them out. It doesn't matter that they are different from all of the other flowers around them. I figure that if they worked hard enough to make it through the previous winter and find a new place to thrive, then they deserve to live. They belong here.

I have two friends with special-needs children. One has a daughter with Down syndrome; the other has a son with autism. Both have told me that they have often felt their child didn't belong at certain places: at concerts, at community holiday celebrations, at the grocery store, and sadly, even at church. If you are the parent of a special-needs child, know that your child does belong—as much as any other child. I'm sorry if people have made you feel unwelcome.

Recently I was at the grocery store when a man and teenage boy walked by me. The boy's arms were drawn up across his chest, and his wrists were limp. With his mouth wide open he stared up at the ceiling as he walked. His dad let him walk independently, but kept a close eye on him. I was impressed that this dad felt his son belonged in the store just as much as the two athletic high school football players who walked by them.

While the boy was looking at a display I asked the man, "Is that your son?"

He turned and looked at me defensively, and yet with sadness in his eyes.

"Yes," he said. "He is."

I smiled and said, "I'm glad you brought him to town today."

"Thank you," he responded, appearing surprised but appreciative.

That dad was a good example of how everyone should feel toward kids with special needs—not with the compassionless judgmental eyes of society, but as God sees them. In His eyes your child is loved, accepted, and treasured. In His eyes, your child belongs.

Lord, thank You that my child belongs. Help me to remember that.

Nancy Canwell

What You Should Know
About Special-Needs Parenting

God has said, "I will never abandon you or leave you." Heb. 13:5, GW.

My beautiful daughter, Makayla, has an absence seizure every two minutes. The experts have told us she will not outgrow them, and so far no medicine is working. She has learning delays, speech delays, and fine-motor delays. Makayla is amazing because although she misses time and information, she continues to learn. We are proud to be her parents.

Here are some things we are learning along the way. Things we would like people to know about our experience parenting a special-needs child.

We are tired all the time. Parenting a child takes time, but a special-needs child takes that to a higher level of fatigue. Yes, we might be lucky to get a good night's rest, but the emotional and physical fatigue leaves us feeling continually drained. Above and beyond attending the many doctor appointments, therapies, research, and the daily routine, we are weary.

The promise we cling to: "Come to Me, all who are weary and heavy-laden, and I will give you rest" (Matt. 11:28, NASB).

We feel alone. Have you ever heard a group of women talking excitedly about their child's accomplishments? "My child was saying the ABCs at 2," or "My child potty-trained themselves at such an early age." Have you ever stopped to consider how that might make a parent of a special-needs child feel? We didn't know if our little girl was going to be able to hug us, or walk. We prayed for more than a year that we would hear the words "Mommy" or "Daddy."

We are still praying for certain milestones, but we are the fortunate ones. Some are still waiting for even the most basic milestone to be reached. Please be sensitive to the feelings of others. Simple words can be so hurtful. The promise we cling to: "And, lo, I am with you alway, even unto the end of the world" (Matt. 28:20, KJV).

Dear Lord, thank You for the strength You provide to keep us going, one step at a time; one day at a time; one milestone at a time. Thank You, too, for helping us to face each day with courage and hope.

Jackie Benwell Hood

Letting God Be Our Strength

I can do all things through Christ which strengtheneth me. Phil. 4:13, KJV.

Raising children is very challenging. In fact, it may well be the hardest job there is. For parents of special-needs children this is even more the case. I discovered that when my third child was diagnosed with autism, a neurological condition that affects language and social skills.

At the age of 3 my son remained nonverbal. Learning that he might never be able to speak to me, or show any feelings of tenderness or connection, was truly devastating. In spite of it being the biggest challenge of my life, I determined to do everything I could to help him develop and reach his highest potential.

I taught him how to roller-skate, and even though I was told he might not have the balance or coordination for it, I taught him how to ride a bike. I showered him with hugs and told him "I love you," whether it meant anything to him or not. I read to him and played with him, even though he never made eye contact. I got a job as a support teacher in the school he attended so I could learn how to teach and interact with special-needs kids.

On my toughest days I held tightly to the promise to "trust in the Lord with all your heart, and lean not on your own understanding: in all your ways acknowledge Him, and he shall direct your paths" (Prov. 3:5, 6, NKJV). Over the past several years I have learned many things. I would never have been able to do it without God's strength. I have learned to trust in God like never before, and I've learned to leave things in His hands. By doing so, I can face each day with the knowledge that I have Someone I can call upon for strength.

My son has made lots of improvement over the years, and even though he still does not communicate verbally, he can communicate through his iPad, sign language, and gestures, and he *loves* to receive hugs. Just because our children may not be considered "normal" by others, and even though we don't always understand them, we should never let this prevent us from showering them with love.

Dear Lord, help us as we face our parenting challenges. In You all things are possible.

Shirley Jones

Mother's Faith and Trust

O keep my soul, and deliver me:
let me not be ashamed; for I put my trust in thee. Ps. 25:20, KJV.

When I was 4 years old, the doctor told my mother I had only four years to live because of a heart problem. My mother dedicated me to God and asked Him to use me as long as I lived. After four years of regular checkups I was, miraculously, still alive. The doctor then told my mother I would last only another three years. Again my mother fell to her knees and petitioned the Lord, "You saved my child before; please save her again." After three years passed by, the doctor was amazed but said, "Mrs. Joy, your daughter has only five years to live."

Five years passed, and I was still alive. Every time my mother visited the doctor he would predict how much longer I had to live. The last prediction was given when I was 20 years old. The doctor said if I made it to 23, I would be out of danger. After I celebrated my twenty-third birthday, my mother was the happiest woman on earth. Her faith moved the hands of God, and the doctor's predictions were proven wrong.

I had no idea during childhood of all God had done for me, but when I was 17 I overheard my mother talking about my case to a family friend. It was only then that I knew how God had preserved my life. At the age of 24, before I got married I went for a final checkup, and the heart specialist finally declared I was completely healed. I know beyond a doubt it was God who healed me, because I was given no medication at all after I turned 12. It was only God, through my mother's earnest prayer and devotion, that healed my heart.

Whenever my mother is asked how I survived, she proudly says, "God is the best physician. He can cure any disease, and He answers our prayers." God answers the prayers of faithful mothers.

Lord, may I not neglect to bring my children before You every day. Use my children, Lord, to be a blessing to others and a reflection of You.

Leonora O. Carado

Things I've Learned From My Special-Needs Child

Verily I say unto you, Except ye be converted, and become as little children, ye shall not enter into the kingdom of heaven. Matt. 18:3, KJV.

People like to be remembered. Many children with special needs, while challenged in many ways, often have an area in which they have special ability. Some excel in music, others in coordination, art, or mathematics. My son's special ability seems to be his prodigious memory. If you tell him your name, he is unlikely ever to forget it. One of his favorite things to do is ask people their name, and then whenever he sees them, he will greet them and remind them who they are. As I've watched him interact with people in his simple, little boyish way, I've noticed that people seem to really appreciate the fact that Corey remembers them.

Bible stories are amazing. Corey loves to be read to. He never gets tired of hearing the same stories over and over and over. His enthusiasm for the stories of the Bible never fades. As adults we lose our sense of wonder over the miracle of Naaman's healing in the Jordan River, or the fire coming down to consume Elijah's sacrifice, or Jesus raising a dead girl to life, or feeding 5,000 people with five barley loaves and two fish. But Corey never forgets that these things were extremely awesome, as his delighted exclamations all through the reading of the story attest.

Everybody needs prayer. In our home we take turns having prayer after family worship. One evening will be the "girls" turn, and the following evening will be the "boys" turn. When Corey has his turn, it is sometimes difficult to get him to find a good stopping spot. Although he usually begins his prayer by asking Jesus to "help us to never, never follow Baal," he follows it up with praying for nearly everyone he can think of. If he's heard that a particular person is sick, he asks for Jesus to "lay a healing hand" on them. He obviously heard someone use that phrase, and he likes it. He prays for all the pastors he can think of, including the ones he has seen on 3ABN. Corey seems to know instinctively that everybody needs prayer.

Lord, help me to come to You as a little child, and to humbly realize what's truly important.

Sharon Monks

OCTOBER 9

Lessons From the Silence

Be still, and know that I am God. Ps. 46:10.

I have a son called Joshua. They say he is autistic. He spoke his first words at the age of 4, and though he can ask for things, he is not conversational. Abstract concepts are beyond his comprehension; he understands only what he can see and touch.

I remember holding him the day he was born, thanking God for the blessing of a new life, vowing to raise him in a Christian home. Three years later I wondered how my son would ever come to know a God he could not see. As he grew older, taking him to church became an incredible challenge. Let's face it, chasing your child through the sanctuary is not viewed as acceptable church etiquette. So, I went to worship on Sabbath morning and he stayed home with a babysitter.

One Sabbath, while preparing to leave the house, I looked at Joshua as a sad expression crossed his face. We decided to give it another try, sending up a prayer as we left for church. We entered the sanctuary, and my heart jumped into my throat as he did the one thing I had prayed he would not do. His eyes locked on the pulpit as he made his way to the front of the church. My whispered protests were of no avail. Joshua was on a mission and would not be stopped.

He reached the platform as the chorister stood to lead the song service. I believe the Spirit of God moved her as she motioned for him to come to the pulpit. She wrapped her arms around his shoulders, and as the piano began playing and the congregation raised their voices in song, Joshua tilted his head, and his expression of uncertainty melted into one of pure joy at the sound of the singing. He raised his right arm and began pumping it in perfect time, directing the "choir" before him.

I believe it was at that moment that my son met God, and if you had seen his expression, you would have thought they were deep in conversation.

Thank You for caring enough to reach into the silence and touch a soul. It is in the silence, Lord, that we know You are God.

Sherry McLaughlin

296

Peace of Mind

Be anxious for nothing, but in everything by prayer and supplication
with thanksgiving let your requests be made known to God.
And the peace of God, which surpasses all comprehension, will guard
your hearts and your minds in Christ Jesus. Phil. 4:6, 7, NASB .

N oah, stop talking and do your homework!" is something I seem to
say a lot. But, as my husband points out, it was not very long ago
we were afraid that Noah would never talk or that his speech would be
so delayed that it would affect all areas of his life. Two years ago I was
battling with insurance companies and doctors to get my son tested for a
disorder that wasn't even on the radar. All I had to go on was the nagging
feeling that there was something wrong with my son and that I had to
have him evaluated. Then came the dual diagnoses of central auditory
processing disorder and developmental apraxia. My immediate relief of
having a diagnosis was quickly followed by anxiety about how Noah would
be affected.

In the midst of my worries, one clear thought came to me: *Doesn't God
love your child more than you could possibly understand? Ask God for help.*
I spent a night pouring out my heart to God, tearfully expressing my fears
and begging for wisdom to help Noah so he would not be held back by the
challenges he would have to face. Finally I asked God for peace of mind so
that I could be the pillar of support my son needed.

When I woke the next morning, all my worries were still there, but
so was my resolve that somehow our family was going to get through this
struggle, no matter how hard. God was going to be right there with us. This
realization gave me the peace of mind I needed to face the day.

Today, after two years of rigorous therapy, Noah has made remarkable
progress. So much so I sometimes forget he has a significant neurological
disorder. Then another hurdle will present itself, and I am reminded that
we are fighting a long-term battle. Though God didn't miraculously cure
my son as I might have wished, He is showing us His steadfast love by carrying us through the rough patches.

*Thank You, Lord, for the special children You give us. Please help us guide
them through their struggles and triumphs. We rely on You for wisdom and
strength.*

Asheley Woodruff

Something Beautiful

And a little child shall lead them. Isa. 11:6, KJV.

I t was love at first sight when my husband and I met. Our deep love for each other and for God, and our gift of music held us especially close during the years that followed. We found it such a joy to share our love for God through music ministry. We dreamed of having a family and spreading the good news together through music.

The Lord answered our prayers and gave us a precious son, Landon, and later a beautiful daughter, Alayna. We felt blessed beyond words, complete as a family, and one step closer to fulfilling our dream. Unfortunately, it soon became obvious that Landon was not meeting the typical developmental milestones in comparison to other children his age. Our love and concern for him prompted us to seek professional help that would allow him to rise above these challenges and to succeed in life. We were devastated to receive Landon's diagnosis of autism at the tender age of 3. Suddenly all our dreams of having a family music ministry painfully crumbled before our eyes. Over the next few years his challenges became overwhelming and almost unbearable. Having no support to relieve us from the demands of his unrelenting needs, we could easily have given up on our dreams and even our faith in God.

Thankfully, our steadfast faith in God, love, patience, determination, prayers, and intensive therapy enabled Landon to overcome many challenges. In fact, our hopes of having a family music ministry were renewed when, to our amazement, we discovered that Landon was gifted with a beautiful singing voice. In fact, not a dry eye could be found after his first performance at church. Now, rather than seeing Landon's autism as an obstacle to our dreams of ministry we see it as a blessing. We firmly believe that God can still make something beautiful out of Landon's life and all of our lives, too, if we allow Him.

We thank You, Lord, for sending Landon into our lives. He has taught us so much about unconditional love and patience and is a daily reminder that with You, all things are possible.

Lisa Arbeau

Gravel Versus Mud

The Lord is my rock and my fortress and my deliverer;
the God of my strength, in whom I will trust. 2 Sam. 22:2, 3, NKJV.

Many years ago a beautiful 5-year-old girl named Tasha came to live at our house. She had been removed from her family for her own safety. She was full of life but also weighed down with some heavy burdens. Have you ever noticed how God will sometimes send you people who need you as much as you need them?

Tasha's first five years were spent in an urban environment surrounded by people who drank too much, used drugs, and were abusive. She was very streetwise when she came to live with us, where she experienced, for the first time, what it was like to live in a family that loved one another. It was difficult at first, because she suffered from fetal alcohol syndrome. Tasha's condition was, fortunately, mild, which meant she could function in life, but things that seemed simple to us were hard for her to comprehend.

Once, for example, we took a trip out to the lake and were walking along the beach. Some parts of the pathway were gravelly, and some were muddy. We were all walking along, and Tasha was following behind, when we heard her scream at top of her lungs in a panic. We turned around to help her and told her if she walked on the gravel she would be OK. Continuing on, we heard her screaming again and asked, "Do you know what gravel is?" We discovered she had no idea what gravel was. We had assumed she understood what we were talking about, but it was in fact beyond her comprehension at the time. Once we showed her the difference by letting her feel the texture of each, and showed her how to keep her feet on the gravel, she was fine and able to enjoy the rest of the day.

Tasha reminds me of myself. As I navigate life's road, too often I panic and freeze, not sure where to place my feet. That's when I need to remember to step out in faith, seeking to place my feet on the Rock. If I do that, I can walk with confidence—unafraid and courageous.

Thank You, Father, for being the Rock of our salvation. If we stand on You, we are safe.

Wanda L. Davis

The Lame Spirit

These are the ones I look on with favor: those who are humble and contrite in spirit, and who tremble at my word. Isa. 66:2.

There is no measuring stick for personal pain. Mephibosheth's nurse must have grieved every time she saw him struggle to survive. As a parent of a child who was diagnosed with Asperger's, not a day goes by that I don't weep internally for what might have been.

I remember reading a book by Patsy Clairmont, *Normal Is Just a Setting on Your Dryer.* I think Patsy was right. We all dream of a life with a white picket fence, two kids—a boy and girl, of course—adequate income, and a dog that behaves! But it doesn't always work out that way.

Most translations describe Mephibosheth as lame, crippled, and disabled. In his culture he was viewed as an outcast and unclean. Fortunately, his story doesn't end in this one verse. Years later, when David's kingdom is at rest, he starts asking about Saul's heirs. He summons Ziba, one of Saul's former servants, to the throne room and discovers Jonathan's son is still alive. Ziba makes sure he knows the son is "lame in both feet" (2 Sam. 9:3). King David immediately sends for the young man to show him "God's kindness" (verse 3). He restores Mephibosheth's inheritance and seats him at the king's table as his own son. David is acting as "a man after God's own heart." From that day on, Mephibosheth never ate anywhere but at the king's table.

In Isaiah 66:2 God is looking for a man who is poor, with a "contrite spirit." Contrite in Hebrew is *nakeh,* and is the exact same word used for "lame" when describing Mephibosheth! In essence God is looking for someone with a "lame" spirit! God told Samuel that people look at outward appearances but God looks on the heart. He sees beyond our disabilities to the potential heirs we are. Our King is frantically searching for those who recognize they are disabled because sin resides deep in the crevices of hearts born lame.

Thank You, God, for Your goodness. Thank You for waiting patiently for us to recognize our need and come to You. For You alone are able to restore us to our inheritance as Your beloved children. Thank You for counting us as Your sons and daughters!

Gail McKenzie

Battle Weary

*Thus says the Lord to you: "Do not be afraid
nor dismayed because of this great multitude,
for the battle is not yours, but God's." 2 Chron. 20:15, NKJV.*

As parents of children with special needs, we often find ourselves in battle mode. We fight to find the right pediatrician, one who understands not only our child's condition, but all the other medical issues that come along with it. We fight with medical insurance companies to secure coverage for the often very costly treatments and therapies our children need. We fight with school administrators to revise IEPs (individualized education plans) to best suit the educational needs of our children. We fight against the ill-informed perceptions and misconceptions society has of our children.

Then there are the internal battles. We fight against the urge to scream at well-meaning family members who criticize our parenting because they think our children's meltdowns are simply evidence of "lack of good home training." We fight against our feelings of guilt; what we did or didn't do that may have caused our child's injury; guilt for our impatience, for our burnout. Sadly, at times we fight against our spouses, the very ones who are in the battle with us. I have spoken with parents who suffer symptoms of PTSD (post-traumatic stress disorder) because of the harrowing experience surrounding their child's condition.

God's Word and His presence have a special potency to parents of special-needs children. His promises have become precious to me. Through it all, our Savior says to us, "Do not be afraid nor dismayed because of this great multitude" . . . of circumstances that seem to work against us. "Be strong and of good courage, do not fear nor be afraid of them; for the Lord your God, He is the One who goes with you. He will not leave you nor forsake you" (Deut. 31:6, NKJV). "Fear not, for I am with you; be not dismayed, for I am your God. I will strengthen you. Yes, I will help you. I will uphold you with My righteous right hand" (Isa. 41:10, NKJV).

Father God, help us to sense Your presence with us in the midst of battle. May we seek You early, before the battle begins, for You promise us that You will be found. Thank You for the courage and strength You offer to all in need.

Lesley Jackson

Special Needs—Special Purpose

It is clear to us, friends, that God not only loves you very much but also has put his hand on you for something special." 1 Thess 1:4, Message.

I believe that each life counts. Each person can make a difference. We all have purpose. I have pondered these truths while thinking of my special-needs daughter. I have asked the Lord "How?" How, when her choices in life are so limited? When her needs are met by caregivers?

With each passing year I see how she has impacted each one in our family. She has stretched us and helped us grow in so many ways. She taught me how to ask for what I need—and want. The longings many women have for their husband to shower them with affection and tenderness. When Candice needs these, she simply climbs onto your lap and relentlessly persists until you cover her with kisses.

She has taught me what true forgiveness is. When she hurts you, she says she's sorry and asks forgiveness. You had better be sure you have truly forgiven before saying yes, because forgiveness means it's over. Done with. No pouting, holding grudges, or rehashing it again and again.

The first book I wrote was about the big things in life I learned from Candi. The book launch was a fund-raiser for her school. We also organized a 100-mile bike ride with her to raise funds. She drew the crowds, we raised the funds, and people were encouraged to see what she could do. They realized that if a special-needs child could do the unthinkable—perhaps their dreams could come true as well.

Her life does have a deeper meaning. She has purpose. She touches lives, and with our help, she is making a difference. Jesus has indeed put His hand on her for something special. I can hardly wait to see what He has planned for her.

Father, thank You that you have a special plan for these special ones. Help us to help them live to give and make a difference.

Emra Wagener Smith

Perfect in Every Way

This is what the Lord says—your Redeemer, who formed you in the womb: I am the Lord, the Maker of all things, who stretches out the heavens, who spreads out the earth by myself. Isa. 44:24.

He is perfect!" We watched as my aunt showed us her new bundle of joy. He wiggled his way out of the blanket. We counted 10 perfect fingers and 10 perfect toes. He had startling blue eyes that slanted upward and ears that were a little low on his perfect face.

"He is, isn't he?" My aunt smiled even as a tear made its way down her face.

He was my new cousin, and his name was Jimmy. He had Down syndrome. I didn't know much about the challenges Jimmy or my aunt would face. I thought he was just perfect.

Bullying was the biggest problem he had to deal with. It didn't come from Jimmy, but was directed at him. He was different to anyone who didn't take the time to really get to know him. For those of us who did, Jimmy was wonderful. He didn't always understand other people's reactions to him, and it broke my aunt's heart. She encouraged Jimmy not to fight back, but to love them in spite of the way they treated him.

So, Jimmy did just that; he made it his mission to tell others that God loved him just fine, and he loved them, too. He'd deliver that line with a sloppy smile and a hearty pat on the back. It didn't take long for the bullies to leave him alone. He met curious glances with that brilliant smile, and it melted the hardest hearts.

As my aunt and uncle saw Jimmy grow into manhood, they realized they had taught him the very best lesson of all. Indeed, God did love Jimmy just fine. By His grace, Jimmy was slowly winning others to Him, just by being the special person God made him to be! Perfect in every way.

Father, thank You for creating each one of us as precious and unique in Your sight. Please help us see that differences are a good thing, and that You create all Your children just perfect in every way.

Kimberley Tagert-Paul

His Plans, Not Mine

For I know the thoughts and plans that I have for you, says the Lord, thoughts and plans for welfare and peace and not for evil, to give you hope in your final outcome. Jer. 29:11, Amplified.

It doesn't take very long on the parenting journey to learn how little control you have over the careful plans you have made for your family. In fact, the longer you live in Christ, the more opportunities He uses to remind you that you are not the Planner or the Way-Maker.

While pregnant with our second child, my husband and I went to the 20-week ultrasound. This was to confirm our hopes for a girl and to make sure there was a heartbeat. We had just been through a heart-wrenching miscarriage and wanted so badly to know all was well. Even though we discovered our baby was a boy, when we saw his strong heart pumping away we were elated. I noticed, however, that the technician became quiet as she continued her examination, and I knew something was wrong. The doctor came in and, without telling us much, scheduled us for another appointment.

After several weeks and another ultrasound we learned that our baby had spina bifida, a birth defect in which the spine doesn't completely close and nerve damage is inevitable. It didn't seem possible that we were going to have to accept this. It wasn't what my plan looked like!

We had a long road that led us into some dark places, but the Lord was always near, gently holding us, reminding us of His promises. The road also led us into a deeper trust in the One who loves us and is powerful enough to make His plans come to be. The incredible, beautiful child who now blesses our home and our family is a daily reminder that God's thoughts and plans are so much better than our own.

Like my family—your family may look nothing like the dream you once had in mind. But we have this hope and promise in Christ that it will be so much more. What a glorious God!

Dear Lord, thank You for Your promises and Your faithfulness in fulfilling them. You have a million ways to make things beautiful, and You are not hampered by our limited human perspective. Help me to see the beauty today!

Kristin Breiner

Raising a Special-Needs Child

Behold, children are a heritage from the Lord,
the fruit of the womb a reward. Ps. 127:3, ESV.

Raising a special-needs child can be beyond challenging. I have a son with autism, and I have learned so much from him.

Special-needs children need patience and love. A lot of it. Though they may seem totally disconnected from the world around them—including us—they are "in there." They just do not know how to socialize or communicate, or understand things the same way we do. When they cannot tell us specifically what their needs are, we need to figure out how to understand what they want. Easily said, I know. Special-needs parenting includes reading and research, and a willingness to go the extra mile to understand and advocate for our children

Many special-needs kids have special talents. Find out where their area of giftedness lies, what their interests are and expand on them. My son loves art and is very artistic in unique ways. Some have a remarkable memory and are good with numbers and organization. Some are musical. It might be that their area of specialty will help them earn a living once they're older. If you recognize their gift and help develop it, it will serve to build their confidence and give them pleasure doing something they are good at. Build confidence in them in any way you can.

I have also learned not to let anyone tell you what your child "can't do." I was told my son would not have the coordination for riding a bike and roller skating, and I taught him both. He is now very good at these things and loves to do them.

Like all children, special-needs kids need to know when they've done something right. And for those times when they do something wrong, I've found that gentle redirection can be really helpful. I know from personal experience that if my son hears impatience in my voice, it makes the situation much worse.

Most important, seek God for help and guidance in raising your child. You cannot do it alone. Put God first in your life, and He will help you with the many challenges.

Dear Lord, in those moments when I want to react and snap, please give me a double portion of Your grace and wisdom. Keep me sweet—especially on the tough days.

Shirley Jones

Where Can a Parent Turn?

*The Law of the Lord is perfect, giving new strength to the soul.
The Law He has made known is sure, making the child-like wise. Ps. 19:7, NLV.*

J ustin has a speech impediment," my mother announced the day before she returned home.

"He does not!" I retorted. "What are you talking about?"

"Listen to him," she insisted. "He says '*b*' at the end of words that end with an '*r*' sound."

She's so quick to point out insignificant imperfections in my children, I thought to myself. *He's only 5. He'll grow out of it.*

However, after my mom left, I began to pay more attention to my son's speech. Sure enough, his lips came together at the ends of words ending with an "*r*" sound. As I listened more carefully, I became concerned.

After exploring options for therapy, we took Justin for a free evaluation at a speech clinic. I observed carefully and took notes when the therapist shared her findings with us and outlined a plan. The cost was outrageous. The time commitment would be huge. I went home very discouraged. Surely there must be another way. Over the next few days I continued to pay attention to my son's speech. I also prayed, asking the Lord how to handle this.

Then one day I read how Jesus obtained instruction from the Father and how every child could do the same. I also reflected on ideas I had heard about Spirit-led parenting. I became convicted that God wanted to be our speech therapist.

"OK, Lord," I said. "Lead me through this." I felt impressed to sit down with Justin and just start. I didn't have any idea what we would do, but I chose to believe that God wanted to instruct me, and instruct Justin through me.

We sat down, and I prayed with Justin, asking the Lord to show us what to do. I suddenly remembered what the therapist had said, and using those cues and allowing the Lord to prompt me, I began to work with my son. We continued doing this for short periods of time each day, and within two weeks Justin was able to say "very, scary, hairy bear" without any "*b*"s in the place of the "*r*"s. It was a watershed experience for me—one that taught me that the Lord is our best teacher and that He wants to teach my kids through me, if I will only let Him.

O Lord, thank You for making wise the simple—for helping me teach my child. You know exactly what we need even before we ask. Thank You!

Cheryl Kronner Wiley

Resilience

*You made all the delicate, inner parts of my body
and knit me together in my mother's womb. Ps. 139:13, NLT.*

There are fantastic videos on YouTube that explain the inner workings of the brain. One of my favorites is a short clip that shows neurons in the brain forming when a new behavior is learned. The connection between the neurons occurs so quickly it is mind-blowing. In moments the brain has "knit" a new pathway for information to move.

Because our son, Noah, has central auditory processing disorder, his brain doesn't process information he hears in the way it should. As a result, one of the major components of his therapy is helping his brain form new connections. It's laborious work, but those neural connections have to be made in order for Noah to communicate with those around him.

For our family, sin is a tangible force, one that has prevented Noah's brain from developing properly. In Noah, the beautiful, delicate weaving that God designed for the human brain has been disrupted. Thankfully, God also designed the brain to be resilient and to form new connections when necessary.

It reminds me of Christ's sacrifice on the cross. The beautiful connection we had with God was broken by Adam and Eve's sin. Yet Christ's death allowed a new connection to be formed. And just as Noah now works to strengthen the new neural pathways forming in his brain, so we must take the effort to strengthen our connection with God so it is never broken again.

Dear Lord, although sin mars this world, You have provided a way that we may remain connected in You. Thank You for the sacrifice of Jesus on the cross.

Asheley Woodruff

What's So Special About 21, Anyway?

For nothing is impossible with God. Luke 1:37, NLT.

I was 23 weeks pregnant, and expecting our first child. It had taken us 10 years to make this dream a reality. Through fertility treatments, a pituitary tumor and neurosurgery on my part, and countless months that turned into years of waiting, it finally happened. We were so excited. But then I got the phone call that would forever change our lives.

"Hi, Becky, I have the results of your blood test, and I want to let you know that the markers show that your baby has Down syndrome. I'm so sorry."

I collapsed on the ground and started to cry. Down syndrome is a genetic condition in which a person has 47 chromosomes instead of the usual 46. It is not an illness or a disease. It is a DNA track record detailing that the baby had an extra copy of the twenty-first chromosome, and because it is a building block of the human genome the effects impact the entire system. One week later we learned that our little boy also had a genetic heart defect that would require surgery. How were we supposed to be happy? Sounds impossible, right? Well, it's not.

In the months that followed I refused to accept the medical literature that prepared me for a lifetime of endless heartache, and I searched and found the testimonials; the happy endings; and the inspiring stories of other parents who had been down this same road. Four months later I gave birth to a beautiful six-pound baby boy. He stayed in the NICU for 23 days and there we fell in love. At 4 months Jacob had open-heart surgery and came through it wonderfully.

We have not let this diagnosis define who our son is and who we are as parents. In our eyes he's perfect. Society places such importance on perfection—but the truth is that none of us are perfect and we live in an imperfect world. Only through Christ can we be made whole.

I've learned through my son's eyes that what makes us different is what makes us special. Our son serves as a witness to Christ's love. Through his never-ending love and acceptance of others; his countless smiles and hugs; his soft brown eyes that tug at your heartstrings—it's through all of this and more that I've learned that God's love is never ending.

Thank You, Lord, for the gift of my son. I praise You—for You truly are an amazing God!

Becky Martinez-Bindernagel

Living the Story

*Therefore you shall lay up these words of mine in your heart
and in your soul. . . . You shall teach them to your children,
speaking of them when you sit in your house, when you walk by the way,
when you lie down, and when you rise up. Deut. 11:18, 19, NKJV.*

My brother-in-law related a cute story about my daughter one afternoon, after he and my sister had been babysitting our kids for us. She was about 5 at the time and had convinced him to play "Good Samaritan" with her. She insisted he be the man traveling to Jericho, and she played all the other parts. First, she jumped out from behind the couch as the robber and beat him up. Then as he lay obediently on the floor, she rode by a couple times on her stick horse pretending to be the Levite and the priest. Finally, as the good Samaritan she tugged him up and helped him onto the back of her trusty steed, and rode him to the inn (the couch) on the other side of the room, and patched him back up with her toy doctor kit.

Who hasn't seen a young child acting out their favorite stories? I know my sisters and I used to do it when we were little. Often the themes were from our favorite TV shows. I am now very glad that we chose not to have a television for most of my own kids' growing-up years, and so most of the stories they acted out were from the Bible.

My son, who has special needs, was especially good at inserting bits from his favorite Bible stories into all his playtime activities. The little creek near our home was "the brook Cherith." Whenever he saw a raven, his first thought was of the birds that fed Elijah. "Ask your God to take away these frogs" was the enthusiastic exclamation he would make whenever he saw a frog. Eating little fish crackers reminded him of the feeding of the 5,000. If we passed a cemetery while riding in the car, he got all excited and always exclaimed, "They will all pop out of the graves when Jesus comes back." To Corey, each Bible character is a friend he eagerly looks forward to meeting someday soon.

Lord, thank You for the reality that the people in the Bible stories will one day be among our dearest friends.

Sharon Monks

Endurance in the Race of Life

I press on to reach the end of the race and receive the heavenly prize for which God, through Christ Jesus, is calling us. Phil. 3:14, NLT.

As a mommy of two, I've prayed for focus. I've prayed for patience. I've prayed for many things, but I never thought to pray for endurance. But mommies and daddies need endurance as we go through this race we call parenthood. We need endurance for work and for the care of our kids, and we need it for the stresses of everyday life.

My 7-year-old is finally potty-trained. That was my stress. I started training her when she was 3½. I asked her pediatrician questions, I read articles about how to potty-train a girl. I read books. I asked for ideas from my friends. Nothing I tried worked. I thought I was doing everything wrong.

Even so, God gave me endurance. I never asked for it, but He gave it to me anyway. I kept asking questions, I kept reading books, and finally found one that described my girl perfectly. Then God gave me the endurance to get through the specialist visits, the physical therapy appointments, and the medicine.

How do we make it to the end? I asked myself this question sometimes on a daily basis. God places people in our lives who know how to give an encouraging word at just the right time: friends, church members, a Scripture verse read during devotionals. Each one helps us to endure for just a little longer. They strengthen us, though sometimes we only realize it when the battle or stress is over, when we look back and see exactly how each one helped us get to the end.

At the end of the race of parenthood we'll receive our reward. Our children become wonderful adults. At the end of the race of life, we will all receive our heavenly prize when Christ comes again. I received my reward: a first grader who continues to come home accident-free at the end of a long school day.

Lord, thank You for giving us things even though we haven't asked. Today, I ask for the endurance to make it to the end of the race, until You take us home.

Tammie Knauff

Developmentally Disabled

We do not have a high priest
who is unable to empathize with our weaknesses. Heb. 4:15.

Developmentally disabled: two tough words for any new parent to hear. Most of us take for granted that our children will thrive. Some don't. There are many things that Satan can whisper to make us bitter.

"You deserve this."

"You don't deserve this."

"It would have been easier to abort, like the doctor suggested."

Is there a bitter phrase you keep fighting off? Here is a secret: Jesus didn't just die for our sin; He died for the things that make us feel like dying, too. Think about it. He could have lived a pain-free life. But He chose rather to know our struggles and feel our pain. Remember, "We do not have a high priest who is unable to empathize with our weaknesses" (Heb. 4:15). No, Jesus understands. He gets it.

Satan said the same things to Jesus:

"You deserve this."

"You don't deserve this."

"It would have been easier to abort this mission, start all over and save Yourself!"

Jesus knew His walk on earth would be hard. Forced to flee the country, as a baby, from those who would take His life; forsaken by the friends who claimed to love Him most; rejected by the very ones He'd come to save, He died alone.

He knows our pain: the pain of every parent who shepherds a broken child through life. The prophet Isaiah tells us in his book that it is "by his wounds we are healed" (Isa. 53:5). Ever struggled with pain for your child? Jesus gets it. He has been there. His heart was broken so we would have the assurance that our story does not end here. He will wipe away all tears. He will heal all brokenness. Hold on to His strength. His promise is sure.

Father, You know what it is like to have a broken child. Please heal my wounded heart. Help me endure and find the peace that comes from knowing You hold us in Your hands.

Jesse Ferguson

Uncharted Waters

If any of you lacks wisdom, let him ask of God, who gives to all liberally and without reproach, and it will be given to him. James 1:5, NKJV.

After an hour of play one beautiful spring morning, I began to secure my happy, 2-year-old twin boys into their stroller. With one boy safely belted and buckled, I turned to do the same to the other, but he was nowhere to be seen. Panic immediately set in. I called his name to no avail. My 5-year-old daughter joined in the frantic search. "Help me, Lord!" I screamed in my head.

After what seemed an eternity, I heard my daughter laugh and say, "There you are, silly boy." Indeed, there he was, standing quietly behind a tree, transfixed by something visible only to him. Prayers of thanksgiving poured from my lips as I held my precious boy close. He didn't respond. He didn't sense my panic. He didn't answer to his name . . . again. This had been happening more and more. A deep, nagging fear had begun to tug at my heart, for I knew something was very wrong.

Despite my intuition, I greeted the diagnosis of autism spectrum disorder with disbelief, then denial, and finally, overwhelming grief. "Why, Lord?" soon changed to "What now, Lord?"

Only one Person knew the answers to all my questions. The lyrics from the old gospel song "If we ever needed the Lord before, we sure do need Him now" expressed my heartfelt need for my Savior, Friend, and Guide, as my husband, my son, and I began to navigate the rough waters of autism. Parenting is challenging. Parenting children with special needs is even more so. It requires a double measure of God's power, wisdom, and strength.

My boys are 5 now. God has answered our prayers for healing, guidance, and strength in ways that leave us with no doubt as to His leading. The way has not been easy, but I am determined to hold on to the hand of the One who "is able to do exceedingly abundantly above all that we ask or think" (Eph. 3:20, NKJV).

Father, teach us to recognize Your voice. May we walk where You lead us with confidence, knowing You will be there to guide and to bless.

Lesley Jackson

Something Else You Should Know

*Let us hold fast the confession of our hope without wavering,
for He who promised is faithful. Heb. 10:23, NKJV.*

Parents of special-needs children are faced with a unique set of challenges. We appreciate so much the understanding from other parents that every day is tough and that a few kind words of support will go a long way in helping us to take one more step forward through the day. A few other things to know about us include the following:

We feel scared. We continually ask questions: Are the doctors right? What treatment is available that we haven't yet heard about? Will it work for our child? We research and talk with everyone and anyone because they might know someone or something that can help.

The questions that plague us personally include: What is going to happen to Makayla in the future? Will she ever talk normally? Will she get married? How will she tell us what she is thinking? It's too soon to know if the fear of these unanswered questions will ever lessen, but until then, we cling to God and claim His promise: " 'For I know the plans I have for you,' declares the Lord, 'plans to prosper you and not to harm you, plans to give you hope and a future' " (Jer. 29:11).

We claim God's promises. We don't feel we did anything wrong. Nor do we think God gave us a special-needs child because we need to learn some lesson. We are not stronger than the average person, but we soon learn to trust God no matter what. And we learn to hold fast to His promises—for He who promised is faithful.

We love Makayla, and we know God will help us as we continue this journey one step at a time; one day at a time; one milestone at a time. And yes, we continue to pray for healing. We will always pray for healing. And we continue to cling to His promise: " 'For my thoughts are not your thoughts, neither are your ways my ways,' declares the Lord" (Isa. 55:8).

Lord, we pray for patient endurance, for unwavering trust in You, and unfailing peace as we meet our daily challenges.

Jackie Benwell Hood

As We Follow

Trust in the Lord with all thine heart;
and lean not unto thine own understanding. Prov. 3:5, KJV.

As a baby, Timothy could stand alone at 7 months. At 10 months he started to run. His mischievous eyes and teasing smile were God's healing balm for us after losing our precious baby girl in a car accident.

Our excitement as he began school, however, soon turned to dismay when we discovered our bright-eyed boy wasn't learning to read or write. Elementary school seemed a maze of dead ends at every turn. The many help programs briefly fanned a flicker of hope, only to burn out and leave us disappointed. Only parents of severely dyslexic children can understand the journey.

Then, unexpectedly, in sixth grade Timothy morphed into a brilliant rugby player. He represented Matabeleland (consisting of three provinces) and was selected to represent his country, Zimbabwe. I had one question: "Will he have to play on Sabbath?" The answer: "Ma'am, he has a rare gift, the makings of a world-class sportsman. It would require him to play most Saturdays."

The tears now flowed freely. How I hurt for my boy, yet how grateful I was to see him take his stand for the Lord. I cried out silently, "Lord, You blessed him with a gift he cannot use and still obey You. Why not just the gift of literacy?"

High school had its own challenges. Our hearts sank when he was offered a place in special ed that would not lead to the equivalent of a GED. And we had to sign that he would attend Saturday sports events. Once again we cried out to God as we called the principal of a boarding school in the Midlands.

We held our breath as Tim was accepted and placed with the other students. The teachers were alerted to the challenges. Fear, mingled with hope, turned into grateful praise when his grades came. He had passed all but one subject. Four amazing, challenging years later, he had his GED and was ready to go on to college. At each step of the way, God has led. What blessings have followed in the train of obedience.

May we faithfully follow through the years; forgive our questions, doubts, and fears.

Helen Louise Hall

Bringing Our Children to the Cross

So do not fear, for I am with you; do not be dismayed,
for I am your God. I will strengthen you and help you;
I will uphold you with my righteous right hand. Isa. 41:10.

One of my favorite parts of the book *Pilgrim's Progress* is the one in which the character Christian finally arrives at the cross with his burden. As he stands there, his unbearable load suddenly falls to the ground, rolls down the hill, and is lost inside an empty tomb.

It may sound strange to say it in this way, but I sometimes think our greatest burdens are our children. I do not mean they are our emotional baggage. I simply mean they are burdens because our children are what we care about most. We lose sleep worrying if they are going to be all right when they are sick. We wake up in the middle of the night if they cry out, and we set land-record speeds to reach them if there is any chance they may be in danger of getting hurt somehow.

Our children are our greatest treasures and our greatest burdens. Doesn't it therefore make sense that we should, like Christian, bring them to the cross?

I remember when our son, Noah, was finally diagnosed with having a learning disorder. I wanted to cry because, even though I am a counselor, I felt overwhelmed by the burden of trying to help my son cope with his disability. Then I remembered that my husband and I weren't alone in raising Noah. God had formed Noah and knew everything about him. If I took my burden for Noah to Jesus, then I would be free of all the fear and stress.

Whether you are the parent of a child with a disability or the parent of a healthy, rambunctious whirlwind, God is there for you. He sees you and He knows your needs. He is waiting to give you the strength and skills you need to raise your son or daughter to be a follower of Christ. He will give you the wisdom you lack. All you have to do is go to the cross and lay your burden for your child at the feet of Jesus.

Lord God, please help us bear our burdens and bring our cares to You, so we may be free to be the parents you call us to be.

Asheley Woodruff

Faith in Action

My help comes from the Lord, who made heaven and earth. Ps. 121:2, ESV.

As a mental health therapist I work with special-needs children and their families every day. I often meet with overwhelmed parents looking for help for their children who are diagnosed with ADHD (attention-defici-hyperactivity disorder) or a PDD (pervasive developmental disorder). I also work with those who are possibly further along the road, struggling to deal with autism or some other mental health diagnosis that communicates their difficulty in how to relate to others or develop in a typical way.

Often these parents are frustrated, angry, and exhausted. They're in crisis because they don't know what to do or where to turn, and they feel judged and rejected by society and their families. So, how do we make peace with those things we can't fix with a Band-Aid or a hug?

We accept our responsibility to care for our children in all aspects of their lives. If our child is hurt, we don't leave them to cry or bleed; we do something to help them. If our child has a learning disability or struggles to maintain attention or behave appropriately, we intervene and find the help of a professional who understands how to work with our child. Seeking help is not a betrayal of your faith—it is faith in action.

We live in a fallen world afflicted by sin, and it is only through faith and trusting that God will use our lives to His glory that we are able to leave the things we do not understand in His hands. Conditions such as a learning disorder, ADHD, or autism are not a reflection upon the individual or family having done or neglected to do something. It is not something they deserve. When undeserved suffering comes to us or our children, it is natural that we are tempted to ask, "How could a loving God allow this?" When we are discouraged, this is the time to reach out to your family and church and ask them to pray for you and help you through the tough times, to be another resource in your time of need.

We are all special-needs children before God, and it is only through the grace of God in our lives that we can overcome the issues we struggle with.

Lord, my help comes from You, and I pray You will give me the strength and wisdom to know when to ask for help from others and the courage to trust in Your will and ability to use my life and my children's lives to Your glory, even when it hurts.

Colleen Duncan

316

Who Cares?

Casting all your care upon Him, for He cares for you. 1 Peter 5:7, NKJV.

Have you ever wondered who cares when your child has undiagnosed seizures and you can't seem to ease their pain? What about having to move again because the neighbors complain about your child's screaming? Have you wondered who cares when you can't communicate with your child and you don't know if it will ever change?

Mary and Martha wondered if Jesus cared. They sent word to Him about Lazarus: "Lord, the one you love is sick" (John 11:3), yet Jesus took His time getting to them. When He arrived at Bethany, they said, "Lord, if You had been here, our brother would not have died" (see verse 21). I'm sure they wondered, If Jesus cares, why isn't He here? Why do we have to experience this pain, this loss?

Jesus knew the end of the story, yet, in His compassion for them, He wept. Jesus demonstrated His care and concern. And He cares for you today. Actually, CARE is a good acronym to remember while parenting a child with a disability.

Collaborate: Build relationships with professionals, educators, church members, and within your community. Seek help and build a network of support for your family. "Two are better than one, because they have a good reward for their toil" (Eccl. 4:9, ESV).

Advocate: Be vigilant in educating others about disabilities, dispelling myths, and increasing supports for resources. "It was not that this man sinned, or his parents, but that the works of God might be displayed in him" (John 9:3, ESV).

Release: Commit your child to the Lord and trust that He cares about you, and for your child, too. "Lord Almighty, if you will only look on your servant's misery and remember me, . . . then I will give him to the Lord for all the days of his life" (1 Sam. 1:11).

Exalt: Choosing to have an attitude of gratitude can displace resentment, anger, and self-pity. "In everything give thanks" (1 Thess. 5:18, NKJV).

Dear heavenly Father, thank You for being a God who cares. Please help me to trust You even when I feel hopeless and alone. Thank You for entrusting me with the care of this special child, who is precious in Your sight. Please help me to care as You do.

Davenia Lea

What Are We Into?

*I tell you, whoever publicly acknowledges me before others,
the Son of Man will also acknowledge before the angels of God. Luke 12:8.*

So we are at the checkout counter at the hardware store and my boys look up and see scores of gross Halloween skeletons decorating the store exit. They look at me and say, "Mommy, that scares me." I tell them to look away. The cashier looks at us in perplexity, and says, "It's Halloween!" My youngest son, Samuel, looks at her seriously and says confidently, "I am into God things."

What are we into? Whatever it is, chances are our children will be into it too. We know they follow more closely what they see us do than what they hear us say. Seeing the look on the cashier's face as she heard those words come from a 6-year-old made me proud my child had chosen to take a stand for God. It meant I was doing something right. They were a reflection of my teaching, but more important, Samuel was speaking his mind and his heart.

That same evening, while snuggling Samuel to sleep, he said, "Mommy, I can't get those scary thoughts out of my head." I prayed with him and had him repeat, "God, come into my heart. Fill me with Your wisdom and knowledge. Redeem my thoughts and fill me with Your peace." This simple request, graciously answered, allowed him to fall asleep peacefully.

In this noisy world, where the roaring lion sets snares to try to devour us and our children, it is crucial that we have our minds set on God. As parents we are responsible for what we allow into our minds and what we set in front of our children to watch. Many TV shows seem harmless, but a single disturbing scene can plant a seed of fear that grows in the minds of our children, causing an unsettled, stressed-out mind and unrest in their hearts.

God did not create fear, nor does He want us to be fearful. Take time to listen to that still small voice, so when the time is right we will speak up for God.

Father, keep me mindful of the things I set before my eyes. May I look to You each day, and guide me as I teach my little ones to do the same.

Tami Faudi

November

The Joys of Grandparenting

The Second Chance

For the Lord is good; his steadfast love endures forever,
and his faithfulness to all generations. Ps. 100:5, ESV.

I'd said for many years that if I were to become a parent again, I'd be a much better one than I was at 21. H'mmm. Be careful what you say. You may be given a second chance. Parenting in my mid-50s is not exactly what I had planned for my life—but God has promised that He will give me what I need to do it well.

The statistics regarding the number of grandparents who now parent their grandchildren is pretty startling. My husband and I are knee-deep in coparenting Chloe, our almost-4-year-old granddaughter, with my son and Chloe's mom. My son and Chloe live with us.

As I help raise this precious child, I am grateful for all the kinks I have worked out in my life. I know now what matters most in life. I have a better grasp on spirituality versus religion. I have something valuable to share regarding what it means to be a Christian. I have learned that it is all about Jesus. It's just that simple.

As I face the last years of my life I now focus on what matters most. As Chloe comes into her relationship with Jesus, she has the innocence and trust as only children can have. I get the opportunity to teach her what a relationship with Jesus looks like through my example. I want to teach goodness, kindness, generosity, concern for others, love, compassion, reverence, joy, peace, gentleness, and faith. I am humbled.

C. Everett Koop said, "Life affords no greater responsibility, no greater privilege, than the raising of the next generation." I can say that I am doing a much better job as a grandparent than I did as a parent, thanks to the life lessons God's allowed me to experience and to His grace and mercy.

So, if you are a grandparent who is parenting . . . hold fast to Jesus. Keep looking up. God has given you a second chance, and He will give you all you need to do it well.

Father, I pray not that You take this responsibility of parenting away from me, but that You work through me to be what this child needs most. Thank You.

Mary Nell Rosenboom

Be With Me!

*Yes, when you get serious about finding me
and want it more than anything else,
I'll make sure you won't be disappointed. Jer. 29:14, Message.*

Because of the multistate distance separating us, visits with my grandchildren are too few and far between. So, whenever we can coordinate a visit, it is a fairly long one. As much as I love my grandchildren, I forget—between visits—how energetic they are, and how old I am getting. Still, I try to throw as much of my energy into those precious moments as I can. Sometimes I fail.

One day during a California visit, I played in the treehouse fort with 2-year-old Zion for two hours, helped 5-year-old Eden roll up and down the block on wobbly in-line skates, made lunch for them, and mediated mealtime bickering. I'd read stories to them and tried to keep one step ahead of their bright, but short, attention spans. When my daughter-in-law returned with the baby from an appointment in town and announced that it was "quiet time," I was there!

Zion went to his bedroom for a nap. Eden went to the homeschool/playroom to read and quietly listen to music. Pam retired to her room to put the baby down, and I lay down on the living room couch. Soon a slight rustling made me open my eyes. Eden was standing over me, holding a handwritten note. She gently, quietly placed it on my chest before disappearing back to her quiet time room to await my response. She'd painstakingly written, "Dear Grammy, my mom is gowing to lay down my mom told me we cood ride in the new pickup my mom says so maybe you could have time with me like some girl time I love you grammy."

That was an offer my heart could not refuse. I slipped out quietly to the quiet time room, where a joyful Eden and I decided to watch an educational cartoon. Eden sat in a little chair beside me and chuckled at the cartoon until she noticed I was thumbing through a magazine. She turned toward me, blocked my page-turning with her little hand, and pleaded, "But I want you to be with me, Grammy. Really be with me. I love you." Little pleading arms encircled my neck.

O my patient God, forgive me for thumbing through magazines and all manner of other distractions instead of hearing You say how much You want to be me . . . because You love me.

Carolyn Sutton

Wait for Me

*Trust in the Lord with all your heart,
and lean not on your own understanding;
in all your ways acknowledge Him,
and He shall direct your paths. Prov. 3:5, 6, NKJV.*

My youngest granddaughter, Emaleigh, is 14 months old. Although she is still learning to walk and talk, she lets us know what she wants and where she wants to go. She takes our hand and begins to walk, and although we are holding her hand she is the one who leads the way. If she sees something she wants she points to it, looks at us, says something no one can understand, and keeps pointing until we give her the toy or book or favorite blanket.

A few days ago we were with Emaleigh and her daddy in the front yard. Her mother, Ashleigh, came out of the house, got in the car, and closed the door. She was rushing to an appointment. Emaleigh, who almost always goes with her mother, pointed to her and started to cry, then talk as if to say, "Wait for me!" She pointed to herself and to the car again. She looked at us and pointed again to herself and then to the car as her mom backed out of the driveway. As she drove off without her, Emaleigh started to cry. Just then her daddy extended his arms and picked her up out of the baby walker. She accepted his loving arms gladly, and as he held her close she stopped crying.

Emaleigh's behavior is entirely appropriate for a 14-month-old. But what about us? Do we tend to take Jesus' hand and try to direct Him where we want to go? Do we chatter away, saying things that no one understands? Are we growing and maturing in our walk with Christ?

The only sure way to grow spiritually is to spend time in His Word, seeking to know Him. As we do this, He will make Himself known and will direct us in the way we should go. We are content to give Him our hand, and let Him lead.

And on those days when we feel abandoned by those we love, God can pick us up in His loving arms and comfort us. What sweet trust! Lord, give me the wisdom I need to place my hand in Yours, and trust wherever You lead, and help me to teach my children to do the same.

Hope Ayala Benavides

Musings of a Grandfather

*Children's children are a crown to the aged,
and parents are the pride of their children. Prov. 17:6.*

I just found another of Cassie's Cheerios," I said to Sue while vacuuming. To my surprise, I felt my heart overflow with a myriad of feelings as I spotted that Cheerio on the floor under the edge of a chair. It began the first time I saw her. Cassandra Elizabeth, that is. I first entered her Alabama home when she was just hours home from the hospital. Her eyes locked on mine as if to say, "I thought I had everyone in this place accounted for. Who are you?" From that moment on, I was a willing captive to her charms.

We live more than 600 miles away, but distance has been only a tiny obstacle to regular visits. Talking with our daughter on the phone while Cassie chirps and chortles in the background adds to the delight of any conversation. I had looked forward to being a grandparent. My own grandfathers had died many years before I was born, but my parents gave me a model to follow as they loved my own children.

As I continue to vacuum, my mind wanders and wonders. What will Cassie's world be like as she matures? In an increasingly unsafe world, will she experience trust, faith, and confidence in her family and friends? What about school? Will she be optimistic? Will this little one, who already offers to share her Cheerios with our dog and cats, grow up to be generous in spirit? Will her precious smile and ready giggle always be so quick to burst forth?

Will she develop a personal relationship with Jesus? She has the opportunity to become a sixth-generation Seventh-day Adventist. Will she see that as a blessed heritage or a burden? Will she follow the Lord with a mature faith that will guide her through the potholes of adolescence and into adulthood? These are the musings of this grandfather as the vacuum discovers another Cheerio left over from summer's visit. She has given me a new passion—that of being a grandfather.

O Lord, what a privilege and responsibility is this gift of being a grandparent. Help me to be faithful.

Don Murray

My Great-Grandmother's Best Gift

I praise you because I am fearfully and wonderfully made;
your works are wonderful, I know that full well. Ps. 139:14.

I picked up a doll in a gift shop in Arizona and read about its creator, Danna. The name of her company is Danna Does Dolls. Each doll comes with a tag that reads "I remember as a young child my grandmother taking me to a field of bright-orange poppies. She showed me how to fold and remove certain parts of the flower and then use my fingernail to carve a face in the soft pod. Suddenly, I had created my first doll . . . Such magic! Maybe because I loved my grandmother so much, and maybe because of the wonder I felt at making those dolls just one month out of the year, I still love to make dolls. Today my Dolls are more permanent, but they too are pure magic."

I exclaimed to the owner of the store, "Why, my great-grandmother taught me how to make dolls out of orange California poppies, too!" I felt an instant kinship with Danna—and the link was our grandmothers.

My grandparents were immensely important to me. They took me into their home when I was almost 3 and, taking on the role of parents, they raised me as their own. It was my great-grandmother who taught me how to make the poppy dolls. She also taught me how to bake bread, make jelly, and expertly shine my grandpa's dress shoes. She could peel an apple in one long, curling serpentine. Then she would tell me to make three wishes as we twirled the apple peelings over our heads, laughing as we made our wishes.

While sharing these memories with a friend one day, she thoughtfully added that perhaps the most important thing my grandmother taught me was that I could do things, that I was capable. I agreed. Many grandparents today find themselves playing the role of parent in the lives of their grandchildren. They need our prayers. Never underestimate the power for good a grandparent can have in the life of a grandchild. I am living proof of that.

By the way, one of Danna's dolls came home with me, and she now lives at our house.

Lord, thank You for godly grandparents who taught me that You created me wonderfully well. Bless grandparents who stand in the place of parents and lead their little ones to You.

Susan Murray

Freeze-frame

I tell you the truth, unless you turn from your sins and become like little children, you will never get into the Kingdom of Heaven. Matt. 18:3, NLT.

There is nothing more miraculous in life than the arrival of a baby. And grandchildren are one of the most precious miracles of all. When that little person pops onto the scene—everything else stops! Beautiful, innocent, and seemingly untainted by the evil of this world, their hearts are like a clear, fresh tablet yet to be written on—unbroken and trusting. If only we could just freeze-frame this moment and make it last forever before the blight of sin makes its mark and takes away their sweet innocence.

Jesus knows the temptations and brokenness of each of our hearts. He has not forgotten the struggles the first parents had with their own disobedience and the pain they felt as they watched their children following in their footsteps as sinners. The whole world still suffers from the consequences of their choice. And Jesus came to rescue us all because, like me, He loves His kids!

There is nothing my new little grandchild could ever do to make me love her less. I love her with all the ability of a grandma's heart. And although I can hardly fathom it, as much as I love my granddaughter, how much more does our Creator love and adore us? How do you measure that kind of love? How strange that we sometimes struggle with wondering whether He loves us. How He longs for us to recognize our need of Him, to be humbled, yet encouraged, by the simple truth that we need Him. We cannot fix ourselves. We are as dependent as little babes on His power and His sacrifice to live for His kingdom.

Eye has not seen, ear has not heard, nor has entered into the mind of man the things He has prepared for us there! Why? Because He loves His kids! Remember to fill your life with His love every day! It makes all the difference. And little ones are watching us.

Dear Jesus, fill us with You, so we can give our children and grandchildren what they need most: Your love, even on the tough days! Thank You for the power You promise to give us—power to be like, to love like, You.

Cheri Gatton

"Girl Talk"

*I pray that your love will overflow more and more,
and that you will keep on growing in knowledge
and understanding. Phil. 1:9, NLT.*

When my first granddaughter, Ashley, was just starting to talk, we began to have "girl talk." When she was younger we talked about things she knew. I asked her about her favorite color or animal and why these were her favorites. We talked about why we liked the shoes we were wearing. We laughed as we talked about the family dogs. We discussed the things that were important to her. I wanted her to learn early that I was a safe person and that I would listen to her. If anyone came near the stairs, she would call out, "Go away! We're doing 'girl talk'!"

As she grew older we continued to talk, often in the car when we were going places. Our conversations changed with her age. We talked about her friendships at school and church. We shared with each other why we loved God and why church was important to each of us. She was open and honest in her opinions, and so was I. But again, there were no wrong answers.

When she got her driver's license she told me, "I'm glad to get my license, but I am going to miss having you drive me places, because that is our time to talk. Maybe you can still drive me once in a while so we can just talk alone."

Now she is almost 18 and ready to graduate from high school. Still she opens her heart readily to me. She knows that I will listen to her thoughts and her feelings. She understands that I will respect her opinions even if I do not agree. I tell her my thoughts without trying to make her accept them as her own. Because there is no pressure, she feels free to agree or disagree. Sometimes I later hear her express my feelings or opinions as her very own!

Our "girl talk" has been important in our relationship, just the way I hoped it would be. It did not happen by chance. It took intentional planning to make it happen and keep it relevant. "Girl talk" has been not only fun but also an important part of my grandparenting. Try it with your grandkids!

Father God, keep us listening to our kids and grandkids the way You listen to us. You are always interested, always take time, and always love being with us.

Ginny Allen

He Is Here

*The grace of God . . . has appeared, . . . teaching us . . . [to look]
for the blessed hope, and glorious appearing
of our . . . Savior Jesus Christ. Titus 2:11-13, NKJV.*

Every night when I put my granddaughter to bed, after reading three books and saying her prayers, she asks me, "Gaga, is Jesus coming tonight?" Then we talk about Jesus. When she wakes up the next morning, her first question is "Gaga, is Jesus coming today?" Morning and evening my answer always includes "I sure hope so, Chloe."

Inevitably our discussions also include Nathan Green's *Second Coming* painting, which is framed and on her nightstand. "Gaga, are we in the picture?"

"No, Chloe, but we will be there the day Jesus comes. So will our angels." And that follows with a discussion about angels.

Oh, how hard it is to look at the longing in her little face, a longing that reflects my own, and know some of the challenges she will yet have to face while living here. How important to remember that this world is not our home. We were created for eternity. We were created to live in a world without sin and pain. But have courage! The world we were created for is coming. Don't take my word for it. Go to God's Word. Soak up His promises and share them with the special little people in your life.

I pray that one day I can look up and say, "Yes, Chloe, Jesus *is* coming today." I know it's possible that I will be at rest on that day, but I love to visualize Chloe and me running into each other's arms, jumping up and down, and hearing her shout, "He's here, Gaga! Jesus is here!" Then, we turn and meet our angels and go to Jesus. Oh, what a glorious day that will be.

Hold fast to Jesus as you lead your precious little people to Him. Remember what C. S. Lewis stated: "There are far, far better things ahead than any we leave behind."

Dear Father, may the promise of Jesus' soon return fill us with anticipation and deepest hope. Keep it real to us—that as we share the promise with our little ones it will become real to them too. One day. One day soon, may we each be able to point heavenward and say, "He is here! Jesus is here!"

Mary Nell Rosenboom

Row With Your Kids, Not Against Them

*I am reminded of your sincere faith, which first lived in your grandmother Lois
and in your mother Eunice and, I am persuaded,
now lives in you also. 2 Tim. 1:5.*

As everyone knows, it's Grandpa's job to provide horsey rides of unlimited frequency; read bedtime stories and pantomime the nightly growly-bear routine; watch *Shark Tale* innumerable times every year, even when the World Series is airing at the exact same time; and hand over to Grandma the seemingly unlimited funds she needs in order to pay for birthday presents, doughnut holes with sprinkles, and airplane tickets for landmark events such as baptisms and first tooth out.

Our grandkids are at the stage of wide-eyed absorption of many details. So I pray daily they'll lock in a picture of a heavenly Father's tender and passionate care whenever Grandpa comes to visit for the weekend. But this is a spiritual river with many submerged rocks.

Grandparents must look in the mirror of time and realize that grandparenting is not parenting; we are not in charge of the spiritual kingdoms established by our children. Directing these children toward a relationship with Jesus is another person's primary role I dare not usurp. First, it wouldn't be right. Second, it could create lasting resentment. Third, it would imply to my daughters that I don't think their own labors are sufficiently diligent or doctrinally sound.

I tend to be a cheerful kind of grandpa. But regarding spiritual things, experience shows how winsome easily morphs into overbearing; family prayers can become a message diverted instead toward lukewarm parents and what we perceive as the Baal worship going on one branch below us on the family tree. This calls for plenty of grace and some sanctified tongue-biting.

The best spiritual grandparenting—speaking of rivers—happens when we graciously row with our children, buttressing and affirming their own efforts. Publicly express that you admire their successes and want to be a welcome ally.

Thank You, Father, for wisdom to know how best to support my children in their role as parents—even when their methods are not what I would choose. Help me to trust that You are at work in them and through them—even as You were with me—back in the "dark ages."

David B. Smith

My Miracle Grandbaby

Behold, I am the Lord, the God of all flesh.
Is there anything too hard for Me? Jer. 32:27, NKJV.

My daughter's first pregnancy ended abruptly at 24 weeks. It found me unprepared—I hadn't bought anything for the baby yet. But shopping was the last thing on my mind the day Michaela was born. As I stood beside the tiny bed where she lay hooked to a respirator and several monitors, the only thing on my mind was Will she live?

My heart ached for my children. When infections invaded Michaela's body and toxins built in her blood, her kidneys shut down, and the doctors gave up hope. But my children didn't. Irytta continued to pump and freeze-store her milk. Courageously my daughter and son-in-law held on to hope. Like the woman of Shunem who could say, "All is well," even though her son had died, Irytta had faith to believe the same. They got a miracle. God healed Michaela.

Many mornings during those uncertain weeks my Bible fell open to Jeremiah 32, and my eyes were drawn to verse 27. It was the promise God gave me and how I clung to it. During the four months my granddaughter was in the hospital I'd visit as often as possible. It was so hard to watch an innocent baby being traumatized by pain. Standing beside her little bed, I asked my Father to hold her in His hand so she would not feel alone and I thanked Him for her life.

It was a happy day when Michaela came home. I would stay over and watch her overnight a couple times each week so her mother could rest. She had to stay at home and away from germs until she was bigger and stronger, so I got to babysit often. Sometimes on Sabbath, while her parents attended church, I would bathe and dress her, then we would rock while I sang her songs about Jesus and His love. Those were special bonding times.

Michaela is a teenager now, and I still commit her to God's keeping every day. What a privilege to be Grammy to both her and her younger brother, Anthony.

Father, nothing is too hard for You, but even if we don't get the miracle we're so desperately praying for, help us to trust You still.

Barbara Ann Kay

Love Across the Miles

*For God is my witness, how greatly I long for you all
with the affection of Jesus Christ. Phil. 1:8, NKJV.*

I never imagined we'd live so far from our grandchildren. My dreams of grandkids included them living nearby. Their parents would drop them off when they went shopping. I'd pick them up from school. We'd play ball and paper dolls. They'd stand on a chair beside me and help me make cookies. We'd be at every school program, wildly clapping their performances. Instead, two grandsons live 600 miles north of us, and one lives 600 miles south. The others, a girl and a boy, live in Kenya, Africa, with their missionary parents. So tell me, what's a grandma to do?

Skype can work well, if you can make it work to fit busy schedules and different time zones. But for us old-fashioned grandmas, letter writing is better. A letter, at least every two weeks, will keep you in their lives. Send a picture you've drawn—young kids aren't critical—pictures to color, stickers, a fun quiz, a stick of gum, or dimes to put in their bank. After a visit, make a booklet of photos of you and them together.

You can read or tell stories for an iPad and send short videos by e-mail. Today's technology gives us so many options. And we can't forget personal visits. Next month I'll go down to babysit Mr. 2-Year-Old, for Daddy will be out of town, and Mama has an uncertain work schedule. Both my husband and I have done this, and we love it.

With the kids in Africa, e-mail is the best option, as Skype has never worked well for us. Even so, year after year we've watched them open Christmas presents, and that's fun for both families. An annual leave brings them back to the States every summer, and several times I've taken courage in hand and have gone to see them. The long flights and layovers are absolutely worth it when I see our granddaughter playing in the violin ensemble for church and our grandson singing in the children's choir.

Dear Lord, thank You for the many ways we have today to keep in touch with our grandchildren. Help us keep connected and relevant in their lives—and may we always point them to You.

Penny Estes Wheeler

The Delights of Grandparenting

Take delight in the Lord, and he will give you your heart's desires. Ps. 37:4, NLT.

What brings you delight in your relationship with the Lord?

It's Sunday morning, my favorite time of the week, for today is the day I get to speak to, see, and delight in Kayla, Ethan, and Zara, our grandchildren. We live in the United States, and they live in Africa—Ghana and South Africa—so we have to make allowances for time zones, sleep times, work schedules, and social activities.

There is only one thing more delightful than being a parent, and that is being a grandparent. Connecting with our children and grandchildren is a priority for my husband and me. At 6 months, 2 years, and 3 years of age, the grandchildren are growing, learning, and developing so quickly we can hardly keep up with them. We are so grateful to have daughters-in-law and sons who value family enough to share the special moments in their children's lives with us and text us from the other side of the globe with video clips and photographs almost every day. We cherish each contact. We check our telephones every morning to see what they have been up to during their day while we have been sleeping.

We delight in every word they speak, every sound or response that we get. We watch them build their tents, have their tea parties, eat their supper, smile their first smiles, roll over, sit for the first time, play with their toes, and take their first steps. While we're not present to give our children the child-care help I am sure they'd appreciate, we can give them support and encouragement and enjoy their delight in being parents.

Taking delight in the Lord and taking delight in children and grandchildren have plenty in common. We can relish our moments with God, savor them, talk about them with one another just as we tell of the latest escapades of our grandchildren. And all the while we can trust that God knows the innermost "desires of our hearts," and He promises to grant those to us.

Heavenly Father, thank You for granting us the desires of our heart, and for understanding the love we have for our grandchildren. What a gift—thank You!

Shirley Allen

Children See, Children Do

Truly I tell you, the Son can do nothing by himself;
he can do only what he sees his Father doing,
because whatever the Father does the Son also does. John 5:19.

I was standing in line to buy breakfast, and just in front of me stood a grandpa and his grandson. Obviously unhappy about the slow service, the grandpa was berating the cashier, who was trying her best to hurry with his order. She was unable to answer his questions to his satisfaction, and he shouted, "What's wrong with you? You work here, and you don't know? Then who are we supposed to ask?" After he was through, the 6-year-old grandson repeated the exact same words while wagging his little finger at the cashier, just like his grandfather had.

Modeling—the best teaching strategy there is on Planet Earth. Good or bad, children learn best by mimicking adults. If parents want their children to pray and read the Bible and have a strong belief in God, then parents—and grandparents—need to be seen praying and reading their Bibles. Often we say, "Don't do as I do! Just do as I say!" That kind of attitude will not work. Our children learn more from our example than from our preaching or teaching. In the religious upbringing of our children we have to be genuine. We must be authentic, and the best way to do that is to live like a Christ follower.

Simply talking about values without living them will never work. Jesus condemned the Pharisees in His day by telling His listeners in Matthew 23:3, "Do everything they tell you. But do not do what they do, for they do not practice what they preach."

On a wall in our office is a chart that testifies to the effectiveness of modeling. A family tree shows Hannah and Gorden Oss, who served in Trinidad from 1934 to 1939. These missionaries started the ball rolling for their family, and eventually four more generations of missionaries served in many parts of Africa.

Jesus is our example. He told us that He does what His Father does. Parents would do well to follow what Jesus did, for without a doubt, what children see, children will do.

May I be ever mindful, Lord, of what I am modeling to the little ones in my life.

Sally Lam-Phoon

The Challenge of the Age

And Jesus increased in wisdom and in stature,
and in favor with God and man. Luke 2:52, RSV.

Within each era, grandparenting has had its own unique challenges, joys, and sorrows. As I contemplate the era I grew up in, my grandparents were creeping out of World War II. I have memories of my grandmother and mother going to the market and standing in a long line as they waited their turn to pay for the few items that were available. My grandfather was unable to find work. In spite of the fact that my grandparents' challenge was poverty, they gave their all to make my journey as comfortable as they knew how. There was never a shortage of love, laughter, and appreciation. I remember helping my grandfather mix cement and playing games with him. My grandmother showed me how to bake cookies, how to knit, and how to play the piano. It was these fond memories that made me determined to give my grandchildren happy memories.

One of the greatest challenge in this era is materialism. Electronics seem to be the monster captivating and devouring our grandchildren's attention, and the enemy is doing all in his power to divert their minds from God's kingdom. Staying on bended knees on behalf of our grandchildren and trusting God for wisdom and guidance on how to bring their interest to the spiritual realm is a journey. One that requires patience—but God never lets us down.

His Word powerfully reveals His special love for His children. As I pondered the words in Luke 2:40, "And the child grew and waxed strong in spirit, filled with wisdom: and the grace of God was upon him" (KJV), I realized that God would do that for our children too. He has a special place for children and says, "Verily I say unto you, Except ye be converted, and become as little children, ye shall not enter into the kingdom of heaven" (Matt. 18:3, KJV).

By introducing them to Jesus from the start, we can give our grandchildren a strong foundation that will help them face the challenge of the age, whatever it may be.

Lord, keep me from becoming discouraged by the challenges of this age. Instead, may I keep my eyes on Jesus, and show my grandchildren a better way.

June Burn

Their Eyes Are Watching

Just make sure you stay alert. Keep close watch over yourselves.
Don't forget anything of what you've seen. Don't let your heart wander off.
Stay vigilant as long as you live. Teach what you've seen and heard
to your children and grandchildren. Deut. 4:9, Message.

The Bible is so practical and helpful for families. Our text today is a challenge for grandparents. Since we don't live in the same house with our extended families anymore, it's sometimes difficult for families to figure out how grandparents fit into the picture.

Four principles cover the parent/grandparent relationship: respect, responsibility, reciprocity, and resiliency. Today's text shows us how this works.

Respect: Keep close watch over yourselves. Children learn by example, so although grandparents are not the primary molder of children, they are watched to see how they interact with the child's parents and if they countermand parental rules.

Responsibility: Stay vigilant as long as you live. Grandparents can't talk about God's faithfulness, mercy, and unfailing love without speaking of how God has been their God throughout their lives.

Reciprocity: Teach what you've seen and heard to your children and grandchildren. A grandparent's relationship with God that is real and vibrant is the priceless legacy a grandparent can pass on to following generations.

Resiliency: Don't forget anything of what you've seen. Grandparents know the stories of their grandchildren's parents as well as their own. Children who know who they are and where they come from can handle anything life throws at them. They know their family has faced challenges in order to be where they are today—that's resilience!

Being a grandparent is delightful—you get to love unconditionally. Yet, you know and understand the challenges of raising children. Grandparents can hold up the hands of the parents when they tire of the day-to-day responsibility of rearing children.

Father God, help me teach my grandchildren all these things by the example of how I treat and love their parents.

Wilma Kirk-Lee

Grandparenting
in the Twenty-first Century

*Only take care, and keep your soul diligently, lest you forget the things
that your eyes have seen, and lest they depart from your heart
all the days of your life. Make them known to your children
and your children's children. Deut. 4:9, ESV.*

Grandparenting has taken on a whole new role in the twenty-first century. According to the National Center for Health Statistics, 60 percent of marriages for couples between the ages of 20 and 25 end in divorce. When children are involved, this takes grandparenting to a whole new level.

In many American homes today it's the grandparents who are helping to raise their grandchildren. If they're not assisting in raising them, they're often left struggling to maintain a relationship with the ex-in-laws. This can make grandparenting extremely complicated.

Our son and daughter-in-law divorced after five years of marriage, shortly after their beautiful little girl was born. This broke our hearts, and we wondered when we would get to see our granddaughter. Fortunately, our ex-daughter-in-law wanted us to stay in contact and be there for her little girl, even though it would be long-distance grandparenting.

We didn't know what that would look like, so we prayed for wisdom. As odd as this may seem to some, we regularly Skype or Facetime with our granddaughter, and even enjoy actual playdates together via the Internet. We read books together, sing songs, play instruments, blow bubbles, and even dance together. She knows who we are and loves our Internet visits.

We were able to drive 20 hours to visit her over the Christmas holidays, and what a joy it was for us to see this tiny little girl run to the door and jump into our arms full of joy, calling us by name. Grandparenting may have taken on a new role for many of us, but love can bridge the miles. It will often take creative thinking to keep a relationship alive with your ex-children-in-law and grandchildren. But just as Jesus went to search for the lone sheep that had wandered away, we too can go after our grandchildren to keep them in our fold. It is worth every effort to keep them part of our lives.

Father, please give us wisdom to know how to stay connected—and keep our families close, in spite of pain and distance.

Kellie Frazier

It's Not All About Me

*Through Jesus we should always bring God a sacrifice of praise,
that is, words that acknowledge him. Heb.13:15, GW.*

A few weeks ago when I walked into church with my 2-year-old daughter we were welcomed by the older couple who faithfully volunteers to greet people at the door. The man knelt down to talk to Ellie. He told her what a pretty smile she had and asked how she was doing. As we left I thought to myself, *This church is fortunate to have such an adorable little girl who brightens everyone's day with her smile!* Almost immediately I heard a voice inside say, "No, you have that backward. You are the fortunate one. You are part of a church family that loves and cares for everyone—even the smallest members."

Unfortunately, this isn't the only time I've had the wrong perspective. I think sometimes it's easy to take for granted the blessings we are given because we are delighted with our own "goodness." Is it possible that we can begin to think we are somehow blessing God with our service, praise? How important to remember there is nothing we can do that compares to what He has given us. The Bible even says that He is not impressed with our sacrifices and burnt offerings, but prefers our loyalty and knowledge of Him—Hosea 6:6.

Maybe I've spent way too much time on the Pinterest quote boards lately, but I've been seeing a lot about the importance of an "attitude of gratitude." I think when we start looking at all we've been given rather than how much we have to offer, our whole outlook on life changes. We become more focused on others and less focused on ourselves.

Last week at church I was aware of the greeters as I walked in the door again, but this time it was because I was thinking how lucky we are to have them. I was conscious of the people who took the time to talk to Ellie as we made our way inside. More important, I was listening for that voice of correction to open my eyes to the blessings around me that I had been missing.

Lord, thank You for not allowing me to remain content to hold on to my treasured—but wrong—perspectives. Thank You for stretching and growing me, and waking me to the blessing of living an others-focused life.

Dena King

My Favorite Person

Love is of God. 1 John 4:7, NKJV.

My earliest childhood memories include times spent with my grandmother. When she visited our family on the weekend Grandmother pulled me onto her lap and read storybooks to me. I soaked up the individual attention, as I had to share Mommy's time with baby brothers.

When I was 4 years old, Grandmother took me camping with my uncles. We pitched the tent beside Spirit Lake in view of Mount Saint Helens. Holding Grandmother's hand, I threw stones into the water. After supper I snuggled with Grandmother by our campfire until I couldn't hold my eyes open another minute. Then we slept together in her sleeping bag in the tent. That night a bear visited our camp and ate some of our provisions, including the raisins for my cereal.

When I was 6, my mother let me stay overnight at Grandmother's house. The next day we rode the city bus, which I thought was fun. We went to the mall and watched people ice skating while we nibbled cashews Grandmother bought us for a treat.

I loved visiting my grandmother's house. She let me play with her plastic flowers, with which I decorated the stairwell. I made a playhouse under a huge fir tree in the backyard, where my dollies and I spent many happy hours. In the summer she'd set up the lawn sprinkler and let me run in and out of its spray.

When I was a little girl, Grandmother was my favorite person because she took time for me, and she understood my heart. She made my dolls clothes that matched the dresses she sewed for me. She let me help her fix things in her cradle roll Sabbath school room. Together we made chocolate-chip cookies. And always she would read me stories.

When I was 8 my family moved far away from where Grandmother lived, and I missed her so much. Grandmother wrote me letters. I wrote her back. And in the summer we would spend time at Grandmother's. I got my love for writing, teaching, baking, cashew nuts, sewing, and working with children from my grandmother. She encouraged me to pursue my interests and stayed in touch with me until her death. I have many books on my shelves that she gave me, including my first Bible. The influence my grandmother had on my life is great. I love her very much and look forward to reunion day when Jesus returns.

Thank You, God, for grandmothers who share time and love with their grandchildren.

Barbara Ann Kay

Beyond the Dirt

But we are all as an unclean thing,
and all our righteousnesses are as filthy rags. Isa. 64:6, KJV.

One morning I rushed out of the driveway and sped off to my midmorning dental appointment. Driving past my eldest son's home, I noticed my 5-year-old grandson, Grant, frantically waving, trying to flag me down. As a loving grandmother I had to stop. I flung my door open, ran across the road, and eagerly squeezed his little hand through the fence.

Grant asked if he could travel with me to the dentist, and while I was thinking about it, I looked beyond his handsome little face and noticed he was covered in mud from the knees down. I didn't want to miss the chance to spend some time with him, so I told him to go and ask his mom if he could travel with me. He ran off, calling for me to meet him in their driveway. Soon he returned and said that his mom had given him permission to come with me. I did not know that my daughter-in-law was in the shower, and had told Grant to change before leaving. Somehow that detail had slipped his mind.

Now my options were to leave him behind or take him along just as he was—mud and all. How could I leave him behind? So, not wanting to be late for my appointment, I scooped him up and placed him in my car. We held hands all the way to the dentist's office. Once there, I introduced Grant to the dental staff, completely oblivious to the fact he was still covered in mud. He was my beautiful grandson and I was his adoring grandmother—that was all that mattered. In my love for him I could see only him. I did not notice his "filthy rags." Everyone else seemed to adore him too. After leaving the dentist's, I bought Grant new pants and shoes and we had a great day together. It was several days later when I recognized the spiritual parallels.

Jesus rushed out and accepted us, despite our mud. His love for us would not allow Him to leave us alone, and He proudly presented us to the Father despite our mud. He has clothed us with clean garments, which He purchased at the expense of His blood despite our mud.

Please, Lord, help us to love the way Jesus does, and to accept each other unconditionally—mud and all.

Shelly Mandy

Beyond Our Wildest Dreams

No eye has seen, no ear has heard, and no mind has imagined what God has prepared for those who love him. 1 Cor. 2:9, NLT.

Being a parent is much like peeling a mango: slow, sticky, and sometimes frustrating. Being a grandparent is much like eating a mango: juicy, delicious, and utterly absorbing. We are the most recent couple in our circle of friends to become grandparents, and though we had often listened with longing to their rapturous reports of grandparenthood, we could never have imagined the joys that awaited us.

My daughter invited me to be with her and her husband in the birthing suite. It was a great honor. She knows that I do not handle blood well, so I was instructed to stay at the head of the bed. My job was to hold her hand and encourage her. I was happy to comply. The labor was, well, laborious and there were many times when I felt utterly helpless. Seeing one's child in pain is almost worse than being in pain oneself, and there were times I wished I could have taken some of her pain upon myself; but of course, that cannot be. I sidled up to the midwife a few times, when my daughter was not looking, to urge her to do something more for my child. The pain and pushing eventually reached a crescendo and suddenly it was all over. The baby was born; the labor was done and the wonder began.

I suspect parents, being so overwhelmed with the day-to-day tasks of caring for a little one, are denied the privilege that we as grandparents suddenly appreciate. We can take "snapshot" memories of specific, wondrous times with our grandchild and frame them in the gallery of our memory. For parents it possibly blurs into one long and sometimes relentless reality. I wonder if preparing for heaven is like parenthood—we become so consumed with the tasks of daily living that we forget that joy lies just ahead. Being a grandparent has tantalized me with the thought: *Heaven might be so much more than I ever imagined!*

O Lord, help me to be ready to embrace the joy that lies ahead when we will taste heaven and find it more to our liking than we could ever have imagined.

Deanna Pitchford

PaPa's Long Shadow

Even to your old age I will be the same, and even to your graying years I will bear you! I have done it, and I will carry you; and I will bear you and I will deliver you. Isa. 46:4, NASB.

My grandfather was tall and thin and old. He was a carpenter. A contractor. Now and then as we rode through Fort Worth, my father driving, PaPa would point out a house and say, "I built that house. Its walls are a foot thick."

But now he lived in one small room behind the house owned by his sister and brother-in-law. There are so many questions I wish I'd asked, such as, How did you come to make your home there? I wish I'd asked about my grandmother, too, but never thought to do it.

PaPa and Annie lost their daughter, Josephine, when she was 3 years old. Dad was born soon after that. Annie died of TB a few years later. A contractor, PaPa's work took him hither and yon, so he took young James, "the baby," as his cousins called him, to live with an aunt and uncle. The cousins were delighted, but for Daddy's whole life he felt the loss of that childhood separation even though his father saw him often.

If he wasn't visiting us, every weekend we drove to Fort Worth to visit PaPa. We'd crowd into his place, sitting on the edge of the bed, in the rocking chair, on the trunk, or just leaning against the door. The first thing my sister and I did was open the lid of his trunk, where we'd find candy, a little tobacco bag filled with pennies, or some other treat waiting for us.

PaPa was a loving, kind man. He leaned toward the Pentecostal religion and never understood how my dad left the church of his youth and became a Seventh-day Adventist. He once told us that when Dad was a boy he'd walked to the front of the church and was "saved." We had an idea that he clung to that as Daddy's salvation.

He spent the last months of his life in our home. The last time I saw him alive he reached out his thin hand and clasped mine. "Always be a good girl," he said. I told him I would. By God's grace, I'll be with him again someday.

Father, thank You for precious memories of precious grandparents. May we never underestimate the impact of a godly life on the life of children.

Penny Estes Wheeler

Teaching Our Children

*Let not your heart be troubled: ye believe in God, believe also in me.
In my Father's house are many mansions: if it were not so,
I would have told you. I go to prepare a place for you. And if I go
and prepare a place for you, I will come again, and receive you unto myself;
that where I am, there ye may be also. John 14:1-3, KJV.*

Three-year-old Kayla followed me round the house chattering away. We had three weeks to spend with our precious grandchildren, children, parents, and friends in South Africa, and we were doing our best to make every moment count.

I had wondered what opportunities God would give me to share Jesus' love with my grandchildren, when Kayla walked into our bedroom one morning and asked, "Is Jesus coming again? Is He coming to take us to heaven?" She had heard it either at home or at Sabbath school, and it had stuck in her head. I could almost see the wheels turning as she seemed to be puzzling over it.

A day or two later she asked me again, and we talked about it some more. She seemed satisfied. The next time she spoke of Jesus coming again it was more a statement of fact. I was fascinated to observe how this truth was becoming part of her thinking.

All too soon we returned to our home in Oregon. We miss them terribly, but feel so blessed to be able to send and receive text messages, video clips, and photographs, and to see them in real time on Skype. A few days after we returned, our daughter-in-law Michelle sent us a text saying that Kayla had woken up twice, asking "Did Jesus come? Is He here yet?" She was excited at the possibility and disappointed to find out that He hadn't come yet. Kayla understands that Jesus is coming again. In her mind it could happen anytime.

Have you noticed how often we teach our children something about God, only to realize that we are the learners? Perhaps we're so busy trying to teach that we've lost sight of how much Jesus loves us and that He's coming to take us home. Soon!

Lord, may we too be so excited that we ask, "Are You coming today, Jesus?"

Shirley Allen

Children of the Heavenly King

*What marvelous love the Father has extended to us! Just look at it—
we're called children of God! That's who we really are. 1 John 3:1, Message.*

Genealogy is very popular today. Everyone wants to know where they come from—whom are they related to and how that relates to who they are today. The Bible tells us, *we are the children of God!* Tracing one's roots and finding the various branches of the family tree can be exciting. We never know who we'll find.

Some people trace their roots to document that they are:
daughters of the Revolution;
descendants of those who came to the United States on the *Mayflower.*

Yet, do we ever think about the fact we are children of God? We are descendants of the God of the universe. We have the heritage of being created in His image. We can tell our children they are children of God. One thing we know for certain—God has no grandchildren. All of us, old, young, and in between, are children of God. What a wonderful heritage.

Parents have the privilege of sharing with their children—whose they are. They are to represent their Creator by being loving, consistent, and thankful parents. Our self-worth is based on the fact that God loves us and calls us His children. Knowing that we are His should encourage us to live as Jesus did—loving, thoughtful, and kind. During the early years of a child's life, we are the only representation of God our child knows.

Parents who represent God will set boundaries—God did in Eden when He told Adam and Eve they should not go near the tree of the knowledge of good and evil. However, when they crossed the boundary, He did not throw them away—He provided Himself for their salvation. Parents show God through consistent, unconditional love with rules. What a privilege we are given—first, we are called the sons and daughters of God; second, He tells us to go and share His love, first at home, then to all the world.

Children of the heavenly King! O Lord, may we rejoice always in the privilege!

Wilma Kirk-Lee

Seven Things I'd Like
My Grandchildren to Remember

In all things show yourself to be an example of good deeds,
with purity in doctrine, dignified. Titus 2:7, NASB.

I didn't meet either of my grandfathers, but I loved to hear about them. Grandpa Nick was a hard worker and an innovative problem solver. Grandpa Shepherd had a heart for God and spent much of his younger years going from town to town to share passionately the Christ he loved so.

Grandma Minnie performed onstage at the age of 15. She wrote poetry and songs, and her "Rocky Mountain Columbine" was a runner-up for the Colorado State song. Grandma Belle was a wonderful cook, immaculate housekeeper, and hard worker, and loved the Lord.

Fond memories fill my mind, and I'm sure my grandmothers had a lot to do with who I am, even more than the red hair and freckles I inherited from Grandpa Shepherd.

I now have eight grandchildren and two great-grandchildren. Here are seven things I hope they'll remember learning from me after I'm gone.

1. Accepting Jesus and following God's Word is the most important thing in life.

2. Guard your mind and resist the devil. If we resist evil, demons will flee.

3. Love God and others, especially those in your family and in the household of faith. Do unto others as you'd have them do unto you.

4. Choose your friends wisely.

5. Develop your talents, and do your best.

6. Establish goals and work willingly with your hands. When you see a need, do it now. Don't wait until tomorrow.

7. Have fun, good friends, laugh often, enjoy your life, seeking Christ first and foremost, and always be ready for the return of the Lord Jesus—your sins forgiven and under His blood.

Finally, a word from my mother for her great grandchildren: "Only one life, 'twill soon be past; only what's done for Christ will last."

Dear Lord—thank You for the gift of godly grandparents, and for the privilege of being a grandparent. May I leave my grandchildren a godly example of what it means to follow Christ.

Ada Brownell

I Know Your Name

I know you by name and think highly of you. Ex. 33:12, CEB.

We sat anxiously waiting for our son-in-law to walk through the doors and take us to meet our newborn granddaughter. I could hardly wait to meet her and hear her name. The four grandparents had come up with a string of possible names for her.

The minutes crept by, and finally we were ushered into the room. There she was, resting against her mommy. A tiny thing with her mommy's curly hair and my button nose. Chubby, sleeping, rosy pink. And then they told us her name. "We'd like to introduce you to Sage Emra."

I stood there with my mouth wide open as tears streamed down my cheeks. My name! They'd chosen to give her my name! I squealed in disbelief. I had no idea how that would impact my life so intensely. This strange name my mother made up had left me alone. Unique—but apart. It now had meaning. I was no longer alone. I was overwhelmed with emotion.

What legacy would I leave behind for her? What story would our shared name carry and tell? How would I inspire her to live a full, rich, happy life? I felt compelled to show her what being a godly woman was all about. The task before me took on a new meaning.

My only other grandchild was a boy, and I thought I could never love anyone quite as much as I loved him. And now here was little Sage Emra. My heart burst with fullness and wonder at such a gift. My capacity to love had expanded. Our name had new meaning through a bond only we would share.

Standing in that room, surrounded by wonder and love, I was given a glimpse of what each of us mean to Jesus. We each are fearfully and wonderfully made. He knows us by our name. He has a new name picked out for each of us in the world without sin. There is power in a name. It represents who we are, the story we share of how Christ transforms our lives. My name will impact my precious Sage Emra. May I represent my heavenly Father well.

Father, may we as parents and grandparents reveal Your character in our names so that our little ones through beholding will be like You.

Emra Wagener Smith

Like a Well-watered Garden

But blessed are those who trust in the Lord and have made the Lord
their hope and confidence. They are like trees planted along a riverbank,
with roots that reach deep into the water. Such trees are not bothered
by the heat or worried by long months of drought. Their leaves stay green,
and they never stop producing fruit. Jer. 17:7, 8, NLT.

There's no degree or license required to be a parent. It's a tough job, and in my estimation the most important one anyone is called to do. Why? Well, much of that is obvious; providing for the sustenance of life—food, shelter, protection, and most important, and usually undervalued—love! Godlike love that's unconditional and ever-present.

My experience as a grandma has been awesome, so far. A little precious child who is beautiful, innocent, and mostly nonmobile. She isn't able to talk back, let alone argue with me. She doesn't demand expensive clothes, or special lessons, or anything hard. I often wonder if there will ever be a day she isn't just simply wonderful. But we know the human predicament of sin will blight her life too, and that things won't be as simple as they are now.

There is nothing I can do to change the fact that life is hard and sin makes raising children less than ideal. But being prepared for the tough times is the game changer. No one is perfect; we will make mistakes, but Jesus promises that He is with us. He draws us with cords of love. He refreshes us like a beautifully tended garden. As we allow the Holy Spirit to change our hearts, we will become good models for our little ones and one day they will follow.

Scary? It doesn't have to be if we will just remember that God promises a life dependent upon Him will flourish even in the face of drought. The longer I live, the more I know this to be truly true.

Lord, I know the drought will come. It always does. But I know, too, that You have promised to be with us always. You are my hope and my confidence. My heart trusts in You, and I am blessed. May I live my life in such a way that this precious little person will have no doubt of Your love.

Cheri Gatton

The Princess Phase

See what great love the Father has lavished on us,
that we should be called children of God! And that is what we are! 1 John 3:1.

Yes, I went through a "princess phase." I received a Cinderella watch for my fifth birthday. My daughter experienced her princess stage, too. Now my granddaughters want everything "princess." I suppose we can blame Walt Disney for this multigenerational recurring fascination with feminine royalty. Tiaras, fancy gowns, coloring books, wallpaper, bedroom furniture, play castles of all sizes, DVDs, glass slippers—is there any end to the princess products being marketed to encourage our little girls in their daydreams and imaginative play?

When I was a little girl, I enjoyed looking at pictures my father took during World War II. The photos that fascinated me most were the pictures of him standing in front of the castle where he lived after the fighting ended, while he served as a guard at the Nuremberg trials. If my daddy lived in a castle, I might truly be a princess, I would reason. Because of my bragging, my father had to remind me he mostly lived in the mud during the war.

It was years before I found out I truly am a princess. As a child of God and joint heir with Jesus, I am a child of the King. It has nothing to do with the fancy clothes I played in as a girl, or the size of my play palace, or the castle where my earthly father resided. It has everything to do with my relationship with the King of kings. As children of God each of us is a prince or princess in the kingdom of God, members of the royal family. Unlike the characters from a Disney movie or the divas promoted by the media, we are set apart to glorify our heavenly Father and to reflect His love and glory to the world around us.

I sure wish someone would have told me this years ago. Now that I know, I will make sure my granddaughters understand they really are princesses, special members of the family of God, the King of kings.

Father, thank You for being my Savior, my Gentle Shepherd, my King of kings and giving me a place in Your kingdom.

Karen R. Hessen

Like Father, Like Son, Like Grandson

Train up a child in the way he should go,
and when he is old he will not depart from it. Prov. 22:6, NKJV.

We married young and had our children soon after. Almost children ourselves, we were young parents, with no training or idea how to raise children. We turned to the Lord for counsel on how to raise our little family—for we both believed that the training of our children would be our most important responsibility as parents.

Our children are grown now, and both of them are married with children of their own. When they were still young, we made it our priority to raise them in the way of the Lord. I was blessed to be able to stay home with them during the day, and when their dad came home from work, he made sure to make time to play with them. After we'd eaten supper, it was time for family worship. As they grew up they loved worship time—that love was formed and established at a young age. As parents, we have to be devoted to God, and family worship is where this can be most beautifully demonstrated.

A year after our daughter was born, my husband decided to go back to school, to study for the ministry. As you know, PKs live in a glass house, where growing up can be a testing time. Our son would come home from school, play with his friends, and then read. He loved to read and would read from the Bible stories every day. Today he is still following the Lord. He preaches and leads out in many departments in the church.

Our daughter is actively serving the Lord and the community as a social worker. They both know that if they ever need anything, to go to the Lord in prayer.

We are blessed to have three grandchildren—but our greatest blessing is to watch their parents raising them to follow Jesus. The daily habits we instill in our children, family worship, Bible reading, prayer, the importance of service in the church and community, all of these become part of their characters. Setting an example of faithfulness in all things is something that can be passed down from generation to generation.

Heavenly Father, thank You for being our teacher, counselor, and guide. Bless our children as they shepherd their children in the way of the Lord.

Linda Naidoo

Grandma Lois

For I am mindful of the sincere faith within you,
which first dwelt in your grandmother Lois and your mother Eunice,
and I am sure that it is in you as well. 2 Tim. 1:5, NASB.

Paul is writing a letter to Timothy, and he is filled with joy when he remembers Timothy's genuine faith. But he says that genuine faith first dwelt in Timothy's grandmother Lois and in his mother Eunice. What a profound spiritual influence those two women had in Timothy's life, that a nonrelative named Paul could say that Timothy's faith had been passed down to him through his mother's and grandmother's influence.

Grandparents can have a mighty spiritual influence on their grand-children. In fact, the most important inheritance you can leave your children or grandchildren is a spiritual one. When eternity is in view, leaving a monetary inheritance means little if the child or grandchild is spiritually unprepared for Christ's return. So our priority needs to lie with the salvation of our children and grandchildren—not how much money we have in the bank or what we own.

Paul's letter reveals that Timothy knew the Scriptures even from child-hood (2 Tim. 3:15). How did he learn the Scriptures as a child? Paul indicates that in the previous verse. Clearly his mother and his grandmother taught him the Scriptures even in his early years.

Parents and grandparents, our job is to teach our children to love reading and studying the Bible. Make the Bible stories interesting and exciting for the kids. In addition to teaching young children the Bible stories, we also need to teach them to hide God's Word in their hearts by memorizing Scripture. Learning memory verses seems like a fading art, but it needs to be revived. As we help our children memorize Scripture, we will probably find ourselves memorizing Scripture as well. One great memorizing tool for this tech-savvy generation is found at www.scripturetyper.com. You can also download the app on your iOS or Android device. Instead of playing games on your devices, teach your kids how to memorize Scripture on them.

Father, help us raise our children and grandchildren to have genuine faith and to know the Bible—just as Timothy's mother, Eunice, and grandmother Lois did.

Jared Miller

The Blessings of Grandparenting

Grandchildren are the crown of the aged,
and the glory of children is their fathers. Prov. 17:6, ESV.

Being a grandparent is a milestone in life that is unparalleled. To think that your child, now an adult, has become a parent produces a joy that is unspeakable. As I held my own grandchild in my arms for the first time, I whispered a prayer that this child would be a disciple of Jesus and a blessing to all around him.

When my husband and I became grandparents, we discussed our new role at great length. We could not agree on one point—that of discipline. My husband felt that discipline was the responsibility of the parents and not the grandparents. He saw his role as a friend to the child, a playmate to him, and when he misbehaved, the discipline should be handed back to the parents.

As a grandmother, I felt that it was as much my responsibility as that of the parents to discipline our grandchild when necessary. While it is true that grandparents need to respect the boundaries that form the sacred circle around their children's home, I believe that in the absence of the parents it is my job to teach, model, and discipline. Grandparents need to have a clear understanding with their children in this regard, respecting their guidelines, so there is consistency in teaching and discipline.

Having learned from the experience of parenting, grandparenting is God's offer of a second chance at parenting another young life. In this day and age of a myriad of distractions, God uses grandparents to reinforce spiritual learning in the home. Their influence, if applied correctly, is a real blessing to their grandchildren, and this blessing boomerangs back to the grandparents, for in giving, we always receive and are rewarded abundantly, just as the Scripture promised.

Father, give us wisdom and tact as we come alongside our children in the awesome task of raising young disciples for You. Keep us ever respectful of our children and the sacred circle of their home.

Sally Lam-Phoon

December

Teaching Children How to Be Like Jesus

Becoming Like Jesus

But we Christians have no veil over our faces; we can be mirrors that brightly reflect the glory of the Lord. And as the Spirit of the Lord works within us, we become more and more like him. 2 Cor. 3:18, TLB.

Living in today's world, parents face an enormous challenge in raising children with good moral values: Children who will grow up to be positive contributors to society. Good examples can seem few and far between. So, where do we as parents turn for guidance on these crucial points? How do we teach our children to become more like Jesus?

The answer lies in the Man Himself. Jesus Christ is the moral gauge in our broken world. As parents, we must take a close look at ourselves if we want to be effective in teaching our children of Jesus. How can we share something we don't know? If we want our little ones to know Jesus—this can only be done by knowing Him ourselves.

As parents, we must lay a sure foundation on the solid Rock. As Jesus so eloquently called the children to His knee, He calls us to His side, to learn of Him. He gave us a perfect example—how to be compassionate, loving, respectful, and obedient. We must learn of Him each day if we want to teach our children to be like Him.

Our children will be the leaders of tomorrow. We need to make certain we connect them, each day, to the One who holds tomorrow; teaching them in a loving manner to mirror the One who gave His life for all.

Let us commit to seeking to know Him for ourselves. There are eternal consequences at stake—for our entire family. May we show, by our example, what it means to spend time in the Word, in prayer, in getting to know Jesus. May we allow the Holy Spirit to change us into loving and lovable Christians. May our joy in serving Jesus and others inspire our children and give them a godly example to follow.

Dear Lord, I want my children to be like Jesus. Please help me to demonstrate Your loveliness each day. Only by Your grace, Lord.

Ronica Smit

Ask God for Guidance

Turn all your anxiety over to God because he cares for you. 1 Peter 5:7, GW.

Raising children and helping to develop their characters for heaven is one of the most important jobs on earth. The Bible says in Proverbs 22:6, "Train up a child in the way he should go, and when he is old he will not depart from it" (NKJV). That is some pretty heavy responsibility. So how can parents know that they're "doing it right," and making the best decisions for their family?

You can read books, go to parenting seminars, and even get counseling, but the first place you should go is to Jesus. Just as your children come to you with their questions, we need to go to our heavenly Father with our questions. Ask God for guidance, wisdom, and discernment, and He will lead and guide each step of the way. God is the very best resource you can find—for any situation.

One of the most important ingredients to being a "good parent" is unselfishness. It means saying no to many things you might want to do, places you want to go, and things you want to buy. It is putting your child's needs above your own wants and desires. Equally as important is the gift of your time. Spend time with your children. Play with them, have fun, laugh often. Hug them and let them know every day how much you love them.

And don't forget to introduce your kids to Jesus. It is critical that they know He is real and that He loves them. The most important task a parent has is to prepare their child to meet Jesus. Your children are precious to you, as well they should be, and I'm sure you would not hesitate to protect them with your life. Now take a moment to remember that you are God's child. He not only created you, He gave His life when He died for you on Calvary. Just as you love your children, never forget how much Jesus loves you.

Dear Lord—it almost seems unbelievable—You love my children even more than I do! Thank You that I can trust them to Your loving care. And thank You, Jesus, for loving me.

Brenda Walsh

Mama's Soup

Kind words are like honey—
they cheer you up and make you feel strong. Prov. 16:24, CEV.

When our kids were growing up I can't say I thought much about how my behavior modeled God. Yet, looking back, I see times I did just that—modeled how God would've handled a situation and other times how He would not. One cold, snowy day I felt cranky and depressed and just wanted to flee it all. "Let's go outside," I told the kids, "and build a snowman." They loved it when I played with them. We made a snowman and a snowlady, and when we finally came back inside all of us were happy.

When I was growing up, my maternal grandmother lived with us, and as our mother worked outside the home, we spent a lot of time with "Mama." She was strict and no-nonsense, but we got along just fine. Mama was a good cook, and she made wonderful vegetable soup. I make mine the same way now, and between you and me, I think it's as good as Mama's. But it wasn't always . . .

I was a teen the time Mama was sick in bed for several days. As she began to feel better my aunt Leona thought that some hot vegetable soup would be good for her, so she brought the ingredients and asked me to make it. I was glad to and, I suppose, a little proud that they trusted me to do it.

Both my aunt and Mama gave me explicit instructions, which I carefully followed. Then I left it boiling on the stove and picked up a book to read. Of course, being the scatterbrained teen that I was, I forgot all about the soup until—I raced into the kitchen. My beautiful soup had turned into an inch of black sludge in the bottom of the pot. I was devastated.

With tears, I confessed what had happened. Mama said that it was OK. "But what are you going to tell Aunt Leona when she asks how it tasted?" I cried.

"Oh, I'll just say that it wasn't as good as hers."

Forgiveness! If that isn't just like God.

Lord, thank You for glimpses of grace that touch our lives with Your love—words of kindness that brighten our day and draw us closer to You.

Penny Estes Wheeler

Show—Don't Tell

Parents are the pride of their children. Prov. 17:6.

The first people children know and learn to trust are their parents. They look up to us. As we look up to our Father in heaven and learn to trust Him, we become more like Jesus. As we seek to disciple our little ones to become more like Him, we can be overwhelmed by the daunting responsibility. We know ourselves to be flawed and imperfect. We need to remember that our first responsibility is to look to Jesus. All else will flow from that place.

If we want our children to know Jesus, the most effective way is for us to show them. One of the rules of writing is to show, and not just tell. It is the same with teaching children. We need to show them and not just tell them about Jesus, and our actions must line up with what we say. Like show-and-tell at school. A child can tell their friends about their cat, but when the child brings it to the classroom, they can see it for themselves.

Through the years I developed a habit of prayer and Bible study every morning. Without my realizing it, my children were watching me. They are now grown and have families of their own, and both have followed my example. Who knew? Our actions reveal what we believe to be true about God. It's important that we reflect the true and living Christ and have an active relationship with Him.

"Hurry up, you slowpoke!" I yelled at my first grader. Tommy ran to the bus, eyes brimming with tears. I felt so guilty. "Lord, I'm sorry," I prayed. The words "Tell him" popped into my mind. I went to the school and asked his teacher if I could speak to him. Once in the hallway, I stooped down, looked into his eyes, and said, "Mommy was wrong to yell at you this morning. Will you forgive me?" Without a pause, he replied, "Yes, Mom. Did you come all this way just to tell me that?" I hugged him and said, "It's important. I love you, son."

Jesus came to show us the Father's love. He calls us as parents to show Jesus' love. Do our children know that Jesus loves them?

Father, You are the only prefect parent. Help us display the character of Jesus as we care for our children, while we are being changed ourselves.

Claudia LeCoure

Oh, Be Careful, Little Lips

Let the message about Christ completely fill your lives,
while you use all your wisdom to teach and instruct each other.
With thankful hearts, sing psalms, hymns,
and spiritual songs to God. Col. 3:16, CEV.

My sister and I were driving together with my 2-year-old and her 4-year-old in the back seat. We were talking about a recent visit with friends who have a wild little boy. We couldn't believe they let their little guy run around and take things from the other children like that. We were really hashing through it when my nephew chimed in, "Nathan is so bad. What else him do?"

Oops. My sister and I looked at each other and realized that not only had he been listening to us gossip—he was joining in! The Bible says clearly that "love does not delight in evil but rejoices in the truth" (1 Cor. 13:6), "love . . . keeps no record of wrongs" (verse 5), and "he who does not love does not know God, for God is love" (1 John 4:8, NKJV). Ouch. Our seemingly innocent conversation didn't sound as loving when it was repeated back to us by a 4-year-old. I worried that our griping would undermine the beautiful job my sister is doing in raising my nephew.

I've heard people talk about showing your children how to be more like Jesus by taking them to volunteer at the food pantry or making blankets together for the homeless. These are wonderful things, and I hope to do them someday with my daughter. However, I think children truly learn to be like Him by the way they see His love demonstrated on a daily basis more than the occasional grand humanitarian gesture.

My nephew's contribution to a gossip session with my sister made me keenly aware of how closely our children are watching and listening to what we say. I want my daughter to see God at work in me through the way she sees me love others—in my conversations with them and about them. Because I am painting a picture of how God loves her, I must be sure it is as complete a picture as possible.

Dear Lord, may our little ones learn about Your love from the example we set. May Your kindness speak through our words and give evidence that we are growing in Jesus.

Dena King

355

Be Like Jesus?

*I have been crucified with Christ and I no longer live,
but Christ lives in me. The life I now live in the body,
I live by faith in the Son of God, who loved me
and gave himself for me. Gal. 2:20.*

"B e Like Mike" was a famous ad campaign for one of the greatest basketball players of all time: Michael Jordan. Kids everywhere wanted to "be like Mike." They wanted his shoes as well as the drinks he endorsed, and tried their best to imitate him on the basketball court.

Thirty years later people are still talking about him. Matt Smethurst wrote an article entitled "Do You Still Want to Be Like Mike?" He quotes Jordan: "How can I find peace away from the game of basketball?" Smethurst responds in the article, "Michael, you never had peace. Triumph and fame, yes, but not peace."

How many of us search for peace in the form of houses, cars, and social status? Romans 12:2 says, "Do not conform to the pattern of this world, but be transformed by the renewing of your mind. Then you will be able to test and approve what God's will is—his good, pleasing, and perfect will."

If someone created a Be Like Jesus ad campaign, what do you think would be part of it? One might quote Exodus 20 and the Ten Commandments. Someone else might use Matthew 22:37-40: "'Love the Lord your God with all your heart and with all your soul and with all your mind.' This is the first and greatest commandment. And the second is like it: 'Love your neighbor as yourself.' All the Law and the Prophets hang on these two commandments."

Can you imagine what this world would be like if everyone were trying to imitate Jesus, following His ten commandments, loving the Lord with all their heart and soul, treating their neighbor respectfully? Second Corinthians 5:17 says, "Therefore, if anyone is in Christ, the new creation has come: The old has gone, the new is here!"

I'll take the new creation, any day!

Lord, help me to be like Jesus. Take the old me and make me Your new creation.

Tamara Michalenko Terry

356

You Are the One

Your eyes saw my unformed body; all the days ordained for me were written in your book before one of them came to be. Psalm 139:16.

Our 4-year-old was looking at the pictures in a Bible story book. On seeing a picture of Jesus on the cross with the two other crosses beside Him, she asked, "Are there three Jesuses?" She saw another picture with Jesus wearing the crown of thorns. "What's in His hair?" she asked.

"Thorns," I told her.

"Why did He have them?"

"People who didn't like Him were listening to Satan and put them there," I said.

"But He didn't want the thorns?"

"No . . ."

What an awesome moment. How thrilling it is, as parents, to be the first ones to explain the story of Jesus' death and the plan of salvation to our children. Sometimes in the day-to-day business of helping our kids with life, potty-training, obedience-training, settling squabbles, and cleaning up the house, we lose sense of the priceless privilege we have as parents: to teach them about Jesus and help them get ready for heaven.

God intends that the primary way our kids learn about Him is through us. That may be scary some days, but it is also an incredibly high calling and a blessing to us. No matter whether you think the church school teacher down the road or the pastor and his wife would do a better job with your kids, remember, God didn't choose them to parent your kids. He chose *you.* He ordained you—set you apart—and planned for today, according to our verse for today.

Parenting is an indescribable journey, understood only by those who have been on it. God uses it as an opportunity to open our eyes to who we really are and to grow us into holiness, if we let Him. So, today, why not embrace every opportunity that comes to love, train, comfort, and be an example to your kids? You are all they have and God's chosen person to parent them.

Dear God, thank You for choosing me and for the children You chose specifically for me. Please give me strength to parent wisely, and pour Your love through me to all those around me.

Heather Krick

DECEMBER 8

An Opportunity to Give Hope

Whatever you do, work at it with all your heart, as working for the Lord, not for human masters. Col. 3:23.

Dinnertime is a great time to talk with our children. One evening we were talking about the importance of helping people. My daughter asked, "I know we should help people, Papa. Who do you help?" I told my children the following real-world example.

"Early yesterday morning I asked God for an opportunity to bring hope to someone." They were all watching me as I continued. "I stopped at a gas station for a large soda, and after I'd paid for it, I took two huge gulps when a complete stranger approached me. Do you want to know what she asked me?" They all nodded their heads.

"She said, 'Excuse me, sir, but I forgot my wallet at home and I'm on my way to my next appointment. Could you help me at all?'" I really had their attention now.

"I froze, because I did have an extra $10 with me that day. And do you know what I said?" I was enjoying their involvement in the story. "I said, 'Sure, I can put $10 on your pump.' And then I waited for her to tell me how she would pay me back. But do you know what she said?" Their eyes grew wider. "She just said, 'Thank you!'"

"That should have been enough, right? But honestly, I was a little disappointed. And then I remembered I'd asked God for an opportunity to provide hope for someone else. He did, but I was hoping I would be repaid for my good deed. My response should have been the same as hers: 'Thank You, God!' Helping people should be its own reward."

God will always give us opportunities to help others. Often they can come at home. Raising children can be a difficult and thankless task—if you are looking for a reward from someone else. The greatest reward will be to hear the words "Well done, good and faithful servant." When you've helped change the diaper for the thousandth time, or cleared the table alone again, remember, God sees you. He is your Master, and He is pleased with you."

Father, please give me an opportunity to bring hope into someone else's life today.

Jason Hanselman

358

Jesus in My Heart

The Lord is my strength and shield. I trust him with all my heart.
He helps me, and my heart is filled with joy.
I burst out in songs of thanksgiving. Ps. 28:7, NLT.

I reached out a hand to stop the thundering footsteps of my precocious little 3-year-old. She was one of several children running up the aisle of the church, around the back and down the side. The adults we were visiting with seemed oblivious to what was happening. The irreverence didn't seem to bother them, but I thought I had already taught my child to respect the sanctuary of God.

Catching her as she raced past me, I knelt by her side, her breath blowing my hair as she impatiently shifted on her feet, anxious to run again.

"Larissa," I reprimanded. "We don't run in God's house."

Her eyes widened with disbelief. I went on to explain that we had to be reverent in God's special house and that did not include running.

Red curls bounced as she shook her head adamantly. Placing her hand dramatically over her chest, she leaned in closer and stage-whispered, "Mommy! In Sabbath school, didn't Teacher say that Jesus comes into our hearts?"

I nodded, and she reached out, grabbed my hand in hers, and placed it firmly over her pounding heart. She pressed her cheek confidently against mine and spoke earnestly.

"Mommy, I'm running in God's house because then I can feel Jesus in my heart! See? He's happy, you can FEEL Him!"

As my hand absorbed the strong beating of her heart, my own heart responded to the realization of how very real Jesus was to my precious child. Oh, for the presence of Jesus to reverberate through my entire being, that I cannot stay silent about what Jesus is doing for me, in my heart, in my life, and for eternity.

Father God, I invite You into my heart in a tangible way. May I feel Your presence in all I do. Help me to share the joy You generate within my heart with those around me!

Carol Bovee

Gratefulness

*See what great love the Father has lavished on us,
that we should be called children of God! And that is what we are! 1 John 3:1.*

Sometimes my children frustrate me to no end, always asking for things, and as soon as they get them they move on to the next thing they really, really need.

I ask, "If you don't get this thing, what will happen? Will you die?"

"No, Mommy," they reply reluctantly. Because we love our children, we enjoy giving them things or surprising them, but the constant nagging for more stuff can make you wonder if your child loves you for you, or for what you can give them. When they complain, I remind myself of the longer view: growing citizens fit for heaven and earth.

Occasionally I do the unexpected. I give them an undeserved treat. When they ask in surprise what it is for, I say, "This is called grace. Getting something we do not deserve." It's a timely reminder for them and for me about how amazing God is.

Am I any different than my children in how I treat God? I run to Him with lists of "asks." Lord, please give me this, or provide me with that, or make this happen for me. Lord, heal my friend, let that lump in my breast go away, get rid of the bully who is bothering my child. We expect God, like the mythical genie in a bottle, to make all our "asks" come true.

Today let's do something unexpected and ask for nothing at all. We can thank Him for who He is, thank Him for the love He constantly lavishes on us. Talk to Him about our hopes and dreams, and share our fears and doubts. Tell Him how our day was and about that funny incident that made us smile. Why not praise Him for His marvelous works, dance with joy for the mighty deeds He has done? Let us clap our hands in exultation for the privilege of being called a child of the King. Worship Him because our hearts beat in rhythm and adore Him as our maker. Talk with Him as a friend! Whisper "Good night" and "I love You" before we fall asleep.

Father, thank You for loving me despite my selfishness. I love You.

Yvonne Rodney

Less Is More

*The Lord is my shepherd; I have all that I need. He lets me rest
in green meadows; he leads me beside peaceful streams.
He renews my strength. He guides me along right paths,
bringing honor to his name. Ps. 23:1-3, NLT.*

Shortly after my husband and I moved our family across country we came to a very startling realization: we were going to have to change our way of living. This was not simply because we had moved from a rural area to an urban one. This change was because of the very real understanding that we had too much stuff and that it was time to simplify our lives.

God provided a place for us to live that was within our means, close to my husband's new job, and within walking distance of our kids' new school—but it had only two bedrooms. How on earth were we supposed to fit into such a tiny space? I was sure it was a recipe for disaster.

Yet I could feel God tapping me on the shoulder, telling me it was time to make a change. I gave in and decided God knew best. As for our children, I should never have worried. We piled all three children into one bedroom and got rid of the excess stuff we had accumulated. As the days turned into weeks, I made another startling realization: no one missed the stuff that was gone. Instead of feeling cramped, our little apartment felt cozy.

A side bonus was that the small space encouraged us to live outdoors more. Instead of spending time in front of a television or computer, we were outside in God's nature. Our children discovered how fun hiking and biking could be, and, best yet, our apartment complex had a pool!

Gone were the things that had cluttered our lives, claimed our attention, and deprived us of family time. Often as parents we want to give our children everything they want. However, what they might actually need is less.

O Lord, You guide us along the right paths, and You bring us to the places where we will find all that we need. Thank You, Lord, thank You for being the Good Shepherd.

Asheley Woodruff

The Broken Doll

*I will ascend above the heights of the clouds;
I will be like the Most High. Isa. 14:14, NKJV.*

When I was a child, I had the privilege of having many toys in spite of the poverty in my country of Cuba. My parents were clever and able to be generous. Ever since I was a child, I have always loved order. After I'd finished playing, I would put everything back into its box.

At that time I had two little neighbors who were sisters. They did not have as many toys as I had because they would break them. They loved to play with my things, but they never helped me put anything away.

Their father, and mine, owned a furniture store. I could not understand why they felt so much envy toward my toys. I had two big baby dolls, a boy and a girl, and one of the sisters coveted them very much. As I said before, I was super careful with my toys. I had learned through my parents and the church that I should share. One day one of them asked to borrow my baby doll. I gave it to her with some mistrust, giving her many instructions. When she returned it to me I put it away. The next day, when I was changing its clothes, I could not believe what they had done. The doll's legs had been sliced! I was so angry, I cried, knowing I could never replace it. How far could envy reach? My mother fixed the doll so you could not tell what had happened. The girls' mother denied what they had done. With the help of God and the encouragement of my mother, I was able to forgive them, and I never mentioned the subject again.

Envy is so harmful! Look at what happened in heaven. It was envy that destroyed Lucifer in his eagerness to be like God. He then planted the same sentiment into Eve's mind, whispering, "You will be like God, knowing good and evil."

Envy displaces God's presence from the heart. It corrupts relationships, destroys friendships, and hurts families. But God's love "covers a multitude of sins." God forgave Adam and Eve and gave them another opportunity . . . the same opportunity He gives to us.

Thank You, Father, for Your immense love that goes beyond all envy and all sin! Thank You for redeeming us of all evil!

Alina Careaga

Love Your Enemies

You have heard that it was said, "You shall love your neighbor
and hate your enemy." But I say to you, Love your enemies
and pray for those who persecute you, so that you may be sons of your Father
who is in heaven. For he makes his sun rise on the evil and on the good,
and sends rain on the just and on the unjust. Matt. 5:43-45, ESV.

Many things about this world make it difficult to avoid becoming overwhelmed by the mess it is in. For me, one of the most disturbing things to hear about is a school shooting. I remember how stunned I was when I heard about the attack on Sandy Hook Elementary School. Watching television images of parents and children reunited outside the school broke my heart. I could only imagine the agony experienced by the parents who waited, only to discover their children hadn't survived.

It's easy to acknowledge that "God is love"—but when unimaginable tragedies such as this occur, how do we love our enemies? Do we know who the enemy is? The person cutting me off on the freeway? The one making my life difficult at work, or the person with a different political viewpoint than mine? Is it the parent of the child who doesn't intervene when their child bullies mine at school? Is the terrorist my enemy?

Jesus tells us we need to love anyone who wants to harm us. I have to admit, I just can't do it. I certainly can't do it in the midst of a tragedy or deep hurt. What I can do is surrender my feelings to God daily and ask Him to help me to love my enemies. I have to remember that God died for my enemies. He loves them every bit as much as He loves me. It is hard to understand, and it is difficult to move from realizing this to acting upon it authentically. As Matthew 5:44 says, we need to pray for those who treat us poorly. In those few words lies the key to transformation.

Father, I pray that You will forgive me for my anger and help me forgive my enemies. Help me demonstrate a Christlike spirit to my children—that we all may be more like You.

Colleen Duncan

Little Imitators

And you should imitate me, just as I imitate Christ. 1 Cor. 11:1, NLT.

Scattered around the stands were parents, grandparents, and friends of two young basketball teams. It was halftime, and someone was giving a devotional talk. Placing his finger against his cheek, the speaker said, "Now put your finger on your chin." Where do you think most people placed their fingers? You got it—on their cheeks.

If we as adults follow what others do more closely than what they say, how much more is this true of our children? I know this all too well. You see, I want my son to make healthful eating choices that will promote his physical, emotional, and intellectual well-being. I teach him that fruits, vegetables, and nuts make wonderful snacks. But when I'm hungry for just a little something to tide me over until dinner, I reach for the candy jar. I'll give you three guesses what my son usually requests as a snack . . .

The propensity for imitation can work for the good as well. When my son sees me taking time to pray about my missing car keys, he learns more about trusting God than if I tell him every day that God will take care of us but then fuss and fret while trying frantically to find the keys myself. When he stops to pray about his lost toy or a friend who hurt his knee, I know that my example is making a difference.

Knowing that someone is watching and imitating us can feel intimidating sometimes. What if I slip up? What if I set a bad example? Centuries ago the apostle Paul had the courage to tell the believers in the city of Corinth to imitate him. How was he able to say such a bold thing? Because he himself was imitating Someone—the best example who ever lived, Jesus Christ.

Like Paul, it is only as we come to Christ in daily fellowship and seek to become more like Him that we can be examples worthy of our children's imitation. Let's commit to seeking Christ first, today and every day.

Jesus, help me to be more like You so when my children imitate me, they are imitating You.

Cheryl Faith Tarr

Learning to Walk

I'll take the hand of those who don't know the way, who can't see where they're going. I'll be a personal guide to them, directing them through unknown country. I'll be right there to show them what roads to take, make sure they don't fall into the ditch. These are the things I'll be doing for them—sticking with them, not leaving them for a minute. Isa. 42:16, Message.

One of my favorite pastimes is people-watching. I do it at the mall, the beach, or wherever I have the opportunity. I am fascinated by people's actions and interactions with one another.

One day I sat watching a young mother with her toddler. The little girl was just learning to walk and was still unsteady on her feet. She would take a few tentative steps forward before losing her balance and falling down. The mother, with outstretched arms, would catch her just before she hit the floor. With a gentle laugh she would say, "Oops! Up you go."

The mother's face beamed with pride as she saw her child progress. The child gave a toothless grin and kept on walking—falling down often. I waited to see if the mother would scold her for being so slow to learn. She never did. She simply reached down to lift her daughter back on her feet each time she fell.

I sat back and mused on the object lesson that had just unfolded in front of me. We have a heavenly Parent who broods over us like a loving mother. He stands with arms outstretched and cries "Oops! Up you go" as we take our first tentative steps onto the road He has called us to walk. We fall down often, but before we hurt ourselves He is there to catch us and keep us safe.

I like to try to imagine the pride on our Father's face as He watches us learning to walk; learning to depend on Him; learning to trust Him implicitly. He never scolds us for falling down. His grace reaches down to lift us up. It holds and sustains us on our journey.

We can safely place our confidence in a Father who cares for us and loves us much more than any earthly parent ever could. He is waiting with outstretched arms. Let Him lift you up and put you back on your feet.

Thank You, Father, for Your outstretched arm that helps when we need it most.

Cordell Liebrandt

To Train Up a Child

I will instruct you and teach you in the way you should go;
I will counsel you with my eye upon you. Ps. 32:8, ESV.

I am always learning from my children: the best ways to be tickled, the necessity of free time, and most important, how to hide chocolate from my 2-year-old super sleuth. Of course, as their mother, I hope that I am teaching them a few things too. Mostly, I hope I am teaching them to love and serve God.

Recently I was driving my oldest son to school. The holidays were in full swing as I turned on the radio to the local Christian station. Strains of "Mary Did You Know" filled our car, but my children, unfamiliar with the song, protested and asked for real "Christmas tree" music. I flipped through the stations until I found one playing "Jingle Bells," but I was bothered by the idea that my children didn't know the real meaning of Christmas. It also made me wonder what exactly I was teaching my children about God and the great gift we have been given through Jesus.

I was flooded with the fear that somehow I was failing in my duties as a parent. If my children didn't know Christmas was the time to celebrate Jesus' birth, what other important lessons was I failing to teach them? However, God spoke to me and reminded me that I wasn't alone in raising my children. After all, they are His children too.

I felt reassured that God would be with me and would make up for my weakness and give me the wisdom I need to train my children to be sons and daughters for Christ. My mind was immediately at peace. I went about the rest of my day confident that God would teach me what I needed to pass on to my kids so their love for Jesus would grow.

Raising our children to know and love the Lord is a daunting task, and it's easy to become overwhelmed. Thankfully, the Lord sees our needs and is ready to provide us with everything necessary to be good parents to our children. All we have to do is ask.

Thank You, Lord, for guiding us in our own walk with You. Please, Father, give us wisdom so that we may also train our children to follow after You.

Asheley Woodruff

Hammer and Pound

*You, Lord, never fail to have pity on me; your love
and faithfulness always keep me secure. Ps. 40:11, CEV.*

The other day, in an effort to be more festive, I decided to hang stockings over my fireplace, but I didn't want to spend the ridiculous price I was seeing in the stores. So I hunted around the house and found three nails that I decided would work—at least while the stockings were empty.

The first nail entered the wood, but after the first two knocks it started to turn up. I had to hold it terrifyingly close with the risk of smashing my fingers. The second was better. The third was a charm. Yet I wasn't particularly satisfied. After I hung the stockings I discovered I could use the loop of the stocking to help pull down on the nail. It would keep my fingers significantly safer. I hammered away again and learned some valuable parenting lessons along the way.

All children are different. I had a lot of problems with one nail, less with the others. Some children obey quickly and easily, while others will offer resistance every step of the way. Each person reacts differently to their environment, even if that environment is the same home. What may stir obedience in one child may raise rebellion in another.

Your fingers will get mashed. As James Dobson said, parenting isn't for cowards. It is impossible to drive the nail of childhood into the wood of the real world without getting hurt yourself. God can identify and He can help. You need help. Let the village help you raise your child, whoever your village may be. Pick a good one.

You have to stay close. It would have been impossible for me to drive the nail in if I hadn't held it close. Parenting cannot be done remotely. For children, and most adults too, love is spelled t-i-m-e.

After the stockings were hung I stepped back to survey my handiwork. Beautiful. Stockings of red gently swayed against a wooden mantel. A perfect Christmas picture. Three stockings—one for each child. Maybe one day their lives will create a beautiful picture in a world of suffering and pain. The smashed fingers would have been worth it.

Lord, thank You for lessons learned in the little things—which really aren't little at all.

Faith A. Hunter

The Gift of Conversation

Make every effort to add to your faith goodness; and to goodness, knowledge, and to knowledge, self-control. 2 Peter 1:5, 6.

In a world in which communication is becoming increasingly electronic, time spent speaking directly with someone is decreasing. Good conversation is an important aspect of creating a strong and healthy family. Sensitive parents focus on creating harmonious parent-child relationships and establish secure attachments between themselves and their children. This, in turn, encourages cooperation from children, and a willingness to listen to their parents' requests. Real conversations are an important part of this mix.

In conversation young children are eager to share their experiences. They don't worry as much as older children about criticism and negative reactions, and the most routine event is fertile ground for a conversation. Storytelling isn't just about telling a story—it's about making a conversation out of ordinary, everyday happenings.

When you talk about rules and the reasons for them, children can understand why they are important. Talking when everyone's emotions are calm increases the likelihood that your child will hear and take in what you are saying. Even a young child who doesn't understand all the words will catch the tone of voice and learn that there is a routine to follow.

Bible verses can be great conversation starters. Revelation 3:21, for example. Ask, "What do you think God's throne is like? What would it feel like to sit next to God? What are some questions you want to ask God?"

The rules of a good conversation are that everyone listens without interrupting, criticizing, or putting down another's responses. With all the choices for Christmas presents this year, how about giving children the gift of conversation? It is a gift that keeps on giving!

Slow me down, Lord, so that I truly give my children the gifts of conversation.

Susan Murray

The Gift of My Daughter

I'm not writing all this as a neighborhood scold just to make you feel rotten.
I'm writing as a father to you, my children.
I love you and want you to grow up well. 1 Cor. 4:14, Message.

When my wife told me we were having a baby girl, I broke into a cold sweat (no lie or artistic hyperbole; my wife can verify beads of chilled perspiration on my anxious brow). I had barely gotten used to the reality of becoming a parent, convincing myself of how great it would be to take a son to a ball game, and then this. A girl. Here are a couple of things I have learned.

Show her you love her mom more than she can imagine. Sure, she has you wrapped around her little finger, but don't give your daughter the notion that loving her means you love her mother less. A dad models respect, service, sacrifice, loyalty, and humility when he lavishes grace-filled love and faithfulness on his wife. The relationship between parents is one of the most profound templates a young girl will have to navigate her own relationships.

Further, don't allow yourself to be pitted against your spouse when there is conflict. Being properly unified in the role you have as parents gives your daughter healthy boundaries and respect for the authority God gave mothers and fathers.

Her "Father in heaven" begins with her "daddy at home." How does she get to know God? She is introduced to Him by you. In bedtime prayers and Bible stories and taking her to church, but also in more powerful and awesome ways, your daughter's view of God is first formed as you express the love He gave you for her. As Jesus Christ lives in your heart, He expresses Himself in life-changing ways as you father your daughter. She gets glimpses of her heavenly Father through a devout daddy who is first in love with Christ.

These are just a couple of tips I can offer from this milestone moment in this journey. I'm still learning, and some of the lessons learned have tumbled me deeper into God's Word for help. In the meantime there's no way I'm blinking away these moments. However, if I did have a time machine, I could maybe whiz right past the whole "walking-her-down-the-aisle-to-give-my-baby-girl-away" part and get straight to the "spoiling granddaughters" part.

Father, thank You for the gift of my daughter, and for wisdom to raise her well.

A. Allan Martin

God's Love Remains

For I am persuaded that neither death nor life, nor angels nor principalities nor powers, nor things present nor things to come, nor height nor depth, nor any other created thing, shall be able to separate us from the love of God which is in Christ Jesus our Lord. Rom. 8:38, 39, NKJV.

The greatest gift you can give your kids is not the newest and best gadget the world has to offer; it is introducing them to Jesus, their best friend. Giving them Jesus is the gift that will enable them to fall in love with their Creator.

Your kids are going to be bombarded with messages and "gifts" from the world, and the "gifts" that the world offers are extraordinarily difficult to resist. In fact, without Jesus at their side, your children will find them impossible to resist. Introduce your kids now to the gift that keeps on giving: the love of Jesus!

And what about you? Do you pursue God with the same fervor with which you pursue the things of the world? Your kids are watching you. As parents we need to take inventory of our priorities. If you asked your child what they thought was important to you, how would they answer? What occupies most of your time? If our children see us prioritizing our relationship with God, they will be encouraged to form their own relationship with Him.

Do your children know that even if calamity or tragedy strikes and everything the world values is lost, there is one thing of value they will never be separated from?

How often do you talk about the love of Jesus in your home? Are you spending more time offering Jesus to your children, or do you allow the world's offerings to take precedence? The more of Jesus you show them every day, the less they will be attracted to what the world has to offer.

Dear Lord, may I give the gift of Jesus to my children. May they follow my example in seeking You first and always, and may they know You and grow in Your love each day, even as I strive to do the same.

Claudio and Pamela Consuegra

When Christmas No Longer Feels Merry

Do not be afraid; just believe, and she will be healed. Luke 8:50, NET.

As I awoke on Christmas morning everything was quiet. I was alone. No longer did I enjoy the anticipation of watching little faces light up at the sight of presents under the tree. I was no longer welcomed when visiting my mother-in-law and my now ex-husband's family for the holidays. This was the first Christmas after the divorce, and the document that now dictated our lives stated that my son was to spend this Christmas with his dad.

There was a huge hole in my heart where once I had felt complete. I felt discouraged. Guilty that my child had to deal with a new, uncomfortable situation that was not of his making, I came to a new realization: Not only had I lost my immediate family during the holidays, I'd lost other family members and friends I'd always enjoyed visiting in years past. I was invited to spend the day with my family, but all I really wanted to do was to crawl back into bed and feel sorry for myself. Christmas no longer felt very merry.

I wish I could say that during this time I had a wonderful relationship with God, that I prayed and gave praise daily, and that God filled all my empty places. Unfortunately, this was not my experience at all. At that time, I had fallen far from the intimate relationship that I now enjoy with God. Looking back, I can only imagine what life would be like had I gone through this time with God at my side.

If you find yourself in a pit, raising a child alone, or going through the drama and heartache of shared custody, God is there to heal you. Put your faith in His Word and believe that He can and will heal any brokenness, if you let Him. Know that, with Christ, you are not alone in your trials.

Lord, please help me to focus on You, rather than on my circumstances. Teach me to lean on You for my innermost needs. When my heart is aching and bruised, when I am too weary and discouraged to keep going, may I remember that You are there beside me, waiting to bestow Your healing touch.

Shirley Troilo

How Many Toys Is Too Many?

By this all men will know that you are My disciples,
if you have love for one another. John 13:35. NASB.

Ever find yourself struggling with a toddler in a shopping cart who wants everything they see? Have you ever been tempted to leave them at home?

Well, actually that won't solve the problem, will it? It might make your shopping a little less stressful, but it won't deal with the child's attitude. Allow me to make some suggestions.

First, I'd suggest you look at your child's toys. Most kids who want everything they see have too much already. Does your child have more than a dozen toys? That's probably too many. That's why they get bored. Aim for just a few and make sure they are the kind that give a child's imagination a good stretch. Blocks or small boxes, play-dough, Legos, and puppets are some good examples. Don't get really young children anything with an off/on switch; toys should make kids think, not just press buttons.

Next, practice with some really short shopping trips. Explain that you need to get just two items and that there won't be time for them to shop today. On the way to the store, explain to them the kind of behavior you expect. If they forget, they go to bed early for a week. At the age of 4 the child will quickly get it.

No generation in history has had the fixation with "stuff" that ours does. Model for your kids the true joy of a Christlike spirit in giving things away. Encourage your kids to think about what gift Mom might like from them, what hints has Dad dropped of something he might like. Help them learn to think of what they can do to make others happy.

"Adopt" a needy family with children of their own, and encourage your kids to help plan what they can give to the other family's kids. Let them help you distribute food baskets with your church. Have them help fill shoe boxes for Samaritan's Purse. The more your kids learn to give, the less they learn to want.

Lord, teach me to model a cheerful, giving spirit.

Don Jacobsen

Basic Training

Start children off on the way they should go,
and even when they are old they will not turn from it. Prov. 22:6.

I have watched my adopted children, both now adults, make decisions and choices that disappoint me. I have stood by while they endured the consequences of bad judgment. At times I wondered if they learned anything from their father and me, or if they embraced any of our values. Likewise, I have seen my adult stepson reject the lifestyle of his father and walk a path leading to hardship, family strife, and dissension.

My children's father and I were together physically, emotionally, and spiritually when they were growing up. My stepson's parents were not. They separated when he was 2 and went through a very long and contentious divorce. My children were raised in a church that taught the truth. My stepson was raised in a church that believed you should do whatever "made you feel good."

My husband has been diagnosed with Dandy-Walker syndrome, an extremely rare condition that has caused him to lose the use of his legs. Life as we know it, and the future we dreamed of, are simply memories. I have not adjusted to what it means to live with a disabled husband, providing care 24 hours a day. I am tired, sad, scared, and lonely.

Christmas was difficult for me. I cried most of the day, knowing this was likely our last Christmas together in our home. On Christmas Eve our tree wasn't up, the gifts weren't wrapped, the groceries were not purchased, the beds were not made, but the guests were here. I'd never known whether my children had learned anything from me at all, yet here they were, folding the clean laundry, trimming the bushes along the sidewalk, replacing the burned-out lightbulbs I could not reach, making beds, peeling potatoes, wrapping gifts, telling me they loved me—all without being asked. I was so proud to be their mom.

My children had learned from me after all. Though it took years, I saw them return to the ways they had been taught. God promises that your children will, too.

Father, we thank You that all Your promises are true. Give us the wisdom to raise our children in the ways You would have them go.

Karen R. Hessen

Some Assembly Required

*Therefore, be imitators of God as dearly loved children and live in love,
just as Christ also loved us and gave himself for us, a sacrificial
and fragrant offering to God. Eph. 5:1, 2, NET.*

The gospel paints a beautiful picture of Jesus for us to model, but it's easier said than done.

One year for Christmas, we got our daughters a Radio Flyer red wagon. It was the ATW (all-terrain wagon) model with a wooden cage surrounding the red metal base, and big rubber off-road tires. The picture on the box looked so pretty that we didn't even notice the fine print at the bottom of the box: Some assembly required.

After we tucked our kids into bed on Christmas Eve, we dragged the big box up from the basement. We tore it open and pulled out the wagon. I examined what appeared to be a large red baking pan with a few dozen little parts nestled inside. Where was the rest of it? I had my doubts that this pile of nuts and bolts would become the pretty picture of the ATW model wagon on the box. My husband dove in enthusiastically, screwing random parts together, doing his best to fit them onto the red metal body. It wasn't long before we realized that without instructions we would never complete the project. Fortunately we discovered the manufacturer's directions hidden beneath the pile of parts. There was even a customer service number I could call during business hours with questions.

The apostle Paul tasked believers with a high calling in his letter to Ephesus: Imitate God. This is especially important for parents, because our children imitate us. We can try as hard as we want to complete this assignment on our own strength, but when perfection is the measure, we all come up short. Thankfully, God doesn't expect us to do it alone. He's given us an instruction manual filled with all the directions we need to assemble our lives to model Christ. We also have a direct line to God through prayer, and His business hours are never-ending. He's always available to us, even at 1:30 a.m. on Christmas morning.

Lord, thank You for giving us such a wonderful example in Jesus. Guide us through Your Word and help us imitate You. As parents, give us the strength to model Christ for our children.

Andrea Michelle Wood

Preparing a Nursery

And Jesus said to him, "Foxes have holes and birds of the air have nests, but the Son of Man has nowhere to lay His head." Matt. 8:20, NKJV.

When I was 14 weeks pregnant, I began to feel the strong desire to nest for our first baby. The beginning of my pregnancy had been stressful and uncertain, so this urging from the Lord brought tender healing to my heart. I cried tears of joy, hope, and relief as I put the soft makings for the perfect blanket in the car. I thought how excited the Trinity must have been during each day of Creation, as They prepared the perfect nursery for Adam and Eve. They filled it full of golden light, vast beauty, tender green, and soft furry animals. Then God created a lovely garden from the most special things He had made. No detail was overlooked. Every care was taken for the most beautiful, lush, nurturing nursery for humankind to be "born."

Yet when Love Incarnate was born, no one made room for Him. Imagine how Joseph's and Mary's hearts must have ached to have so little to offer their baby. How does one make a nursery in a stable? Joseph probably had carved a lovely crib for the baby at home, but couldn't bring it on their 70-mile journey. Far away from family and friends, Jesus' parents leaned completely on God's provision for them. How the shepherds and Wise Men must have cheered their hearts.

My Joe and I are traveling medical workers, and finding short-term housing was very difficult for our four-month assignment. It will end a few weeks before our baby is due, then we won't have any guarantee for work or home. We'll have to lean on God to prepare, lead, and provide for us and our baby. Thankfully I won't have to ride a donkey, nor deliver in a stable.

In the meantime my heart toward God is deepening in love and growing in understanding of His heart. He provided creation with the richest blessings, and yet He went through severe deprivation. Whatever may come in the days ahead, I have absolute confidence He knows the longings of my heart. He created me in His image and He will completely provide for our little family.

Heavenly Father, I open my heart and ask Jesus to make His home here. I praise You for Your gentle care for our hearts, so we can trust You completely to help us provide for our baby.

Jessica Earl

Praying for Our Children

Early in the morning he would sacrifice a burnt offering for each of [his children]. . . . This was Job's regular custom. Job 1:5.

When my children were very young I found it difficult to take time to commune with God. The busyness of motherhood kept me on my toes, so I hardly had time to think. One evening before going to bed I prayed: "Lord, I need an extra hour to spend with You." The next morning I woke up to the strong smell of something burning. It sent me bounding to the kitchen to see if the stove had been left on. Though I could smell smoke distinctly—there was none to be found. I looked at the kitchen clock. It read 4:00 a.m.—exactly one hour earlier than my normal time for rising.

For several days the Lord continued to waken me in this way, until I formed the habit, which is with me even now. What a blessed time this became. A time when I bring each child and grandchild before the Lord. He understands the concerns of every parent for their children, and promises: "I will not forget you! See, I have engraved you on the palms of my hands; . . . I will contend with those who contend with you, and your children I will save" (Isa. 49:15-25).

When, at times, our children seem to wander, let us pray more earnestly. "Prayer and effort, effort and prayer [must] be the business of your life" (*Sons and Daughters of God*, p. 345).

Thank You, Lord, that the strength and wisdom to train and influence our families are not in ourselves, but in the mighty power of a risen and interceding Savior!

Sheila Williams

Like Sponges

Your word have I hidden in my heart,
that I might not sin against You. Ps. 119:11, NKJV.

Children learn so much, so fast, during their first seven years that it's like a dry sponge eagerly soaking up water. As parents we shouldn't be afraid to "soak the sponge" a bit. We've all heard that children learn other languages more easily than adults, so why not apply that principle to learning Scripture?

There are lots of fun and unique ways to memorize Scripture. When my kids were about 5 and 8, I decided to have them memorize Ephesians 6, about putting on the armor of God. When I found a toy set of armor at a local Christian bookstore, I knew the kids would love it. Sure enough, they had a grand time dressing up in the various pieces as they practiced reciting the corresponding verses.

One of the best ways to memorize Scripture is by setting it to music. Sign language is another good method to help the words stick in their memory. Finding pictures to go along with the verses is another way to jog the memory. Fortunately, for those of us who don't write music, there are numerous great Scripture song CDs out there. Some Christian bookstores even have children's books with illustrated Scripture passages and CDs to go along with them. I used several of those when my kids were young.

Don't be afraid to "squeeze the sponge" to see how much is in there. Encourage your kids to show you how much they remember. Quiz them. Let them quiz you. Help them find the meaning of difficult words. Train them to apply the passages to modern-day life. I remember hearing a friend tell how they'd been in a bad storm while on a hike, and how their children were very frightened. Then they remembered a Scripture song they had learned, and they all began singing, "Whenever I am afraid I will trust in You." Just remembering God was with them, by singing that song, helped their kids calm down.

Lord, soak our hearts with Your Word. May its transforming power be drawn into our lives like water to a sponge.

Sharon Monks

Passing It On

*Do not forget the things your eyes have seen
or let them fade from your heart as long as you live.
Teach them to your children and to their children after them. Deut. 4:9.*

Whether we like it or not, our children inherit a lot from us, from hair color down to the shape of their big toes. But we don't just pass on our physical characteristics—what about matters of faith? What is it that we can pass on, in spiritual matters, to our children?

Our lives as believers are defined by our relationship with the living God. By the dictionary definition, relationship is a connection between people. As Christians, each of us must develop our own relationship with God. We must experience a personal encounter with Him. As parents, we need to expose our children to God encounters. So how do we lead our little ones into these encounters so they can grow their own relationship with Jesus?

Make God real. Talk to Him often and speak about Him often so your children can see God at work in your life. Share what God is doing in your life and the lives of others. Point out the beauties of nature, reminding them that they come from God.

Share the Bible. Expose them to every opportunity to hear and study the Bible. This happens best at home but also at church and school. Remember that the main point of every story is about God and His dealings with His people. As we retell history we rekindle the living presence of a mighty God.

Share your joy. Children are attracted to and will imitate your passion for God. If it is joyful and important to you to worship, it will be for them also.

Love unconditionally. In loving them as Jesus did, they will know God's love. Teach them to obey you while they are young, and they will learn to naturally obey God as they grow.

Know that He will provide an abundance of grace as you lead your children to Him.

Heavenly Father, may our love for You flow sweetly into the lives of our children. May we pass on to them our hunger and longing to be like Jesus. May our home be a little heaven on earth—because Jesus is there.

Elvera Blake

I Would Be Like Jesus

For you created my inmost being; you knit me together in my mother's womb. I praise you because I am fearfully and wonderfully made; your works are wonderful, I know that full well. Ps. 139:13, 14.

Teaching my little one about how we grow and change can be a bit daunting. At the 4-, 5-, and 6-age mark, they pride themselves in growing up, but still relish in being Mama's baby. They learn to hold bonafide conversations, graduate from Velcro to actual tie laces, and realize the world around them. It's scary and exciting at the same time.

In the midst of all the human changes I've witnessed in my children, I pray daily that my children also grow spiritually and become more like Jesus. I pray that the bond never severs.

Throughout my experience in planting seeds, and the prayerful yearning for my children to have the desire to be like Jesus, I also experienced change within my own personal relationship with Jesus. I am growing and becoming more like Jesus!

Just as we were formed in the womb, protected and nurtured, our spirituality and relationship with Jesus should also be protected and nurtured within the heart. In each instance, there is growth and maturity. Every day we stay connected to Him, as every day we become more and more like Him.

"Be like Jesus, this my song,
In the home and in the throng;
Be like Jesus, all day long!
I would be like Jesus."

Dear Lord, thank You for creating me in Your image. Help me to continually grow and be more like You.

Jocelyn D. Zvosechz

God's Love

Cast all your anxiety on him because he cares for you. 1 Peter 5:7.

My daughter was 3 years old and she wanted a rag doll more than anything else. The doll was all the rage at the time, and it seemed as though every little girl had one—except Chere. The trouble was, we couldn't afford to buy her a doll. We had two children and I was the sole breadwinner, as my husband had gone back to school. Life was tough and we had some heavy commitments. There were bills to pay, food to buy, school fees due. You get the idea.

So I said to her, "Honey, we don't have the money to get you the doll, but we will ask Jesus about it and if it's His will, you will have it." So we prayed about it.

A few weeks went by, and my neighbor's little girl, Lisa, came by our home to ask, "Do you have a rag doll?"

My daughter said, "No."

A week or two went by, and when it was Chere's birthday, Lisa came over with a beautiful big 20-inch rag doll. It was absolutely adorable. Lisa told us, "My friend wanted to give me one of her rag dolls because she had two. I thought about Chere."

God is so good. He works in mysterious ways to show us He loves us. He invites us to trust and believe in Him. He wants us to teach our children to do the same. He tells us that if we cast all our care on Him—He will care for us. There is nothing about us that God does not notice. Anything that matters to us matters to God. And He invites us to bring everything to Him in prayer.

That was an important moment in my daughter's life. She never doubted that God loved her after that—to think that He had answered her prayer. Jesus had given her the desire of her heart and she was bubbling with joy.

God is good, don't you think? He answers prayer! From that day my daughter believed that Jesus loved her very much to think about her and answer her prayer. Jesus gave her her heart's desire and she was bubbling with joy.

Today, my daughter is a social worker. She works with children and young adults and helps them to make good life choices. She enjoys sharing stories with the kids about when she was a little girl. And she is still bringing all her cares to the Lord.

Heavenly Father, thank You for drawing near and showing Your love to us all.

Linda Naidoo

Here He Comes!

They [will] see the Son of Man coming on the clouds of the sky. Matt. 24:30.

As a young missionary wife and mother in Africa, daily responsibilities nearly overwhelmed me. If things didn't run like clockwork—I'd never cover all the bases. Rising before dawn, I'd study my Bible by candle—or kerosene lantern-light. Then after boiling water for the upright filter so we'd have drinking water for the day, I'd make porridge on either the propane or the wood-burning stove—depending on which one we had the most fuel for that week. After my husband, a full-time teacher, left for his classes, I'd awaken Kent, our 4-year-old for breakfast.

Often, during breakfast I'd hear a timid tapping on the front door. Opening it, I'd find an indigenous mother or two camped out, waiting with their hungry babies. They would cry at the sight of me, a stranger with a heart that hurt for them. I'd share what food or clothing I could.

When my local girlfriend, Kerina, arrived to help with some of the work and to babysit Kent for a couple hours, I had to be dressed and ready. Ready, with lesson plans, to hike up to the sparsely-furnished classroom where I taught English as a second language.

One morning, in the midst of the daily rushing routine, my little Kent awakened earlier than usual. He padded out onto the back screened-in porch to play for a few minutes before breakfast. Suddenly he ran back into the kitchen, so breathless he could hardly talk.

"Sweetheart, what is it?" I asked in alarm.

"Oh, Mom! Here he comes! He's almost here!" Sudden joy wreathed his small face.

"Who's almost here?" I asked, glancing over my son's head toward the porch.

"Jesus is almost here!" he announced. "Come with me and I'll show you the small, dark cloud in the sky that He's riding on." I went with Kent and saw a small cloud on the horizon. Tenderly, tactfully I shared with my disappointed child that, because so many people still needed to hear about Jesus, maybe that cloud wasn't the exact one He'd ride in on.

"Oh, well, Mom," said Kent, "that's OK. Jesus may not be almost here on that cloud. But I know He's already here with us here in our house, right?"

Thank You, God, for a child's reminder that You come to be with me—every day.

Carolyn Sutton

Biographies

Ginny Allen is a retired school nurse from Vancouver, Washington. She has been happily married to her husband, Pastor David Allen, for almost 50 years. A mentor to many women, Ginny founded Joy! Ministries, dedicated to bringing joy to the heart of God. She is committed to God's will for her life: nothing more, nothing less, nothing else! **Nov. 7.**

Shirley Allen serves as associate pastor of Sunnyside church in Portland, Oregon. Previously she served for almost 10 years as the church ministries director for the Cape Conference in South Africa. Skyping her children and grandchildren is her favorite pastime, as well as spending time with her husband, Dave, who also serves in the Oregon Conference. **Nov. 12, Nov. 22.**

Lisa Arbeau resides in beautiful Nova Scotia and works full-time as a dental hygienist. Her first loves are the Lord and spending time with her precious family. She also enjoys playing and teaching the piano, photography, writing, and walking in nature. **Oct. 11.**

Marilyn Armayor was born in North Carolina, the second of twin girls into a family of three girls and three boys. She was blessed by God-led, loving parents who taught her to walk with God. She now serves as a helpmate to her husband, a Seventh-day Adventist pastor for 37 years. She is mother to two wonderful young adult sons. She works as a nurse anesthetist. **Mar. 25, Apr. 20.**

Ryan Ashlock is an Adventist pastor and father of three daughters. He and his family live in Charlotte, North Carolina. **Aug. 20.**

Amy Austin is a stay-at-home, homeschool mom from Alpena, Michigan. She is a pastor's wife and mother of three. **Aug. 25.**

Karen Barnett is the mother of four and a 15-year veteran of homeschooling. She has been happily married for 21 years. Her hobbies include photography, horses, country living, and everything about nature. **Apr. 16, May 7, May 18, Aug. 10.**

Hope Ayala Benavides was born in Phoenix, Arizona. She is retired, although her husband of 63 years is still working as a pastor in the Redlands Spanish church in California. They have four grown children, nine grandchildren, and three great-grandchildren. **Nov. 3.**

Sophie Berecz enjoys the outdoors, homeschooling, and rearing five daughters for God's kingdom with her husband, Monty. **Mar. 3.**

Elvera Blake was born to missionary parents in Zimbabwe. She is the mother of two sons and wife of a pastor, and currently works as an associate pastor for women and children at the Fletcher church among the beautiful mountains of North Carolina. **Dec. 28.**

Olivia Bomester has been happily married for eight years to Stafford Morgan Bomester. They have two children, Tristan, 5, and Isabella, 4. She is senior lecturer in psychology at Helderberg College, South Africa, and is involved in the children's department at Kuils River SDA Church. Her hobbies include reading and writing, hiking, and spending time with her family. **Aug. 17.**

Jean Boonstra recently joined the Voice of Prophecy as associate speaker alongside her husband, Shawn, who serves as speaker/director. Jean has authored eight books in the Adventist Girl series. While working at It Is Written, she created My Place With Jesus, an online series of interactive Bible studies for children. Jean has two daughters, Natalie and Naomi. **June 17.**

Debby Botes is wife to Andy and mother to Vicky-Lee and Angela. Originally from South Africa, she now resides in Maputo, Mozambique. She is an author and speaker who loves to share the message of God's goodness. Her book, *"but, I AM with you,"* recounts her journey through breast cancer. **Jan. 25, May 10.**

Carol Bovee is a wife, mother, teacher, cancer caregiver, writer, lover of music and nature, and child of the King who longs for heaven, where there will be joy in the presence of our Father! **Aug. 24, Sept. 8, Dec. 9.**

Kristin Breiner, the mother of three amazing boys, lives on the frozen prairie of Minnesota. The noise can be deafening, but the joy is undeniable, and she feels blessed every day to get to be on this journey. **May 3, Oct. 17.**

Jeffrey O. Brown, Ph.D., is president and family ministries director of the Bermuda Conference of Seventh-day Adventist. He is the author of *Single and Gifted: Making the Most of Your Singleness* and coauthor with his wife, Pattiejean, of *Total Marriage: Guide to a Successful Marriage* and *A Guide to Parenting: On the Winning Team With Your Children*. Their two children, Kristle and Jamel, are now young adults. **Jan. 6, Sept. 1.**

Louise T. Brown is a single mother living, working, and studying in Jamaica. She currently serves as administrative assistant in the Office of the Provost at Northern Caribbean University. Her beautiful 4-year-old daughter, Jordanique Alisa Nunez Brown, is her source of inspiration. **July 8, July 13.**

Pattijean Brown is director of clergy spouses and family ministries assistant for the Bermuda Conference of Seventh-day Adventists. She is the author of *What on Earth Am I Doing? Leadership Lessons for Clergy Spouses* and coauthor with her husband, Jeffrey, of *Total Marriage Guide to a Successful Marriage* and *A Guide to Parenting: On the Winning Team With Your Children*. Their two children, Kristle and Jamel, are now young adults. **Jan. 23.**

Ada Brownell is a retired journalist from the Pueblo *Chieftain* in Colorado. She has written for Christian publications since age 15, and is the author of *Imagine the Future You*; *Joe the Dreamer: The Castle and the Catapult*; and *Swallowed by Life*. **Nov. 24.**

June Burn was born in South Africa and married Walter Burn. The immigrated to America in 1994. June is grandmother to five, ranging in age from 6 to 15. She is retired and lives in Michigan. **Nov. 14.**

Christine Gillan Byrne, Ed.D., works in the Office of Education at the Pacific Union Conference. **Apr. 7, Sept. 5.**

Z. Kathy Cameron teaches at a hospital in Michigan. She served as women's ministries director and health ministries coordinator of the Lake Union Conference and is married to a retired church administrator. They have a beautiful daughter, Chelsey. Kathy's motto is "Hide me behind the cross; I am just a vessel." **Feb. 23, Mar. 22, Apr. 18, May 9, May 25, June 4, July 27.**

Nancy Canwell has served as a children's and youth pastor, and chose to take a leave of absence when her daughter was born. She is currently a freelance writer and author. She has written the 2015 junior/earliteen devotional book for the Review and Herald titled *He's Got Your Back*. **Oct. 4.**

Leonora O. Carado lives and works in the Philippines. She is a mother of two and wife of a professor in the Religion Department at Central Philippine Adventist College. **May 8, Oct. 7.**

Alina Careaga is Cuban and along with her husband, Pastor Pedro Coreaga, ministers in Oregon. They have three children. She is a pioneer of the Hispanic women's ministry in the Oregon Conference, which she has directed since 2005. **Sept. 7, Dec. 12.**

Cindy R. Chamberlin serves as communications director for the Illinois Conference of Seventh-day Adventists. She studied journalism at Walla Walla University and now lives in Chicago. **Feb. 12, Apr. 26.**

Lisa O'Connor Clark lives in Brantford, Ontario, with her husband, Delwin; son, Braedan; and daughter, Kailey. She has been an advocate of the Adventist education system and has served as a teacher, principal, presenter, and curriculum writer for more than 12 years. **Aug. 5.**

Lori Colwell lives in Berrien Springs, Michigan, and has worked at Andrews University for almost 25 years. She has a 19-year-old son, Curtis, who is in college. She loves hosting social events at her house, NFL football, games, and cooking for family and friends. **Mar. 12, Mar. 29.**

Claudio Consuegra, D.Min., serves as the director of the Family Ministries Department of the North American Division of the Seventh-day Adventist Church. **Jan. 2, Jan. 12, Feb. 8, Feb. 22, Apr. 13, Apr. 25, May 23, May 30, June 2, Aug. 2, Dec. 20.**

Pamela Consuegra, Ph.D., serves as the associate director of the Family Ministries Department of the North American Division of the Seventh-day Adventist Church. **Jan. 2, Jan. 12, Feb. 8, Feb. 22, Apr. 13, Apr. 25, May 23, May 30, June 2, Aug. 2, Dec. 20.**

Lisseth Davis is a proud wife and mother of a son, 6, and daughter, 2. She is a licensed clinical social worker, with a specialty in children's mental health. She enjoys waterskiing and snow skiing with her family and using the outdoors to teach them about God's love. **Apr. 5.**

Wanda L. Davis graduated college with a business/accounting degree and has worked mostly in not-for-profits for the past 15 years. Creative, artistic and musical, Wanda loves to sing and write about what God has done for her. She enjoys nature photography and hiking. **Jan. 19, Feb. 18, July 10, Aug. 23, Oct. 12.**

Heather Thompson Day is working on her Ph.D. at Andrews University. She is the author of *Cracked Glasses, Hook, Line and Sinker, How to Feed the Mediavore,* and *The God Myth . . . and Other Lies.* She teaches at Southwestern Michigan College, Andrews University, and Ferris State University. She and her husband, Seth, live in Berrien Springs, Michigan, with their two children. **Sept. 11.**

Cheryl Woolsey Des Jarlais is coordinator of the two-year early childhood degree at Southern Adventist University. She has six children and six grandchildren. She holds a doctoral degree in educational leadership, and taught many years in tribal colleges. **July 18.**

Candy Graves DeVore is editor of *Kids' Ministry Ideas* magazine, and her passion is to equip parents and teachers with the resources and training need to share the love of Jesus with children effectively. She and her husband are preparing for the second stage of parenting—the "grand" one. Now, if they could just get their kids on board. **Mar. 7, Apr. 30, May 28, Sept. 21.**

Nephtaly Dorzilme lives in Toronto, Ontario. He graduated from Andrews University with an M.Ed. **Aug. 26.**

Rene Drumm is dean of the School of Social Work at Southern Adventist University. **Jan. 29.**

Colleen Duncan is originally from Bulawayo, Zimbabwe. She is a crisis-level family therapist in Portland, Oregon. When not at work, she enjoys cycling and camping with her husband, Bobby, and spending time with her children, Grant and Emma. **Jan. 5, Mar. 2, Sept. 22, Oct. 29, Dec. 13.**

Dorothy Duncan grew up as the oldest girl among seven siblings. She received a degree in nursing, and with her husband, Elmer, served 30 years in the mission field, in schools and orphanages. Now retired, she enjoys living near her three biological granddaughters. She waits anxiously for a family reunion in heaven with all her "children" from around the globe. **Jan. 15.**

Jessica Earl is a phlebotomist and is married to Joseph Earl, a traveling medical technologist working in California. They are the brand-new parents of Jonathan. Jessica loves nature and all things creative, especially writing, music, art, and cooking. **Feb. 21, Sept. 10, Dec. 25.**

Joseph Earl is a traveling medical technologist currently working in Novato, California. He enjoys nature photography, rock and tree climbing, and teaching. **Feb. 10.**

Tami Faudi is passionate about nurturing and homeschooling her two vibrant boys with her loving husband. She enjoys life on the land and sea of Nova Scotia and respectfully loving God. **Feb. 20, Mar. 16, Aug. 14, Sept. 28, Oct. 31.**

Jesse Ferguson was rebaptized after attending a series of meetings at the Washington Conference camp meeting. He and his wife have served as church-planting pastors in Seattle, Washington. During the past year they have started a family. Jesse has begun writing and loves to express his passion for Jesus through creative communication. **Feb. 6, Oct. 24.**

Sandra Fletcher, Ed.D., has been a teacher for more than 30 years. She has worked in the Inter-American Division and the North American Division as a teacher (kindergarten through college) and dean of women (NCU). She has been married to Oswald for 31 years, and they have three adult children. **May 12, July 7.**

Elario Belita Coombs Fortune has been an educator since 1970 and is presently teaching in the foundation phase at the Riverside primary school in Cape Town, South Africa. She loves the Lord and looks forward to His soon return. **Aug. 22.**

Kellie Frazier loves God. She founded Connecting LLC, a leadership development company, in 2005. She is a best-selling author and certified trainer who inspires women to know God and to overcome a victim mentality. Her books include *Connecting Faith, Hope and Love,* and *God's Miracles: True Stories of Healing and Restoration.* **Mar. 15, Apr. 17, Nov. 16.**

Elizabeth Fresse is honored to be the wife of an amazing husband who serves as a pastor. She is also prileged to the mother of five beautiful children. Together they seek to live out a life of service to God that will be a blessing to all those in their sphere of influence. **Feb. 13, Aug. 30, Aug. 31.**

Barbara Frohne is a full-time mother of two teenage children. She has bachelor's degrees in education and religion. She delights in sewing, painting in watercolors, playing her harp, and tending her garden. **Sept. 24.**

Cheri Gatton is an enthusiastic, high-energy retreat speaker. She is currently the women's ministries leader for the Idaho Conference of Seventh-day Adventists and owns and operates her own business: Abundant Life Ministry and Sales. Cheri is mother of two grown children and a new grandma. Her message is simple: "God found me, so I know He wants to bring hope and healing to all His kids." **Nov. 6, Nov. 26.**

Carol Wiggins Gigante lives in Beltsville, Maryland, with her husband, Joe. A retired day-care provider, she enjoys reading, writing, and photography. She is currently writing a book about her maternal ancestors, *Looking for That Blessed Hope.* **Mar. 20.**

John Gold wrote the devotions for **June 21, July 29.**

Carrol Grady is a pastor's wife, mother of three, and grandmother of 15. She loves quilting, reading, and writing. She leads a ministry for families of gay and lesbian people. **Jan. 22.**

Heidi Ok Kyung Ha, originally from Korea, now serves as assistant chaplain at Hong Kong Adventist Hospital. Her husband, Paul K. Cho, is currently serving Hong Kong Adventist International Church as senior pastor. They are blessed with one son, Paul Do Hyun. **May 16.**

Kelli Haines is a freelance writer who resides in Mishawaka, Indiana, with her husband and stepson. She is a full-time hairstylist who enjoys bringing encouragement and inspiration to others. She has published articles in *Evangel.* **July 5, July 15.**

Helen Louise Hall is wife of Basil; mom to Matt, Nate, Tim, and Sarah; and grandmother to two gorgeous granddaughters, Hannah-Rae and Evie Rose. **Oct. 27.**

Joy Hank writes from Cape Town, South Africa. She is a wife, mother, grandmother, teacher, missionary, but most important, a daughter of God. **Mar. 21.**

Jason Hanselman is a devoted father of three children. He and his wife, Mary, have been married for 18 years and have served in ministry for most of that time. Jason loves to write, speak, and help others unlock their God-given potential. **Mar. 6, Sept. 4, Dec. 8.**

Jeanne Hartwell is the family ministries director and associate ministerial director for the Pennsylvania Conference. She is married and has two grown children. Among her hobbies are gardening, crossword puzzles, playing racquetball, and enjoying her Westie dog, Nessie. **Jan. 7, Jan. 24.**

Beth Helm graduated from Andrews University in 2013 and now works as a school psychologist in South Bend, Indiana. She is mom to Katie, age 18 months, with a second baby due shortly. She is married to Herbie, her high school sweetheart. **Apr. 8.**

Beverly Henry is an educator and speaker in the Seventh-day Adventist school system who has taught to the university level. She enjoys writing and contributes to the *Collegiate Quarterly, Cornerstone Connections,* and the lesson guide for new SDA new believers. She enjoys mentoring young people. She is a mother of three sons and four grandsons. **July 31.**

Karen R. Hessen is an Oregon speaker and author of inspirational non-fiction and humor. She has been published in numerous anthologies and writes the monthly column Out of the Ark, for *The Seaside Signal* and the Lincoln City *News Guard.* **Apr. 2, June 14, July 4, Aug. 4, Sept. 23, Nov. 27, Dec. 23.**

Kelly D. Holder, Ph.D., is a wife and mother of three young children. She serves her community as a clinical psychologist. Kelly blogs to encourage moms on their parenting journey at projectencouragemom.com. **Feb. 11, Feb. 28.**

Kirsten Holloway is a stay-at-home mom to three rambunctious but very sweet boys. Her days are filled with homeschooling, lots of laundry, and breathtaking moments. She lives with her family in beautiful northwestern Montana. **Jan. 13, Jan. 21, June 10, June 22.**

Jackie Benwell Hood lives in Nampa, Idaho, with her husband, Todd, and their three children, Jayden, Jeffrey, and Makayla. She taught in church schools for 21 years in Canada and the U.S.A. Now she is a stay-at-home mom and loves it. She volunteers at the school her boys attend as home school coleader. She loves to travel, camp, swim, and read (when given an opportunity). **Oct. 5, Oct. 26.**

Kristen Hoover is a homemaker and mother who is aspiring to live the fully abundant life in Jesus. **June 24.**

Peggy Horne was a child when she first caught a glimpse of God's amazing love from her mother. She has adopted four children and has had two of her own. She is passionate about writing and writes her church newsletter. **Sept. 20.**

Faith A. Hunter is an associate editor in the Sabbath School and Personal Ministries Department. She and her husband, Cliff, are the parents of two teenage sons, Orion and TJ, and a preteen daughter, Tahlia. A cat and a cockatiel (who get along!) complete the family. **Dec. 17.**

Nancy Beck Irland lives with her husband, Gary, in Hillsboro, Oregon. She is a registered nurse, mother of three children, and grandmother of one. Her writings include junior devotionals *Out of This World* and *Little Talks With Jesus.* **June 5.**

Lesley Jackson is the COO of the Jackson household, which includes four precious children ages 8, 5, 5, and 9 months. Along with ensuring the smooth running of all things Jackson, she homeschools her twin boys and, as a nod to her former life as a musician, teaches a handful of piano students. **Oct. 14, Oct. 25.**

Cindy Lynn Jacobs decided long ago that surviving the wonderful world of parenting came much easier with God and a little bit of humor. She raised three kids in northern Indiana, where she currently teaches journalism at a collegiate level and works on her freelance writing and marketing on the side. **May 15.**

Don Jacobsen is husband to Ruthie, father of two sons, grandpa to two adult granddaughters, and a great-grandpa. He has spent more than 50 years counseling and coaching parents and kids. Don is an educator, clergyman, certified parent master coach, and sought-after speaker. His third book, *Rare Kids: Well Done,* was recently released. **May 27, Aug. 3, Sept. 2, Sept. 17, Dec. 22.**

June Jepthas lives in the beautiful Cape, South Africa. She has two sons and loves being Ma June to her three gorgeous grandsons. She enjoys reading, running, and taking long walks on the beach. **Jan. 30.**

Madeline Steele Johnson served as a missionary in South Korea and the Philippines. She is the mother of four and grandmother of six, and the wife of one seminary professor. For 20 years she was the secretary of the Department of World Mission of Andrews University. She is an author, knitter, and associate head elder of Pioneer Memorial church in Berrien Springs, Michigan. **Aug. 21.**

Shirley Jones is married with three teenage sons and lives in Laurel, Maryland. She is a member of the Beltsville SDA Church and serves as an administrative assistant in the North American Division Retirement Office. She loves to play games with her family, read, take walks, bake, cook, and try new recipes. **Feb. 3, Apr. 12, Oct. 6, Oct. 18.**

Desiree Julies is wife to Pastor Jonathan and mother of two adults, Jonathan, Jr., and Debbie. She has taught for more than 20 years and currently works at the VOP Bible School as children's instructor. **Apr. 9.**

Barbara Ann Kay is married to a farmer and delights in phone calls and visits with her grown children and grandchildren. She has written a book entitled *Who Is God?* Visit her Web site at www.gardenofgraceandhope.com. **Jan. 29, Mar. 10, June 23, Aug. 12, Nov. 10, Nov. 18.**

Nami Kim, Ph.D., is wife of a pastor at Seoul English Institute. She serves as assistant professor at Sahmyook University and is director of Urisai Personal Relationship Research Center. **Mar. 28.**

Dena King left a career of fund-raising in Texas to pursue her dream of opening a mountain boutique with her sister in Colorado. Dena lives with her husband and daughter in Estes Park. They are expecting their second child in September. **May 26, Nov. 17, Dec. 5.**

Thandi Klingbeil is the mother of three beautiful boys. She homeschools and writes from Collegedale, Tennessee. **May 31.**

Tammie Knauff is the mommy of two little girls, ages 7 and 4. She works as a freelance copy editor in Nampa, Idaho. **Oct. 23.**

Elaine Koen is a stay-at-home mom and homeschools her daughter Nicky. Her husband works on a humanitarian project with ADRA in Madagascar. Her oldest son lives in South Africa. Elaine believes we are all missionaries, and are called to serve wherever we are. **July 14.**

Heather Krick is originally from South Africa and now lives in California. She is the happy wife to her husband in ministry and homeschool mom to their two girls, ages 8 and 10. She enjoys traveling, teaching, music, and home arts. **Feb. 5, June 12, Aug. 9, Sept. 9, Dec. 7.**

Sally Lam-Phoon serves the Northern Asia-Pacific Division of Seventh-day Adventists in Korea as children's, family, and women's ministries director. Her passion is pointing people to the Lord who can unleash their potential. Married for more than 40 years to Chek Yat Phoon, a pastor, they have two married daughters and two grandchildren. **Aug. 15, Nov. 13, Nov. 30.**

Davenia Lea, Ph.D., currently serves as the associate director of early childhood education in the Office of Education at the North American Division. She has extensive experience in early childhood and special education as well as in working with families. **Oct. 2, Oct. 30.**

Ketty R. Leal is a pastor's wife and mother of two. She lives in Garland, Texas, and enjoys traveling with her husband, conducting marriage and parenting seminars. **Aug. 6.**

Ruber J. Leal is the pastor of the Garland Faith community church in Garland, Texas. He has been joyfully married for 18 years to Ketty Leal. They have been blessed with two children, Yarianni and Jeriel. He and his wife travel all over the country conducting marriage and parenting seminars. **Apr. 4.**

Claudia LeCoure is a mother of two and grandmother of five. She is currently writing children's books to help parents train their children in the ways of the Lord. **Apr. 23, June 30, Aug. 28, Dec. 4.**

Wilma Kirk-Lee has been married to her pastor husband, W. S. Lee, for more than four decades. She is the mother of three adult children. She currently directs the Center for Family Wholeness (CFW), located in Houston, Texas. Mrs. Kirk-Lee also serves as codirector of Family Ministries of Southwest Region Conference along with her husband. **Nov. 15, Nov. 23.**

Sharon Leukert writes from Jefferson, Texas. She loves to copresent marriage seminars with her husband, teach adult Sabbath school classes, and write words that inspire and encourage. Mother of three, she is currently in denial that her oldest child is now an adult. **Apr. 29.**

Cordell Liebrandt lives in Kuils River, South Africa, with her husband, Allistair. She graduates with a degree in theology from Helderberg College in December 2014. **Dec. 15.**

Beverly Thorp Logan was a single mom to two amazing boys for seven years. She and her husband, Hudson, are the parent/stepparents of five adult children. **July 28.**

Jenny Lovemore lives in South Africa and is a farmer's wife and mom of three kids, ages 18, 16, and 14. She loves wilderness places (where she can sense God's presence) and spending time with her family. **Feb. 2, May 11.**

Shelly Mandy is the wife of Neville and mother of four married children. She is passionate about brisk walking and entertaining her children and grandchildren. **Nov. 19.**

Deborah Marschner lives in Pottstown, Pennsylvania. She is a wife and a mom of four who tries to see opportunities of learning about God's love in everyday situations. **Aug. 27.**

A. Allan Martin, Ph.D., was a professor at the Theological Seminary at Andrews University for several years before taking a call to return to pastoral ministry. He previously served as a pastor in the Orlando, Florida, area and is currently the young adult pastor for the Arlington, Texas, Seventh-day Adventist Church. **Dec. 19.**

Aaron and **Jennifer Martin** live in Nampa, Idaho. Aaron loves to spend time with his family. He also enjoys woodworking, flying, and hiking. He works as an avionics technician in Boise, Idaho. Jennifer is a music teacher and mom of their young son. **Feb. 16.**

Becky Martinez-Bindernagel lives in Paradise, California, with her son, Jacob, Jr., and her husband, Jacob. After completing her M.B.A., she took time off to be with her son. She currently works part-time as a bookkeeper. Both she and her husband advocate with their Treasures-21 support group to bring awareness and support for families of children with Down syndrome. **Oct. 21.**

Darla L. McCarty is the mother of three adult children and lives in Kelowna, British Columbia, Canada. She has worked in the early childhood education field for 25 years. She has found that being a mother and working with children has shown her God's grace and love and has helped her on her Christian journey. **Jan. 9, Feb. 27, Mar. 5, May 20, June 7.**

Gail McKenzie lives in Madison, Tennessee, with her pastor husband, Mike, and serves as women's ministries director for the Kentucky-Tennessee conference. Her passions are small groups, prayer, and Bible study. She served as interim pastor for GracePoint church for a year and now hosts two TV programs on a local cable channel, *Health Hope* and *Truth and Wellness*. She is a sought-after speaker. **Oct. 13.**

Sherry McLaughlin is a 1990 graduate of Andrews University and the president/founder of the Michigan Institute for Human Performance in southeastern Michigan. She is a physical therapist and national speaker. She resides with her son in Birmingham, Michigan. **Oct. 9.**

Lynn Meadows has a degree in journalism and enjoys freelance writing. She currently teaches at a community college in Washington. **July 21.**

Jaclyn S. Miller is an early childhood educator and freelance writer. She lives in northern Indiana. **Apr. 10.**

Jared Miller serves as the family ministries director for the Iowa-Missouri Conference in addition to his pastoral responsibilities. He and his wife, Katie, have two beautiful daughters: Angela Grace and Andrea Faith. **Aug. 13, Nov. 29.**

Katie Miller loves to spend time with Jesus, go on dates with her hubby, and have tea parties with her girls, Angela Grace, 3, and Andrea Faith, 1. In her spare time she loves to take elementary students magabooking. **July 24.**

Sharon Monks is a part-time employee at Pacific Press Publishing Association. She and her husband, Gerald, are the parents of two amazing young adult children. She enjoys going for regular walks, reading stories out loud, playing table games, and cooking. Her son, Corey, was diagnosed with Fragile X syndrome at age 3. **Oct. 8, Oct. 22, Dec. 27.**

Don Murray loves young people and spent 42 years as a dean of men at both the academy and university levels. He is a certified family life educator with the National Council on Family Relations and author of *Called to a Ministry of Caring: A Dean's Guide to Residence Hall Leadership,* now in its third edition. He and Sue have four treasured grandchildren who call him Grampie. **Sept. 15, Nov. 4.**

Susan Murray served as an associate professor of family studies at Andrews University. A columnist for the *Lake Union Herald,* she coauthored *Mom to Mom: Heart to Heart,* and cofounded Adventist Engaged Encounter. She is a certified family life educator (National Council on Family Relations) and a licensed marriage and family therapist. **Jan. 4, Jan. 11, Feb. 17, June 18, June 27, Aug. 11, Oct. 1, Nov. 5, Dec. 18.**

Linda Naidoo is originally from Johannesburg, South Africa, and now lives in Vancouver, Canada, where she serves as the women's ministry director of the British Columbia Conference of Seventh-day Adventists.

She also works as a domestic violence counselor for a women's safe home. She has two adult children and loves to bake, decorate, and garden. **Nov. 28, Dec. 30.**

Bill Neely is married to Edwina. He is a board-certified chaplain and is currently employed as campus chaplain with Brooke Grove Retirement Village in Sandy Spring, Maryland. He has a B.S. in electronics technology from Hampton University, and an M.Div. from Andrews University. **Mar. 19, Mar. 31.**

Edwina Grace Neely is a wife, mother of four, and grandmother of two. She and her husband, Bill, have been married for 45 years. Edwina is an educator, author, seminar presenter. Her passion is parent education. She strives to empower parents and help them to be the best parents they can be. **Mar. 17, May 13, June 3, June 13, June 28.**

Rebecca Swinyar Neff is a human resources professional, a blogger, and a writer. She is passionate about helping people become who God created them to be, either in the workplace or wherever God leads her. **July 3, July 17.**

Arthur E. Nowlin and **Kim Logan-Nowlin**, Ph.D., are a husband-and-wife Christian counseling team and owners of the Kim Logan Communications Christian Family Counseling Clinic in Detroit, Michigan. They also serve as the family life directors of the Lake Region Conference. **Mar. 4, Sept. 16.**

Patty Froese Ntihemuka is the author of 13 novels. Currently she is writing under the pen name Patricia Johns for the Christian, Love Inspired line for Harlequin. She is a loving wife, a doting mother, and a joyful Christian. You can find her work at http://pattyfroese.com and http://patriciajohns romance.com. **Jan. 26, Apr. 15.**

Bonnie Nyachae is a freelance writer and artist residing in Florida. She has an associate's degree in professional writing and is a self-taught artist. When she is not tapping on computer keys or drawing on everything within reach, her favorite occupation is just simply mom. **May 6, June 20.**

Nicole Crosier Parker lives in Collegedale, Tennessee, with her husband, Alan, and their three children. Nicole is a writer and sought-after speaker. **May 19.**

Carey Pearson writes from Seattle, where the winters are mild and the flowers bloom in February—paradise after nine frozen winters in Michigan, where she graduated with a degree in vocal performance. When she is not writing, Carey can be found racking up noise complaints from the neighbors for singing opera too loudly. **Jan. 14, Jan. 27, Mar. 11, Apr. 3, May 2, Sept. 18.**

Deanna Pitchford is a clinical psychologist in private practice in Brisbane,

Australia. She keeps her eyes open for the unexpected ways in which God often manifests in daily life and considers her most important work the building of God's kingdom. **Sept. 25, Nov. 20.**

Pierre Quinn currently serves as a pastor in the South Central Conference. He and his wife, Coleen, are having the time of their lives raising two daughters, Briana and Ella. **Mar. 30, May 5, Sept. 3.**

Gary Reinbold is the father of two grown sons and spent 14 years teaching middle school in Arizona and Idaho. He's spent countless hours volunteering in nursing homes, schools, churches, and youth programs sharing yo-yo tricks. Currently he's an air-quality analyst in Boise, Idaho. **Feb. 15.**

Verna Reinbold is in her third decade of teaching in the Seventh-day Adventist school system. She taught in Glendale, Arizona, and she's currently teaching in Boise, Idaho. As a recipient of the Don Keele Excellence in Education award she was able to visit the Amish community of Lancaster, Pennsylvania. **Jan. 28, Sept. 12, Sept. 19.**

Lynn Ripley is a mother, grandmother, wife, and pastor. She serves too far away from her family in the Northern Asia-Pacific Division, but finds joy in ministry to pastors, their spouses, and their families. **Mar. 23, Sept. 14.**

Yvonne Rodney is a wife, mother, author, playwright, speaker, and consultant who enjoys most things creative. She lives in Toronto with her husband and two children and attends the Toronto West church. **Jan. 20, Jan. 31, Aug. 8, Dec. 10.**

Mary Nell Rosenboom works as a family service coordinator at Lory's Place and as bereavement coordinator at Hospice at Home. She has a graduate degree in social work from Andrews University. She lives with her husband, Tim, in Berrien Springs, Michigan. **Mar. 13, July 11, Nov. 1, Nov. 8.**

Maurette Saint Fleur is the mother of 6-year-old Farrah and 5-year-old Prince. She graduated from Andrews University with a B.A. in political science and French studies. She currently lives in Smyrna, Georga. She says that her faith in God helped her through some tough times after she became a parent. **July 25.**

Jennifer Jill Schwirzer lives in the Philadelphia area, where she runs Abide Counseling and involves herself in various other creative endeavors under her nonprofit organization, Michael Ministries. She lives to communicate the love of God through every means possible. Find her at www.jenniferjill. org. **Jan. 10.**

Cynthia L. Simmons is a mother, Bible teacher, and author. She encourages women with glimpses of history combined with a sensible approach to Scripture. Her Web site is www.clsimmons.com. **Feb. 4.**

Jill Simpson is a single mom of two wonderful children. After living apart from Christ, she came back two years ago and rededicated her life to God. She has found that although at times she may grow weary, He always gives the strength to carry her through. **Apr. 11, July 12, July 20.**

Ronica Smit is an accountant at the Cape Conference in South Africa. She is married to Pastor Sarel Smit, and together they minister to two churches in Port Elizabeth. She is currently studying for a B.A. in anthropology and psychology. She is a mother to one beautiful 11-year-old daughter. **Dec. 1.**

David B. Smith is a math professor at San Bernardino Valley College. He blogs at www.davidbsmithbooks.com. His current writing project is a series of books set in his childhood home of Bangkok. **Mar. 18, Apr. 27, Nov. 9.**

Emra Wagener Smith teaches women to reclaim their life story and shows them how to walk in God's purpose for their lives, finding real joy and peace. She lives in Savannah, Georgia, and is now grandma to Lianro's two children. **Jan. 16, July. 23, Oct. 3, Oct. 15, Nov. 25.**

Nick and **Deanne Snell** have been married for four years and currently live in Philadelphia, Pennsylvania. Nick is an associate pastor of the church plant REACH Philadelphia, where he specializes in music ministry. Deanne is a stay-at-home mom for their daughter and son. She is also studying for her M.S. in speech-language pathology. **Apr. 22.**

Dan Solis serves the College Place village church as the youth and young adult pastor. He and his wife have three adult children and two grandchildren. His interests include coaching cross-country and track and field, gardening, writing, and music. He praises God for the gifts of his family, the Bible, salvation through Jesus Christ, and the promise of His soon return. **July 1, July 26.**

Belinda Solomon is a homeschooling mom of two children, ages 5 and 11. She lives with her family in Bloemfontein, South Africa, and enjoys reading, walking, swimming, gardening, and outdoor life. **Feb. 7, Feb. 26.**

Kimberly Spare grew up in Berrien Springs, Michigan, where she is now the owner of an imprinting promotional and apparel business where she loves to be creative and design logos and imprints. She also loves to spend time with her darling 4-year-old girl, energetic 3-year-old boy, and her loving firefighter/EMT husband. **July 22.**

Tawny Sportsman is a speaker for the Oregon Conference of Seventh-day Adventists and an associate chaplain. She serves on the conference prayer team and worked as a pastoral assistant in Oregon and Alaska and coordinated women's retreats for many years. She has a ministry for widows and women alone. **Feb. 25, Apr. 21, Apr. 28.**

Maike Stepanek is a stay-at-home mom raising two feisty little boys, ages 3 and 1, in Thailand, where her husband, Brian, is currently a student. When she is not potty-training, changing diapers, or saying "No," she enjoys reading, drawing, walking, writing, and making memories with her family. **June 16.**

Angela Ruth Strong lives in Idaho with her husband and three children, fondly known as J-Dog, Cat, and Mouse. Besides taking care of her zoo, she writes women's fiction and teaches group fitness classes. You can visit her at www.angelaruthstrongblogspot.com. **Mar. 8, June 6.**

Garry Sudds has, during his career in Adventist education, been an assistant boys' dean, chaplain/Bible teacher, principal, associate superintendent, and superintendent of schools in the New Jersey and Rocky Mountain conferences. He has served for the past 19 years as associate director and then director of education for the Lake Union Conference. **Sept. 27.**

Carolyn Sutton is a retired missionary teacher and editor living with her husband, Jim, on their small goat farm in Alabama. They're active in their local church and serve as volunteer field reps for Adventist World Radio. Carolyn also enjoys three grandchildren, writing, and music. **Nov. 2, Dec. 31.**

Cheri Swalwell is a wife, mother, and avid reader, but first and foremost she is a Christ follower. She has a heart for marriage, parenting, and relationships from a Christian perspective. She blogs at http://journeysfromthe heartofawifeandmother.wordpress.com. **Jan. 8.**

Kimberley Tagert-Paul writes from Michigan. When not writing, she loves crafts, photography, cooking, and reading. She loves to enjoy the sounds and beauty of Lake Michigan with her husband. Her life goal is to make it to heaven and take as many people with her as she can. **Jan. 1, Jan. 17, Mar. 26, Apr. 6, May 4, May 22, May 29, June 19, June 25, Aug. 18, Sept. 13, Sept. 26, Sept. 29, Oct. 16.**

Cheryl Faith Tarr is a wife and mother of one, living in North Carolina. Her son is a special blessing and miracle from God after years of infertility. By day she enjoys teaching English to speakers of other languages, but her real passion is loving God and her family. **Apr. 24, June 15, Dec. 14.**

Tamara Michalenko Terry is a freelance writer and designer. She and her husband, Randy, have three boys: Joey, Jonathan, and James. Their characters continue to build through life situations. **Jan. 3, Mar. 27, Apr. 14, May 14, May 21, Dec. 6.**

Jerry D. Thomas is the author of *Messiah* and *Blessings* and the Detective Zack children's series. He lives with his wife, Kitty, in Nampa, Idaho, and works at Pacific Press Publishing Association. **Feb. 1, Mar. 1, Mar. 24, Apr. 1, May 1, June 1.**

Shirley Troilo lives in Guntersville, Alabama, with her husband and best friend, Steve. They have a blended family of three his-and-her boys. She is thrilled to share her wonderful relationship with Christ to encourage others who also struggle through life. **July 6, Dec. 21.**

Jenny Trubey lives in Ooltewah, Tennessee. She is a middle school teacher but currently stays at home with her son Thatcher. **June 8.**

Jude Urbanski writes fiction as well as nonfiction. People and places are her passions. Find her at http://www.judeurbanski.com. **Jan. 18.**

Neal J. VanderWaal is a former teacher and semiretired Realtor living in Battle Creek, Michigan. His book, *Looking for the Good*, was published in 2004. **June 9.**

Brenda Walsh is the producer and host of a daily children's program on 3ABN called *Kids' Time*. She is an author, speaker, singer, registered nurse, and artist, and has authored several vegetarian cookbooks with her sisters, Linda and Cinda, of the Micheff Sisters. Brenda is married to Tim and has two daughters, Rebecca and Linda Kay, and two grandsons, Michael and Jason. **Aug. 19, Dec. 2.**

Penny Estes Wheeler, retired book and magazine editor and mother of four, writes from western Maryland. She loves to travel, which is a good thing, because her grandkids live all over the map. **May 17, Nov. 21, Nov. 22, Dec. 3.**

Ellen G. White lived from 1827 to 1915. During her lifetime she wrote more than 40 books. Her classic, *Steps to Christ,* has been published in more than 160 languages. **Aug. 1.**

Cheryl Kronner Wiley enjoys sunbeams, garden-ripe tomatoes, home-made bread, homeschooling her kids, studying the Word, prayer, and Spirit-filled worship. She's so grateful to God for His many blessings; her husband, Craig; and their four children, Brianna, Justin, Kierra, and Joshua—whom she prays the Lord will use to change the world. **Apr. 19, Oct. 19.**

Cheryl Williams teaches at Riverside primary school in Cape Town, South Africa. She has been married to David for 24 years and has two daughters, Ashleigh and Andrea. Her hobbies include reading and gardening. She aims to live within God's will and to bear witness to the loveliness of Christ's character. **Feb. 19.**

Robyn Logan Williams is married to Carlos and has two children, a daughter, Jordyn, and a son, Logan. She is a department head at Wells Fargo Bank, and in her spare time she enjoys running and scrapbooking. **July 29.**

Sheila Williams has four children, 11 grandchildren, two stepdaughters, and two step-grandchildren. She taught for 30 years and is now retired in Chinhoyi, Zimbabwe. She and her husband, Ron, enjoy their large garden and the many birds that visit. **Dec. 26.**

Chidi, Lissie, and **Tyreke Wilson** wrote the devotional for **Mar. 14.**

Linda Wolfaardt lives in Somerset West, South Africa. She has been married to Francois for 22 years, and they have two children, Ben, 18, and Katelyn, 16. She is a trading manager at a marketing company that exports fresh fruit globally. **Aug. 7.**

Andrea Michelle Wood, former journalist turned novelist, focuses her speaking, teaching, and writing on her passion for faith, family, and fiction. She resides with her husband and three daughters in North Dakota. **Feb. 9, Sept. 6, Dec. 24.**

Asheley Woodruff is a writer and licensed clinical counselor. She lives with her husband and three children in Washington, D.C., where they spend their free time exploring the great outdoors. **Feb. 14, Feb. 24, Mar. 9, May 24, Aug. 16, Oct. 10, Oct. 20, Oct. 28, Dec. 11, Dec. 16.**

Michelle Yeager spent four years as a single mom telling God, "No, thank You," to getting married again. God and Brian convinced her that was a silly idea. Boy, is she glad they did! She has four beautiful girls that range in ages from 5 to 19. She lives in Boise, Idaho, where she cohosts the morning show on the local Christian radio station. **June 11, June 26, July 2, July 9, July 16, July 30.**

Jocelyn D. Zvosechz is a wife of 22 years and mother of four. She has enjoyed many years of experience in children's ministry as well as Pathfinder and Adventurer clubs. She is also a Master Guide. **Aug. 29, Sept. 30, Dec. 29.**